DANCING ON THE EDGE

Stephen Poliakoff [was]
appointed writer in [...]
1976 and the same [...] t
Promising Playwri[ght ...]
Sugar. He has also won a B[AFTA ...]
Play for *Caught on a Train* in 1980, the *Evening [Standard]*'s
Best British Film Award for *Close My Eyes* in 1992, the
Critics' Circle Best Play Award for *Blinded by the Sun* in
1996 and the Prix Italia and the Royal Television Society
Best Drama Award for *Shooting the Past* in 1999.

His plays and films include *Clever Soldiers* (1974), *The
Carnation Gang* (1974), *Hitting Town* (1975), *City Sugar*
(1975), *Heroes* (1975), *Strawberry Fields* (1977), *Stronger
than the Sun* (1977), *Shout Across the River* (1978),
American Days (1979), *The Summer Party* (1980), *Bloody
Kids* (1980), *Caught on a Train* (1980), *Favourite Nights*
(1981), *Soft Targets* (1982), *Runners* (1983), *Breaking the
Silence* (1984), *Coming in to Land* (1987), *Hidden City* (1988),
She's Been Away (1989), *Playing with Trains* (1989), *Close
My Eyes* (1991), *Sienna Red* (1992), *Century* (1994), *Sweet
Panic* (1996), *Blinded by the Sun* (1996), *The Tribe* (1997),
Food of Love (1998), *Talk of the City* (1998), *Remember This*
(1999) and *Shooting the Past* (1999). *Perfect Strangers* (2001)
won the Dennis Potter Award at the 2002 BAFTAs and
Best Writer and Best Drama at the Royal Television Society
Awards, and *The Lost Prince* (2003) was the winner of three
Emmy Awards in 2005 including Outstanding Mini Series.
Friends and Crocodiles (2006) and *Gideon's Daughter* (2006)
won two Golden Globes and a Peabody Award in 2007.
His most recent work for the BBC includes *Joe's Palace*,
Capturing Mary and *A Real Summer* (all 2007). His latest
feature film, *Glorious 39*, was released in 2009 and his latest
stage play, *My City*, was staged at the Almeida in 2011.

Works by Stephen Poliakoff published by Methuen Drama

Plays and screenplays

Friends and Crocodiles *and* Gideon's Daughter
Glorious 39
Joe's Palace *and* Capturing Mary
The Lost Prince
Perfect Strangers
Remember This
Shooting the Past
Sienna Red
Sweet Panic
Sweet Panic *and* Blinded by the Sun
Talk of the City
My City

Collected works

POLIAKOFF PLAYS: 1
(Clever Soldiers, Hitting Town, City Sugar,
Shout Across the River, American Days, Strawberry Fields)

POLIAKOFF PLAYS: 2
(Breaking the Silence, Playing with Trains, She's Been Away,
Century)

POLIAKOFF PLAYS: 3
(Caught on a Train, Coming in to Land, Close My Eyes)

See also

Poliakoff on Stage and Screen by Robin Nelson

DANCING ON THE EDGE

Stephen Poliakoff

With an introduction by the author

Methuen Drama

Methuen Drama, an imprint of Bloomsbury Publishing Plc

10 9 8 7 6 5 4 3 2 1

Methuen Drama
Bloomsbury Publishing Plc
50 Bedford Square
London WC1B 3DP
www.methuendrama.com

First published by Methuen Drama in 2013

Cover photography by Cathal McIlwaine and Laurence Cendrowicz
© Ruby Film and Television (DOTE) Limited 2013

ISBN: 978 1 408 18559 9

A CIP catalogue record for this book is available from
the British Library

Available in the USA from Bloomsbury Academic & Professional,
175 Fifth Avenue/3rd Floor, New York, NY 10010.
www.BloomsburyAcademicUSA.com

Typeset by Country Setting, Kingsdown, Kent
Printed and bound in Great Britain

Caution

This book is produced using paper that is made from wood grown
in managed, sustainable forests. It is natural, renewable and
recyclable. The logging and manufacturing processes conform to
the environmental regulations of the country of origin.

Contents

Introduction

Ten years ago, I made my drama *The Lost Prince* about Johnnie, the youngest son of George V and Queen Mary. While researching the show, I became very intrigued by Prince George, a rebellious and musical child, who was the only one of Johnnie's siblings to show any interest in the epileptic and autistic boy. George, the Duke of Kent (sometimes confused with his elder brother, the future George VI, who was in fact called Albert), grew up to become a playboy prince with an absolute passion for jazz music. I discovered that he used to patrol the clubs in London with his eldest brother, David, the Prince of Wales, exploring the music of different bands. The two princes were thrilled by what was an entirely new sound to them and found themselves irresistibly drawn towards the charged atmosphere of the clubs. They mixed with the musicians and singers, some of whom they befriended and invited into their homes.

For me, coming across this single anecdotal fact was like going through a door and seeing a totally different side of the thirties. It was almost as if one was entering a hidden garden and discovering an oasis among the extreme hardship of that time. Britain in the early thirties was struggling to recover from the worldwide financial meltdown of 1929. There was mass unemployment, hunger, an enormous gulf between rich and poor, and society was riven by racism and anti-Semitism, especially among the aristocracy and the ruling class. Yet at the same time certain black musicians were mingling with the aristocracy, playing at their parties, even having love affairs with them, for the fashionable attraction towards black music was not just limited to royal princes. Visiting American musicians, like Duke Ellington and Louis Armstrong, were given an enthusiastic welcome in London, and there were several flourishing home-grown black jazz musicians – who are currently being reclaimed in various histories of popular culture after many years of neglect.

As a dramatist, I find this a truly fascinating period, for it was a time when certain musicians could find themselves one week on the verge of being deported and the very next week fraternising with the ruling elite at one of the great country houses. Of course, this glimpse of a more tolerant society, apparently moving towards being free of prejudice, where penniless musicians were welcomed into wealthy homes and became the lovers and friends of the aristocracy, was not destined to last. In reality, it was a total illusion soon to be violently obliterated by the rise of fascism in Europe and the build-up to war in Britain. But it did happen, and some of these brief, intense relationships that occurred across the class divide lived on in the participants' memories for many decades.

In *Dancing on the Edge*, I wanted to create a story set against this background, inspired by these true incidents and vivid memories. I wanted to follow the fortunes of a fictional band and see this time of dramatic change through their eyes. We watch the band strive for success and then just as they achieve it, performing for royalty on a regular basis, a sudden terrible event changes all their lives. The most extreme effect is on Louis, the bandleader, who finds himself an outcast and forced to try to escape the country to save his life.

In writing this story I wanted not just to look at this pivotal period in a different way, but also to show all the main characters in the drama being confronted by a moral choice. The dilemma they face – whether to help Louis or not – is the sort of choice our forebears would certainly have been compelled to make if we here in Britain had been invaded like the rest of Europe. The reverberations from that time still echo loudly in our lives today as we watch all of Europe once again in financial turmoil and racist political groups flaring up in different countries.

The characters in *Dancing on the Edge* do not know they are heading straight towards the Second World War. On the contrary, most of them believe the world is full of possibilities, that life would get better, that society was changing and becoming more tolerant, and that a lasting peace in Europe was going to happen after the catastrophe of the Great War.

As in the other period stories I have made, I try hard to remain on the same level as the characters throughout, seeing the action in this case almost exclusively through the eyes of Louis or of Stanley, the music journalist who champions the band's music. We only go where they are allowed to go. This is the reason why we are constantly moving with the characters through the back corridors of the hotel, or entering the kitchens of a country house in the dead of night or accompanying them through the tradesmen's entrance of the Imperial, past large dustbins that are piled high with uneaten food from the ballroom.

We are backstage with them, right there in a doorway waiting to go on and perform, rather than peering at them from a great height, weighed down with the hindsight of history.

Stephen Poliakoff
December 2012

Dancing on the Edge was produced by Ruby Films for BBC Television and was first screened in February 2013. The cast (in order of appearance) was as follows:

Louis	Chiwetel Ejiofor
Stanley	Matthew Goode
Rosie	Jenna-Louise Coleman
Deirdre	Caroline Quentin
Wesley	Ariyon Bakare
Thornton	Miles Richardson
Pamela	Joanna Vanderham
Julian	Tom Hughes
Sarah	Janet Montgomery
Donaldson	Anthony Head
Jessie	Angel Coulby
Carla	Wunmi Mosaku
Ryall	Richard Cunningham
Prince George	John Hopkins
Masterson	John Goodman
Hannah	Katherine Press
Schlesinger	Mel Smith
Mrs Mitchell	Maggie McCarthy
Sarah's Father	Rob Edwards
Mr Wax	Allan Corduner
Prince of Wales	Sam Troughton
Lady Winnet	Ruth Gemmell
Lady Cremone	Jacqueline Bisset
Boxley	Ian Swann
Hardiman	Richard Teverson
Sergeant	Liam Fox
Gunson	Gerard Horan
Eric	Sam Hoare
Horton	David Dawson
Mrs Luscombe	Jane Asher
Violetta	Madeleine Smith
Emily	Isabella Blake Thomas
Portly Young Man	Calvin Dean
Lady Altringham	Heather Chasen
Josephine	Laura Haddock

Writer/Director Stephen Poliakoff
Producers Nicky Kentish Barnes and Faye Ward
Music and Lyrics by Adrian Johnston
Director of Photography Ashley Rowe
Film Editor Chris Wyatt
Production Designer Grant Montgomery
Costume Designer Lindsay Pugh

PART ONE

LONDON 1933

EXT. A STREET. NIGHT
A figure is moving towards a lighted entrance in a row of dark buildings. He is wearing evening dress, tails and a black cape, but we cannot yet see his face. We track behind him across the road and pause with him in the shadows. A subjective shot of the building's windows. We can hear distant dance music from a radio.

We see a curl of smoke as the figure lights a cigarette in the darkness.

*The front door opens, a teenage boy (*MICK*), a messenger, comes out into the street and the figure moves quickly and catches the door before it closes. The boy's head turns and watches with idle curiosity as the man slips into the building.*

INT. MUSIC EXPRESS OFFICES. NIGHT
*We pause for a moment in the hall of the building. The figure drops his cigarette calmly into an ashtray. Then a subjective shot moving rapidly up the steep staircase and on to the first landing where we can see, through a half-open door, a portly man in his sixties (*MR WAX*), hunched over some papers on his desk and eating a sandwich.*

The figure moves past the door and up a further flight of stairs, past framed covers of a magazine, Music Express, *different bandleaders staring out at us. We track subjectively with him. The camera stops abruptly again as a secretary passes across the landing below. We then move with the figure towards the door of the main office on the second floor; loud dance music is pouring out of the room. We can see through a crack in the door that the office is crammed with piles of books, newspaper cuttings, gramophone records, paper everywhere. At a desk alone in the office is* STANLEY, *a man in his early thirties, who is*

typing and smoking. The figure pushes open the door and
STANLEY *looks up very sharply. We see real surprise in his eyes,*
as if the figure was the last person he expected to see.

We cut round and see the figure fully for the first time: a tall
black man, LOUIS, *also in his thirties, immaculately dressed*
and holding a pair of white gloves. One of his hands is bleeding
badly and there is blood on the gloves, but his manner is
contained, not desperate. There is a glamorous aura about him
as he stands in the doorway, meeting STANLEY's *startled look.*

STANLEY: Louis?! What on earth are you doing here?
LOUIS: I needed somewhere to come to. (*He smiles.*)
Naturally I thought of you, Stanley.
STANLEY: You might have given me a little warning . . .
LOUIS: That wasn't easy.

LOUIS *moves past* STANLEY's *desk to the window and*
stares down into the street. There are two parked cars and
a young couple walking along laughing together.

STANLEY: You've cut your hand.
LOUIS: You noticed . . . I had a little trouble getting here.
STANLEY: Anybody follow you?
LOUIS: I don't think so . . . not yet.
STANLEY: And nobody saw you come in here?
LOUIS: No.

He turns from the window and moves towards the desk.
I need you to get me out of the country, Stanley.
STANLEY *tries to appear calm. He knocks some ash into*
the ashtray.

STANLEY: Ah! . . . That will be an interesting challenge,
considering how many people are looking for you,
Louis.

Time cut. A few minutes later.
ROSIE, *a young woman in her twenties, is bandaging*
LOUIS' *hand with some white cloth, a makeshift bandage.*
The radio is off, there is a tense silence in the room.

STANLEY: You can trust Rosie.

LOUIS: I know. (*Watching her bandage the cut.*) That's a fine bandage.

ROSIE: I just cut up a pillowcase . . . it's all I could find.
She indicates the adjoining darkened office where there is a crumpled bed in the corner. LOUIS *glances at* STANLEY.

LOUIS: Still sleeping at work I see.

STANLEY: Sometimes. Of course. And tonight that might be where we're putting you.

ROSIE (*finishing the bandage*): That'll do for now, but you ought to see a doctor.

LOUIS: Thank you . . . and I will see a doctor, yes. (*Calmly.*) As soon as I've got out of the country.
Dominating one of the walls of the office is a large photograph of LOUIS *sitting at a grand piano on stage, looking dazzlingly successful. He is staring out of the photograph with a cool confidence.*

LOUIS: I've always liked that picture.

STANLEY (*moving towards the darkened office next door*): It's terrific, yes, one of the best we've got of you. You stay there a moment Louis, I need to make sure of something . . .
STANLEY *indicates* ROSIE *should follow him, and they disappear into the dark office, carefully closing the door.* LOUIS *can hear their voices for a moment, then all goes quiet.*
Suddenly the phone in front of him on the desk tinkles as if someone has picked up the extension and is dialling. We track in on the phone. LOUIS *stands over it.*
He very carefully lifts the receiver and hears STANLEY*'s voice.*

STANLEY (*voice-over*): No, I'll wait . . . I'll be here till then, no, it's better I wait . . . Yes I will.
LOUIS *replaces the receiver just at the moment* STANLEY *re-enters the room.* STANLEY *is holding a bottle of whisky,*

he is alone. He sits behind the desk and reaches down to
produce a glass.

STANLEY: I've only got one clean glass . . . (*He smiles.*) So
   I'll have the bottle. (*He begins to fill the glass.*) We need
   to have a plan, don't we, Louis?

LOUIS: We do, yes.

STANLEY: Because we can't have you being caught.

LOUIS: That's not going to happen.

STANLEY: I hope not.

LOUIS: Who were you calling just then?

STANLEY: Calling? Oh, I was just making sure Mr Wax
   knew I was staying late and that I would lock the
   front door . . . You happened to have turned up on a
   copy night, this week's edition goes to press in the
   morning, so everybody's working late. (*He takes a swig
   of whisky from the bottle.*) We don't want Mr Wax
   popping his head round the door do we!
   Their eyes meet.

   Why would I lie to you Louis?

LOUIS (*calmly*): You're always lying to me. (*He drinks more
   whisky.*) When didn't you lie?

STANLEY (*grins*): Not about anything important.

   LOUIS *looks disbelieving.*

STANLEY: No I haven't . . . and that must be true, mustn't
   it, otherwise you wouldn't be here.

LOUIS: I ran out of possibilities. It had to be you, Stanley.
   STANLEY*'s expression changes, he suddenly becomes more
   tense, serious.*

STANLEY: Have you got any idea what we should do?

LOUIS: Not yet, no.

STANLEY: I'm not sure I like you being this calm. (*He
   suddenly jumps up.*) Well, we're pretty sure nobody
   knows you're here, and we want to keep it that way,
   so we should play the loudest record we've got
   shouldn't we?! To help us think, and stop us being

heard . . . (STANLEY *moves to gramophone.*) It has to be
one of yours doesn't it . . . (*He puts on a record.*) This
seems appropriate.

*An up-tempo jazz number starts, full of energy and
movement.*

LOUIS: Good choice . . . (*He smiles at* STANLEY.) You lied
about this too.

STANLEY: I lied about this?!

LOUIS: Absolutely. You never saw us play that first time . . .
It was a blatant lie.

STANLEY: That is not true!

*The camera is moving into the record as it plays, so it fills
the screen. We keep moving closer, it gets bigger and bigger,
so we are right into the surface of the record.*

STANLEY (*voice-over*): I'd been unavoidably detained . . .

I ran! I've never run so fast in my life. I dashed across
the city to see you!

INT./EXT. STANLEY'S OFFICE AND ROOFTOP. LATE
AFTERNOON

*We dissolve from the surface of the record to bright sunlight. The
sun shines straight into the lens as the camera moves, so it flares
vividly. As the dissolve finishes the camera is moving across*
STANLEY*'s office, which is much less cluttered than in the
previous scene and there are no pictures of* LOUIS *on the wall.
The camera keeps moving fast across the office towards the open
window; we can hear voices and the sound of typing. Without a
cut the shot passes through the open window, brushing through
the window box. As we pass through the flowers, there is a
caption.*

EIGHTEEN MONTHS EARLIER

*As the caption disappears, the camera is still moving; it is now
through the window and out on to the flat roof beyond, which*

we see STANLEY *has turned into an extension of his office. He is typing at a little trestle table which is covered in papers, papers are also all around him on the roof as well. Next to him* ROSIE *is typing rather more calmly at another trestle table. She is retyping pages.*

Behind them is a cityscape of chimneys and roofs.

ROSIE: You have to go, Stanley.

STANLEY (*typing furiously*): Any minute, any minute now, just got to finish this. (*He yells.*) Mick! . . . Out here, Mick!

ROSIE: You'll never do it, unless you go now.

MICK, *the young messenger, climbs through the window negotiating the window box.*

STANLEY: Mick, she's finished those pages.

ROSIE: Almost finished those pages

STANLEY (*pulling a page out of his typewriter*): And you can take this too.

ROSIE: No he can't! (*Intercepting the page.*) I have to retype everything, Stanley, because you go at such a rate . . .

STANLEY: She thinks I make mistakes! (*Grins at* MICK.) I never make mistakes –

ROSIE: You have to go! You've got to get to the Olympia, and the Café Royal and the Apollo, and then there's that little club in Lyle Lane you want to fit in too –

STANLEY: That's the only important one –

ROSIE: And you can't possibly cover them all unless you go now.

STANLEY (*pushing back his chair, stretching his legs out*): It's a lovely evening, too good to waste on Jack Paynton at the Olympia. (*Softly.*) We could have a drink, Rosie . . .

ROSIE: You've got to run, Stanley!

EXT. LONDON STREET. NIGHT

It is night now. STANLEY *is walking along some railings as he approaches a steep flight of metal steps leading to a basement club. The street is dingy and deserted, not quite a back alley but clearly away from the West End. We can hear music as he nears the club, the same tune that he played* LOUIS *in his office. Just as* STANLEY *reaches the top of the stairs the music stops. He clatters down the steep steps but as he opens the door at the bottom members of the audience begin to leave, brushing past him.* STANLEY *dodges into a small darkened office and lights a cigarette as voices buzz around him.*

We cut to him emerging from the little office and moving down the now almost empty passage. The club's owner, DEIRDRE, *a working-class woman in her forties, is watching him approach.*

STANLEY: That's a tremendous sound Deirdre, they were sensational.

DEIRDRE: Don't you dare, Stanley, you've only just arrived! You missed them!

STANLEY (*unabashed*): I missed them?! They've finished? That's impossible!

He kisses DEIRDRE *and smiles.*

I heard enough to be interested . . .

He begins to move further down the passage.

DEIRDRE: You liar! Where are you going?

STANLEY: I'm going to see them.

DEIRDRE: Well, don't try your usual with them, Stanley, it won't work, I warn you . . . they'll know you missed it!

STANLEY (*stops, looks back at her*): You think they're terrific though, don't you?

DEIRDRE: I think they are very exciting, yes. And unusual too.

STANLEY (*grins, moving on*): That's good enough for me then.

STANLEY *reaches the door at the end of the passage. He knocks once loudly and without waiting he enters.*

INT. DRESSING ROOM. NIGHT

STANLEY *is greeted by the sight of the band all in different states of undress, a group of black musicians, changing in a shabby room full of piled-up chairs.*

We recognise LOUIS, *looking less assured and affluent but he has nevertheless a confident air about him. Standing near him is a man of the same age,* WESLEY, *who has a searching combative manner.*

As STANLEY *enters, the band members look up with surprise and hostility at him barging into their dressing room.*

STANLEY: Forgive this intrusion, gentlemen, but I just couldn't stop myself. I just had to tell you that was terrific, absolutely terrific.
There is silence.

WESLEY: And you are?

STANLEY: Stanley Mitchell, of *Music Express* . . . That was a very exciting evening, tremendous. (*He smiles.*) And unusual.

WESLEY: We didn't see you in there, where were you sitting?

STANLEY: Ah, I have a habit of slipping into places unnoticed.

LOUIS (*sharp*): So you're a critic then?

STANLEY: Amongst other things, yes, I write profiles, features and reviews.

WESLEY (*giving him a penetrating stare*): So you'll be reviewing us, will you?

STANLEY: I will, most certainly.

WESLEY: What were we playing when you 'slipped in'?

STANLEY: A lovely little number, I didn't get its name.

They are all staring at him.

I'm looking for a band for the Imperial Hotel to play
next Friday night. I wouldn't be about to recommend
you for that job without having seen you would I?!

WESLEY (*immediately*): We're out of London next Friday,
on tour.

STANLEY: On tour? Really? Where are you going?

LOUIS *is staring at* STANLEY *impassively, giving nothing
away.*

WESLEY: We're on tour. And even if it was possible to
change that, the Imperial? That old place! They want
a coloured band? I don't think so!

STANLEY: The Imperial is incredibly stuffy, that is certainly
true . . . but it is changing. (*He grins.*) After all,
they've hired me to spot bands for them. (*He suddenly
takes a fountain pen and notebook out of his pocket.*)
Remember I know what you are getting to play
here . . . and I know what they pay at the Imperial –

*He writes down a figure, tears the page out, folds it and
holds it out to them.*

Who do I give this to?

LOUIS: You give it to me . . .

He takes the folded page, and then indicates WESLEY.

And you also give it to him . . .

LOUIS *looks at the figure, he betrays no surprise. He
hands it to* WESLEY, *who doesn't look at it for a moment.*

WESLEY: Louis writes the music and leads the band, and
I deal with everything that comes up, and that means
everything . . .

WESLEY *now glances at the figure. He looks up, very
startled, then tries to cover his surprise.* STANLEY *watches
this, he smiles.*

STANLEY: And you'll get a free meal as well! Obviously
that figure is for the first booking, if there was a
second booking it's possible it could even increase.

WESLEY: We'll let you know.

STANLEY: Of course. (*He hands him his card.*) You do that.
(*He begins to leave.*) By nine o'clock in the morning or
I will have to move on . . . (*His head appears back
round the door.*) You'll need full evening dress of
course, I can arrange a very good rate if you would
like me to?

EXT. LONDON STREET/IMPERIAL BACK ENTRANCE. EARLY
EVENING
*A long-lens shot of the band coming directly towards us in a
London street. They are all in dinner jackets and are carrying
their instruments. A horse and cart is following with their set of
drums and the double bass; a couple of band members are
riding on the cart. There are trees behind them, suggesting they
have just skirted a London park.*

*A lemon-coloured Bentley is parked in the front of shot,
framing their approach.*

*We then cut to them moving through the back courtyard of
the Imperial Hotel, past large metal rubbish bins bulging with
hotel debris. A young man is pouring a large amount of discarded
food into the bin. One of the band members can't stop himself
turning longingly towards the food as it disappears into the bin.*

INT. BASEMENT PASSAGE. EVENING
*We cut to the band moving cautiously along the tiled basement
passage by the Imperial's kitchens. They pass a line of trolleys
piled high with different desserts, meringues and gateaux.*
WESLEY*'s hand drifts very close to the trolleys but he manages
to resist. The sound of a waltz as played by a dance band is
drifting from elsewhere as they move further into the bowels of
the hotel. Suddenly a voice yells at them.*

THORNTON: Hold it there!

> *A short, officious-looking man with glinting glasses,*
> THORNTON, *has appeared behind them in the passage.*

LOUIS: We were looking for our dressing rooms . . . we're the Louis Lester Band.

THORNTON: The Louis Lester Band? Yes, I was warned you were coming.

> *He indicates a doorway they have already passed.*

Musicians booked for one night only usually wait in this room here . . .

INT. THE PARLOUR. EVENING

The band spill into a tiled parlour to be greeted by a long table dominated by a very large metal bowl of gungey-looking soup. Next to it is a pile of small enamelled bowls.

THORNTON: By all means help yourselves gentlemen, the soup should still be reasonably warm.

> *Time cut. The band is sitting round the table in silence eating the grim vegetable soup, most of them clearly very hungry.* LOUIS *is sitting in a corner reading a book.* JOE, *the lead trumpet, is standing leaning against the wall, looking very tense. Suddenly* STANLEY *erupts through the door, the languid waltz clearly audible behind him.*

STANLEY: Hear that . . . the hot sound of the Jack Paynton Orchestra, the most overbooked band ever. You'll be going on after the dullest music in London – shouldn't be difficult to wake them up in there!

WESLEY: Maybe they don't want waking. I've got a bad feeling about tonight.

STANLEY: Absolutely not! Here, look at this . . . (*He waves a copy of* Music Express.) You're in here already! One of my tips of the week.

He gives WESLEY *the magazine. We see the by-line*
'Stanley Mitchell's Picks'. WESLEY *scours the page.*

WESLEY: Where are we? I can't find it.

STANLEY (*lightly*): Oh, it's quite near the bottom of the
page.

LOUIS (*looking up from his page*): Near the bottom?
Somebody was taking no chances, were they?

STANLEY *has sat at the table and is tasting the soup.*

STANLEY: This soup is disgusting, I'm sorry. We'll have
to do something about that. (*He looks up and smiles.*)
But it's going to be exciting in there . . . I can promise
you that.

INT. HOTEL PASSAGE. NIGHT

We cut to the band moving along the passage that leads to the
ballroom, they are being led by JOE, *the burly trumpeter. The*
decor all around them is shabby and old-fashioned, the curtains
are heavy and the furniture Victorian, the passage lit by
mournful old lamps. The whole place has the feeling of a
mausoleum.

Just outside the entrance of the ballroom they pause on a
small landing. A very old lady, sitting in an armchair, is
laboriously looking for something in her heavy handbag. She
is totally oblivious of the band standing just a few feet from her,
clustered round, waiting to go on.

The band members' faces are very tense.

STANLEY: This is where I leave you – good luck.

LOUIS (*as* STANLEY *moves off*): They haven't ever had a
coloured band here before, have they?

STANLEY: It's even better than that . . . I don't think
they've ever had jazz music here before!

STANLEY *smiles at their astonished faces and disappears*
into the shadows.

INT. THE BALLROOM. NIGHT

We move in one urgent sustained shot through the doors of the ballroom, snaking round the back of the stage with the band, and then follow them on to the stage itself as the light suddenly gets much brighter and stabs straight into their faces. We see the drums and the bass have already been arranged on the stage in readiness. The band move to take their positions and then stare out. We see the audience for the first time, seemingly a long distance away, sitting at round tables at the other end of the large ballroom. Pale, hostile faces, a mixture of ages but mostly middle-aged and elderly, sitting in a sepulchral atmosphere staring back at us with incomprehension. There is a look of distinct discomfort on some of the faces, as if they have been taken completely by surprise at the entrance of a black band.

We cut to a close-up of LOUIS *as he adjusts his seat at the piano. He is trying hard not to betray his nerves.*

We cut to STANLEY *joining* THORNTON, *standing at the back at the other end of the ballroom from the stage. Both of them are watching the audience's reaction keenly.*

We cut back to LOUIS, *who glances at the audience one more time, then at* JOE *the trumpeter. The band begins to play.*

It is a highly energised up-tempo number, raw and exciting, led by JOE *on the trumpet. There is a dramatic contrast between the music's velocity bursting from one end of the ballroom, and the chilly silent audience at the other. Separating them is the chasm of the empty dance floor. Absolutely nobody gets up to dance.*

We cut to STANLEY *standing next to* THORNTON *in the shadows. There is excitement in* STANLEY*'s eyes as he watches the band play for the first time, and he senses how talented they are.*

THORNTON: Goodness knows why Mr Schlesinger let you do this, Stanley, it's a disaster.

STANLEY *is staring across at the deeply conservative-looking diners.*

STANLEY: He let me do it because of them . . .

THORNTON *turns, bewildered.*

Look at them Harry, look at your clientele! Something's got to change . . .

We notice an elegant-looking middle-aged man, DONALDSON, *sitting at a table surrounded by younger people. A beautiful brother and sister in their twenties,* JULIAN *and* PAMELA. *Next to* PAMELA *is a second young woman,* SARAH, *who has sharp humorous eyes, a slightly bohemian air.*

STANLEY *catches sight of them and moves to their table. We intercut between* LOUIS *playing the piano glancing up at the audience, and* STANLEY *talking to* DONALDSON.

DONALDSON: Hello, Stanley . . . I read your column and you see here I am.

STANLEY: It's tremendous somebody believes what I write!

STANLEY *greets* JULIAN *and* SARAH *as the music plays; he clearly knows them too.* JULIAN *encourages him to sit at their table but* STANLEY *is too energised to sit.*

DONALDSON *is watching the band, intrigued but surprised by them, undecided.*

STANLEY: I'll be very interested to hear your opinion Mr Donaldson . . .

DONALDSON (*smoking his cigar*): I hope I will have an opinion, Stanley.

The band finishes their number. There is a stunned silence. Then DONALDSON*'s table starts clapping quite loudly,* STANLEY *joining in. There is a tiny reluctant ripple of applause from some of the other diners.*

The band starts their second number. Immediately an elderly couple get up to leave, with much scraping of chairs and commotion.

Suddenly PAMELA *stands up and asks* STANLEY *to dance with her. A moment later* SARAH *and* JULIAN *are dancing together as well, the only two couples on the dance floor as the other diners stare uneasily, half repelled, half unable to take their eyes off the band.*

We settle on DONALDSON *as he takes in the band, preparing his verdict.*

INT. THE PARLOUR. NIGHT

We cut inside the tiled parlour. The band have just entered and are coming down after the session, their instruments strewn across the long table. They are looking dazed and bewildered. LOUIS *is standing on his own deep in thought, rather shocked by the hostile reaction.*

JULIAN*'s eager young face appears round the door.*

JULIAN: I'm Julian! Everybody decent? Can we come in?
LOUIS: Of course.

DONALDSON *enters with* JULIAN, PAMELA *and* SARAH. STANLEY *is bringing up the rear.*

DONALDSON *exudes an air of elegant authority, a man of consequence. The group stands at the other end of the room from the band, the women in their fine evening gowns looking incongruous against the kitchen tiles.* PAMELA *has a fragile beauty; in repose she seems very aristocratic but she has a sudden flirtatious smile.* SARAH *is much more direct, less grand, she has a natural warmth.* JULIAN *radiates energy and easygoing charm.*

The band members are all standing now, facing their guests across the parlour.

JULIAN: This is my sister Pamela and her friend Sarah . . . and this is Mr Donaldson, who is a connoisseur of your kind of music.
STANLEY: A great authority in fact!

DONALDSON *takes a puff of his cigar, but initially doesn't say anything. There is an awkward pause.*

SARAH: That was terrific music to dance to, thank you!

LOUIS: Well thank you for dancing. I thought nobody was going to.

PAMELA: Don't be silly, it was the least we could do, gentlemen. It was divine.

WESLEY: I think that was the most disastrous booking we've ever had.

DONALDSON (*effortlessly, delivering his verdict*): No, gentlemen, the audience maybe were a little surprised –

SARAH: They couldn't believe their eyes!

DONALDSON: But I thought you were excellent. No, I did. Sometimes my friend Stanley here exaggerates, but in your case I don't think he is. You have an intriguing line-up of musicians, and no sign of the dreaded banjo, it was very interesting and unusual. A pleasing sound . . . exciting music, I think.

WESLEY (*surprised*): Well, thank you.

STANLEY: What did I tell you?! It's not easy to get praise from Mr Donaldson.

DONALDSON: This is true. (*Smiles charmingly.*) Whether it is of any consequence is quite another matter! But I do as it happens have one piece of advice . . .
WESLEY *and* LOUIS *turn sharply.*
Get yourself a singer.

LOUIS: A singer?

DONALDSON: Yes, I think it might make all the difference to your chances.

WESLEY (*quickly*): It might, yes. But we don't have the money to bring a singer over from America.

DONALDSON: Well, that's a problem certainly. But then you can always try looking for someone here . . . Who knows, you might be lucky. (*He smiles.*) It's just a thought gentlemen, merely a notion, I don't want to interfere, naturally. (*He is moving to the door.*) I must leave you now.

PAMELA, SARAH *and* JULIAN *are leaving too, they smile at the band.*

DONALDSON *turns in the door.*

I will of course spread the word . . .

STANLEY (*turning to* LOUIS): Talking of which – want to come and watch me write my review?

INT. MUSIC EXPRESS OFFICE. NIGHT

The sound of loud typing. We cut to the collage of photographs and drawings that are spread all over the wall of STANLEY*'s office at* Music Express. *We see photographs of people dancing in different settings: some are in grand ballrooms, others are dancing in the street on New Year's Eve.*

We cut wide, STANLEY *is typing vigorously at his desk, a cigarette in his mouth,* LOUIS *and* WESLEY *are watching him from across the room. A small plump man,* ALBERT, *is sitting quietly in the corner.*

STANLEY: Help yourself . . . Louis, Wesley, there are some cigars over there, some whisky somewhere, poke around and help yourself.

WESLEY (*glancing round for the cigars*): Do you let a lot of bands watch you write your reviews?

STANLEY: No, absolutely not. I wouldn't let most musicians anywhere near this office.

LOUIS: So why us?

STANLEY (*fast, as he types*): Because you're different – you're not Jack Paynton for a start! And because I've been given the job of making the Imperial a little more fashionable, it's the sort of challenge I like. So my reasons are purely selfish. (*He grins.*) Naturally.

WESLEY (*finding a cigar among the newspapers*): How many
people read your magazine? Because I never have . . .

STANLEY: More than you might think, and we're growing.
If you're asking me does it matter what I write? I think
it probably does!

*On saying this he slides his chair along his desk and starts
working on something else, a series of drawings which are
spread in front of him. He begins writing captions.* LOUIS
looks slightly alarmed, in case WESLEY *has stopped*
STANLEY *writing the review.*

STANLEY: Forgive me, I've got to do this as well, I always
do two things at once. (*Indicating the half-finished
review in the typewriter.*) Come and have a look, see
what you think so far . . .

WESLEY (*leaning over typewriter, reading*): 'Louis Lester
Band makes storming debut at the Imperial.'

STANLEY (*as he writes captions*): Not bad for a headline, eh?!

WESLEY: 'The atmosphere was simply electric as the Louis
Lester Band took to the stage in the old ballroom at
the Imperial – '

LOUIS: 'Electric'? They hated us! That wasn't electric!

STANLEY: It was for me. (*He grins.*) And that's what
matters.

WESLEY: 'One of our first-ever home-grown coloured
bands shook the room with their intensity, and
showed that this kind of music could appeal to a
much larger audience than it presently enjoys – '

STANLEY (*still busy writing on the drawings*): You are home-
grown, aren't you? That's right, isn't it?

LOUIS: In a way, yes . . . I was born here.

WESLEY: And so was I –

LOUIS: But he's lost his birth certificate!

WESLEY: Yes, somewhere it's gone missing. Got to find it
one day! I was born in Cardiff, but my father took us
off to Chicago when I was four.

STANLEY: So you're from the Midwest, Wesley . . . ?

WESLEY: Yes . . . until I had to leave in a bit of a hurry!
He stares at STANLEY, *challenging him to ask more.*
STANLEY *continues to type his review.*

LOUIS: We met in a club in Harlem. I was there five days
without a break, watching every act –

WESLEY: We never left the club, we never saw daylight –

LOUIS: I was on shore leave, I was working on a liner, the
Aurora. I told Wesley to come to England and see if
we could make something happen in the clubs in
London –

WESLEY: And we did!

LOUIS: Nearly all the band have worked on the ships at
one time as sailors, or cooks –

WESLEY (*lightly*): Or stowaways! . . . And all of us have to
report every week to the Alien Registration Office –
except for Louis, of course, because he's got the right
documents.

STANLEY (*looks up, startled*): You have to do that every
week?

WESLEY: Every week, yes! To get a work permit, they will
only give them to you week by week.
He smokes the cigar and looks straight at STANLEY.
Of course, if we suddenly got a longer booking at the
Imperial that would help us.
STANLEY *smiles at* WESLEY*'s blatant pressure.*

STANLEY: Then I better make sure I finish my review,
hadn't I . . .
*He slides his chair back along the desk and resumes
typing.* LOUIS *picks up one of the drawings* STANLEY *has
been writing on. We see it is a strip cartoon.*

LOUIS: What is this?

STANLEY: Oh, I just have to do the speech bubbles for our
strip cartoon, 'Farquhar and Tonk'. (*He grins.*) You
mean you haven't heard of it?

He indicates the small round man in the corner.
Albert here draws it, and he can't finish it until I've
done the bubbles. It's one of the most important
things we've got!
We begin to see the drawings.

LOUIS: Is it for kids?

STANLEY: No, it's for everyone. I'm trying to make this
much more than just a music magazine . . .
*We see the strip cartoon, a tall slender aristocratic young
man with a monocle and a very squat, strange-looking
companion. They are visiting the races.*

STANLEY (*voice-over the drawings*): Farquhar is an inquisitive
aristocrat and Tonk is his valet who happens to be from
outer space, and together they have adventures . . . We
take them to all sorts of places, don't we, Albert?
LOUIS *stares down at the drawings, Farquhar and Tonk
causing havoc in the Royal Enclosure at Ascot.* LOUIS
laughs.

STANLEY: You like it? Good. (*He continues to type fast.*) We
need a big finish here, to the review! What I really
should say is . . . (*He looks up.*) Get yourself a singer,
Louis.

INT. THE STRIP CARTOON: FARQUHAR AND TONK
*The drawings from the strip fill the whole screen in a series of
fast cuts, as we see the vivid caricatured faces of the guests in the
Royal Enclosure, a scramble of aristocrats pursuing Farquhar
and Tonk along the race track, people scattering in all directions.*

EXT. PEABODY BUILDINGS. AFTERNOON
*We dissolve through the drawings to the camera travelling fast
down an alleyway with old dark walls on either side. It comes*

out into the central courtyard of some East End tenements, a
Peabody building.

    There is the sound of a female voice singing to a piano
accompaniment ringing from somewhere in the estate.

INT. BASEMENT PASSAGE/BASEMENT ROOM. AFTERNOON
We cut to STANLEY *moving along a grubby passage in the*
basement of the tenement building, full of boxes and rotting
discarded furniture. The singing is getting louder. STANLEY
enters a long basement room where a black girl is singing in an
exaggerated minstrel fashion. She is standing at the far end of
the room being watched by some members of the band, who are
slumped in the shadows.

    LOUIS *and* WESLEY *are sitting near the front. The girl is*
being accompanied by one of the members of the band on an
upright piano. There is an atmosphere of despondency in the
room, the girl is singing on regardless. In the corner is a very
*pretty black girl of about twenty (*JESSIE*), dressed immaculately*
in her Sunday best. She is sitting very straight, staring ahead.

    STANLEY *sits next to* WESLEY *and* LOUIS. *He winces at the*
girl's caricatured singing.

LOUIS (*quietly*): I know, I know, we're not having any of
    this terrible West End singing.
WESLEY: They think that's what people want!
STANLEY: Some of them do unfortunately.
    We cut to a montage. A very young fragile-looking girl of
    about fifteen sings quietly, as if she is terrified; a very old
    man sings, a once beautiful voice; and a very large middle-
    aged woman sings very loudly and very badly. All the time
    JESSIE *is sitting in the corner staring ahead.*
    We cut wide as the middle-aged woman is leaving,
    beaming with satisfaction at her own singing.
WESLEY: She looked as if she should be able to sing.

LOUIS: Until she opened her mouth . . . (*He turns.*) Wesley you've got to go. (*He looks at the other members of the band.*) You've got to go, everybody . . . (*To* STANLEY.) it's the day they have to report.

WESLEY: There's plenty of time . . .

He glances across to JESSIE.

LOUIS: She's waiting till her friend arrives, she won't sing till then . . .

The band members are beginning to leave. WESLEY *is reluctant to move.*

Go, Wesley, go! You've got to get to Woburn Square, it's nearly four o'clock! (*To* STANLEY.) They like to cut it as fine as they can . . .

WESLEY (*moving to door, anarchic grin*): I think the old man was best . . . maybe we should hire the oldest singer we can find!

LOUIS (*lightly*): Run, Wesley!

WESLEY *leaves.* LOUIS *and* STANLEY *are alone in the basement room with the young girl* JESSIE *sitting demurely, not looking at them.* STANLEY *takes in the dismal room.*

STANLEY: Is this where you have to rehearse?

LOUIS: Who said anything about rehearsing?! . . . (*Then, more serious.*) Yes, this is the only place we've got – sometimes it's full of coal . . .

JESSIE *suddenly stands up; another young black girl,* CARLA, *is standing in the doorway dressed as if she was going to church.*

JESSIE: I can sing now.

Time cut. LOUIS *is at the piano accompanying* JESSIE, *playing the first notes.* JESSIE *doesn't look at him. She starts to sing, a glorious sound comes out of her.*

STANLEY *is immediately riveted,* LOUIS *is more deadpan in his expression, but we can see a glint in his eye.*

JESSIE *takes a step back, and* CARLA *sings the second verse. She has also got a good voice, though it is not as naturally strong as* JESSIE*'s.*

  JESSIE *steps forward again and they sing the last verse together.*

STANLEY (*calling out*): You're going to get your second booking now, Louis!

  The two girls turn and stare at LOUIS *with a demure look.*

CARLA: She's got the better voice, I know.

  JESSIE *turns to* LOUIS; *her manner is determined, showing steel despite her innocent appearance.*

JESSIE: It's both of us or nothing.

LOUIS: Both of you?

  He pauses, glances from one girl to the other, then he smiles. I don't think that will be a problem.

INT. MUSIC EXPRESS OFFICE. NIGHT

The camera is tracking across the empty Music Express *office towards the small room next door. It is night. We can see in the distance* STANLEY *is in bed with someone, their naked bodies entwined. As we approach the small room the phone in the main office begins to ring.*

  We cut inside the small office. STANLEY *is in bed with* ROSIE, *both of them naked, half covered with a crumpled sheet.* STANLEY *is kissing* ROSIE*'s bare shoulders.*

  The phone keeps ringing.

ROSIE: There's nobody here to answer that, Stanley.

STANLEY: It will stop. It's got to stop soon!

  He starts kissing her again. The phone doesn't stop.

ROSIE: Someone really wants you, Stanley . . . They are not going to give up!

STANLEY: It can't be for me at this time of night.

He gets out of bed, naked, the phone is still ringing. There is an old overcoat hanging on the back of the door, he puts it on. ROSIE *smiles, amused at his modesty.*

STANLEY: Can't answer the phone naked, you never know who it might be.

INT. MUSIC EXPRESS OFFICE/STUDY. NIGHT
STANLEY *answers the phone on his desk.*

STANLEY: *Music Express.*

DONALDSON: So you are still at work, Stanley.
We intercut with DONALDSON *sitting in a book-lined study. On hearing* DONALDSON's *voice* STANLEY *instinctively does the middle button up on the coat.*

STANLEY: Mr Donaldson! Yes I'm still at work. (*He smiles.*) I think.

DONALDSON: One of the nights you sleep there, is it?
ROSIE *is laughing, watching* STANLEY *from the bed in the little room.*

STANLEY: That seems to be the case, yes.

DONALDSON: I need your help, Stanley.

STANLEY: But of course.

DONALDSON: I'm having a lunch party in five days' time –

STANLEY: Am I invited?

DONALDSON: You could be, Stanley, that depends if you can help me. I have a very important – and I mean extremely important – guest coming who loves jazz music –

STANLEY: Who is it?

DONALDSON: I can't tell you that . . .
STANLEY *looks very surprised.*
I am afraid I can't. I had booked Lesley Thompson Oliver Russell's band, but they can be so dull, and they're so –

STANLEY: White? Yes, they are.

DONALDSON: I don't quite know what to do, Stanley.

STANLEY (*immediately*): Well this is perfect timing, Mr
   Donaldson, the band you saw at the Imperial the
   other week, they've taken your advice, they've hired
   a fabulous singer, two in fact –

DONALDSON: Well, that was quick work I must say . . .
   (*Doubtful.*) And they're your top recommendation are
   they, Stanley? I was looking for somebody a little
   more established I have to say, somebody from the
   US, but there's nobody around at the moment. I can't
   make the wrong choice . . . It would be extraordinarily
   embarrassing if this went wrong.

STANLEY: They won't disappoint you, Mr Donaldson.

DONALDSON: Are you certain Stanley?

STANLEY: Am I certain? (*He hesitates for a split second.*)
   Absolutely.

INT. PEABODY BUILDING. DAWN.
Close up of LOUIS *asleep in a small, cramped bedroom in the
Peabody building. Suddenly there are yells in the passage, the
door bursts open and a torch is trained straight at his face. We
see the silhouettes of two policemen yelling at him to get up
immediately. For a moment* LOUIS *is totally disorientated but
then he sits up in bed unhurriedly, refusing to panic.*

INT. PASSAGE. PEABODY BUILDING. NIGHT
*Various members of the band are in the passage, barefoot. Some
are half-naked, covering themselves with blankets.*

POLICEMAN: We're taking all of you down to the Alien
   Registration Office . . . Those that aren't dressed, get
   dressed!

WESLEY (*bare-chested, coming out of his room*): It's five in the morning, what the hell are you doing this for at five in the morning?!

POLICEMAN (*aggressively*): You get dressed, or we'll take you like that.

LOUIS *comes out of the passage half-dressed, wearing a jacket over his bare chest.*

LOUIS (*to* WESLEY): You didn't report did you?

WESLEY: It was shut! They were shut early!

LOUIS *looks disbelieving.*

I swear to you.

LOUIS: I told you not to leave it to the last moment.

POLICEMAN (*to* LOUIS, *very sharp*): It's quite all right by us if you want to go like that. (*Moving towards him.*) Come on then!

LOUIS (*calmly*): I am a British Citizen.

POLICEMAN: Since when?

LOUIS: Since I was born here.

POLICEMAN: Is that right? Show me your birth certificate then.

LOUIS *immediately flicks it out of his jacket and holds it right up close to the policeman's face.*

LOUIS: I always have it handy, especially at five o'clock in the morning.

The POLICEMAN *examines it.*

I've got used to the idea that I might have to prove who I am at any moment.

WESLEY *watches* LOUIS' *boldness with the policeman.*

So you see, I don't need to come with you, but I will all the same, I'm not going to leave the others . . .

I just need to make one telephone call.

The policeman reluctantly gives the birth certificate back to LOUIS.

POLICEMAN: And who are you going to find to ring this early in the morning?

INT. ALIEN REGISTRATION OFFICE. MORNING
*We cut to the Alien Registration Office, a large low room, with
lines of plain wooden benches and dark-green walls. The band
is sitting along two benches watched over by a police officer. On
the other benches are two elderly black men, a Turkish-looking
man and a couple of Eastern Europeans. Their haggard faces
look very tense in the early morning light.*

A sharp-featured man, RYALL, *comes into the hall. There is
an icy authority about him.* WESLEY *whispers out of the corner
of his mouth.*

WESLEY: This is not looking good . . .
RYALL: Are you gentlemen the musicians?
WESLEY: That is us, yes.
RYALL: Do you have a spokesman?
LOUIS: That would be me.
RYALL: Could you please follow me?

INT. RYALL'S OFFICE. MORNING
*We cut inside a small office at the far end of the central room.
It has a frosted glass door.* RYALL *is seated, staring down at
some papers on his desk.* LOUIS *is standing in front of him.*
RYALL *is holding a silver fountain pen which hovers
menacingly over the papers.*

RYALL: You can have a seat, Mr Lester, if you would prefer.
LOUIS (*determined to remain calm*): I'll stand thank you . . .
    I've done a lot of sitting already.
    He drops his birth certificate sharply on to RYALL*'s desk.*
RYALL: I don't require that Mr Lester . . . I know you have
    a birth certificate. (*He looks up sharply.*) Under the
    terms of the work permits granted to the performers
    in your band they have to report every week. This
    week that did not happen.

LOUIS: Well, it's the first time they've ever missed a week.

RYALL: If we allow that to be an excuse the system would quickly fall apart, would it not? If people could choose the week they wanted to report . . . (*He writes something on the papers in front of him with a brisk flourish.*) We can't have that.

LOUIS: What do they need to do?

RYALL: Normally we require proof in writing that they have employment as musicians for the following week before we can issue a permit, but because there has been this transgression of the rules – I now require written proof of three weeks' employment, as an absolute minimum. If I don't receive that by the end of this working day your colleagues will be detained in custody, pending possible deportation.

LOUIS' *eyes flick, this is worse than he was expecting.*

LOUIS: Proof of three weeks' employment?

RYALL: Yes, starting immediately. (*He looks up, his beady eyes studying* LOUIS.) If you don't think you can produce that, Mr Lester, it would save us all time if you told me now.

LOUIS: I will be able to produce that.

RYALL *puts the top back on his fountain pen.*

RYALL: Today we close at 5.15.

INT. MAIN HALL. ALIEN REGISTRATION OFFICE. LATE AFTERNOON

We cut wide to the Alien Registration hall, which is splashed with late-afternoon light. The band are now spread around all the benches, the large clock is showing it is 5.03.

A black couple are sitting watching their two small children run around the hall.

In the distance the door of RYALL's *office is open; he is packing up his briefcase.*

LOUIS *is reading a book, while* WESLEY *is sitting fidgeting beside him. He produces a cigar from his pocket.* LOUIS *looks surprised.*

WESLEY: I kept one from when we were in the magazine office. (*He clamps it in his teeth but doesn't light it.*) It's getting late, Louis.

LOUIS: Don't worry.

WESLEY: Don't worry?! He just reads his book! (*He watches the children.*) I didn't know they brought people here with children . . . Nobody's safe – I better find my bloody birth certificate!

LOUIS: Yes you had.

WESLEY *looks across at the severe-looking female clerk.*

WESLEY: Because I don't want to go back to the US. (*He talks directly to the clerk*). Do you want to know why? (*She ignores him*). Shall I tell her the truth?

LOUIS (*under his breath*): Wesley . . .

WESLEY: Had a little difficulty in Chicago. (*To the clerk.*) Lies were told . . .

LOUIS (*under his breath*): Don't be stupid Wesley – stop this . . .

WESLEY (*lowering his voice, his eyes glinting*): You don't think she wants to hear I was accused of sleeping with a white woman . . . ? That the white woman's husband said I had raped his wife . . . and that carries the death penalty in Chicago . . . You don't think she would be interested in that?! (*He smiles, raises his voice a little louder.*) I think she might be very interested in that . . . (*He looks across at the clerk*). But I was born here, and that makes me English – Welsh in fact! (*He grins.*) So nobody has to worry about it, do they?!

Suddenly we hear STANLEY*'s voice.*

STANLEY: There you are!

STANLEY *enters the hall flourishing a piece of paper.*

So, gentlemen, I have here a four-week booking, in
writing, from the Imperial for their inspection.

LOUIS (*surprised*): Four weeks?

STANLEY: Yes, I told you I'd fix it.

WESLEY (*little suspicious*): Why was it that easy?

STANLEY: Did I say it was easy? It certainly was not, you
don't know Mr Schlesinger!

LOUIS: Thank you.

LOUIS *takes the paper from* STANLEY *and moves towards*
RYALL*'s office,* RYALL*'s beady eyes watching him
approach. The clock shows it's eleven minutes past five.*
STANLEY *sits next to* WESLEY.

STANLEY: There is a little extra as well. Mr Donaldson's
garden party . . . with a special guest of honour whose
identity is being kept secret even from me.

WESLEY (*disbelief*): A secret guest? Who is it? Clark Gable?

STANLEY: There is a nice fee . . . but Wesley, whatever else
you do, you have to be on time. I've given my word.

WESLEY: You've given your word Stanley, have you?
(*Sharp grin.*) We better be on time then.

EXT. LONDON STREET. DAY

*The band are coming towards us down a leafy London street.
Behind them loom large stucco villas. They are dressed in dinner
jackets though they are walking in the midday sun. This time
they are without their instruments.* JESSIE *and* CARLA *are with
them, walking together, dressed in their very proper Sunday-best
clothes.*

*They come to a high brick wall with large trees behind it. In
the wall there is a small wooden door.*

WESLEY: Is this it?

LOUIS: It must be. He said the little door in the wall . . .

*He turns the handle of the door. It is very stiff; he gives the
door a vigorous shove.*

EXT. DONALDSON'S GARDEN. MIDDAY

The door flies open, revealing a large town garden, with plenty of shrubs and tall trees and full of flowers. A subjective shot takes them into this secluded private space. In front of them is a small marquee open at the side, forming a bandstand, with a piano and music stands and all their instruments laid out waiting.

Next to the instruments is a table with bowls of fruit and jugs of soft drinks. Facing the marquee across a piece of lawn is the back of the house with its french windows and terrace. They approach the marquee.

LOUIS (*whistling, impressed*): It is all waiting for us . . . just like he said.

JESSIE and CARLA move along the flowerbeds, exploring the garden, full of wonder.

CARLA: What a garden! Does it belong just to one house?

JESSIE (*staring towards the french windows*): Do you think we are dressed right?

They can see the shadows of people drinking and eating in the room beyond the french windows.

Suddenly STANLEY is running towards them from the house.

STANLEY: Here you are! Exactly on time.

LOUIS: Of course.

STANLEY: Then start playing!

LOUIS: Is the mystery guest of honour here yet?

STANLEY: Start playing, and if he likes you you may get to see him.

We cut to the band playing in the empty garden, their music pouring towards the french windows. JESSIE is standing in front of them as they play the intro, calmly waiting for her cue. Then she launches into her first song, her big voice carrying towards the house. Her singing is very expressive; she commits to the emotion in the song totally, holding nothing back. We see a close up of WESLEY, *deeply impressed by her singing.*

LOUIS *is watching the house as he plays the piano. We cut between* JESSIE *singing,* LOUIS *and* WESLEY *watching for signs of life from beyond the terrace, and silhouetted figures glimpsed through the glass of the french windows but not coming out.*

We see a close up of DONALDSON *through the window, looking rather tense.*

Suddenly one figure comes out of the french windows. It is SARAH; *she has a camera with her and she starts taking photographs of the band and* JESSIE *singing.*

The song finishes. There is distant applause from inside the house but nobody else has come out.

The band launches into the second song, a vibrant catchy number.

Now some figures start to appear on the terrace to watch them more closely. There are JULIAN *and* PAMELA, *who looks radiant in a beautiful dress, there is* DONALDSON, *with a small cluster of other guests behind him, and a tall rather sinister-looking man of about fifty,* MASTERSON, *who has a very reserved manner.*

And then we cut to a figure, dressed casually in flannels, appearing out of the shadows of the room. He leans nonchalantly in the mouth of the french windows and sips his drink. He is a fleshy young man with piercing sensual eyes and a rather decadent air. The other guests deferentially move out of his way as he steps on to the terrace. JESSIE *finishes singing. The fleshy young man beams and starts clapping vigorously. The other guests follow suit immediately. We cut to* DONALDSON *looking very relieved.*

We cut to STANLEY *coming across the lawn to the band, with the guests watching from the terrace.*

STANLEY: He wants to meet you.

The band stare at the fleshy young man.

WESLEY: Who is he?

STANLEY: Prince George! (*They look blank.*) The fourth son of the King!

JESSIE: The son of the King!

CARLA: What do we call him?

LOUIS: Your Royal Highness, and you're not meant to speak to him until you're spoken to.

STANLEY (*laughing, impressed*): How do you know that?

EXT./INT. DONALDSON'S HOUSE. DAY

We cut inside the room that leads on to the terrace. PRINCE GEORGE *is sitting in a large chair drinking and eyeing the band as they approach.* LOUIS, CARLA *and* JESSIE *are first, but they pause, not wishing to come too close to him.*

PRINCE GEORGE: Come here, come here, please . . . You must tell us all about yourselves. (*He stares at* JESSIE.) Where on earth did you learn to sing like that?

JESSIE *looks startled, not sure how to reply.*

CARLA: Jessie's always been able to sing, right from when she was tiny at school.

JESSIE: Yes . . . (*Nervous laugh.*) Since school.

PRINCE GEORGE: Since you were tiny at school, is that right? I was always awful at everything at school . . .

There are deferential murmurs of disbelief from some of the guests.

Oh no, I was bottom at everything, resoundingly bottom, every term! Except for music . . . I can play a little as it happens . . .

LOUIS: You must show us, Your Royal Highness.

PRINCE GEORGE*'s eyes flick towards* LOUIS, *surprised at him piping up uninvited.*

PRINCE GEORGE: Maybe I will.

LOUIS (*deadpan*): That would be tremendous . . . (*Then remembers.*) Your Royal Highness.

PRINCE GEORGE (*studying* LOUIS, *intrigued by his confidence*): In fact I would love to . . . but when I've had a lot more to drink and therefore won't have to worry quite so much about making a complete fool of myself!

We cut to DONALDSON *standing with* STANLEY. *In the background we can see the band helping themselves to the fine spread of food, the buffet that is arranged deeper in the room. They are heaping food on to their plates.*

DONALDSON: You were right about the singer, Stanley.

STANLEY: Yes, she is even better than I thought she was.

DONALDSON: But your band are clearly absolutely starving.

We see a shot of WESLEY's *plate completely groaning with food.*

DONALDSON *looks across at* LOUIS *mingling with the guests.*

And I like the look of your Mr Lester. It's quite surprising really, he seems an educated man, doesn't he . . . ? The way he conducts himself, the way he talks.

STANLEY (*grins*): Unlike me, you mean?! Yes, he's quite a character.

DONALDSON: I like people who have that natural authority about them, who know who they are.

His gaze crosses over to PRINCE GEORGE, *who is flirting with* JESSIE *and* CARLA.

And clearly His Royal Highness is very happy indeed.

We cut to SARAH *coming up to* LOUIS.

SARAH: I couldn't take your picture out in the garden, could I? And any other members of the band who would like to . . . ? I want to do some portrait shots.

LOUIS: Of course. (*Glancing across at the buffet.*) But I'm not sure I can stop them eating right at this moment . . .

JOE, *the trumpeter, stands up having finished a very large plate of food.*

JOE: I'll come.

We cut to JULIAN *and* PAMELA *coming up to* STANLEY, *who is just serving himself from the buffet.* JULIAN *is in an exuberant mood.*

JULIAN: It's not just the Prince that's here today you know . . . (*He indicates* MASTERSON.) Some say he's one of the richest men in the world . . . He's from the US, managed not to lose everything in the Crash, in fact he even made money while it was happening. I'm working for him at the moment, just helping out, but he said he might have something bigger for me . . .

STANLEY (*watching* MASTERSON, *intrigued*): I must try to talk to him.

PAMELA: You won't have any luck. He never says more than five words at any party. It's impossible to know what he's thinking . . .

We see a shot of MASTERSON *surveying the room with an impassive stare.*

We then see PRINCE GEORGE *really close to* JESSIE *and* CARLA, *full of drink, laughing and coaxing them.*

PRINCE GEORGE (*to* JESSIE): Go on, sing something more for me now . . . a little song, just right here, please.

CARLA: You want her to sing now? . . . Your Royal Highness?

JESSIE: Sing what?

PRINCE GEORGE: Anything you like?! Sit here . . .

He encourages her to sit on the arm of his chair. JESSIE *begins to sing softly, unaccompanied, as we cut back to* PAMELA *and* STANLEY *across the room.*

PAMELA: So, Stanley, you really do have an eye for talent.

STANLEY (*lightly*): Of course I do, don't you read the magazine?

PAMELA: I read *Music Express* every week, as it happens.

STANLEY (*surprised*): You do? I didn't know you were so
keen on music?

PAMELA: I'm interested in all sorts of things Stanley. (*Self-
mocking smile.*) Not just clothes and men! I read your
magazine from cover to cover. And it all seems to be
written by you.

STANLEY: Most of it. Yes.

PAMELA: Even the diary of the chorus girl in the West End
show!

STANLEY (*unabashed*): Well, that was a sort of
collaboration.

PAMELA: Don't you have an editor who orders you
around?

STANLEY: I do have an editor, a Mr Wax. (*He smiles.*) But
he seems to like what I do.

PAMELA *laughs, an infectious laugh. She looks straight at*
STANLEY *flirtatiously.*

PAMELA: Stanley, you know you always surprise me.

STANLEY: That's good. (*He returns her gaze.*) Isn't that
good?

PAMELA: Yes. I like daring people.

STANLEY (*obviously pleased*): You think I'm daring, Pamela?

PAMELA: Maybe . . . almost. (*She smiles.*) What a pity you
won't be able to write about this, the Royal Prince
and a jazz band, that would make a story! (*Their eyes
meet.*) But even you can't do that.

EXT. DONALDSON'S GARDEN. DAY
We cut outside to the garden where SARAH *is taking photos of*
JOE *among the flowers, under the shade of a tree.* LOUIS *is
standing next to her, watching.*

SARAH (*to* LOUIS): Stanley told me about your trouble with
the immigration authorities.

LOUIS: Yes, well, the rules are very strict, especially if you've worked on ships . . . so they have to report every week. Some of them even get followed sometimes, people checking to see if they really are employed as musicians.

SARAH: Followed, in the street? Really?

LOUIS: Not many people realise that's what goes on . . . but it's a tough regime, the Alien Registration Office.

SARAH (*checking her camera*): Well, my father's Russian and he gets some strange looks sometimes . . . (*She laughs.*) People thinking he might be a Soviet spy! (*She turns towards him.*) So maybe I understand a little more than you think.

A shot of PAMELA, *in her beautiful dress, staring across at them from the house.*

LOUIS: Sorry, I didn't mean to –

SARAH: Don't worry.

SARAH *is not offended, she points her camera at* PAMELA. *We see her framed in* SARAH*'s lens, then she moves back on to* JOE.

SARAH: Maybe I see a bit more of the world than Pamela. I'm her friend but I work for her really. I choose her clothes, and I design some of them. (*Self-mocking smile.*) Which means I actually have to go into shops, warehouses even, looking for material! I'm sure you guessed, but I'm no aristocrat, Louis.

LOUIS (*smiles*): I don't think I had guessed that.

SARAH (*takes last picture*): Thank you Joe . . . you're next, Louis.

LOUIS *steps forward to be photographed but at that precise moment* JULIAN *yells across the garden, hurtling towards them.*

JULIAN: The band must play again . . . Prince George has requested it!

We cut to LOUIS *moving back towards the marquee to play.*
JULIAN *is by his side, full of warmth and enthusiasm.*

JULIAN (*suddenly turning to him*): I love your music . . . I hope you don't mind me saying that . . . I love your band!

We cut to the band playing again, with PRINCE GEORGE *actually sitting in amongst the band, on the drums, with the drummer next to him.*

As the drummer starts drumming so does PRINCE GEORGE, *laughing rather drunkenly, but trying to keep in time. He is enjoying himself immensely.*

PRINCE GEORGE (*yelling out as he drums*): I'm hopeless! Is it hopeless? . . . I think this really is hopeless isn't it?!

LOUIS (*calling from the piano*): Of course not, Your Royal Highness.

The rest of the guests are standing watching, making approving noises and clapping PRINCE GEORGE, *as he drums enthusiastically.*

STANLEY *finds himself standing next to* MASTERSON.

STANLEY: I don't suspect you ever thought you'd see something like this.

MASTERSON (*impassive, sipping his drink*): It's possible I've seen it before.

WESLEY *helps himself to a drink from a passing servant. He watches* PRINCE GEORGE *in amongst the band. He mutters to himself.*

WESLEY: Well, what do you know, we have a new member of the band! (*As if announcing to the audience.*) And on the drums . . . the Royal Family!

PRINCE GEORGE *and the drummer are now in a drumming solo together, both drumming faster and faster. We move in on* PRINCE GEORGE *as he drums furiously.*

INT. IMPERIAL HOTEL. NIGHT

It is night. We cut from the loud drumming to the sound of
JESSIE *singing with the band. We hear it from a distance, as we*
track across the lobby of the Imperial towards the doors of the
ballroom. As we get near we can see a group of uniformed hotel
staff are straining to look into the ballroom through a crack in
the door. Two fashionable women glide towards them to re-enter
the ballroom and one of the hotel staff holds the door open for
them, allowing us to glimpse JESSIE *singing at the far end of the*
room. Our view is partially obscured by a group of men standing
at the back drinking and watching her sing. JESSIE *is in a*
shimmering new evening dress. The atmosphere in the ballroom
is already more glamorous.

Suddenly THORNTON *joins the hotel staff, who are*
continuing to hold the door ajar, watching eagerly. THORNTON
surveys the diners.

THORNTON: A little more full tonight . . . not bad at all.
It's been building all week . . . I knew I was right to
tell them to get a singer.

INT. IMPERIAL HOTEL. BASEMENT PASSAGES AND
PARLOUR. NIGHT

We cut to a fast tracking shot as we follow JESSIE *and the band*
immediately after they have come offstage. They are pouring
down the back stairs and into the basement passage. They are
in ecstatic mood, excited chatter and laughter, and the camera is
right in amongst them as they come down after their performance.

INT. PASSAGE/LOBBY. NIGHT

LOUIS *is following them, looking quietly pleased. He pauses by*
a door that has a round window that looks on to the main
lobby. He sees images of the rich clientele moving through the

hotel, glimpses of society. We see a shot of an elderly dowager accompanied by a much younger man, we see a group of men in dark coats all carrying small boxes disappearing through a side door.

INT. PASSAGE/PARLOUR. NIGHT
We cut back to the fast tracking shot as the band approaches the parlour. WESLEY *is standing in the doorway calling to them. He helps himself to a jam tart from a trolley.*

WESLEY: Come and look at this.
    We cut inside the parlour. The band are confronted by the sight of a silver platter of steaming lamb chops sitting in the middle of the long table, with a large bowl of peas next to it and several bottles of red wine.
Meat for the first time! (*He grins.*) We must be doing something right then!
    The band fall on the lamb chops ravenously.

INT. PASSAGE/LOBBY. NIGHT
We cut back to LOUIS *staring through the window into the lobby. He is just about to move on when he sees* JULIAN *and* MASTERSON *huddled in a corner.* MASTERSON *is standing over* JULIAN *talking to him in a serious, confidential manner, as if he is giving him instructions.* MASTERSON *moves off and disappears into the shadows.*

INT. THE PARLOUR/PASSAGE. NIGHT
The lights are now low in the parlour. WESLEY *and* LOUIS *are alone. They are sitting at the long table surrounded by the clean bones of the lamb chops and empty bottles of wine. Both men are in mellow mood, full of drink.* WESLEY *pours out the last drops of wine from the final bottle.*

WESLEY: We've never been given wine before . . . Maybe this Mr Schlesinger, or whatever he's called, is beginning to like us.

LOUIS: And maybe we'll get to meet him one day . . . if he exists, that is!

JULIAN's head suddenly appears round the parlour door.

JULIAN: Louis, sorry to butt in like this, but can you come here a moment? I need your help. (*His tone is urgent, his face rather tense.*) Please.

Both men stand up in response to the urgency of his request.

No, just Louis . . . (*To* WESLEY.) That's very kind, but I just need Louis . . .

We cut to LOUIS *joining him in the passage.* JULIAN *turns to him.*

Thank God you were still here!

INT. THE IMPERIAL. BEDROOM PASSAGE. NIGHT

We cut to JULIAN *leading* LOUIS *along a wide passage past the bedrooms on the third floor of the hotel. The passage is deserted, just the lines of shoes outside the bedrooms waiting to be polished.*

LOUIS: Where are we going, Julian?

JULIAN: Just a little further, just round the corner . . . Something I need a little help with . . . Mr Masterson has asked me to do something.

They go round the corner and stop by a door that says 'The Minotaur Suite'.

JULIAN (*searching his pockets*): This is Mr Masterson's suite, he gave me the key, I've got it somewhere . . . he's left the hotel. (*He finds the key.*) Now Louis if you feel you are unable to help, you must say so at once, and of course I'll understand . . . but if you do feel able to help, I'd be so terribly grateful.

JULIAN opens the door of the suite.

INT. MASTERSON'S HOTEL SUITE. NIGHT

JULIAN *and* LOUIS *enter the darkened suite.* JULIAN *switches on a side light. Everything in the main room of the suite is smashed, tables upturned, food squashed into the carpet or smeared over the mirrors, glasses broken, china ornaments shattered all over the floor.*

LOUIS *surveys the wreckage of the room.*

LOUIS: What happened here?

JULIAN: I don't know . . . he said it would be like this. I don't know what he's been doing . . .

There is a sound, a low moan from the darkened bedroom beyond. LOUIS *instantly moves towards the dark bedroom. The curtains are drawn, there are just pinpoints of light. For a moment all he can see is a shape moving slightly on the bed. He switches on a lamp. The bedroom is also smashed up.*

Lying on the bed is a young woman in her petticoat, her head turned away from us. LOUIS *moves towards her.* JULIAN *is hovering in the doorway, he can see the girl. He calls out urgently.*

JULIAN: Is she all right?

LOUIS *looks down at the girl* (HANNAH). *She turns her eyes towards him; they look glazed, like she is high on drugs and alcohol. She seems to be breathing heavily. She beckons* LOUIS *closer.*

HANNAH (*whispers*): Hello . . .

LOUIS (*calling to* JULIAN): I don't know . . . she isn't really awake –

JULIAN (*standing in the doorway*): What a mess! Mr Masterson said would I clear this up . . . I didn't think it would be this bad, I mean not quite as bad as this! I knew I shouldn't involve you, Louis, but I can't do it all on my own. (*He cries out.*) I didn't know what to

do! (*He looks across at* LOUIS.) Please leave if you need
to Louis . . . please leave if you want.

LOUIS *looks back at* JULIAN, *his anguished young face.*

LOUIS: What do we need to do?

JULIAN: We need to get the girl out of the hotel . . . Mr
Masterson will pay for the damage to the room of
course, but we need to get the girl away from here
without being seen. Can you help me do that? If we
use the kitchen entrance? If I get a taxi, and you take
the girl? I have to do this for Mr Masterson . . . his
reputation and everything. (*Heartfelt.*) Can you do
that, Louis?

LOUIS *approaches the girl.*

LOUIS: Do you need help to get up?

HANNAH (*softly*): Maybe . . .

LOUIS *lifts her into a sitting position. She leans against
him.*

HANNAH: I just need my dress . . . (*Softly.*) And perhaps a
shoe or two . . .

JULIAN (*watching from the doorway*): Oh my God, what a
business this is!

INT. PASSAGE. OUTSIDE BEDROOM. NIGHT
LOUIS *is supporting* HANNAH *as they walk towards the lifts.
She is a tall, striking girl with long dark hair spilling down over
her shoulders. As they stand by the lift, she is breathing heavily.*

LOUIS: What's your name?

HANNAH (*softly*): Just call me Hannah . . .

INT. HOTEL LIFT. NIGHT
We cut inside the lift. They are alone for a moment. HANNAH
looks up at LOUIS, *and for the first time he can see her clearly.*

*The side of her face and her arm are covered in very heavy
bruises as if she has been assaulted.* LOUIS *looks startled. At
that very moment the lift stops at the second floor, the doors
open and a couple get in. A tall man accompanied by a young
woman, both in evening dress as if setting off for a nightclub.*
HANNAH *lifts her finger to her lips to silence* LOUIS *and turns
her face to the wall. The couple stare beadily at* LOUIS, *a black
man in a lift with a white woman. There is a tense silence before
the lift stops at the foyer and the couple leave.* LOUIS *presses the
button for the basement. As soon as the doors close he moves
across to* HANNAH.

LOUIS: What happened? Are you all right?
HANNAH (*whispers*): I'm perfectly fine . . . Please, no
    questions.
    She slides down the wall of the lift.
HANNAH: Just had a little too much to drink that's all . . .
    (*Softly.*) Just too much room service . . .
    The lift doors open at the basement level.

INT. BASEMENT PASSAGE. NIGHT
LOUIS *moves along the kitchen passage. He is now carrying*
HANNAH *in his arms because the basement is seemingly
deserted. He can see the exit in the distance, and has to get there
unseen. We are moving with him as he carries* HANNAH.
    *Halfway down the passage he hears voices. He moves into
one of the darkened rooms, a pantry room, and watches from
the shadows, still holding* HANNAH. THORNTON *appears round
the corner with two young chefs; he's upbraiding them viciously
for taking too long over a room service order. One of the boys
suddenly runs away from* THORNTON *as soon as he's finished
talking. The boy is very upset, he glances for a second into the
doorway where* LOUIS *is with* HANNAH *as he runs past, and
then disappears down the passage.* LOUIS *can't tell if he was*

seen. He lies HANNAH *down on a table in the dark pantry. The moment he has done this, he sees* THORNTON *coming towards him. He decides to brazen it out. He stands in the doorway and lights a cigarette.*

THORNTON: Still here, Mr Lester?

LOUIS: Yes, I'm just leaving now. I've been going through the music for tomorrow . . .

>HANNAH *is lying in the shadows behind him, but it is very dark in the room.*

THORNTON: I see. (*Peering at him.*) I will be writing a report for Mr Schlesinger. I think he might be quite pleased with tonight.

LOUIS (*can't stop himself*): Do we ever get to meet Mr Schlesinger?

THORNTON (*a piercing stare*): That depends, Mr Lester, that depends. (*He moves off.*) Good night.

>*We cut to* LOUIS *lifting* HANNAH *back into his arms.*

LOUIS (*whispers*): I don't think he saw us . . .

>*We see* LOUIS *moving down the empty passage with* HANNAH *in his arms and out into the night.*

EXT. STREET AT BACK OF IMPERIAL. NIGHT
We cut to LOUIS *and* HANNAH *in a side street in the shadow of a dark wall. A street lamp behind them.* HANNAH *is leaning against the wall,* LOUIS *is gazing up the empty street.*

LOUIS: He should be along any minute . . .

HANNAH (*softly*): That's good.

LOUIS: Do you need a doctor?

>HANNAH *shakes her head.*

>You don't think we should take you to hospital?

HANNAH: No, no, please don't worry about me . . . (*Her glazed eyes stare at him.*) Remember . . .

She lifts her finger to her lips in a gesture of silence.
Promise me . . . (*Before* LOUIS *can reply.*) Oh look,
I think my car is coming!
The lights of a taxi are approaching. She touches his arm.
Thank you. You mustn't worry about me . . .
The taxi pulls up with JULIAN *inside. He throws open the
door.*

JULIAN: There you are. Marvellous!

LOUIS (*as he helps* HANNAH *into the taxi*): She's hurt, she
needs a doctor.

JULIAN: A doctor, oh my God! (*Then, recovering himself.*)
I will make sure she gets looked after, the very best
care . . .
He leans out of the window and clasps LOUIS' *hand, very
heartfelt.*
Thank you Louis, Mr Masterson will be pleased . . .
I'm incredibly grateful! You're wonderful my friend!
The taxi drives off into the night, with LOUIS *staring
after it.*

INT. MUSIC EXPRESS OFFICE/IMPERIAL BASEMENT. NIGHT
*An abrupt cut to the strip cartoon Farquhar and Tonk, an image
of them on the deck of a great liner, climbing out from under a
tarpaulin on a lifeboat. We see a close-up of* STANLEY *writing the
speech bubbles. We then see another panel of the strip, Farquhar
and Tonk entering the grand ballroom of the liner where a black
jazz band are performing, watched by the diners, huge fleshy men
in dinner jackets and tiny elderly women encrusted in jewels.*

The phone on the desk rings. STANLEY *picks it up sharply,
rather testily, resenting being interrupted.*

STANLEY: *Music Express*? (*Sharply.*) What can I do for you?
We intercut with LOUIS *on the phone in the basement
passage in the Imperial.*

LOUIS: Stanley, it's Louis, something strange has just happened with Julian and Mr Masterson.

STANLEY (*breezily*): Something strange involving Mr Masterson? That doesn't surprise me in the least.

LOUIS: There was a girl in Mr Masterson's suite at the hotel. She was in a bad way, the room was all smashed up too.

STANLEY: So they'd been having quite a party –

LOUIS: I helped Julian get her out of the hotel.

STANLEY: And where was Mr Masterson when you were doing this?

LOUIS: I don't know, I didn't see him. He asked Julian to clear up for him.

STANLEY (*lighting a cigarette*): People like that always can vanish when they want to can't they?!

LOUIS: Stanley, I'm thinking, I don't know if I should've helped, I mean the girl, she was hurt –

STANLEY: You're worried about her?

LOUIS: Yes . . . I am.

STANLEY: If you're worried about her Louis, then we'll have to find her.

INT. JULIAN AND PAMELA'S HOME. DAY
We cut to LOUIS *and* STANLEY *sitting in the main reception room of a grand London town house. They are sitting apart and rather tense, waiting. We see them in a wide shot, both of them feeling rather incongruous.*

A MAID *appears at the far end of the room.*

MAID: Mr Julian knows you are here, he will be with you in a moment.
She leaves. STANLEY *suddenly jumps up from his chair and begins restlessly to examine the room.*

STANLEY: One day, Louis, you'll have a house like this!

LOUIS: Of course . . . (*He glances around at the magnificent room.*) As a matter of interest how do you see that happening?

STANLEY: Well, it won't be long before your records are available in every store in the land –

LOUIS: That'll be good, considering we haven't made a single one yet.

STANLEY: It'll be impossible to get away from you – I'll be just walking down the street and your music will be coming out of every other window. And when I turn up to see you, when you've got a house like this –

LOUIS (*grins*): You'll be shown straight to the tradesmen's entrance.

STANLEY: Naturally, yes! And a maid will come in and say 'Mr Louis will be with you in a moment, but he can only spare you five minutes.'

LOUIS: Five minutes?! It might well be less than that.

JULIAN: Stanley! Louis! I'm so glad you're here.

JULIAN *and* PAMELA *sweep into the room, the brother and sister looking glowing, both fashionably dressed.*

PAMELA: There you are! What a lovely way to start the day.

STANLEY (*meeting her flirtatious look*): Start? It's nearly two o'clock, Pamela!

PAMELA (*self-mocking smile*): Oh it's as early as that is it? I thought it was later! It's wicked I know, but I've only just got up.

JULIAN (*to* LOUIS): What a strange evening that was last night. (*To* STANLEY.) Louis was absolutely wonderful, has he told you?

STANLEY: He has. (*He pauses.*) We were just wondering what happened to the girl?

HANNAH: She's here.

HANNAH *is standing in the doorway in a demure summer dress. The bruises round her eye and on the side of her face are hugely visible.*

JULIAN: With her gigantic bruises –

HANNAH: I was so clumsy last night, and so utterly drunk! (*Indicating her bruises.*) I just kept falling over, goodness knows what people must think! (*She looks at* LOUIS.) I'm enormously grateful to you. (*Adopting a discreet tone.*) And so is Mr Masterson.

PAMELA: Oh yes, Mr Masterson is having a picnic next week and you really must join us.

HANNAH: Yes, he would love you to join him – in fact the whole band if they're available . . . (*Pointedly.*) To be his guests. (*Confidentially.*) It's his way of saying a huge thank you.

LOUIS (*startled*): The whole band? Really? They're all invited?

HANNAH (*breezily*): Well, whoever wants to come . . . they might enjoy it. He plans them very carefully . . . I won't be there myself. (*She smiles.*) Sadly my parents are coming to town.

LOUIS: What reason do I give the band, why they're invited?

PAMELA (*smiles*): Just tell them Mr Masterson really likes them.

JULIAN: Oh, you must come, please say you will. It would make his picnic so much more jolly!

PAMELA (*looking straight at Louis*): And in case you were wondering – Sarah will be there, yes.

LOUIS *is taken aback by the implication of this remark.*

PAMELA *turns her gaze on to* STANLEY.

PAMELA: And you'll come, Stanley, won't you?

STANLEY: Ah, I am invited too, am I?

PAMELA: Of course. (*Pointedly.*) I'm inviting you. (*She turns to* LOUIS.) Mr Masterson tends to picnic on a grand scale . . . it's not something you would forgive yourself for missing.

STANLEY: On a grand scale? Does that mean a lot of Rolls-Royces setting off for a mystery destination that only he knows?

JULIAN: You are nearly right. There is going to be some interesting transport – but it's not a line of Rolls-Royces.

INT./EXT. TRAIN. AFTERNOON
A train is hurtling along in bright sunlight. We cut directly inside the carriage and see STANLEY *and* LOUIS *exuberantly exploring the wood-panelled sleeping car with its luxury private compartments.*

STANLEY: This is amazing.

LOUIS (*laughing*): Our own private train!
    He sticks his head out of the window. And we cut to the exterior of the train, with LOUIS *leaning out as it roars through the English countryside: a large engine pulling just four carriages, two sleeping cars and two Pullman cars. We cut back inside the train.*

LOUIS: I didn't think I'd have a compartment to myself!

STANLEY: Yes, we really are his guests. Don't have to sing for our supper . . . (*Smiles at* LOUIS.) Not unless we want to –

LOUIS: Well, you don't, Stanley!

STANLEY: What's your compartment like?

LOUIS: Velvet cushions and a bowl of chocolates.

STANLEY: A bowl of chocolates? Not sure I've got that!
    SARAH *appears at the end of the corridor.*

SARAH: Isn't this tremendous?! We've got this train all to ourselves.

STANLEY: It's like a royal train, yes.

SARAH: I have three different sorts of soap in my compartment! And we have no idea where the

train's going, where we're going to end up! At least,
I haven't –

A door of one of the compartments opens and WESLEY
sticks his head out. He is eating a peach.

WESLEY: I've got a nice bowl of fruit in here!

INT. THE TRAIN. DINING CAR. EVENING

We cut to LOUIS *and* WESLEY *entering the dining car, dressed
in dinner jackets. The dining car is a beautiful old carriage with
decorative panelling and with flowers on each table. The low
evening sun is catching the walls and making the carriage glow.*
MASTERSON *is sitting at a table with* JULIAN. JESSIE *and*
CARLA *are sitting together at another table,* DONALDSON *is
sitting with* PAMELA. STANLEY *is at a table on his own which
he has covered with papers. There are four or five members of
the band sitting at other tables, including* JOE *the trumpeter.*
SARAH *is sitting at a table on her own. Everybody has dressed
for dinner.*

LOUIS *and* WESLEY *hesitate for a moment in the doorway.*

MASTERSON: Come in, gentlemen . . . the soup is about to
be served.

PAMELA (*merrily*): And we're all absolutely starving!

LOUIS (*approaching* SARAH's *table*): Is anybody sitting here?

SARAH: No. (*She looks up and smiles at him.*) By all means . . .

Liveried servants enter with bowls of soup on silver trays.

WESLEY *sits with members of the band and whispers.*

WESLEY: What do you know? We're going to be waited on!

*One of the band members can't stop himself standing up
and taking the soup from the waiter as he approaches their
table. The soup, a rich-looking lobster bisque, is served in
beautiful china.*

We cut to LOUIS *and* SARAH *facing each other across
their table. The train is travelling fast.*

LOUIS: Nobody knows where we're going?

SARAH: Nobody, no.

LOUIS (*glancing towards* MASTERSON): Do you really think that can be true?

SARAH: Yes, he likes his mystery picnics.

> LOUIS *stares across at the strange figure of* MASTERSON *as he sits impassively with* JULIAN. *We cut to a close-up of* LOUIS *watching* MASTERSON *keenly. We cut back to* MASTERSON *eating his soup. Their eyes meet.*

LOUIS (*suddenly*): Is it easy Mr Masterson to hire a private train?

MASTERSON (*pauses for a second, then continues with his* soup): Oh it's quite easy if you know who to ask.

LOUIS: But you have to tell someone the exact route you are going to take? You must have to do that surely?

MASTERSON (*a faint smile*): What makes you think that?

EXT. THE TRAIN. NIGHT

Night. We see a wide shot of the train, which is now stationary. It is stretched out under the night sky in the middle of the countryside, glowing out of the surrounding blackness with all its lights on. There is the sound of a single trumpet being played and JESSIE *singing softly. We track towards the train fast and peer in through the lighted windows of the dining car.*

INT. TRAIN. DINING CAR. NIGHT

We cut inside the dining car. Candles have been lit on the tables, the dinner is finished, some of the guests have left the carriage, including STANLEY *and* MASTERSON. JESSIE *is singing softly in a corner, with* CARLA *joining in,* JOE *is accompanying them on the trumpet. The atmosphere is very mellow, everyone is rather drunk.* JULIAN *is standing leaning against a table watching the girls singing, absolutely entranced.*

DONALDSON *is presiding over the carriage, drinking brandy and smoking a cigar.* PAMELA *is sitting next to him and* LOUIS *is opposite, also drinking brandy.*

SARAH *is stretched out on a seat staring at the ceiling and smoking. In the corner* WESLEY *is watching everybody very beadily.*

DONALDSON: I think what you've done, Mr Lester, is truly extraordinary.

LOUIS: What I've done? What is that, Mr Donaldson?

DONALDSON: How you've made this band from nothing.

WESLEY (*muttering to himself*): How he's made it?

DONALDSON: I am very intrigued by how you've managed to meld it all together in a very sophisticated way, if you don't mind me saying so. You've taken the best of what you've heard from America, but you've made it your own. How did you learn to do that? (*Suddenly correcting himself.*) I'm sorry, that sounded much too patronising – forgive me, but I think you know what I mean . . .

LOUIS (*not offended, smoking a cigar*): Well I think it was my experience on the ocean liners that helped me so much . . . playing on those, even if most of the time we were just playing foxtrots! I got a chance to meet a lot of other musicians, I learnt from them. We always rushed straight to Harlem when we docked, Wesley and me. We saw Duke Ellington play. It opened my eyes to what was possible . . . (*Drinking his brandy.*) But I always remembered one thing, you need to make music people want to dance to –

PAMELA (*lighting a cigarette*): And you certainly do that!

SARAH: And when you were playing on those liners and people were dancing in front of you, did they ever say things to you?

LOUIS: Say things?

SARAH: When you were on a big ship together . . . with all those people –

WESLEY: Rich people!

SARAH: Yes, you must have bumped into them when you weren't playing, like when you were leaving the stage. Did you have to put up with them being rather horrible?

DONALDSON (*delicately*): You must have got used to dealing with a lot of prejudiced people?

LOUIS: Of course, yes. (*He sits back with his cigar and brandy.*) You never know where it's going to come from either.

PAMELA*'s pale aristocratic face.* WESLEY *watching* LOUIS*' expansive mood closely, how he's enjoying the attention.*

Sometimes it's the people you don't expect. (*To* SARAH.) You're right, you know, I remember bumping into a table when I was leaving the stage on one crossing, and the couple nearest to me – and the lady, she was all covered in jewels but she was very young and charming looking – and both of them, this couple, started wiping their cutlery with their napkins, rubbing their knives and forks, even though I hadn't even touched them, wasn't even near their knives and forks! But there they were, rubbing them clean . . . (*He empties his glass.*) They changed them a few minutes later too – just to make sure!

DONALDSON: Oh, that's very revealing, wiping their cutlery.

SARAH: You should do that to them next time! When certain people walk really close to your table you should start cleaning your fork, see how they react to that!

DONALDSON (*filling* LOUIS*' glass*): There is so much ignorance isn't there, and you're right, Mr Lester,

sometimes those that seem to be the most educated
turn out to be quite the most ignorant, the most
prejudiced. (*Smoking his cigar.*) But then we don't
know what's going to happen next do we?!
LOUIS *is looking at him intrigued.*
If six months ago one had gone around saying we're
going to have a National Government with the Tories
and some of the Labour politicians actually working
together, people would have said you're absolutely
mad! But now we've got that. Maybe things are about
to change. Despite all the hardship there is, I feel –
and I hope this is not too optimistic Mr Lester – but
I do feel anything is possible now. There are no limits.
LOUIS *clinks his glass in a toast with* DONALDSON.
PAMELA: I wonder why Mr Masterson has left us? (*She gets
up a little unsteadily.*) What do you think he is up to?

INT. TRAIN CORRIDOR. SLEEPING CAR. NIGHT
PAMELA *is moving along the corridor of the sleeping car. She
stops at the door of one of the compartments. She knocks and
without waiting for an answer she opens the door.*

    MASTERSON *is sitting in his compartment, surrounded by
a pile of gold cigarette cases, gold snuff boxes and other gold
objects. He has them laid out carefully on the seat next to him,
as if he is counting them.*

PAMELA (*unabashed*): Oh, I am sorry, I got the wrong
compartment, Mr Masterson! Please forgive me.
MASTERSON (*looking at her impassively*): Gold . . . gold is
the safest thing at the moment. I like to have some
with me at all times, small enough to carry around –
so I know if something happens I will still have a roof
over my head.

INT. STANLEY'S COMPARTMENT. NIGHT
We cut to STANLEY *working in his compartment, surrounded by papers. He has a portable typewriter on his knee. The door of his compartment suddenly opens,* PAMELA *is standing there.*

PAMELA: There you are! (*She laughs, seeing the typewriter.*) You're not writing about this before it's even happened?

STANLEY (*surprised*): Before what's even happened?
    PAMELA *sits opposite him, looks straight at him and smiles.*

PAMELA: I love trains, don't you?!

STANLEY: Absolutely.

PAMELA: Please go on working, Stanley . . . I like to see that. (*Self-mocking smile.*) I so rarely watch anybody work. (*She lights a cigarette.*) I'm not putting you off, am I?
    She looks really beautiful in her evening dress, her uninhibited manner.

STANLEY: You most certainly are . . .

PAMELA: Well, try not to be. I'm sure you overcome most distractions, Stanley.

STANLEY (*staring back at her*): Usually that's true!

PAMELA (*meeting his look*): You don't think I can be serious do you, Stanley? About anything?
    STANLEY *hesitates.*
    Go on, lie. Why not?

STANLEY: Of course you can.
    PAMELA *laughs.*
    I mean it.

PAMELA (*smiles*): Thank you. (*She picks up a piece of paper at her feet.*) Oh, is this some of the strange cartoon you have in your magazine, Farquhar and Tonk? I rather like that!
    We see part of a new strip in her hand.

They went on an ocean liner last week, didn't they, and met a jazz band? So Mr Lester is having an effect on your strip cartoon, Stanley!

STANLEY: Well, I grab material from anywhere I can, I'm afraid, always have done.

He takes the typewriter off his knee. PAMELA *suddenly sits next to him.*

PAMELA: So we could find ourselves in it soon? I might be there?!

STANLEY: You might.

PAMELA: And you can send your Farquhar and Tonk wherever you want in the world just like that, to the moon even?! (*She smiles, she is very close to him.*) And we could all follow them there . . .

Their lips close.

STANLEY: It's quite possible. I could do that . . . if I wanted.

PAMELA: Then what's stopping you? It might be fun.

STANLEY *kisses her gently.*

INT. DINING CAR. NIGHT

LOUIS *is playing the piano softly in the corner of the dining car.* JESSIE *is humming lazily, drunkenly.* CARLA *is joining in intermittently.*

DONALDSON *and* JULIAN, *both drinking, are watching the two girls.*

SARAH *is standing near the piano.*

SARAH: You don't have to play now, you know.

LOUIS: You want me to stop?

SARAH: No, of course not, but you were invited as a guest, weren't you? You don't need to play for your supper.

LOUIS: You're telling me they didn't expect any music?

SARAH: Well, maybe a little, yes!

WESLEY *is sitting in the corner, full of drink, but watching everything closely. He mutters darkly.*

WESLEY: Of course they did. And more than a little. But I've got some plans for tomorrow . . .

The train suddenly lurches forward, the loud sound of its whistle. It sets off into the night.

INT. STANLEY'S COMPARTMENT. NIGHT

The train is picking up speed. STANLEY *and* PAMELA *are naked together, curled on the bottom bunk, making love.*

STANLEY: The train's moving!

PAMELA (*giggling*): Do you have to stop because the train's moving?! (*She kisses him.*) It's lucky, isn't it, at least we don't have to worry about all the noise we're going to make . . .

STANLEY: Yes. (*He kisses her.*) It's just I have no idea where we are going.

PAMELA: Why does that matter? I think it's marvellous not knowing!

EXT. THE TRAIN. NIGHT

We cut to a wide shot of the train moving through the night landscape.

INT. STANLEY'S COMPARTMENT. MORNING

Morning light. The train is stationary. We cut to STANLEY *waking, seeing* PAMELA *curled up beside him. She is watching him in a sleepy, hazy way.* STANLEY *lifts his head, glances towards the window.*

PAMELA: Are we in the middle of nowhere, Stanley?

STANLEY *turns.*

STANLEY: It looks like it, yes.

PAMELA: Splendid. I can't imagine a better place to be. (*She looks at him for a second, then she asks pointedly but with a smile.*) Are you wondering something?

STANLEY (*meeting her gaze*): I don't think so, no.

PAMELA: I'm glad you aren't. Because you don't need to, Stanley.

INT. THE TRAIN. MORNING

We cut to all the characters in the luxurious morning carriage, tucking into a full English breakfast surrounded by rugs, silverware and servants. MASTERSON *is watching all the characters as they tuck in.*

MASTERSON: You must excuse my idea of how to picnic, but I've invented my own version since I do feel the cold whenever I'm outside, even in summer . . . I always have indoor picnics, always. But I make sure the view outside constantly changes – that's why picnicking in a train is such a good idea.

PAMELA: It really is the perfect way to picnic! (*She looks across at* STANLEY.) And it's funny how the trains always make me ravenous for some reason . . .

SARAH (*whispering to* LOUIS): We get a proper English country-house breakfast even though we're in a field!

LOUIS: Of course. Wherever you are you have to have a proper breakfast.

JULIAN (*suddenly*): And Mr Masterson would like you all to know, in case you are wondering where you are going, there is no destination!

DONALDSON: No destination?!

JULIAN: None, no. We'll eat lunches in the middle of woods and have candlelit dinners by the sea, but we'll be on a train all the time.

MASTERSON (*dryly*): And maybe we never go back to town.

CARLA (*laughing*): Yes, let's live on the train!

SARAH (*getting up*): I'm going to risk getting frozen and go outside, if that's not forbidden!

MASTERSON (*genially*): That is allowed, yes.

SARAH (*to* LOUIS, *lifting her camera*): I would really like to do the portrait we never had time to do . . . if you could spare a moment?

LOUIS (*in the middle of a mouthful*): I expect I can.

EXT. EDGE OF WOOD. DAY

We cut to Sarah taking photographs of LOUIS *among the trees on the edge of the meadow. They can see the train and the picnic spread out below them.* JOE *is sitting on the steps of the train improvising on the trumpet.*

   LOUIS *is leaning against a tree as* SARAH *photographs him.*

LOUIS: Is this all right?

SARAH: It's good, yes.

   LOUIS *glances across at the train. They can see the servants scuttling along outside the edge of the train, carrying the new linen and carpets they have been beating in preparation for the rest of the journey.*

SARAH (*quietly*): I know you think there is something wrong with all of this, with Mr Masterson's hospitality.

LOUIS: Did I say anything?

SARAH: You didn't have to . . . but maybe he really means it, it's not just a rich man's whim.

LOUIS: And he won't move on to something else next week?

SARAH: No, I don't think so. Mr Donaldson really loves your music, and so does Mr Masterson.

   LOUIS *stares towards the train. He can just make out* MASTERSON *holding court in the breakfast carriage.*

LOUIS: Really? He does? Who would have guessed!

SARAH: He looks a dry old stick I know, but he goes to every party he can, never goes to bed! He likes watching the young people.

LOUIS (*darkly*): Not just watching them.

SARAH stands next to him.

SARAH: Pamela told me about Hannah . . . (*She stares down at* MASTERSON.) I wouldn't want to be alone with him certainly, but she adores him apparently.

We see MASTERSON *leaning back on the cushions and lighting a cigarette.*

(*With feeling.*) People's private lives, one never really knows what goes on, does one?

INT. TRAIN — BREAKFAST CARRIAGE. DAY
We cut back to the breakfast on the train. STANLEY *is scribbling in his notebook.* CARLA *and* JESSIE *are piling more food on to their plates.*

CARLA: I'm going to keep eating, I may never have a breakfast like this again the whole of my life.

JESSIE: Yes, we could be in the gutter tomorrow.

JULIAN: Oh, please don't say that! Of course you won't!

WESLEY (*suddenly*): But that could happen quite easily, couldn't it, Mr Donaldson?

DONALDSON: I am sure that won't happen, no, Mr Holt, not after you've made such a start.

WESLEY (*his tone is very sharp, businesslike*): I'm glad you think that, but there is a way we can make very sure that doesn't happen, isn't there?

STANLEY: And what is that?

WESLEY: By having a proper contract, not a week-by-week arrangement.

DONALDSON: I am sure in time that will happen, these things tend to evolve naturally.

WESLEY: They 'evolve naturally', do they? Well, I agree –
and since we have only two weeks left of our booking
with the Imperial – I think it will be natural, very
natural in fact, to ask Mr Schlesinger for a six-month
contract, so we become the regular band at the Imperial.

STANLEY: Six months?! Nobody gets six months! Jack
Paynton doesn't get six months, Wally Dix doesn't get
six months!

WESLEY (*implacable*): We get a six-month contract or we
will go and offer our services to the Savoy . . . or to
the Cecil Hotel. (*Looking at* STANLEY.) With the sorts
of write-ups we've been getting, I'm sure they'll be
interested!

A shot of MASTERSON *staring at* WESLEY *impassively.*

JULIAN: Wesley, my dear friend, breakfast is a little too
early to do business.

DONALDSON: It doesn't really mix with kippers and
scrambled eggs, this is true. Let's leave this to another
day.

STANLEY (*urgently*): This isn't the time, Wesley.

WESLEY: This is definitely the time. What better time
could there be than when we're all together?

STANLEY (*sharply, trying to shut him up*): I will talk to Mr
Schlesinger as soon as we're back and see what he
thinks he can offer.

WESLEY (*raising his voice*): You will not talk to Mr
Schlesinger! I am the manager of this band, I will talk
to Mr Schlesinger, who has not even bothered to meet
us so far, not even bothered to put his head round the
door. (*His voice getting really loud.*) So I will be very
interested to meet him, and I will tell him what I
think! Exactly what I think.

WESLEY *stares at them for a moment. The atmosphere is
hushed.* JESSIE *and* CARLA *are looking down, everybody's
embarrassed, except for* WESLEY.

So let me put it very simply, we meet Mr Schlesinger, and he makes us a new offer – or I will start talking to the Savoy.

EXT. FIELD/OUTSIDE TRAIN. DAY
SARAH *taking photos of* LOUIS *outside the train.* MASTERSON *appears above them, leaning out of the door of the train.*

SARAH: Mr Masterson!
MASTERSON: Just wondered how you were doing?
SARAH (*she smiles at him*): Come out and have your picture taken . . . (*Suddenly she raises her voice.*) In fact, everybody come on out and I'll take your picture!
We cut to the breakfast group, JULIAN, CARLA, JESSIE, PAMELA *and* DONALDSON *being led by* MASTERSON *towards the locomotive. They all stand and have their photo taken by* SARAH. *We see* JULIAN *standing very near* CARLA *and* JESSIE, MASTERSON *watching the young women.*
    WESLEY *is moving on the edge of the group looking preoccupied.* LOUIS *watches* WESLEY.
LOUIS (*to Sarah, as she takes photos*): I wonder what he's been up to during breakfast . . . I ought to remember it's not wise to leave Wesley on his own.
    WESLEY *looks straight at* LOUIS, *smiles and gives him a thumbs up.*

EXT. PEABODY BUILDING. DAY
A black Daimler draws up outside the Peabody Buildings. A huge fleshy man with sharp penetrating eyes gets out, SCHLESINGER.
    He is accompanied by DONALDSON *and* STANLEY.

INT. BASEMENT ROOM. DAY

We cut to the basement room where the auditions were held.
SCHLESINGER *and* DONALDSON *are sitting facing* WESLEY
and LOUIS *across a small table. They are surrounded by boxes
and stacked chairs.* STANLEY *is watching from the shadows.*

SCHLESINGER: A three-month contract is my final offer.
WESLEY: Six.
SCHLESINGER: Six months is out of the question. Three
   months or I find another band to take your place.
WESLEY: Six months.
SCHLESINGER: I won't do business like this, young man.
   I have come to meet you as you asked, something I've
   rarely done for any other band, and three months is
   my final offer.
DONALDSON: And, Mr Holt, it is in fact a very good offer.
   My advice would be to consider it very carefully.
WESLEY (*implacable*): Six months, or we go to the Savoy,
   Mr Schlesinger.
SCHLESINGER (*his eyes flick*): The Savoy won't take you.
   I can tell you that now. You won't find it nearly as
   easy out there as you think. You are not a minstrel
   band, your music is – how shall I put this – very
   particular. Some might say it's just for the connoisseur.
WESLEY (*unfazed*): Why do you want us at all then?
   WESLEY *and* SCHLESINGER *stare at each other, there is a
   tense pause.*
LOUIS (*suddenly*): Four months.
WESLEY: Louis!
LOUIS (*silencing him*): No. (*To* SCHLESINGER.) Four
   months or we will go elsewhere.
   DONALDSON *is watching intently.*
SCHLESINGER (*impassive*): Four months? . . . I may be
   able . . . just . . . to consider four months.
WESLEY: And our accommodation of course.

SCHLESINGER (*icy*): What about your accommodation?

STANLEY: I am sure, Wesley, that can be looked at separately.

WESLEY (*ignoring* STANLEY): We will need new accommodation, that goes without saying.

SCHLESINGER: And where might that be?

WESLEY: At the Imperial of course.

SCHLESINGER *looks startled.*

The Jack Paynton band have rooms there when they play, so why shouldn't we?

INT. THE IMPERIAL. BACK STAIRCASE. AFTERNOON

High shot staring down the main back staircase of the Imperial. The band, including JESSIE *and* CARLA, *are climbing the staircase carrying suitcases and their instruments.*

A voice is suddenly calling down to them. THORNTON *is right at the top of the staircase.*

THORNTON: Come on, it's this way! Right up here. Keep coming all the way up!

INT. PASSAGE BY STAFF BEDROOMS. AFTERNOON

The band are moving along the passage at the top of the hotel by the staff bedrooms. THORNTON, *carrying a clipboard, is leading them. He suddenly turns sharply.*

THORNTON: So these are the rooms usually given over to performers. Accommodation here can only be granted for four weeks. We will be reviewing the situation after that. I will call out your room numbers and give you your keys – but first I want you to pay particular attention to the rules of the hotel. You may under no circumstances use the main entrance or the main lobby at any time, or go into any of the lounges or dining rooms or any of the bars, except of course

when you are performing there. And you may not
entertain guests of any kind, I repeat of any kind, in
your rooms. I hope that is clear.

LOUIS: Absolutely clear, Mr Thornton.

THORNTON: It is under these conditions that Mr Schlesinger
has kindly agreed to you staying in the rooms. Now
Mr Lester, you have a room to yourself, No. 708, the
rest of you will be sharing, ladies you are in 722 . . .

INT. CARLA AND JESSIE'S ROOM. AFTERNOON

CARLA and JESSIE *burst into their hotel room, overjoyed.
It is a modest enough room but with fine fittings.*

CARLA: Our own room! In a hotel! I never thought that
would happen –

JESSIE: And just think of the meals. Hot meals every day!

CARLA (*throwing herself on the bed*): Yes, I've been hungry
ever since I can remember, I really think I have. But
I won't be any more! (*Adding hastily.*) All being well.

JESSIE (*staring at herself in the mirror*): Tonight I think we
should look fabulous . . . (*Close up in mirror.*) really
fabulous.

CARLA: Yes . . . (*Looking across at* JESSIE.) To make sure
they don't change their mind!

INT. MAIN PASSAGE. IMPERIAL. NIGHT

We cut to JESSIE *and* CARLA *in splendid new show costumes,
elegant but sexy, moving straight towards us. In a key sequence
we see them journey through the hotel towards the main bar
area where they are going to perform. They turn heads as they
go, whether it is the hotel staff or two old colonels muttering
together in the passage.*

They get to the double doors of the central bar.

INT. MAIN BAR AREA. IMPERIAL. NIGHT

JESSIE *and* CARLA *enter the main bar, standing for a moment
on the edge of the area. The bar is an old-fashioned space, full
of large plants and dark wood. The band is waiting for them on
a little stage at the end of the room. We see the occupants of the
bar turn towards* JESSIE *and* CARLA, *who are looking radiant
in the doorway. The clientele are mostly elderly and sitting in
deep armchairs, with a few young couples sprinkled among
them. The bar falls silent as the girls progress towards the stage.*

*We see sharp cuts of the elderly disorientated faces watching
them.*

In a corner are SARAH, JULIAN *and* PAMELA. SARAH *is
watching keenly as* JESSIE *and* CARLA *pass very close to the
tables, weaving their way through, their dresses almost brushing
members of the elderly audience. One of the old dowagers
flinches as they get close.*

As JESSIE *begins to sing, the audience stare at her, startled,
some disapproving or disconcerted, but all compelled to watch.
They are so much closer to the band in this intimate space.*
WESLEY *is standing in the shadows watching* JESSIE *cast her
spell.*

JULIAN: She's incredible, isn't she? Can't take my eyes off
   her!
PAMELA: We had noticed, Julian.
   JULIAN'*s eyes are shining as he watches* JESSIE.
   Sarah helped them choose their new clothes, you
   know.
SARAH: Mr Donaldson paid for them . . . She looks good,
   doesn't she?
JULIAN: She looks wonderful! Do you think she will ever
   like me? You know show-business people, they live in
   a world of their own and change their mind every day.
   I have to find a way of really impressing her.

SARAH: Well, the picnic was quite a good start, Julian!
    Suddenly STANLEY *appears next to them.*

PAMELA (*whispering*): You're always late, Stanley.

STANLEY: I still have a magazine to write, remember.
    He sits next to them, staring at JESSIE.
    She's magical isn't she . . . ? (*He looks across at the audience.*) This is terrific, look at their faces!

SARAH: Yes, the dear old hotel doesn't know what's hit it.

JULIAN: That's so true! (*Staring at the imperious old ladies sitting with elderly men.*) Some of those old dowagers have had apartments here for thirty-five years.

PAMELA: Yes, goodness knows who's hidden away here.

STANLEY: That's exactly why Schlesinger wants to make this place more fashionable . . .
    We see JESSIE *singing, her powerful voice.*

JULIAN (*whispers*): You know the Freemasons have temples here!

STANLEY: They don't?!

JULIAN: Oh yes, in the basement. I wouldn't make that up would I?! Those that don't use the temples under the Café Royal come here. (*He grins.*) I wonder what they'd think of this?!

SARAH (*watching two old dowagers*): Some of those dresses are from before Queen Victoria died you realise!

STANLEY: Ah, talking of strangely dressed people . . . my mum wants to meet Louis.

PAMELA: Really, Stanley? That's very charming. How come?

STANLEY: Because she likes the sound of him, that's why.
    We cut to the band playing, LOUIS *looking up from the piano at the wax-like audience, and* JESSIE*'s heartfelt singing.*

EXT. SURBURBAN STREET. EVENING
JESSIE's *singing carries across the cut as we see* STANLEY *and* LOUIS *walking up a steep hill on the edge of the city, a street of small Victorian terrace houses.*

STANLEY: So, Louis . . . I sprang from here, this humble dwelling right here.
He stops by one of the houses and knocks on the door.
LOUIS (*staring at the house*): It's not that humble . . .
A small plump woman opens the door. She has dressed up for the occasion but the clothes are old-fashioned and ill-fitting.
STANLEY: Mum, this is Louis.
MRS MITCHELL: Hello . . .
She looks at LOUIS *very startled, clearly taken aback.*
So you're Stanley's friend?

INT. MRS MITCHELL'S PARLOUR. EVENING
We cut to the small parlour where LOUIS, STANLEY *and* MRS MITCHELL *are having a modest meal.* LOUIS *is tucking in.*

MRS MITCHELL (*rather anxiously*): The food is to your liking is it? Not going to disagree with your digestion?
STANLEY: It's all right, Mum . . . Louis eats everything.
LOUIS: It's delicious, Mrs Mitchell.
MRS MITCHELL (*suddenly*): Oh I quite forgot the lemonade!
She gets up, LOUIS *stands up too.*
No, no, you stay there, I must get the lemonade, I made it specially.
LOUIS (*as soon as she's gone*): Didn't you tell her?
STANLEY: Tell her what?
LOUIS: That you were bringing a black man to the house?
STANLEY: Of course not! It's good for her to have a surprise.

LOUIS: But I thought you'd said you'd told her all about
our music?!

STANLEY: I did, but she thinks all dance bands are white –
MRS MITCHELL *is in the doorway with lemonade.*

MRS MITCHELL: I hope to hear your music, Mr Lester,
I would be very interested to hear it.

STANLEY: Well, I'm going to try and persuade Louis and
the band to come and play in the back garden here
one Sunday afternoon.

LOUIS *looks up startled.*

MRS MITCHELL: Well, maybe not in the garden, the
neighbours might not like that, not on a Sunday.

STANLEY: Who knows, we might get the whole street
dancing!

MRS MITCHELL (*to* LOUIS): Though of course I can tell
them you played for royalty, that would impress them.
You did play for royalty didn't you, Prince George?

LOUIS: We did, yes.

MRS MITCHELL: And did he like you? I do hope he liked
you.

LOUIS: Did he like us, Stanley?

STANLEY: Oh yes, very much.

MRS MITCHELL: So has he asked for you again? (*She looks
hopeful.*) To play for him?

STANLEY: Not quite yet. He is being a little slower than
I thought. (*He smiles.*) But I have other plans in that
direction . . .

INT. STANLEY'S BOYHOOD BEDROOM. NIGHT
STANLEY *is looking for something behind the bed in his small
childhood bedroom. The room, including the bed, is packed with
boxes, records and old magazines.* STANLEY *produces a bottle of
whisky from behind the bed.*

STANLEY: I always keep a bottle hidden away for when
I drop by . . . my mother doesn't approve of liquor.
There's only one glass. (*He grins.*) So I'll have the
bottle.

LOUIS: Some of these records are really old – are they the
first ones you ever bought?

STANLEY: Yes, snoop away by all means. It's always a good
idea to see people's childhood bedrooms, you can tell
a lot from them!

*STANLEY is putting an early jazz record on a wind-up
gramophone.*

LOUIS: You probably started a magazine at school, didn't
you?

STANLEY: Of course I did. I wrote and performed music
there as well, formed my own little band, and then
gave it rave reviews in the magazine I'd started!

LOUIS: You were in a hurry even then.

STANLEY: Yes, I've always been in a hurry. You need to
have a lot going on, so at least something has a chance
of working! It's taken me quite a while to get this far –
so there's no time to lose. At the moment, as well as
writing most of the magazine, I'm working on a movie
scenario about King Arthur, an Edgar Wallace sort of
thriller for the theatre, I'm trying to get Farquhar and
Tonk turned into an animated cartoon for the cinema
or else a series on the wireless, and I want to make
Music Express the top-selling music magazine in the
country. I want to beat *Melody Maker*!

LOUIS: Not enough, that's not enough, Stanley!

STANLEY: You're right, it isn't! And of course I'm going to
make you the number-one band in Britain, naturally!
(*He smiles.*) I'm very ambitious. And so should you
be, Louis.

LOUIS: You think I'm not?

STANLEY: I don't know yet. Maybe underneath that calm
exterior you're more ambitious than you seem.

LOUIS: I want to reach a really big audience, of course
I do. But some things are meant to take time, Stanley.

STANLEY: I don't believe that. Very few things are meant to
take time.

LOUIS: How do you plan to make us the number-one band?

STANLEY: I have to get you on the wireless somehow.

LOUIS: Only the white bands get to play on the wireless.

STANLEY: So far . . . but not everybody is completely
unimaginative, and not everybody is prejudiced.

LOUIS: Of course not, just a lot of people.

STANLEY: Quite a few, yes. (*Drinking from bottle.*) But we
don't need them . . . there is another audience out there.

LOUIS: Really? Look what happened when we played in the
bar the other night, they hated it, they loathed being
that close to us – that's what most people are like.

STANLEY: Some of them. At the moment.

LOUIS (*laughing*): You're going to change the world, are
you, Stanley?!

STANLEY: Probably, but it will take a few months I grant
you! (*He grins.*) Though things can change quicker
than you think . . . (*He drinks.*) Talking of which, is
Wesley your permanent manager?

LOUIS: Why?

STANLEY: Just wondered.

LOUIS: Yes, he is. Definitely.

STANLEY *gives him a searching look.*

He argues a lot I know, but he's very effective.

STANLEY: Don't get me wrong, I have no desire to be your
manager, having to worry about your transport and
all that, I'd hate it!

LOUIS: Wesley has done a lot for us. He doesn't believe
in being too grateful to people, being humble and
knowing his place. He's absolutely without fear.

STANLEY: Without fear? That's a tremendous thing to be.
   He sounds perfect then.

INT. THE IMPERIAL. PASSAGES. NIGHT
The silent grand passages late at night at the Imperial. WESLEY
*and a white girl of around twenty are walking towards us down
one of the main bedroom passages. They pass the lines of shoes
outside the bedrooms.* WESLEY *drunkenly picks up a pair of
shoes and drops them outside another door several bedrooms
away. A room-service trolley is sitting outside one of the doors,
a lot of the food uneaten.* WESLEY *helps himself to a couple of
eclairs, giving one to the girl. A maid passes across the landing
in the distance, she doesn't seem to see them.*

   We cut to WESLEY *and the girl in the much narrower passage
by the staff bedrooms. The girl is still eating the eclair.* WESLEY
starts to unlock his bedroom door. At that moment, CARLA,
hearing a noise, opens her door a crack and sees WESLEY *and
the girl.*

CARLA (*whispers*): What are you doing?
WESLEY: I just met a friend. (*The girl laughs.*) And Joe's
   out tonight, so we won't get interrupted. (*He grins.*)
   It's perfect!
CARLA: It's against the rules.
WESLEY: I think you'll find not many people keep to that
   rule, Carla. (*As he closes the door.*) Don't worry,
   remember who got you here!

INT. ALIEN REGISTRATION CENTRE. RYALL'S OFFICE.
LATE AFTERNOON
   We cut to RYALL's *office, a dark afternoon. Through the
   frosted glass of his office we can see the shapes of people
   waiting to see him.* RYALL *is studying papers on his desk,*

*signing documents with his silver fountain pen, as a tall
male official stands waiting.*

*RYALL suddenly pauses over a document, his pen
hovering.*

RYALL: Ah, those musicians at the Imperial Hotel . . . a
four-month booking now? (*He's about to sign the
document, then stops.*) We just need to check if that
includes all of them. (*He looks at the official.*) I feel we
need proof of that, don't you?

INT. THE IMPERIAL. SCHLESINGER'S OFFICE. EVENING
SCHLESINGER *is sitting in his office, a huge brooding figure
behind his desk.*

*The wireless is on in the corner, and we hear a voice
announce: 'And now over to the Savoy hotel and the Jack
Paynton Orchestra . . . !' We then hear the comforting sound of
a foxtrot.* THORNTON *is standing, waiting obediently in front
of the desk.*

SCHLESINGER: I never make mistakes, Harry, as you know.
THORNTON: No sir, you do not.
SCHLESINGER: Very occasionally I take risks, and they
pay off.
THORNTON: They do sir, very much so.
SCHLESINGER (*indicating the sound of the foxtrot*): Like not
always having that! But maybe I've made a bad
mistake with this Louis Lester band – their kind of
music, as we know, is not to everybody's taste. (*He
looks up.*) Is it?
THORNTON: Not to everyone's taste, no sir. This is true.
SCHLESINGER: And they're not even a minstrel band!
(*Beadily.*) But business is still picking up is it?
THORNTON: For the main dining room, yes sir. At the
moment.

SCHLESINGER: Will it last?

> THORNTON *just blinks politely.*

And have there been any serious complaints?

THORNTON: There have been a number of complaints, of course. Not always from where one would expect . . . (*He pauses.*)

SCHLESINGER (*impatiently*): Yes? What's this about, Harry?

THORNTON (*his tone grave*): The most serious complaint has not been from a guest, sir.

EXT. LONDON STREET. AFTERNOON
We cut to LOUIS *approaching a line of red-brick houses in a leafy street. The houses are not particularly large and have tidy gardens.* LOUIS' *manner is relaxed, almost carefree. He rings the bell.* SARAH *opens the door.*

SARAH: There you are. I thought you might not come.

LOUIS: Why did you think that?

SARAH: Because I invited you completely out of the blue!

LOUIS (*lightly*): Well, I heard there were some rather good photographs of me here . . .

INT. HALL. SARAH'S FATHER'S HOUSE. AFTERNOON
SARAH *and* LOUIS *move through the small hall of the house.*

SARAH: We don't actually know that yet, how good the photos are . . .

LOUIS: What do you mean?

SARAH: Because I haven't developed them.

INT. SARAH'S DARK ROOM. AFTERNOON
We cut to a photograph floating in a tray of developing fluid in

SARAH's *dark room. The image is ghostly, just beginning to take shape.*

SARAH: I thought you'd like to see it happen.
LOUIS: Yes . . . I've never seen this before.
SARAH: Never?

> LOUIS *is staring at the image as it begins to appear. All around them in the dark room photographs are hanging.*

LOUIS: No, in fact I've not had many photographs taken of me at all. (*He laughs.*) Maybe once before . . . !
SARAH: That'll soon change, I expect.
LOUIS: You sound like Stanley.
SARAH: Well, Stanley's a bit of a rogue, of course, but he's not always wrong.

> *She moves the picture to a second tray. Her manner is very professional.*

LOUIS: Your father doesn't mind you having these chemicals in the house?
SARAH: Oh no, in fact he likes the idea of his daughter being artistic. (*She laughs.*) He's Russian, remember!
LOUIS: And there're some tremendous pictures here . . .

> *There is one in particular, a striking-looking older woman* (LADY CREMONE), *dressed in dark clothes staring out with fierce eyes.*

LOUIS: Who is that?
SARAH: Oh Lady Cremone, she's an interesting lady, but she's a recluse. Maybe we can find a way of introducing you somehow . . . (*She lifts the picture of* LOUIS *out of the second tray.*) What do you think?

> LOUIS *stares at the image of himself, looking rather glamorous, leaning against a tree at the picnic.*

LOUIS: I like it.
SARAH (*businesslike*): Yes, I think it's quite good.

> SARAH *pins the photo up.* LOUIS *watching* SARAH *closely, her professional manner.*

LOUIS: Are there any more?

A montage begins of photos appearing, magically looming into view as SARAH *and* LOUIS *stare into the developing tray. They are all from the picnic: more images of* LOUIS, *and then of* PAMELA *looking fragile and beautiful, and* CARLA *and* JESSIE *laughing together,* JULIAN *watching them closely, clearly fascinated by them. The photo reveals more than we have seen before, there is a longing in* JULIAN*'s face.*

And then we see MASTERSON, *a close study of him, his strange long face, his inexpressive eyes, his whole demeanour very unsettling and mysterious.*

In between these images taking shape, we see LOUIS *watching* SARAH, *her face framed by the photos and the low light in the dark room. He is strongly attracted to her, but she seems to be so completely concentrating on the photographs and he doesn't move too close, not wishing to break the spell.*

At the end of the montage, as MASTERSON*'s face takes shape in the developing tray,* LOUIS *stands closer to her. They both stare at the image of* MASTERSON.

SARAH: He really is spooky, isn't he?!

LOUIS: He is.

SARAH *turns, their eyes meet.*

We suddenly hear a voice calling, 'Sarah are you there?'

INT. STAIRCASE AND HALL. SARAH'S FATHER'S HOUSE.
AFTERNOON

SARAH *appears with* LOUIS *at the top of the stairs that lead down into the hall.* SARAH'S FATHER, *a man in his sixties, is standing in the hall, having just taken his coat off. A maid rushes into the hall to take the coat.* SARAH'S FATHER *looks truly startled to see his daughter standing on the stairs with* LOUIS.

SARAH (*calmly*): Hello Daddy, I was just showing Mr
    Lester my photographs in the dark room. Louis, this
    is my father.

LOUIS: Delighted to meet you, sir.
    Her father is still speechless for a moment.

SARAH: Mr Lester is the bandleader I was talking to you
    about . . .

SARAH'S FATHER: Good afternoon. I had no idea you had
    a guest, Sarah – no idea at all. If I'd known I would
    have hurried home an hour earlier . . . (*He stares up
    at them.*) Made sure we had some cake for tea.

INT. THE IMPERIAL. THE BALLROOM. DAY
The empty ballroom. A high shot of JESSIE *and* CARLA *rehearsing
together, singing alternate verses of a song, accompanied by*
LOUIS *on the piano.* WESLEY *is sitting watching them. They
seem to be alone in the ballroom. But then, high above them in
the gallery, we see* SCHLESINGER *is staring down at them.
A close-up of* SCHLESINGER's *jowly face, his beady eyes staring
at the four of them.*

INT. THE MUSIC EXPRESS OFFICE. AFTERNOON
We cut to MR WAX *looking through the latest edition of* Music
Express, *watched by* ROSIE, STANLEY *and* ALBERT *the
illustrator.*

    The cover screams JACK PAYNTON STORMS THE SAVOY.

MR WAX: Yes . . . yes . . . everything seems in the right
    place. Not bad at all, Stanley . . . just remember, give
    enough space to the West End shows and you can't go
    wrong. (*He moves.*) Don't work too late tonight, will
    you?!

STANLEY (*watching him go*): And off he goes to his bridge party . . .

ROSIE (*pointedly to* STANLEY): And are you working late tonight?

STANLEY looks up, their eyes meet.

STANLEY: Not tonight Rosie, I don't think I am. I need to be elsewhere . . . There's so much happening.

ROSIE (*sharply*): I'm sure there is Stanley, yes!

We cut to the images of the new edition as STANLEY *flicks through the pages. We see pictures of white bands playing, headlines about shows and broadcasts.* STANLEY *mutters to himself.*

STANLEY: It's much better than 'not bad' . . .

We see Farquhar and Tonk in the latest strip, boarding a train, the Paris sleeper The Golden Arrow, surrounded by an extraordinary collection of faces on the platform. They are aristocrats, bishops, children begging for money, aviators, movie stars.

Suddenly a silver trowel drops on the page. STANLEY *looks up from the magazine with a start.* JULIAN *is standing in front of him, beaming.*

STANLEY: Julian!

JULIAN: Hello, my dear friend, sorry to interrupt you so rudely. (*Excited smile, indicating the trowel.*) But do you know what this is?

STANLEY: No, what is it?

JULIAN: Go on, have a guess.

STANLEY (*reluctantly*): A little shovel, for somebody's town garden?

JULIAN: You couldn't be more wrong. I am now a Master Mason. I have been lifted into a new category and that tiny shovel is part of it, as is this . . . (*He produces a small dark box.*) My little Mason's box, what we use in our rituals!

STANLEY: Well, congratulations, Julian.

JULIAN: Thank you, my friend.

STANLEY: I had no idea you were a Freemason.

JULIAN: Oh yes, I'm going along to the temples tonight as it happens – you know, in the sub-basement of the Imperial, just as I told you. And I was wondering, knowing how you are interested in so many things, Stanley, I thought you might want to come and see me go in, in my full regalia?!

STANLEY: I can't, can I? It's highly secret, isn't it?

JULIAN: Ah . . . (*He grins.*) That depends . . .

INT. LOUIS' HOTEL BEDROOM. LATE AFTERNOON

LOUIS *is lying on his bed, flicking through the latest edition of* Music Express *with Jack Paynton on the cover. There is a sharp knock. Before* LOUIS *has time to reply,* STANLEY *has walked into the room.* LOUIS *casually flicks the magazine away.*

STANLEY: Don't worry, I know you read my magazine from cover to cover, no need to be bashful.

LOUIS: I won't be reading it much longer, it gets worse every week.

STANLEY: It does not!

LOUIS: What is Jack Paynton doing on the cover, for Christ's sake?

STANLEY: Because he sells copies. I can't put you on the cover, not just yet. At the moment the king of the foxtrots still rules!

LOUIS: Why are you here, anyway?

STANLEY: Your presence is required in the sub-basement. I'm told it's a once-in-a-lifetime opportunity.

INT. SUB-BASEMENT PASSAGE. LATE AFTERNOON
We track with STANLEY *and* LOUIS *down a sinister-looking passage in the sub-basement. It has no natural light. A voice suddenly calls from behind them.*

JULIAN: What do you think?
> *They turn.* JULIAN *is standing in his full Masonic regalia, a leather apron, a sash, strange white stockings and buckled shoes.*

LOUIS: You look tremendous, Julian.

STANLEY: You're not meant to be seen in those, are you?

JULIAN: No, I'm not, only by fellow Masons. (*Lowering his voice.*) I've just popped out of the special robing room. (*Cheerily.*) We'll see if I get fined, or maybe something infinitely worse . . . Now, follow me, come on . . . !
> LOUIS *and* STANLEY, *intrigued, follow* JULIAN *down the dark passage.*

JULIAN: I need to remember which is the right door.
> *He pulls open the door to a linen cupboard and steps in.*
> LOUIS *and* STANLEY, *surprised, hesitate.* JULIAN's *head pops back round the door.*

JULIAN: I think this is the one!

INT. LINEN CUPBOARD. LATE AFTERNOON
We cut to JULIAN *beckoning them on in the large linen room. They are surrounded by laundry baskets, piled sheets and pillows.* JULIAN *is moving deeper into the shadows.*

STANLEY: Where are we going Julian?

JULIAN (*holding his finger to his lips*): Shhh . . . I'm trying to remember where it is.
> *He stops by the far wall and begins moving laundry baskets.*
> You've got to promise me you won't write about this, Stanley.

STANLEY (*lightly*): I never promise that.

JULIAN: Promise?

STANLEY *nods.*

And you, Louis, you won't tell anybody?

LOUIS: Whatever it is, I will take it to my grave, I swear.

JULIAN *moves the last laundry basket. Behind it is revealed a spy-hole in the wall.*

JULIAN: There it is . . . (*He looks through the spy-hole and then turns.*) Come on have a look, very few people get to see this ever.

STANLEY *applies his eye to the hole. We see shapes of figures in their strange aprons, some very close to the spy-hole, some more distant, moving in their secret temple which is a private dining room decorated with Masonic symbols, including on the floor. We only catch half-obscured details.* STANLEY *is watching the shadowy figures with their sashes. He whispers.*

STANLEY: That's wonderful.

He steps back to let LOUIS *have a look.*

JULIAN (*indicating the spy-hole*): I think it was made as a dare, many years ago, and people have forgotten it's here.

LOUIS *puts his eye to the hole. At that moment a fleshy aristocratic face is right up next to the hole on the other side of the wall, coming so close, totally unaware.*

JULIAN: There are dukes in there – see if you can spot the Duke of Bedford . . . or the Head of the Foreign Office! No members of the Royal Family sadly today, not even minor ones, they tend to use the temples under Piccadilly anyway. But it's quite a good selection none the less!

LOUIS *is watching as the rituals begin and voices intone.*

JULIAN: I'm late now, I should be in there! I'll try to do a little secret signal to you . . . (*As he moves off.*) Remember, if you breathe a word, we're all for it!

*He mimes his throat being cut and then disappears into
the shadows.* LOUIS *looks into the spy-hole again, just in
time to see* JULIAN *slip into the temple behind the dark
figures, and do a tiny surreptitious wave towards him.*

STANLEY: They like using hotels for their temples – they
can go and get violently drunk immediately afterwards.

LOUIS: What if a maid came in right now?

STANLEY (*back at the spy-hole*): I like to think I can explain
anything!

INT. KITCHEN PASSAGE. EVENING

We see LOUIS *and* STANLEY *emerge from the sub-basement into
the kitchen passage.*

LOUIS: That was the best time I've ever had in a linen
cupboard.

*A young chef's head turns sharply as he passes with a
tray of desserts.*

STANLEY: You know, if I succeed in making this place
really fashionable, they may feel they've got to move
on, find a more sleepy hotel.

LOUIS: You'll flush out the Masons, will you, Stanley!

They turn a corner in the passage. THORNTON *is
standing there.*

THORNTON: Mr Schlesinger wants to see you, Mr Lester.

STANLEY: What about?

THORNTON: Not you, Stanley, I said Mr Lester.

INT. SCHLESINGERS'S OFFICE. EARLY EVENING

SCHLESINGER *is seated at his desk, staring straight at* LOUIS,
who is standing.

SCHLESINGER: I have received a message from the
immigration authorities that they require a letter from

me stating that Mr Wesley Holt is essential to your performances as a band.

Their eyes meet.

I will not write that letter.

LOUIS (*calmly*): Then I will have to write it.

SCHLESINGER: You can write as many letters as you like, Mr Lester, but unfortunately it is from me they wish to hear. And I know Mr Holt's presence isn't necessary for the success of the band –

LOUIS: His presence is absolutely necessary. He is our manager – without him the band could easily break up.

SCHLESINGER: You don't believe that.

LOUIS: I do believe that.

SCHLESINGER (*staring unflinchingly at* LOUIS): I thought you ought to know what I am going to write . . . I'm going to inform the authorities that in my view Mr Holt is an undesirable, destructive personality, who is utterly superfluous to the entertainment operation of this hotel.

LOUIS: That is not true.

INT. HOTEL PASSAGE. EVENING

We cut to STANLEY *in the passage watching the door of* SCHLESINGER's *office.*

INT. SCHLESINGER'S OFFICE. EVENING

We cut back to SCHLESINGER, *who is now reading from a list on his desk.* LOUIS *is smoking, tugging at his cigarette.*

SCHLESINGER: Mr Holt has stolen food on more than five occasions –

LOUIS: Food? That's ridiculous. What food has he stolen?!

SCHLESINGER: Various cakes and other desserts . . . he's brought back female companions to his room in complete contravention of the rules –

LOUIS: And no musicians at this hotel have ever done that before?! You can look me in the eye and tell me that, can you?

SCHLESINGER (*looking him in the eye*): You wanted accommodation in this hotel, I got you the accommodation – and then your manager behaves like this. Are you going to tell me you're happy with that, Mr Lester?

LOUIS: I will inform Wesley of these allegations –

SCHLESINGER: These aren't allegations! He was seen by members of staff!

LOUIS: And I will tell other members of the band there is an attempt to prevent Mr Holt from working with us any more – and in the event of that happening, we may regrettably be forced to move to another hotel.

SCHLESINGER (*not taking his eyes off* LOUIS): I met Harold Voight from the Cecil the other night. He could not believe, absolutely could not believe, I had coloured musicians staying at this hotel! (*His voice rising.*) Just down the road at the Savoy Theatre, there are people walking out of *Othello* as we speak, because that coloured actor, what's his name – Robeson – is kissing his Desdemona . . . and yet I have given you four months' work in this hotel! People are amazed at what I've done. (*He looks at him.*) I wouldn't be so sure you'll get another booking, Mr Lester.

LOUIS: I'm sure about one thing. If Mr Holt is prevented from being here with us, there's no possibility of us carrying on without him.

SCHLESINGER *looks at* LOUIS *sceptically. Their eyes meet.*

SCHLESINGER: Isn't there?

INT. HOTEL PASSAGE. EVENING

LOUIS *comes out of* SCHLESINGER*'s office. He sees* STANLEY *leaning against the wall, waiting for him. The camera whip pans to the right.* WESLEY *is there too, he is coldly angry.*

WESLEY: I've been looking for you everywhere, where've you been?

LOUIS: I had to see Schlesinger.

WESLEY: Yes . . . (*Indicating* STANLEY.) he told me that! (*Very sharp.*) So what's going on?

LOUIS: I don't think we should do this here, Wesley.

WESLEY: What's wrong with here?

STANLEY (*trying to move* WESLEY *out of the passage*): Let's go for a drink –

At that moment SCHLESINGER *comes out of his office and walks straight past them, heading down the passage that leads to the main staircase.*

WESLEY: I want to know what's going on, Louis?

LOUIS: The authorities want a letter from him . . . (*Indicating the receding figure of* SCHLESINGER.) About you, saying you are needed here.

SCHLESINGER *disappears through the doors at the end.* But because you have been behaving like an idiot he's not going to write it.

WESLEY: I've been doing what?! What did you say?

LOUIS (*furious with him*): I don't know how you can have been so stupid Wesley, I really don't, stealing food, bringing women back?

STANLEY: Let's not do this here, OK, we don't want the whole hotel to hear –

WESLEY: What's it to do with you? I don't believe it's got anything to do with you, has it?! (*Turns to* LOUIS.) Is that what he told you I'd done? Right! (*He stares down the passage for a moment.*) I'm going to get to speak to him right now!

WESLEY *sets off down the passage fast towards the double doors, with* STANLEY *and* LOUIS *running after him. In one continuous shot we follow them through the doors and on to the grand main staircase, as they hurtle past people. The shot is fast, powerful, the dialogue overlapping, and the scene happens in the full view of people in the lobby.*

WESLEY: How dare he talk to you rather than to me! I'm the manager . . . If it's about me, he should talk to me . . . nobody else! No one!

STANLEY: Wesley, calm down, for Christ's sake! Louis, you've got to stop him, we'll find a room to do this –

WESLEY: They think I'm not necessary do they?!

LOUIS: Nobody thinks you're not necessary. I told him that, I told him just now we wouldn't go on without you –

WESLEY: I don't believe you! You're lying. (*He suddenly stops on the stairs, halfway down.*) You would be finished without me! Who's going to fight for you, get things done?! Who got you the contract here? Who got you the rooms?!

LOUIS: It was you, of course –

STANLEY: Wesley, everybody knows what you do –

WESLEY (*indicating* STANLEY, *his voice rising all the time*): You think he's going to do it . . . ?! These people, let me tell you, these people, him and Mr Donaldson and all the rest, they'll drop you in a couple of weeks, move on to somebody else, *they'll drop you so fast –*

LOUIS: I know that.

WESLEY: You don't know that! (*Indicating* STANLEY.) You think he's going to make you a star, do you?! Going to make you famous, put you on the cover of his fucking magazine . . . ? And you think I'm the idiot here?! *You know nothing, Louis.*

LOUIS (*desperately trying to calm him*): And that's why I told Schlesinger you had to stay, that's why I told him that.

WESLEY (*setting off again to find* SCHLESINGER): He can't stop me working with you . . . I helped build the band, it's my work as much as yours –

LOUIS: If you went and got your birth certificate none of this would be happening –

WESLEY: When have I had time to do that?!

People are passing them on the stairs, stunned by the shouting.

When've I been able to do that?! When haven't I been working with you?! Come on, tell me?! Night after night I've been –

LOUIS: Go now and get it, for Christ's sake. Go down there – go to Wales, get the authorities to look up the records –

WESLEY: This is all about a fucking birth certificate, is it?

Astonished faces turn in the lobby.

One fucking birth certificate?!

LOUIS: Yes, that is what it's about.

WESLEY: One fucking piece of paper! And what if they can't find it?! What if there is no record? . . . What then?! I get sent back to the US, is that what'll happen? That can't happen . . . !

STANLEY: Nobody is talking about sending you back to the States –

WESLEY: Yes they are! That is what they want, and that is what they'll do . . .

They have reached the foot of the stairs. An astonished huddle of guests watch the scene, keeping a distance from this enraged man. WESLEY *is still moving, this time towards the entrance to the dining room.*

He turns abruptly in the mouth of the dining room, some diners look up horrified from their tables. WESLEY *is now crying, his anger has turned into a desperate hysteria.* LOUIS *and* STANLEY *try to approach him.*

WESLEY: I can't go back to the US! (*He shouts.*) Don't you realise that . . . because they will arrest me as soon as I get off the boat!

LOUIS: That won't happen . . . even if you went back, that wouldn't happen –

WESLEY: And do you know what they'll do to me then?! They're going to try me, and then they'll probably execute me! Do you realise that? – THEY WILL SEND ME TO THE CHAIR. THEY WILL! And all because I stole a piece of cake, is that what you're telling me?! Is that what Schlesinger wants, because of a fucking piece of cake . . . ?!

He sends a dessert trolley hurtling across the front of the dining room. It hits a vase of flowers, which topples over and shatters on the floor.

WESLEY *turns, tears pouring down his cheeks.*

I can't go back there, don't you understand?! I won't go back. (*He screams.*) I WILL NOT GO BACK!

Hotel staff descend on him from all sides and surround him.

INT. THE PARLOUR/KITCHEN PASSAGE. NIGHT

LOUIS, STANLEY, JESSIE *and* CARLA *and the other musicians are in the tiled parlour. The band are getting ready to perform, but they are all shocked, dazed. In a series of dissolves we see their disorientation, a feeling of numbness.*

We settle on LOUIS *who is looking very upset.*

THORNTON *and* SCHLESINGER *enter the parlour. The band all stand.*

SCHLESINGER: Gentlemen . . . (*Seeing* CARLA *and* JESSIE.) And ladies of course . . . I thought I should inform you Mr Holt is now in custody.

CARLA: He's in prison?!

SCHLESINGER: He is being detained at the Alien
   Registration Office, where the authorities are taking
   a keen interest in him.

LOUIS (*under his breath to* STANLEY): I'll go there first thing
   tomorrow.

SCHLESINGER: Well carry on . . . (*He moves.*) Glad to meet
   you gentlemen at long last . . . Oh, and ladies too. You
   are all doing well. Mr Lester, can you just come out
   here for a moment.

   LOUIS *and* STANLEY *follow* SCHLESINGER *and*
   THORNTON *into the passage.*

SCHLESINGER: I asked just Mr Lester to come out here,
   Stanley.

STANLEY: So you did. What you got to tell us, Nathan?

SCHLESINGER: I've received a message –

LOUIS: Another message from the Alien Registration
   Office?

SCHLESINGER: Not exactly, not unless they are now running
   their operation from Buckingham Palace – (*He looks
   straight at* LOUIS.) I have received a message that next
   Friday, His Royal Highness the Prince of Wales, is
   coming to dine here, for the first time, with the
   express purpose of listening to the Louis Lester Band.
   His brother must have liked you, mustn't he? (*Close-
   up of* LOUIS.) I do hope you will be here, Mr Lester,
   to entertain our future King.

INT. CELLS. ALIEN REGISTRATION OFFICE. DAY
Morning light. LOUIS *is moving down a narrow passage in the
basement of the Alien Registration Office. He passes two cell
doors that are closed. A policeman opens the third cell door
where* WESLEY *is lying on a narrow bed.* LOUIS *is holding a
box.*

WESLEY: Brought me a present, have you?

LOUIS: I've brought several presents, from me and the
boys. (*He puts the box down.*) Some cigars . . . and of
course some cakes and eclairs.

WESLEY (*grins*): I hope you stole them from the kitchen.

LOUIS (*sitting at the end of the narrow bed*): We're going to
find that birth certificate in Cardiff. Mr Donaldson is
involved now, he has contacts at the Home Office . . .

WESLEY: Good, that's good . . . yes. I know you think if
I'm so afraid about going back – why didn't I find it
before? But I did mean to find it!

LOUIS tries not to look sceptical.

It does exist, you know, you've got to believe me.

LOUIS: I do believe you.

WESLEY (*smiles*): I'm not going to lose my freedom
because of an eclair.

LOUIS: No! We had some dramatic news last night – the
Prince of Wales is coming to see us play.

WESLEY looks impressed.

And you've got to be there . . .

INT. RYALL'S OFFICE. DAY

*A tracking shot through the frosted-glass door, which is half
open, towards RYALL at his desk. He is bent over his papers.
He looks up sharply. LOUIS is in the doorway.*

LOUIS: They said I could have a word with you.

RYALL: Yes, Mr Lester, what is it?

LOUIS: Mr Holt is a British citizen – he has a birth
certificate which is lost, but there must be a record of
it in Cardiff. We are going to produce that proof.

RYALL: Produce it by next Friday, by nine o'clock in the
evening, and naturally he will not be deported. If he
is a citizen he has every right to stay here, of course.

LOUIS: And if it takes longer?

RYALL: It can't take longer. The deadline cannot be extended, nor is there any other process of appeal. (*He looks up at* LOUIS.) But I like to think I am not an unreasonable person, I am here at the end of a telephone, I am always available. The authorities in Cardiff have merely got to ring me. It is as simple as that, Mr Lester.

INT. PASSAGE LEADING TO SCHLESINGER'S OFFICE. DAY
DONALDSON *and* STANLEY *are approaching* SCHLESINGER'*s office. The door is open and we can see* SCHLESINGER *in the distance, a brooding presence at his desk.*

DONALDSON: You will let me do the talking, won't you, Stanley?

STANLEY: I always let you do the talking.

DONALDSON: I'm not sure that's true, Stanley.

    SCHLESINGER *calls from a distance, seeing them approach.*

SCHLESINGER: I won't discuss this matter in front of the press.

STANLEY (*calling back*): I'm not here as a member of the press, Nathan, I am here as the person who discovered the band.

DONALDSON (*stopping in the passage*): I think maybe it is best if I deal with this Stanley . . . (*He lowers his voice.*) I'll get old Nathan to drop his charges against Wesley, and I am in touch with the authorities in Wales, they will be making a telephone call very shortly to the immigration authorities . . . (*Softly.*) Don't worry, everything's in hand.

    DONALDSON *goes alone into* SCHLESINGER'*s office and closes the door.*

INT. THE IMPERIAL. BALLROOM. LATE AFTERNOON
*We cut to a high shot of the ballroom. It is now full of flowers
and special decorations in preparation for the Prince of Wales'
visit. A long, thin blue carpet is being unrolled leading from the
lobby across the ballroom to where the Prince is going to sit.*

*We start a series of dissolves gathering in pace and intensity,
as the preparations mount.*

INT. PASSAGE/PARLOUR/DRESSING ROOM/BALLROOM.
EVENING
*We dissolve to the blue carpet being rolled down the kitchen
passage that leads to the parlour.* LOUIS *is standing with*
THORNTON, *watching the carpet come towards them.*

LOUIS: He's not going to come back here?!
THORNTON: It has been known . . . at other hotels. We
　　have to be prepared for everything.
LOUIS: Is there any news about Wesley?
THORNTON: I believe he is going to be released, yes.
　　LOUIS *looks relieved. We dissolve to a small tiled parlour*
　　where JESSIE *and* CARLA *are making up, staring into a*
　　mirror. They are both in their petticoats, looking very
　　nervous. We dissolve again as they transform into their
　　show costumes and with their full show make-up.

　　We dissolve again, we see special trays of soaps and
　　hairbrushes being carried towards the lavatories in the
　　main lobby.

　　We dissolve again to see SCHLESINGER *and* STANLEY
　　standing together in the middle of the empty ballroom.
SCHLESINGER: Are we ready, Stanley?
STANLEY: I think we're ready, Nathan.
SCHLESINGER: You know what they say about the Prince –
　　what he likes today, the whole of London likes
　　tomorrow.

STANLEY (*grins*): Well that was always the plan wasn't it –
somehow to get him here!

SCHLESINGER: If it misfires, if he doesn't like them, if he
walks out, half the diners will leave too of course!

We dissolve to a track with STANLEY *along the kitchen
passage. He passes* JOE *the trumpeter, standing nervously.*

STANLEY: Have you seen Louis? Has anybody seen Louis?

JOE *shakes his head, lifts his trumpet nervously to his lips,
plays a few notes.* STANLEY *turns a corner.* PAMELA *is
coming towards him. She smiles.*

STANLEY: Pamela! What are you doing back here?

PAMELA: I was looking for you.

STANLEY: For me? Why?

PAMELA: I came to warn you.

STANLEY: To warn me?

PAMELA: The Prince may not come, just be prepared, he
always accepts five invitations for every night. He may
even get here, and then change his mind at the last
minute and leave without even getting to the dining
room.

STANLEY: Right!

PAMELA (*smiles*): I will be doing my best to stop that
happening of course . . . (*She stares at him, there's a
warmth in her eyes.*) Stanley I want this to go well for
you.

STANLEY: So do I! I forced Mr Schlesinger to follow this
plan.

PAMELA: I know. (*She touches his cheek.*) I've been thinking
about the picnic a lot, more than I thought I would.

STANLEY (*lightly*): I'll take that as a compliment. It was a
compliment, wasn't it?

PAMELA (*she gives him a little kiss*): I believe it was.

We cut to JESSIE, *sitting in front of a mirror, mouthing a
short prayer.*

JESSIE: Dear Lord, in a few minutes I'm going to be singing for the Prince of Wales, the son of the King. Please forgive me for asking for help but I do need help, so please give it to me if you feel able and let me sing in a way that will please him – and you of course too. Amen.

We cut to STANLEY *going into a small room full of china and silver serving bowls.* LOUIS *is standing alone in his dinner jacket, studying a piece of paper.*

STANLEY: There you are!

LOUIS: Just getting prepared. Checking the order . . .

STANLEY: I came to wish you good luck, Louis. (*Grins.*) But I know you don't need it.

THORNTON *appears behind* STANLEY, *looking at* LOUIS *in the tiny room. He is very flustered.*

THORNTON: Remember – and this is important, Mr Lester. The Prince's table . . . you mustn't address the Prince's table directly, you understand. If you say anything from the stage, you mustn't look straight at his table.

We cut to the whole band moving up the short staircase that leads to the entrance of the ballroom.

We are in among them; there is nervous chattering, excited laughter, the musicians keep checking their instruments, JOE *lifting his trumpet to his lips again and again.* STANLEY *and* DONALDSON *appear above them, at the top of the staircase.*

STANLEY: He's here! He is actually in the building!

The band go quiet. Tense, serious faces.

DONALDSON: He's just arrived, yes. (*He smiles charmingly.*) I am really looking forward to this, everyone.

The band begins to move forward, up towards the ballroom door. As LOUIS *passes* DONALDSON, *he takes his arm and says in a confidential tone.*

DONALDSON: I just thought you'd like to know that
    important telephone call is taking place as we speak . . .

INT. IMPERIAL BALLROOM. NIGHT
*The band move on to the stage. The ballroom looks magnificent
with its flowers and decorations and more glamorous lighting.
The diners are sitting at round tables with the dance floor
stretching between them and the band. We see* JULIAN, PAMELA
and SARAH *sitting at a table together.* DONALDSON *joins them.
The Royal table is right at the front, but there is nobody sitting
at it. There is a commotion among the diners, hardly anybody is
looking at the stage, most are turned away, looking through the
double doors into the lobby. There we can see a cluster of people
surrounding the* PRINCE OF WALES, *a dapper, complacent-
looking little man, clearly used to being the centre of attention.
He is talking to a group of fashionably dressed women who
surround him. Next to him is* PRINCE GEORGE, *his fleshy face
eyeing the women.*
    We cut to STANLEY *next to* SCHLESINGER, *at the side of the
ballroom watching* SCHLESINGER *through the doors.*

STANLEY: What is the bastard doing?!
    *We see one of the women pointing back across the lobby as
if saying she sadly has to leave, and the* PRINCE OF
WALES *looks as if he may well follow her out.*
STANLEY: He can't do that!
    *We see the indecision in the lobby. The band start to play,
an intro to a song. It makes no difference, the* PRINCE OF
WALES *and his entourage begin to move away across the
lobby towards the street.* LOUIS *is watching all of this as he
sits at the piano playing.* JESSIE *is standing by the
microphone, ready for her cue.*
    Suddenly LOUIS *stops playing, the band break off in
confusion, he boldly walks over to the microphone.*

LOUIS: Ladies and gentlemen, you must excuse me . . .
I forgot to introduce our first number, usually I don't
do much talking from up here . . .

The PRINCES *and their entourage have paused in the*
lobby and are looking back towards the ballroom.

But tonight being such an important night, I thought
I would make an exception. This is a new number for
us, what we're going to play now, something I've just
written, hot off the press. It's about a train . . . we
all have favourite train journeys don't we and this is
ours . . .

We see STANLEY *watching* LOUIS, *intrigued:* LOUIS'
ambition kicking in, his command of the audience.

It's called 'Dead of Night Express'.

He returns to the piano. We see PAMELA *is now among the*
PRINCE OF WALES' *entourage, having left her table, and*
she is guiding him into the ballroom, laughing and flirting
with him. The PRINCE *seems oblivious to the commotion*
he is causing. He sits at the table with PRINCE GEORGE
and some of the fashionable women from the lobby. As
PAMELA *begins to move away, he asks her to stay and sit*
at his table. She sits next to him. The band plays the intro
of the song, the PRINCE OF WALES *is talking loudly and*
smoking and generally only half looking at the stage, and
then JESSIE *begins to sing.*

As soon as he hears her voice he looks up and
immediately stops talking. We move in on his face. The
other diners, who have also been chatting and clinking
their cutlery loudly, notice the PRINCE's *reaction, and they*
begin to fall silent and listen to the singing.

We move closer still on the PRINCE OF WALES. *We cut*
to PRINCE GEORGE *watching* JESSIE *with lazy, sensual*
eyes. Behind JESSIE *on stage,* CARLA *is moving like a*
backing singer, joining in the chorus. We cut to LOUIS
playing, and PAMELA *glancing towards* STANLEY *and*

catching his eye, as he stands in the shadows on the edge
of the room.

INT. ALIEN REGISTRATION OFFICE/BALLROOM. NIGHT
We cut to RYALL *sitting in his silent office. We track in on his*
phone.

We begin to intercut between the dark office and the glowing
ballroom.

We cut back to JESSIE *and the band getting to a really fast*
part of the song, full of propulsion, we see the PRINCE OF
WALES, *his glass half raised to his lips, his foot tapping.*

We cut back to WESLEY *being led from the cells up to the*
main hall in the Alien Registration Office. In the hall there are
a group of about ten very frightened-looking people; about six
of them are black and there are some from Eastern Europe,
including a very Jewish-looking couple in the corner. We see the
clock is showing it is ten to nine.

We cut back to JESSIE *reaching the climax of the song. She*
finishes. There is a moment's silence, all the audience watching
the PRINCE OF WALES, *and then the* PRINCE *smiles. He starts*
clapping vigorously and mouths a bravo. STANLEY, *encouraged*
by this, shouts out from the corner.

STANLEY: Bravo! Bravo!
PRINCE OF WALES (*leaning over to* PAMELA): What a
    gorgeous little singer! I love this jazz sound don't you?!
PRINCE GEORGE (*dryly, to* PAMELA): He went to see
    Florence Mills forty-seven times . . . (*Indicating* JESSIE.)
    it's possible she could be a very busy young woman!
    The rest of the diners are now clapping enthusiastically,
    following the PRINCE OF WALES' *lead. We see* JULIAN
    beaming and standing up and clapping, and SARAH
    watching the Royal table fascinated. We also see at a table
    in the corner that MASTERSON *is one of the diners.*

Among the guests at his table is HANNAH.

LOUIS *walks up to the microphone. He stares straight at the Royal table and makes direct eye contact with the* PRINCE OF WALES.

LOUIS: So I think we have left the station now haven't we?! Left it right behind!

The PRINCE OF WALES *smiles at this. A woman at the back of the ballroom calls out 'Yes!'*

I'm glad you agree with me, madam . . . and now we've got to get you dancing, because that's why we're here, after all! So here's another new number . . . which I hope you will like . . . it's called 'Dancing on the Moon'.

The band start to play and JESSIE *begins to sing the new song.*

Immediately JULIAN *gets up and invites* SARAH *to start dancing, but just as they are about to reach the dance floor the* PRINCE OF WALES *turns to* PAMELA *and invites her to dance.*

JULIAN *and* SARAH *immediately hold back, and the diners watch the* PRINCE OF WALES *dance with* PAMELA *in the middle of the dance floor as some of the audience begin to clap in rhythm.*

INT. ALIEN REGISTRATION OFFICE. NIGHT

We cut back to the Alien Registration Office. WESLEY *is standing staring across the hall, a woman is crying in the corner, stifled small sobs.* RYALL *comes out of his office, he is wearing a coat and is holding his umbrella.*

RYALL: It's time to leave . . . time to catch the bus . . .

People begin to move across the hall. WESLEY *reaches* RYALL *but before he can speak –*

There has been no telephone call I am afraid, Mr Holt.

EXT. YARD AND BUS. NIGHT
We cut to the single-decker bus that is standing in the yard.
  WESLEY *whispers to the woman next to him as they
approach the bus.*

WESLEY: At least it's not a police van . . .
    *He gets on the bus. The faces of the occupants are pale and
    frightened. Everybody except for the old Jewish couple are
    sitting on separate seats, spread through the bus.*
WESLEY (*quietly, to himself*): We could almost be going on a
    trip to the country.

INT./EXT. BALLROOM/NIGHT BUS. NIGHT
We cut back to the dance floor at the Imperial with JESSIE *and*
CARLA *singing together. The dance floor is now getting fuller
and fuller as couples get up to follow the* PRINCE OF WALES'
example. PRINCE GEORGE's *gaze moves from* JESSIE *and*
CARLA *to* LOUIS *on the piano, his sensual eyes studying* LOUIS
for a moment.

PRINCE GEORGE: He's a striking-looking fellow, isn't he?
    *He looks at the dancing couples and then turns to one of
    the fashionable women on his table.*
    We are in danger of being left behind in the rush!
    *He invites her to dance and they move on to the dance
    floor. We intercut between the diners dancing, really
    responding to the jazz music, and a shot of* WESLEY's *face
    staring back out of the window of the bus as it moves off
    into the night. We see a receding shot of* RYALL's *neat
    figure, standing holding his unopened umbrella, watching
    the bus go. And then we see* WESLEY's *face, we move close
    on to his eyes. He stares back at us for a moment.*
    And then we cut to the ballroom and see MASTERSON
    standing up at his table, and moving with HANNAH *to*

join the dancers. We see JULIAN *dancing with* SARAH, *full of energy and excitement. We see a close-up of* STANLEY *surveying the scene; he can't stop himself grinning broadly.* SCHLESINGER *is standing next to him.*

SCHLESINGER: Not bad, Stanley . . . not bad.

We cut to JESSIE *singing,* LOUIS *playing.*

We then cut to a high shot of the dance floor with all the characters dancing.

INT. KITCHEN PASSAGE. NIGHT

We cut to the band all standing to attention in a line-up in the kitchen passage. The Royal entourage is coming round the corner towards them, the PRINCE OF WALES *and* PRINCE GEORGE.

PRINCE OF WALES: Wonderful, this is wonderful, I love seeing the kitchens, I love going backstage!

He pauses, the two PRINCES *stare at the line-up waiting for them down the passage. The* PRINCE OF WALES *calls out to them.*

I can't express how much I enjoyed myself, I just can't express it. (*He turns.*) Can you Georgie?

PRINCE GEORGE: It was sublime.

PRINCE OF WALES: It was. That is the word . . . and let me meet you all, by all means! I must meet you all . . .

We dissolve through the excited faces of the band bowing to the two Royal PRINCES, *to a tracking shot moving into an almost empty kitchen, where two young boys are washing the dirty dishes, and* STANLEY *is sitting typing vigorously.*

LOUIS, SARAH *and* PAMELA *appear in the door.*

PAMELA: What are you doing, Stanley?!

STANLEY: What do you think I'm doing? . . . I'm writing about the Princes and the jazz band . . . I can do it now, it's happened in public!

DONALDSON *puts his head round the door.*

DONALDSON: You must come and see this.

> *They all spill out of the kitchen and into the passage.*
> *Some of the musicians are improvising; they have started*
> *playing music among the trolleys in the passage. And in*
> *the distance, on the blue carpet, but with the kitchen staff*
> *all lined up watching, the* PRINCE OF WALES *is dancing*
> *with* JESSIE *and* PRINCE GEORGE *with* CARLA. *We see*
> *shots of* LOUIS, SARAH *and* STANLEY *watching this*
> *extraordinary image.*

DONALDSON (*turns to* LOUIS): You see I was right, anything
is possible now . . .

> *We track past* DONALDSON *and* LOUIS *and see*
> MASTERSON *standing in the shadows of the passage with*
> HANNAH. STANLEY *suddenly notices him there.*
>
> *We move in on* MASTERSON, *his long, thin face*
> *watching them all closely.*
>
> *And then we see* JULIAN *watching the dance, absolutely*
> *mesmerised by the scene.*
>
> *We then cut back to the shot of the two* PRINCES
> *dancing with* JESSIE *and* CARLA.
>
> *The image slows, as they move together at the end of the*
> *passage, and then it fades suddenly to black.*

PART TWO

EXT. LONDON STREET. NIGHT

*It is night. We are tracking fast across a London street and up
to a window, the only lighted window in an otherwise dark
building. As we move towards the window a caption appears.*

LONDON 1933

When we reach the window we see the curtain stir, and
STANLEY's *face appears glancing down into the empty street.
He then draws the curtain tightly shut.*

INT. MUSIC EXPRESS OFFICE. NIGHT

STANLEY *turns from the window.* LOUIS *is standing on the
other side of the office near the large photograph of him sitting
at a grand piano.*

STANLEY: I don't think there's anybody watching the
building.

LOUIS (*calmly*): Not yet anyway.

STANLEY: Not yet, no! Better keep away from the window
just in case . . .

We cut to STANLEY *switching on the light in the small
outer office where there is a crumpled bed in the corner.*

Do you think you can sleep?

LOUIS: I don't know, usually I can sleep anywhere, but
tonight I'm not sure . . .

STANLEY: So you're not as calm as you look, Louis, that's
good . . . It was beginning to make me really nervous!
(*Indicating* LOUIS' *bandage.*) How's the hand?

LOUIS: It's OK.

STANLEY *turns to move out of the room.*

Where you going?

STANLEY: Don't worry, I'm just going to try and get us
something to eat . . . Mr Wax usually has some food
hidden away in the basement so he can tuck in

whenever he wants to. (*Turns in door.*) And of course
I've also got to try to work out a way of getting you
out of the country.

STANLEY *leaves.* LOUIS *is alone in the small room. He is
sitting on the bed. The walls of the room are covered in
photographs of himself,* SARAH, JULIAN *and* MASTERSON.

We begin to track in on LOUIS' *face. A powerful
montage starts of images and moments telling the story of
Part One, ending with* WESLEY *shouting on the stairs and
being driven away in the bus to be deported, as all the
characters and the* PRINCE OF WALES *dance in the
ballroom at the Imperial.*

We cut back to LOUIS' *face – the camera still moving,
right into his face, into his eyes.*

INT. THE IMPERIAL BALLROOM. AFTERNOON

We cut from LOUIS' *eyes filling the screen to the mouth of a
trumpet, and we pull back in the Imperial Ballroom to see the
jazz band playing: a smaller ensemble than normal and
without the singers. They are in white evening dress and* LOUIS
is looking distinctly ill at ease.

A caption appears.

LONDON 1932

*We then cut round and see the audience the band is playing to.
The ballroom is entirely deserted except for a group of about
fifteen upper-class children in smart party clothes, the little boys
in velvet suits, the girls in fluffy dresses. It is a birthday party,
there are decorations and balloons. An over-dressed woman,*
LADY WINNET, *clearly the mother of the birthday boy, is sitting
presiding with a worried smile. She is surrounded by her two
simpering daughters in their late teens and there is a group of
four nannies in uniform sitting in the shadows. Some of the
children are dancing together, little hopping movements. The*

birthday boy, who is six, is sitting on a large chair in the middle of the dance floor. He is repeating over and over:

BIRTHDAY BOY: When do we get the cake, Mummy, it
   must be time for the cake?! . . . When do we get the
   cake? (*Suddenly he yells really loudly.*) WHERE IS THE
   CAKE?!

LADY WINNET (*indulgently*): Just be patient for a moment
   longer, darling, listen to the funny music. (*She turns to
   one of her daughters.*) I think they like the music . . .
   I thought it would make a change, Jennifer Fairchild
   had them play at her daughter's party and it was a
   success.
   Two children are sitting crying in a corner.
   But maybe some of them find it a little frightening . . .
   *The music stops, the velvet-clad children stare blankly at
   the band.*

LOUIS (*to the band*): I'll be back in a moment.

INT. THE KITCHEN PASSAGE. IMPERIAL. AFTERNOON
LOUIS *is moving along the kitchen passage, desperate to have a
break from the children's party. He pauses to light a cigarette.*
STANLEY *is coming along the passage in the opposite direction.*

LOUIS: What are you doing here?

STANLEY (*breezily*): I have some business with Mr
   Schlesinger. Anyway that's not much of a greeting,
   Louis.

LOUIS: Well you're the last person I want to see.

STANLEY: Why, what have I done?!
   *They have met a series of trolleys covered in desserts that
   line the passage.*

LOUIS: That's exactly the point, you've done nothing,
   Stanley!

STANLEY (*unabashed*): Remind me what I was meant to be doing?

LOUIS moves on past the desserts towards the parlour.

LOUIS: Don't try that, Stanley, you know perfectly well. We are without a manager still, I'm having to do all that myself! We're playing at kids' birthday parties –

STANLEY: You're still the top featured band in this hotel. And of course nobody need worry about being deported while you're here –

LOUIS: We've not been on the wireless, we've not made a record yet . . . Every time I switch on the wireless Jack Paynton is playing! (*He turns, his face close to* STANLEY.) I seem to remember somebody boasting they could make us the number-one band in Britain –

STANLEY (*smiles*): And I will. I haven't changed my mind about that, but these things take time. I thought that's what you believed in, Louis, things taking time! Mind you, I like seeing you a bit impatient –

LOUIS: You do, do you?! Well maybe you'd like to go in there and finish the children's party.

They are now in the parlour. STANLEY *almost helps himself to a cherry tart.*

STANLEY: Better not . . . (*He stops himself.*) Not after what they did to Wesley –

LOUIS: Yes, and that's the most serious of course – I still don't know what really went on.

STANLEY (*innocently*): How do you mean?

LOUIS: You know what I mean! I don't understand what happened with Wesley . . . I don't know why he was thrown out of the country. Mr Donaldson told me he was handling everything . . . he lied to me.

STANLEY: That's a serious charge Louis. (*Calmly.*) Want the chance to say it to his face?

LOUIS: I certainly do.

STANLEY: Then you must.

SCHLESINGER *suddenly appears in the doorway.*

SCHLESINGER: Ah there you are, Stanley! (*Turns to* LOUIS.)
Mr Lester, Lady Winnet says they are ready for 'For
He's a Jolly Good Fellow' now . . .

STANLEY: Oh, you can't keep her waiting Louis.

LOUIS *gets up.*

I've got to see this . . . your rendition of 'For He's a
Jolly Good Fellow'!

INT. IMPERIAL BALLROOM. AFTERNOON

We cut to LOUIS *rejoining the band. All the children are standing
watching him; accusatory stares for keeping them waiting.*

LOUIS *begins to pick out the tune on the piano and the band
join in.* LADY WINNET *starts waving her hands in an agitated
fashion and beckons towards* SCHLESINGER.

LADY WINNET: I am not sure they are used to playing 'For
He's a Jolly Good Fellow', are they? It's much too
fast, almost unrecognisable! Tell them to play it
properly, Mr Schlesinger.

SCHLESINGER: Mr Lester . . . a little slower please . . . Slow!

LOUIS *reluctantly starts to play it again, very slowly. The
upper-class children's voices sing out.* STANLEY *smiles
sharply at* LOUIS *and joins in the singing. A very large
birthday cake on a silver trolley is wheeled into the
ballroom by liveried hotel staff.*

The children run around squealing at the cake.

BIRTHDAY BOY: It's a nice cake Mummy!

*He stops and stares at the band playing 'For He's a Jolly
Good Fellow'.*

But why haven't the band got those black-and-
white faces? . . . You said they would have black-
and-white faces!

EXT. THE IMPERIAL HOTEL. BACK ENTRANCE. MORNING
We cut to LOUIS *walking towards the Imperial front entrance;
he is wearing a daytime suit. A maroon Rolls-Royce is standing
waiting and* MASTERSON, *looking immaculate, is about to get
in. As* LOUIS *passes we catch a momentary view of the inside of
the Rolls; on the back seat there is a flash of gold, gold cigarette
and cigar cases.* MASTERSON *gives* LOUIS *a nod and climbs
into the car, the sun is hitting the interior and the glow of gold
is visible for a second on* MASTERSON's *face.*

The hotel commissionaires watch LOUIS *skirt to the side of
the hotel – he still has to use the back entrance.*

We cut to LOUIS *crossing the backyard of the Imperial. A
young cook is throwing away whole trays of cakes and other
desserts, pouring them into the bins. He is being supervised by*
THORNTON, *who is keeping a check on the cakes even as they
are being thrown away.* LOUIS *calls out breezily to* THORNTON
as he passes.

LOUIS: Check with me, Harry, before you do that next
time.

INT. THE IMPERIAL BAR. MORNING
We cut to LOUIS *moving into the hotel bar, which is closed and
empty except for some cleaners polishing the brass railings and
dusting the deep old armchairs. A sharp-faced young bartender
is cleaning glasses behind the bar.*

*Right at the far end of the room, with the light behind him
so he is initially silhouetted, is* DONALDSON. *He is smoking a
cigar, the smoke curling above him. He has a cup of coffee in
front of him. He watches* LOUIS *approach.*

DONALDSON: So you wanted to see me, Mr Lester?
LOUIS: Yes, I did, very much.

LOUIS *sits in front of him.*

DONALDSON: As you may have noticed, the bar is closed
but perhaps I could use my influence, since it is
almost the legal hour, and get you a glass of wine?

LOUIS: No thank you.

DONALDSON: You must let me get you a cup of coffee at
least.

LOUIS: No thank you, I don't need anything.

DONALDSON: Except to know if I lied to you?

He smiles through the cigar smoke, meeting LOUIS' *gaze.*

Whether I ever really tried to stop your friend from
being deported? You would like to know that,
wouldn't you?

LOUIS: I would, yes.

DONALDSON: Well, I did try. (*Watching* LOUIS *carefully.*)
But I can see you don't believe me . . .

LOUIS *hesitates.*

Don't worry, you don't need to answer that –
whichever way you look at it, I failed. And for that I
am truly sorry. Sometimes one overstates what one can
do, maybe out of arrogance or a desire to please . . .

The sharp-faced bartender watching with interest.

It's a terrible thing to be suddenly thrown out of the
country –

LOUIS: It is, yes . . . and I've not heard what happened to
him. I probably never will.

DONALDSON: And now you have no manager and you're
stuck playing in this old place –

LOUIS (*choosing his words carefully*): Well it's good to have a
regular job of course, but I really thought after the
Prince of Wales heard us play, and all that excitement –

DONALDSON: You were going to be making records? You
were going to be on the wireless?

LOUIS: Yes, I did think that.

DONALDSON: The trouble is, Mr Lester, the people in
charge of those places are quite unbelievably

conservative. Sir John Reith for instance at the BBC detests jazz music . . .

An old dowager comes into the bar leaning on two sticks, she is accompanied by a severe-looking younger woman.

LOUIS: So it's never going to happen then? My band won't get on the wireless or be able –

DONALDSON: On the contrary I think your band and that young singer Jessie, who we all like . . . I'm sure you are both going to become very famous.

LOUIS *looks sceptical.*

That's the second thing I've said you don't believe?

LOUIS: I don't believe you, no.

DONALDSON: Mr Lester, I know you find me – how shall I put this – a trifle baffling. Why am I interested in you at all? (*He looks straight at him.*) You do find that strange don't you?

LOUIS: A little, yes.

DONALDSON (*smiling charmingly*): Well, bit by bit I'm sure we'll get to know each other more – but for the time being just let's say I'm a man of leisure who is addicted to the new, whose chief excitement in life is spotting and encouraging new talent, and sometimes becoming their patron.

I do want to help you. Will you let me do that?

LOUIS: It depends in what way.

DONALDSON: Ah, funny you should say that! I've actually come with a request right now, and this will surprise you I warn you . . . Lady Cremone, who is an old friend, would like you to play at a funeral.

LOUIS (*calmly*): To play at a funeral? Really? And that's going to help us?

DONALDSON: Yes. (*He smokes his cigar.*)

LOUIS: Whose funeral is it?

DONALDSON: Her estate manager, who was a tremendous jazz enthusiast. She is a very interesting woman,

Lavinia, somebody of great taste, we tend to get
excited by the same things. She's become a bit of a
recluse recently, lives in an appalling remote spot! But
somehow she keeps in touch with everything that's
happening . . .

LOUIS: How does she do that?

DONALDSON: I don't quite know. (*He smiles.*) If you
discover that you can tell me. You will be staying in
her house, but that is no guarantee you will get to
meet her. (*He leans forward.*) But if you do, Mr Lester,
this is someone who knows even more people –
important people – than I do.

LOUIS: Is that possible?

DONALDSON (*smiles*): You flatter me, but that is possible.
Stanley is going to go to the funeral to try to get to
meet her . . . (*Pointedly.*) And so is Sarah. (*He looks
straight at* LOUIS.) Will you go?

LOUIS: I think so . . . yes.

DONALDSON: It might just be the best decision you've ever
made.

EXT. OUTSKIRTS OF VILLAGE/HILLSIDE CHURCH. DAY
*A wide shot of the funeral procession, the coffin is being drawn
by sturdy horses. The cortège is moving through the edge of a
mining village. Behind are dark hills and a brooding landscape.
There is a group of mourners following the coffin, retainers from
Lady Cremone's estate and villagers; they are followed by the
band who are playing a slow number, mainly on brass, and
then* CARLA *and* JESSIE, LOUIS, STANLEY *and* SARAH.

*We see images of acute poverty, pale undernourished children
in doorways, a small group of villagers staring at the band with
curiosity as they pass. The village buildings are stark, a slate-
grey hamlet surrounded by hills. The landscape is powerful
rather than pretty, windswept and isolated.*

We cut to the graveside, a cemetery on a hill next to a small church. As the mourners stand waiting for the priest to start the service the band are still playing. A black car draws up at the bottom of the hill and a distant figure in black gets out, an older woman, LADY CREMONE. *She stands watching the ceremony from a great distance.*

The images of the funeral dissolve into each other, the priest beginning the ceremony and then JESSIE *and* CARLA *singing a lament over the grave, accompanied by* JOE *on the trumpet. All the time* STANLEY *and* LOUIS *can't stop staring over at the dark figure watching from a distance.*

We cut to after the funeral. The mourners are just beginning to disperse.

The widow, MRS LEE, *comes up to* LOUIS.

MRS LEE: I want to thank you, from the bottom of my
    heart, for coming all this way and playing for Charlie.
LOUIS: We're delighted to be here, ma'am.
MRS LEE: He would be so thrilled, he is so thrilled. I am
    sure he could hear the music! You know he always had
    the latest gramophone records sent over from America,
    he did. (*She whispers.*) There's one in his coffin, yes
    there is! Now you will come and play in the village?
    Please, I know they would so like that. Do say yes!

EXT. THE VILLAGE. DAY
We cut to the wake, which is happening in the street and in the village hall. We see people watching from the doorway of the hall. The band are playing outside in the main street; some of the children are dancing around. The villagers are watching the band, fascinated. Some of them are clearly drawn towards the music, excited by it.

SARAH *is holding her camera, uncertain if taking pictures would be considered disrespectful.*

SARAH: Do you think they'll mind me taking photographs?
It is a funeral after all.

STANLEY: I don't know . . . (*He is watching the villagers.*)
I don't expect they've ever seen black people before.
He watches LOUIS *mixing with the villagers. They are
coming up to him and asking him about the band and the
music.*

Then out of the corner of his eye STANLEY *sees* LADY
CREMONE*'s black limousine driving towards the village.
It stops some distance away at the end of the street,
watching from afar. She doesn't get out.*

STANLEY: Do I dare?

SARAH: Dare what?

STANLEY: Do I dare run over there?

SARAH (*laughs*): I don't know what's stopping you,
Stanley?!

STANLEY *stares at the black limousine sitting at the end of the
street. He then makes a decision and starts to walk
towards it at a very sharp pace. We see a subjective track
as he gets closer. He hears the engine start as if the car is
about to move off; he breaks into a run and reaches the
car.* LADY CREMONE *is sitting in the back.* STANLEY *taps
on the window. She winds it down reluctantly halfway.*

STANLEY: Your Ladyship, forgive me, I just wanted to
introduce myself, I'm Stanley Mitchell, I'm a friend
of the musicians and I –

LADY CREMONE (*sharp*): Are you a journalist?

STANLEY: It's that obvious is it! Yes, I am.

LADY CREMONE: I have nothing against journalists, Mr
Mitchell, I just never talk to them, and certainly not
at funerals.

STANLEY: Of course. I understand that, but actually we
might bump into each other later today because you
are kindly allowing the band to stay on your estate.
(*He smiles breezily.*) And I've always wanted to meet

you, and so just in case we do run into each other
later . . . I wanted to say hello . . .
LADY CREMONE: And now you've done it, and at a
considerable length. Hello, Mr Mitchell. (*She begins to
wind the window back up.*)
STANLEY: I don't expect it will mean anything to you, but
I am deputy editor and chief writer on *Music Express*,
a magazine that concentrates on –
LADY CREMONE (*her head turns sharply*): Are you, Mr
Mitchell? How very interesting.
STANLEY *can't tell if she is being sarcastic or not.*
Why don't you come to tea at four o'clock? You and
the bandleader, Mr Lester? I'm sure that's a better
way of doing things than trying to bump into each
other.

EXT. LADY CREMONE'S HOUSE. LATE AFTERNOON
We cut to LOUIS, STANLEY *and* SARAH *walking towards the
front entrance of* LADY CREMONE*'s house, a rather severe grey
mansion nestling in the hills.* JESSIE, CARLA *and the band are
behind them and are moving off towards the outbuildings
carrying their instruments.*

SARAH: Did she invite me too, do you think? To tea?
LOUIS: Of course! You know her anyway.
SARAH: I don't know her . . . I photographed her once in
London, and she didn't like that.
STANLEY *is staring at the forbidding house as they get
closer.*
STANLEY: I like to think it takes a lot to scare me, but this
tea – I'm terrified!

INT. LADY CREMONE'S DRAWING ROOM. AFTERNOON
LOUIS, STANLEY *and* SARAH *are sitting together on a sofa*
facing LADY CREMONE *across her fine drawing room. There*
are modern pictures on the wall, the furniture is new – it is an
unusual interior for a manor house.

    There are plates of sandwiches in front of them and the clink
of fine china as they drink tea.

LADY CREMONE: You have an exciting band, Mr Lester.
LOUIS: Thank you, Your Ladyship.
LADY CREMONE: It was the perfect funeral for Charlie.
    (*She drinks her tea.*) I know there is the view that your
    kind of music can only appeal to a very small
    audience . . . but we saw just now in the village how
    all sorts of people can respond.
STANLEY: Absolutely right, Your Ladyship.
LADY CREMONE (*to* LOUIS): I'm sure you're wondering if I
    know anything about music – your music – somebody
    of my age . . . .
LOUIS: No, Your Ladyship, I wasn't wondering –
STANLEY: No, he knows you do!
LADY CREMONE: Mr Mitchell, if you could be so kind, just
    over there in the bookshelf . . .
    STANLEY *follows her instructions.*
    On the second shelf, you see that binder, that dark
    red one – if you could take it down, and open it.
    STANLEY *opens the binder. He is astonished.*
STANLEY: I don't believe it! Blimey . . . ! (*He holds up the*
    binder.) Bound copies of *Music Express*! I've never seen
    that before in somebody's house!
LADY CREMONE: Of course not. I don't suppose anybody
    else would be mad enough.
LOUIS (*whispering to* SARAH): So that's one of the ways she
    keeps in touch . . .

STANLEY (*standing in front of* LADY CREMONE): I know
　　what I'm about to say is very stupid . . . but I can't
　　stop myself saying it.

LADY CREMONE: And what is it Mr Mitchell?

STANLEY: You wouldn't . . . you wouldn't, would you . . .
　　let me interview you? Now? I've always wanted to
　　interview you.

LADY CREMONE: Well it would depend on the quality of
　　the questions, Mr Mitchell.

STANLEY (*thrilled, immediately turns*): Sarah, Louis, you
　　want to have a look at the garden don't you?! (*They
　　look blank.*) Go and look at the garden. Now!

EXT. LADY CREMONE'S GARDEN. AFTERNOON
SARAH *and* LOUIS *emerge into the large garden that surrounds
the house, formal gardens surrounded by woodlands. They are
both laughing.*

SARAH: Stanley! He's incorrigible – he is such a rogue!

LOUIS: Why's he always wanted to interview her?

SARAH: Because she's known so many great artists and
　　musicians, she encouraged them, discovered them,
　　and now nobody sees her any more.

INT. LADY CREMONE'S DRAWING ROOM. AFTERNOON
We cut back to STANLEY *pacing in front of* LADY CREMONE.
He stops and pulls out a notebook.

STANLEY: Don't change your mind.

LADY CREMONE: I think I've already changed my mind.

STANLEY: No, no, you can't.

LADY CREMONE: I hate talking about myself, always have.

STANLEY: I am going to say – is it true? And you're
　　going to agree, or rather if you would be kind enough

to agree, or not. (*He smiles.*) And I'll see how many
I get away with before you stop me. Is it true Noël
Coward sends all his plays to you to read before he
puts them on?

LADY CREMONE: Yes.

STANLEY: Is it true that you told MGM to sign Greta
Garbo after you saw her in a Swedish film?

LADY CREMONE: When I was living in America I spent time
both in New York and in Los Angeles, and so I got to
know all sorts of people, some of them in the film
business, and sometimes they asked for my opinion.

STANLEY (*writing in notebook*): I am going to say that's true
then! Is it true you have put money into seventeen
West End successes in a row and did that without
even leaving this house?

LADY CREMONE: No, that certainly isn't true, that would
be ridiculous, nobody could have a record like that.

STANLEY (*grins*): I'll say fifteen hits in a row then, shall I?

EXT. WALLED GARDEN. AFTERNOON
SARAH *pushes open a small metal gate, and steps with* LOUIS
*into a sunken garden which is surrounded by high walls. There
is a piece of modern sculpture in the middle of the garden with
a plaque.*

SARAH: I think this must be a memorial garden for her
sons . . .
*They stare across at the sculpture which has a plaque with
three names inscribed, 'Lionel, Ralph, Thomas'.*
All three of her sons were killed in the war.

LOUIS: All three . . . ? That's terrible.

SARAH: Yes . . . How do you get over that?
They are standing close together, affected by the garden.
Are your parents alive, Louis?

LOUIS: No, they're not. My father did fight in the war, but he didn't die in it.

SARAH *looks at him very surprised.*

Yes, there were some coloured soldiers, Sarah!

SARAH: Sorry, I didn't mean to look surprised, I've just never heard that before, but of course there must've been.

LOUIS: Yes, he survived the war, my dad, but then both my parents died in the flu epidemic. It happened very quickly.

SARAH: I'm sorry. (*She touches his arm gently.*) Suddenly you were an orphan. What did you do?

LOUIS: That's when I started travelling, went to all sorts of places . . . I spent time in Paris playing in bars, time in New York, and a lot of time on ocean liners as you know.

SARAH: So you've seen a lot more of the world than I have?

LOUIS (*smiles*): Yes, I must have.

SARAH (*turns, really close to him*): I want to hear everything Louis, all about America! About New York especially, I so want to go to New York. To photograph all those buildings, that would be fantastic. You will tell me everything won't you?! . . . (*She kisses him.*) Tell me.

INT. LADY CREMONE'S DRAWING ROOM. AFTERNOON
STANLEY *is now sitting on the edge of a chair in front of* LADY
CREMONE, *a cigarette in the corner of his mouth, scribbling in
his notebook, talking at the same time.*

STANLEY: Is it true that you've been trying very hard to get some different things played on the wireless, a more exciting repertoire? Especially jazz music?!

LADY CREMONE: Maybe, but I've been extremely unsuccessful – so far. Now this has got to stop, Mr

Mitchell, it's been oddly enjoyable, but that's quite
enough.

STANLEY: Just one more, please! (*Without waiting.*) Is it
true that famous artists have trekked across the world
to see you, and just turned up here on the doorstep
totally unannounced?

LADY CREMONE: That's not true, no.

STANLEY (*disappointed*): Are you sure?

LADY CREMONE: That's not true, Mr Mitchell. Now
shall we –

STANLEY: But it's possible somebody could come here,
almost by accident, who was extraordinary? (*He looks
at her.*) And then you'd want to see them properly?

LADY CREMONE: You mean Mr Lester and his band?

STANLEY: Yes, but also the singer Jessie.

LADY CREMONE: That young girl? I saw her sing at the
funeral –

STANLEY: Yes, but you were an awfully long way away! (*He
looks straight at her.*) Can she sing for you again in the
morning?

INT. LADY CREMONE'S HOUSE. PASSAGE/SARAH'S
BEDROOM. NIGHT
We cut to a dimly lit upstairs passage in LADY CREMONE'S
house. The sound of the wind and the creaks of the old house.
We cut inside SARAH'S *bedroom. She is lying with the
blankets right up to her chin.*
*She's wide awake, her teeth chattering, absolutely freezing.
She sits up in bed.*

INT. LADY CREMONE'S HOUSE. PASSAGE/KITCHEN. NIGHT
We cut to SARAH *in a dressing gown moving along the dark
passage and down some stairs. Ahead of her she can see light*

spilling from the basement. She reaches the basement and pushes open the door of the large kitchen. She is startled to find STANLEY *and* LOUIS *already there.* LOUIS *is in some stylish silk pyjamas;* STANLEY *is in some striped pyjamas but is wearing his jacket over the top.*

STANLEY: You too! God, it's freezing isn't it!

He cradles the warm teapot.

LOUIS: It's so cold we just had to have some tea.

SARAH: Yes, I don't think I've ever been so cold in my life.

STANLEY (*takes a cup of tea, sips it, moves to the door*): That's perfect . . . I am going back with this, and we'll see if I can make it through the night!

LOUIS *and* SARAH *are alone.*

LOUIS: Isn't it funny, a lady with such modern taste and yet her house is this cold.

SARAH: And it creaks too! . . .

She puts her arms around him.

That's a little warmer isn't it – (*She stares into his eyes.*) Maybe the only way to get through the night . . .

LOUIS: Is like this?

He kisses her, they hold each other tight, a long sensual kiss. SARAH *slides her hand across his chest, wrapping her body close. They move against the wall, their kissing getting more and more passionate.*

LOUIS *slides his hand inside her nightdress.* SARAH *sits down on the edge of the table, they are kissing all the time, she lies back on the table. Suddenly there is a very loud and rather terrifying creak on the stairs and they hear footsteps.* SARAH *sits bolt upright.* STANLEY*'s head appears round the door.*

STANLEY: I think she might be awake! Best not to take any chances!

INT. LADY CREMONE'S HOUSE. PASSAGE/CONSERVATORY.
MORNING

We cut to morning light. We see JESSIE *walking along a passage towards the conservatory in* LADY CREMONE*'s house.* CARLA *is following just behind her. They can see in front of them* LADY CREMONE *sitting at her breakfast table drinking coffee and eating something in a bowl.*

They reach the conservatory. LOUIS *is sitting at a small upright piano in the corner,* STANLEY *and* SARAH *are sitting behind* LADY CREMONE.

CARLA: We're not late are we, Your Ladyship?

LADY CREMONE: No, no, any time during my breakfast will do.

CARLA: I am just here to watch . . . It's Jessie –

LADY CREMONE: Yes, this is about Jessie, I understand.
(*She looks straight at* JESSIE.) So, my child, do you want to sing something for me?

JESSIE *is extremely nervous confronted by* LADY CREMONE *at her breakfast table.*

JESSIE: I'll try yes . . . (*Looking across at* LOUIS.) I'll do a bit of 'Dead of Night Express', shall I?

LADY CREMONE *is eating a large artichoke for breakfast, dipping the leaves into melted butter which is in a separate white dish.* JESSIE *prepares to sing.*

LADY CREMONE: I do hope this old nursery piano is still in tune.

LOUIS *begins to play; the piano is in tune.* JESSIE *starts to sing the first verse of the song,* CARLA *egging her on.* STANLEY *and* SARAH *are watching* LADY CREMONE, *very intrigued. But as* JESSIE *sings she can't stop staring at the strange vegetable* LADY CREMONE *is eating – the spiky leaves, the soft heart of the artichoke, the way* LADY CREMONE *is dipping leaves into the butter and then eating them with her fingers.*

JESSIE *becomes mesmerised by the extraordinary vegetable, so distracted she suddenly stops.*

LADY CREMONE: What's the matter, child?

JESSIE *is staring.*

STANLEY: I don't think Jessie has ever seen an artichoke before!

LADY CREMONE: Have you not my dear? Then you must have one of course, at once!

EXT. LADY CREMONE'S HOUSE. DAY

LADY CREMONE *is standing on the steps outside the french windows at the back of her house, posing reluctantly for a photograph.* SARAH *is taking the photograph;* STANLEY, LOUIS, CARLA *and* JESSIE *are watching. The rest of the band are waiting at a respectful distance.*

SARAH: That's very good, Your Ladyship, just hold it like that.

LADY CREMONE: Are there going to be many more? I'm beginning to wonder why I ever agreed to this . . .

SARAH: Just one or two more.

LOUIS (*to* STANLEY *as he watches*): Did she say anything about Jessie?

STANLEY: No. Not a thing.

LOUIS: Have we done ourselves any good do you think?

STANLEY *stares at the stylish, imperious* LADY CREMONE *as she poses.*

STANLEY: It's quite hard to tell.

We see LADY CREMONE *framed in* SARAH*'s camera. She is staring straight into the lens.*

INT. MUSIC EXPRESS OFFICE. DAY

We cut to the cover of the latest edition of Music Express.

LADY CREMONE *is on the cover standing on the steps of her*

house, and she is surrounded by smaller photos of musicians and writers she has championed, they are encircling her. The headline in huge letters says:

THE FIRST LADY OF JAZZ AND MUCH MORE

We cut from the cover to STANLEY *staring down at it with a smile of satisfaction. Across the room is* MR WAX *who is waving the magazine around, and* ROSIE *who is sitting at her desk.*

MR WAX: I really don't know what she is doing on the cover . . . Lady Cremone! Of course I've heard of her, I know who she is, but she's not a bandleader, she's not a musician of any sort. What on earth is she doing on the cover?!

STANLEY (*trying not to sound exasperated*): You agreed to it, Mr Wax.

MR WAX: I don't believe I did, Stanley, you must have misheard me . . .

He turns the pages of the magazine.

And yet again there is an article about the Louis Lester Band . . . ! I've lost count of the number of articles you've done on them –

STANLEY: They are going to be the biggest band in Britain and we will have helped create them.

MR WAX (*beginning to leave*): There he goes again! He always exaggerates . . . Stanley, you make me laugh with all your claims, you really do!

STANLEY *and* ROSIE *are alone.*

STANLEY: You think I'm exaggerating?

ROSIE: Maybe. Mr Wax is right, you often do.

STANLEY (*lightly*): You're still angry with me, Rosie, aren't you?

ROSIE: No, I know what to expect from you Stanley, after all I've seen enough of it over the last two years, quite enough.

STANLEY (*startled*): You're not quitting are you?

ROSIE: Of course not. I know this magazine is going to
     really grow – and soon you won't be able to write it all
     yourself, you'll be looking round for another writer.
     (*Looks straight at him.*) And there'll be one right here
     in the office. (*Looking for his reaction.*) Won't there?

STANLEY: And so there will, Rosie.

INT. IMPERIAL HOTEL. STAFF BEDROOM PASSAGE/JESSIE'S
ROOM. DAY

JESSIE *and* CARLA *are walking together down the staff bedroom
passage at the Imperial. They see in the distance* JULIAN, *who
is standing holding a huge bouquet of flowers in one hand and
a smaller bunch in the other.* JULIAN *calls down the passage.*

JULIAN: There you are! (*Watching with delight as they
     approach.*) Just dropped by to give you this . . .
     He hands JESSIE *the big bouquet.*
     They're for you, Jessie.

JESSIE: Thank you, Mr Luscombe, they're beautiful.

JULIAN: Yes, and these are . . .
     He hesitates with the smaller bunch.

CARLA: For me?

JULIAN: Yes, I know it looks smaller Carla, and, well,
     I suppose it is smaller, but I meant to get them the
     same size . . .

CARLA: They're lovely. Don't worry about that Mr
     Luscombe.

JULIAN: I would have bought the whole shop if I could,
     and then there would have been no problem! But I
     had nobody with me to help carry them . . . (*He
     smiles.*) So I couldn't buy the whole shop.
     JESSIE *and* CARLA *move into the bedroom.* JULIAN *stands
     in the doorway.*

JULIAN: Oh this room! No, I won't come in, thank you,
	but this room is not nearly good enough –
JESSIE: We love this room!
CARLA: Yes, it's the best room I've ever slept in.
JULIAN: No, no, I want to arrange a better room for you
	both, I can do it easily!
CARLA: No, no, please don't, we're happy here.
JESSIE: Please don't, Mr Luscombe!
JULIAN: Well if you really don't want me to . . . (*He smiles.*)
	then I won't. Soon of course you'll have the absolutely
	biggest suites in the most fashionable hotels all over
	the world!
JESSIE (*laughs*): That's not going to happen, Mr Luscombe!
JULIAN: Oh yes, people are going to be crossing the
	Atlantic just to attend one of your concerts – and
	they'll wait for nights in the street just to get a glance
	of you driving away in a car.
CARLA: You mustn't do this, Mr Luscombe! –
JULIAN: Why not?! It's going to happen! And when you go
	abroad, even in the most faraway places, people will
	come running out of their houses into the street when
	they see you, calling your name and blowing kisses!
	A voice calls out 'Julian'. JULIAN *turns in the doorway
	and sees in the distance* MASTERSON *standing down the
	other end of the passage, his tall sinister figure.*
MASTERSON: I've been looking everywhere for you, Julian!
JULIAN: I'll be with you in a minute, Walter.
MASTERSON: We haven't got long.
JULIAN (*more tersely*): In a minute, Walter.
JESSIE: You have to go?
JULIAN: Not quite yet, no.
	He glances back at MASTERSON, *then turns to the girls.*
	It's just it's nearly time to go down to the spooky
	temples – you know the Freemasons have temples in
	this hotel, all these old dukes and other boring people

putting on strange clothes and doing peculiar things
in the basement . . .
The girls laugh.
No, it's true! So he is letting me know we ought to get
down there . . . (*He smiles at the girls.*) But they can
wait a bit, can't they?!
We cut back to MASTERSON *standing waiting in the
shadows in the passage.*

EXT. MUSIC EXPRESS. THE ROOF. LATE AFTERNOON
We track towards STANLEY *on the flat roof of the* Music
Express *building, the cityscape of chimneys and rooftops behind
him. He is typing furiously. We can hear a brass band playing in
the distance.* MICK, *the young messenger, is standing by*
STANLEY *who is calling out what he is typing in a defiant tone.*

STANLEY: 'This is a Call to Arms! The audience are crying
out for a more exciting choice of music on the wireless,
and this has to be delivered now! At the moment they
are being fed a tired and endlessly familiar diet, the
same bands every night of the week!' What do you
think of it so far, Mick?
MICK: Quite strong stuff, Mr Mitchell.
STANLEY: 'Listeners will be soon switching off in their
droves or else hunting with their dials to find more
exciting sounds, which are readily available from the
rival stations abroad!' (*He looks up.*)
PAMELA *is standing by his desk, the sun behind her. She is
exquisitely dressed.*
Oh it's you!
PAMELA: Oh it's me, yes.
STANLEY: Mick, take this to Rosie, let her have a look at it,
see if she approves. (*He turns to* PAMELA.) Sorry, you
took me by surprise.

PAMELA: Don't worry, most people don't say 'Oh it's you'
when they see me, so I suppose you can.

STANLEY: I'm just a little behind, that's all –

PAMELA: I'm interrupting, forgive me.

STANLEY: No, you're not. I'm always behind . . . and I
always catch up. I'm very glad to see you.

PAMELA: And I'm glad to see you, Stanley. I think about
you every week when I read your magazine.

STANLEY: You think about me just once a week? Is that all?

PAMELA: Yes, but that's quite good isn't it? (*She picks up a
copy of* Music Express *from the floor.*) I know you think
I'm not really interested in your magazine –

STANLEY: Did I ever say that?

PAMELA: No, but you think it. (*She flips through the
magazine.*) I do spot a few things though you know . . .
like it's changing, isn't it? It's getting more political –

STANLEY: I wouldn't quite go that far, I still have to get
everything past Wax!

PAMELA: But you're sneaking more and more things in . . .
(*She holds up the cartoon strip.*) Like Farquhar and
Tonk running a soup kitchen!

*We see the strip cartoon, Farquhar and Tonk serving a
queue from their soup kitchen in the slums. In among the
line of destitute people are members of the House of Lords,
wearing their robes, joining the queue because they have
spotted a free meal.*

STANLEY: That's right. We got that past Mr Wax!

Their eyes meet. Despite wanting to work, STANLEY *is
strongly attracted to* PAMELA*'s febrile beauty.*

PAMELA: You look surprised I've noticed, Stanley! (*She
lights a cigarette.*) You'll laugh at me, but as it happens
I know what it's like to be hungry.

STANLEY (*solemnly*): You do?

PAMELA: You don't have to look quite that serious! (*She
moves.*) I starved myself for ten days a couple of years

ago – I could say it was to understand how it felt to
be really hungry, but actually I was just trying to
shock my parents who are quite the dullest people in
England. (*She turns.*) Don't say anything to that
Stanley!

STANLEY: Probably best I don't say anything, no.

PAMELA: So now you can put me in this cartoon . . .
looking like a skeleton, mad eyes popping out, dressed
in a ball gown with a coronet on my head!

STANLEY: You think I'd do that?

PAMELA (*looking at him with her sensual gaze*): Yes Stanley,
I really think you would!

MICK (*calling from the open office window*): There's a
telephone call for you, Mr Mitchell.

   STANLEY *climbs through the window.* ROSIE *looks up
   from reading 'Call to Arms'.*

STANLEY: What do you think of it so far?

ROSIE: It's much milder than I thought it was going to be.

STANLEY: That's not good!

   STANLEY *answers the phone. Intercut with* LADY
   CREMONE *in her drawing room.*

LADY CREMONE: I am on the cover of your magazine, Mr
Mitchell. You never said you were going to do that!

STANLEY: It was too good an opportunity to miss. I hope
you don't mind.

LADY CREMONE: It's an extraordinary thing to do, I'm not
a performer – who wants to see what I look like?

STANLEY: More people than you think.

   ROSIE *watches beadily as* PAMELA *climbs through the
   window from the roof.*

LADY CREMONE: I should be furious with you, in fact
I am furious with you, but that's not why I'm ringing
you. I have another reason, something a little more
interesting . . .

STANLEY: That's a relief!

LADY CREMONE: I may be coming to London shortly.

STANLEY: Really?! You are!

LADY CREMONE: Don't sound so astonished, Mr Mitchell. I may be.

STANLEY: That's tremendous news! You must come. Can we meet?

LADY CREMONE: It's possible we will. It depends on everything falling into place. I've had a notion, Mr Mitchell.

INT. THE PARLOUR. IMPERIAL. DAY

LOUIS *is alone sitting at the big table in the tiled parlour. Pieces of paper and music sheets are spread all around him.* STANLEY *appears in the doorway.*

STANLEY: Hello, Louis. (*Glancing at the paper.*) Writing something good?

LOUIS: Not sure yet. (*He smiles and covers the papers.*)

STANLEY: Now you're not going to like what I am about to say at all.

LOUIS: Same as most days then . . .

STANLEY: You've got to go back to the club where we first met.

LOUIS: Says who?

STANLEY: Says me . . . You're going to play the most important session of your life.

EXT./INT. BASEMENT CLUB. NIGHT

STANLEY *dressed in a dinner jacket rattles down the stairs of the basement club and into the passage.* DEIRDRE, *the club owner, is standing in a splendid red dress.*

STANLEY: Deirdre, you look magnificent!

DEIRDRE: Thank you, Stanley, I don't usually get a chance
to dress up like this.

STANLEY *is running his hand along the edge of the bar.*
What are you doing?

STANLEY: Just looking to see . . . (*He turns.*) I hate to say
this, Deirdre, you need to clean this place.

DEIRDRE: It's been cleaned! What do you think I've been
doing?!

STANLEY: Well, I'll give it a quick extra clean myself . . .
(*He grins.*) We're not going to leave anything to chance.

INT. PASSAGE AND BACK STAIRS, IMPERIAL HOTEL. NIGHT
*The band are moving down the back stairs at the Imperial in
their dinner jackets, carrying their instruments.* MASTERSON
suddenly appears above them and calls down.

MASTERSON: Mr Lester, can you just spare me a minute?

LOUIS: I can't, Mr Masterson, not tonight, we're just off to
an engagement –

MASTERSON: I need to tell you something about tonight,
Mr Lester, it's important.

LOUIS (*hesitates, calls after the band*): I'll catch you up.

INT. MASTERSON'S SUITE. THE IMPERIAL. NIGHT
We cut to LOUIS *and* MASTERSON *entering the Minotaur Suite.
This time it is in an immaculate state, no traces of the violence
we saw before.* LOUIS *follows* MASTERSON *in cautiously. There
are many gold objects and ornaments in the room.*

MASTERSON: You've been here before, of course.

LOUIS (*pointedly*): I have, yes.

MASTERSON: I like this suite, there are bigger suites than
this in the hotel, of course, but I'm fond of this one.

When you've seen as many hotel rooms as I have, you get a feeling for one that really fits.

LOUIS *is glancing at a particularly beautiful gold clock.* MASTERSON *notices.*

Yes, you may have heard about my interest in gold, Mr Lester, keeping it close . . .

LOUIS *looks up.*

You can think you have covered every possible eventuality, how things can go wrong, but you never have. There will always be something that comes up from behind and tries to destroy everything one's created, however powerful one's position appears to be . . . (*He smiles.*) So one has to be ready . . . I like to know I can fight back.

He stares at LOUIS, *his tall, rather frightening figure.*

LOUIS: Mr Masterson . . . I have an urgent engagement tonight, so if we –

MASTERSON: I know, yes. Julian will be at the club tonight, won't he?

LOUIS: Maybe . . . I don't know who's going to be there, we haven't been given the guest list, to be honest with you I have no idea why we're playing there.

MASTERSON: Would you just tell Julian – (*He stares straight at him.*) Not to worry, I have completely taken care of it. And would you give him this . . .

MASTERSON *hands* LOUIS *an envelope.* LOUIS *puts it in his pocket.*

You will remember to do it?

LOUIS: I will, yes. I really must go now.

MASTERSON: If you were wondering –

LOUIS: I wasn't wondering.

MASTERSON: It's a little debt I've taken care of.

As LOUIS *reaches the door,* MASTERSON*'s tone becomes more urgent.*

You will tell him that and give him the envelope?

EXT. STREET NEAR CLUB. NIGHT
We see LOUIS *walking along the dark side street and alley that leads to the basement club. A large car is parked at the mouth of the alley. A chauffeur is standing next to the car watching* LOUIS *as he moves towards the club.* LOUIS *runs down the metal steps.*

INT. BASEMENT CLUB. NIGHT
As LOUIS *enters the club he is confronted by* STANLEY *and* DEIRDRE, *who are standing in the passage looking frantic.* STANLEY *starts shouting.*

STANLEY: Where've you been Louis?!
LOUIS: Something came up –
STANLEY: Are you mad?! This is the one time you couldn't be late!
   LOUIS *is about to enter the auditorium but* DEIRDRE *intercepts him.*
DEIRDRE: Let me look at you Louis . . . (*She straightens his bow tie.*) You can go in now.

INT. CLUB THEATRE. NIGHT
LOUIS *moves into the intimate auditorium, a club theatre painted red with a stage at one end, café tables and behind those some raked seating. The band are waiting on the little stage with* JESSIE *poised to sing.* LOUIS *stops in surprise: the café tables are completely empty. He begins to laugh, assuming it is all a joke. Then he turns and sees sitting in the shadows behind him in the raked seating are* DONALDSON, PAMELA, JULIAN, SARAH, *and* PRINCE GEORGE. *Along the walls on one side are the* PRINCE*'s entourage, thin-faced courtiers looking completely out of place; along the opposite wall are lined the club's staff, sturdy Londoners looking like bouncers.*

   LOUIS *for a split moment is rendered speechless by the strange scene.*

LOUIS: Your Royal Highness, I'm sorry I am so late.
Something happened and I . . .

PRINCE GEORGE: Please, you're here now, Mr Lester, and
that's what matters.

DONALDSON: You have nearly disrupted the whole plan,
Louis.

PRINCE GEORGE: And it's the most delightful plan.

LOUIS *moves straight to the piano, glancing at the band.
The* PRINCE *is lolling in his seat, his legs stretched out,
obviously revelling in the informality of the space.*

LOUIS *moves his seat closer to the piano and is about to
start to play.*

Suddenly the PRINCE *calls out.*

PRINCE GEORGE: No, no, no what are you doing? Has
nobody told him? We're not starting yet.

LOUIS: We're not?

EXT. ALLEYWAY. NIGHT

*A second large car draws up at the end of the alleyway. A
chauffeur leaps out and holds the door open.*

LADY CREMONE *emerges from the car. She is accompanied
by a plump middle-aged man,* BOXLEY, *and a thin bespectacled
donnish-looking man in his late thirties,* HARDIMAN. LADY
CREMONE *sets off at a brisk pace, the two men follow.*

LADY CREMONE: This way, gentlemen.

BOXLEY: Is it really down here?

LADY CREMONE: It is. And we need to be brisk, you took
so long over your pudding.

HARDIMAN: I've never been to a club like this, we usually
send junior staff to these sort of places.

BOXLEY: We don't even do that now, I swore I would never
visit these kind of venues again.

We cut to them descending the metal stairs gingerly, following LADY CREMONE.
At least we will be able to have a drink before the performance, they can't object to waiting for that, can they?

INT. BASEMENT CLUB PASSAGE. NIGHT
LADY CREMONE, BOXLEY *and* HARDIMAN *are moving along the passage in the club, the bar is ahead of them. But between them and the bar is* DEIRDRE.

DEIRDRE: There you are! The last ones! Please hurry.
BOXLEY: Hurry? She's not going to stop us getting a drink, is she?!
DEIRDRE: Straight into the auditorium please!
HARDIMAN (*glancing through the door*): It seems a trifle empty . . . What on earth is the hurry?

INT. THE AUDITORIUM. NIGHT
LADY CREMONE, BOXLEY *and* HARDIMAN *enter the auditorium. They see the band, then the bouncers, then the courtiers and then the audience.*
At first BOXLEY *and* HARDIMAN *are totally disorientated.*

LADY CREMONE: I think you've met Arthur Donaldson. I'm not sure you know anybody else. But maybe you've met His Royal Highness Prince George before?
BOXLEY *and* HARDIMAN *are stunned, poleaxed with embarrassment at having kept royalty waiting.* LADY CREMONE *addresses the* PRINCE.
LADY CREMONE: This is Mr Boxley from His Master's Voice recording company, and Mr Hardiman from the BBC.

BOXLEY: Your Royal Highness . . . please accept our
apologies . . . I am so dreadfully sorry to be so late,
we had no idea . . .

HARDIMAN: No idea at all! No! Lady Cremone didn't warn
us, please accept my abject apologies . . . I didn't have
an inkling.

BOXLEY: Not an inkling, no!

JULIAN (*blurts out*): It's very rude to be late! I am never
late!

There is a rumble of thunder and sound of torrential rain.
And now it's raining!

BOXLEY: Let me apologise again, sir, I was –

PRINCE GEORGE: No, no please, why don't we stop all
these apologies and listen to the music . . . (*Pointedly.*)
That's why we're here, isn't it?

BOXLEY *and* HARDIMAN *promptly sit down under the
frosty stare of the courtiers who are lining the wall.* LOUIS
begins to play.

JULIAN (*calling out*): Don't let the rain put you off!

JESSIE *begins to sing, her voice is tremendously powerful
in this small space.* BOXLEY *and* HARDIMAN *realise
everybody is staring with rapt attention at* JESSIE *and
therefore they assume an expression of extreme concentration,
but can't stop themselves sneaking glances at the* PRINCE.

We see STANLEY, *who is standing at the back, slip out
into the passage and light a cigarette. He turns to* DEIRDRE
who is in the door of the auditorium.

STANLEY: So far so good . . . Look, my hand's shaking!

DEIRDRE: I've never seen you nervous before, Stanley.

STANLEY: Well you have to admit this is a fairly unusual
audience!

We cut back to the band reaching the climax, CARLA
*joining in. Despite the sound of the torrential rain they are
making a huge noise in the small theatre, the music full of*

raw vibrant energy. As soon as they finish PRINCE GEORGE
begins clapping really loudly.

PRINCE GEORGE: Marvellous, absolutely marvellous! (*As
the others applaud.*) Wouldn't you agree, Mr Boxley?
All of them look at BOXLEY *and* HARDIMAN.

BOXLEY: Oh yes, Your Royal Highness.

PRINCE GEORGE: And you Mr Hardiman, just right for the
wireless is it not?

INT. LOBBY/BAR AREA. BASEMENT CLUB. NIGHT
*We cut to a high shot of the bar area and the lobby of the club.
The atmosphere is febrile, full of euphoric energy and intimacy.
All the characters are squashed together in this small space, having
a drink. The door into the yard at the back of the club is wide
open and the rain is pouring down in sheets making the scene
seem even more intense. We see in a series of dissolves the characters
full of drink getting more and more uninhibited. The* PRINCE *is
the centre of attention with the band members all around him,
his entourage watching from a discreet distance but mixing with
the bouncers of the club.* JULIAN *is exuberantly standing by the
rain calling out to people, filling their glasses with champagne.
Only* BOXLEY *and* HARDIMAN *are isolated, sheltering in a
corner.* LADY CREMONE *is standing with* DONALDSON.

DONALDSON: Lavinia, I think that could be counted as a
triumph!

LADY CREMONE: Well, let's hope so. (*She looks across at*
BOXLEY *and* HARDIMAN.) Poor little chickens, they
look so mortified still.
PAMELA comes up to STANLEY, *who is watching the scene
fascinated.*

PAMELA: It's just like one of your cartoons come to life,
isn't it, Stanley?! (*She smiles.*) Except it's a little
sexier . . .

We cut to SARAH *and* LOUIS *together close at the bar,*
watching BOXLEY *and* HARDIMAN.

LOUIS: Do you think they liked us?

SARAH: They have to because the Prince did!

We cut to LADY CREMONE *sitting on the stairs with*
JESSIE, *who is staring fascinated at the crowd, real*
excitement in her eyes.

LADY CREMONE: You sang wonderfully, my dear.

JESSIE: All those important people . . . and they were so
close!

LADY CREMONE: Well, I'm not used to crowds either.
(*Her hand is on the banister.*) So I'm holding on tight!

We cut to DONALDSON *near* LOUIS *and* SARAH, *the*
PRINCE, *the band and the courtiers are swirling all*
around them.

DONALDSON: This is what I love Louis, even if I didn't
arrange it all myself, such a wonderful mix of people.

A shot of a bouncer talking to the PRINCE.

I have dreams like this, I really do . . . of unlikely
crowds mixing together.

SARAH: He dreams about you, Louis!

DONALDSON: Well let's not misunderstand each other! (*He*
smiles.) What I like best is how music links people
across the classes . . . I had such a conventional life
when I was young, my father was a general!

LOUIS *looks intrigued.*

Yes, not a very good one, but he was, and my mother
was the daughter of a marquis. The idea of royalty
muddled up with coloured musicians in a basement
club – they would have absolutely loathed it!

We cut to BOXLEY *and* HARDIMAN *huddling in their*
corner, watching the band laughing and joking with the
PRINCE.

BOXLEY: How are we ever going to escape?

We cut to PRINCE GEORGE *approaching* LOUIS. *They are in the doorway of the club's office surrounded by posters for past attractions.*

LOUIS: Your Royal Highness?

PRINCE GEORGE *stares at* LOUIS *closely, his eyes searching him with a flirtatious sexual look.*

PRINCE GEORGE: Mr Lester, we must get to know each other a little better.

LOUIS: That would be an honour, Your Royal Highness.

PRINCE GEORGE: You mean that? (*His face very close to* LOUIS.)

LOUIS (*trying to remain polite*): Of course I do.

STANLEY *is watching them from across the room.*

PRINCE GEORGE: Well, I wonder when we can do this? I'm going to be here a little while longer yet, and then maybe we can move on to another place of entertainment? Or whatever takes one's fancy?
He grins at LOUIS *and indicates* BOXLEY *and* HARDIMAN. Look at those poor fellows! Shall we put them out of their misery? They cannot leave until I do. (*He smiles.*) That's protocol, but maybe we've tortured them long enough. We don't want to make enemies of them, do we?! (*He calls out.*) Mr Boxley! Mr Hardiman! You really don't need to be here a moment longer than you want to be.

HARDIMAN: Oh no, Your Royal Highness, we're enjoying ourselves greatly, we've no wish to leave.

PRINCE GEORGE: Michael! (*He turns to his entourage.*) Arrange a taxi for Mr Boxley and Mr Hardiman. I know they want to make telephone calls in private to their superiors about tonight.

STANLEY *suddenly appears by* SARAH *and* LOUIS.

STANLEY: You go too, you go now . . . I'll get them to order another taxi. (*He whispers conspiratorially.*) It's best to slip away before the Prince gets too interested.

SARAH (*smiles*): That's unless of course you want that,
    Louis . . .

LOUIS: We'll go back to the hotel.

STANLEY: No, he'll probably follow you there.

> *He presses a key into* LOUIS' *hand.*

Here's a key to the *Music Express* office . . . Nobody's
there and that's one place he won't look for you.

EXT. STREET NEAR CLUB. NIGHT

SARAH *and* LOUIS *run in the torrential rain for the taxi that is
waiting at the end of the alley. They jump in. In front of them is
another taxi.* BOXLEY *and* HARDIMAN *are approaching it,
escorted by the* PRINCE's *courtiers with umbrellas, who herd
them into it. We cut inside* LOUIS' *taxi:* SARAH *and* LOUIS
already very wet, they are excited, full of adrenalin. SARAH
watches BOXLEY *and* HARDIMAN *through the window.*

SARAH: Look at them! They won't be able to sleep for
    weeks because of tonight, the embarrassment of it all,
    they'll wake up screaming!

LOUIS: I hope so!

SARAH: You know Mr Hardiman sometimes introduces the
    bands himself on the wireless . . . It'd be so funny if
    he had to do that for you!

LOUIS: Oh my god, I forgot Julian! I forgot to give him the
    message!

SARAH: What about Julian?

LOUIS: I have to do this. I said I would. I won't be a
    moment!

> LOUIS *charges back through the rain.*

INT. BASEMENT CLUB. NIGHT
LOUIS *pushes through the crowd towards* JULIAN. *The* PRINCE, *now very drunk, is surrounded by the band and is not looking in his direction.* LOUIS *reaches* JULIAN.

LOUIS: I have a message for you from Mr Masterson.
JULIAN*'s head turns. We see something approaching panic in his eyes.*
JULIAN: Have you? When did he give it to you?
LOUIS: Tonight. (*He gives him the envelope.*) And he says everything is taken care of . . . I think that's what he said.
JULIAN: He did, did he?!
He rips open the note and then looks up at LOUIS *with a very relieved smile.*
You got soaked for me! My heartfelt thanks, Louis, my dear fellow! All is right with the world . . . I thought it would be, but sometimes you never know!
He gazes across at JESSIE *and* CARLA *and the whole scene in the bar.*
But then look at this . . . of course it had to be!

INT. TAXI. NIGHT
LOUIS *gets back into the taxi,* SARAH *looks enquiringly. The rain is pouring down.*

SARAH: Everything all right?
LOUIS: Yes, let's go, let's go now!
SARAH: Yes, before they come after us! The Prince and his courtiers, he is going to notice you've left any minute!

INT. MUSIC EXPRESS BUILDING. NIGHT
We cut to LOUIS *and* SARAH *going up the darkened staircase in the* Music Express *building. It is very shadowy as they*

pass the framed covers of the magazine on the stairs, the white
bandleaders peering out.
  LOUIS *stops and stares at the bland face of Jack Paynton.*

LOUIS: One day it should be my band up here.
SARAH: What do you mean, 'one day'?! Much sooner than
    that! (*She smiles.*) Next week perhaps . . .

INT. STANLEY'S OFFICE. NIGHT
LOUIS *moves into* STANLEY*'s office, which is in darkness. It is*
still raining incredibly hard. SARAH *is in the doorway.*

SARAH: This is exciting, I've never been allowed in
    Stanley's domain before . . .
    LOUIS *switches on a table lamp.* SARAH *sees the collage of*
    all the images on the wall, the mass of photographs and
    the sketches and finished cartoon strips of Farquhar and
    Tonk.
    Oh there are some terrific photographs here.
    She moves up to the wall. There are photos of people
    dancing in lots of different locations, on rooftops, in the sea,
    on the factory floor, on railway tracks, on the edge of a
    cliff.
LOUIS: Everything that's ever interested Stanley is right
    here, this room is like being inside his brain.
    They are standing close to each other staring at a strip of
    Farquhar and Tonk causing havoc at a society wedding
    which is being besieged by villagers. LOUIS *moves over to*
    the small outer office and switches on the light.
        SARAH *follows him, then catches sight of the bed from*
    across the room. She stops.
SARAH: Oh goodness, there's a bed!
LOUIS: Yes . . . (*His manner is very relaxed, he smiles warmly*
    at her.) I think this is the nearest Stanley gets to a

home . . . I don't think he has a proper house or flat at all. He sleeps here or at his mother's – or he doesn't sleep at all.

SARAH: And he's got all my photos up! (*She's very surprised, they are directly above the bed.*) He asked me for some big copies, but I thought he was just being polite, I didn't realise they'd be on display!

We see large images of the picnic, MASTERSON, JULIAN, DONALDSON. STANLEY *is sitting quite close to* PAMELA. SARAH *stares into* PAMELA*'s eyes.*

SARAH: You know they slept together on the train, Stanley and Pamela!

LOUIS: They didn't?! I didn't know that. Are you sure?

SARAH: Yes, I don't know what's happened since though . . . You couldn't get two more different people, could you?!

LOUIS: And here are all the others – (*He is standing in front of* DONALDSON, MASTERSON *and* JULIAN.) About to cause havoc with the band.

SARAH: Don't say that! I told you, it's all real, their enthusiasm. They absolutely love your music. (*She touches him.*) And so do I.

There is suddenly an extraordinary noise. The sound of the rain has turned into an intense rattling sound at the window, the whole room seems to vibrate with the noise.

LOUIS: What on earth is that?

SARAH: It could be another earthquake!

LOUIS *laughs.*

Don't laugh, there was an earthquake in London last year . . . It was quite a bad one actually! Where were you?

LOUIS: We must have been on tour . . .

They are both moving to the window and they pull back the curtain. A terrific hailstorm is lashing the glass. SARAH *is thrilled with the intensity of it. She throws open the*

*window and scoops up the ice as it settles on the window
ledge.* LOUIS *is next to her; he scoops some up too. Both of
them hold the ice in their palms, their hands stretched out
towards each other, watching the ice begin to melt.*

SARAH: What an incredible storm . . .

*She lifts her hand full of the melting ice and spreads some
gently across his forehead.* LOUIS *takes her in his arms
and they start kissing passionately by the wall, their bodies
wrapped together.*

You know . . .

She continues to kiss him.

You know . . . I've been lying awake at night thinking
where could we meet like this?

LOUIS: So have I . . . It couldn't be the hotel, it couldn't
be your home . . .

SARAH (*laughing and kissing him*): And now Stanley's
arranged it.

INT. BASEMENT CLUB. NIGHT

*We cut back to the club. The hailstorm is falling in the yard, all
the characters are grouped in the open doorway watching the
hailstones rattling and dancing on the dark stones.* JULIAN
suddenly turns to them.

JULIAN: We've got to go out in that! We can't let the
chance go . . . we'd never forgive ourselves!

He runs into the yard, the hailstorm all around him.

Come on . . . (*He calls back at them.*) It's a wonderful
feeling . . . Come on, everybody!

PAMELA: My dear brother . . . always so quiet and well
behaved!

STANLEY *watches* JULIAN's *febrile intensity as he dances
around in the hailstorm, waving his arms and calling for
people to join him.* JESSIE *and* CARLA *suddenly run out to*

be with him, laughing and screaming in the hail. CARLA
calls out to PRINCE GEORGE.

CARLA: Come on, Your Royal Highness! You must come
too!

PRINCE GEORGE *hesitates.* JULIAN *is yelling for him to
come. The courtiers stare, stern-faced.*

PRINCE GEORGE: Well why not? He's right, it's not the sort
of thing you get the chance to do every day!

He goes out into the storm, moving wildly with JULIAN,
CARLA *and* JESSIE, *waving their arms and swirling around.*

JULIAN: There, you see! Royalty in a hailstorm! It's
amazing being here tonight isn't it! (*He calls out to*
DONALDSON.) Come on, Arthur, you're next!

PRINCE GEORGE: Oh yes, you must join us, Mr Donaldson.

DONALDSON: The royal command! Then I have to obey . . .
(*He smiles at* LADY CREMONE.) Last chance to be
young . . .

DONALDSON *walks out more gingerly. The girls are
screaming and dancing, the band start to improvise in the
bar.* JOE *runs out with his trumpet and starts playing in
the storm.* PAMELA, *exquisite and bone dry, watches her
brother.*

STANLEY *is standing in the doorway watching with*
LADY CREMONE.

STANLEY: See what happens when you come to London.

LADY CREMONE (*smiles*): Everybody goes quite mad . . .

INT. SMALL OFFICE. MUSIC EXPRESS BUILDING. NIGHT
We cut back to LOUIS *and* SARAH *naked together on top of the
bed in the small office. They're kissing passionately, the sound of
the hailstorm playing on the window. Suddenly* SARAH *stops
kissing* LOUIS.

LOUIS: What's the matter?

Louis Lester on stage at the Imperial.

The band passing the front entrance of the Imperial.

The band entering by the back entrance of the Imperial.

Jessie and Carla singing in the garden for Prince George.

Sarah, Julian, Pamela, Donaldson, Stanley and the Prince
watching the band perform.

Wesley in the Imperial Ballroom.

The picnic: the characters pose for Sarah
in front of Masterson's private train.

Sarah about to photograph Louis at the picnic.

Masterson and Julian together at the picnic.

Jessie and Carla singing 'Dead of Night Express'.

The Prince of Wales and Pamela dance to the band's music.

Lady Cremone watching the band play at the funeral.

Stanley in the basement club.

The private performance for Prince George and the BBC.

The night of the hailstorm.

SARAH: It's just a little strange . . . (*She indicates the photos above the bed staring down at their naked bodies.*) Being watched by all of them.

LOUIS: Well, I could take them all down.

SARAH: No you don't, they're my photographs remember! (*She laughs.*) On second thoughts I can easily cope with them . . .

She begins to kiss him again, their bodes entwined.

She looks at LOUIS *with real love as she kisses him, holds him tight.*

INT. BASEMENT CLUB. NIGHT

We cut to the bar of the club, the hail has now turned back into torrential rain. All the characters who went into the storm are completely soaked. DEIRDRE *has supplied towels and they are drying their hair and trying to get warm. The* PRINCE *is being treated by three courtiers, rubbing his wet trousers, his arms and his shoes.*

PRINCE GEORGE: Stop fussing for God's sake, I will survive, don't worry!

He looks across at JESSIE.

Why don't you sing for us Jessie?

JULIAN: Yes that will warm us up!

JESSIE *turns to look at the* PRINCE. *She is completely soaked but she stares at him with confidence.* STANLEY *notices her poise and ambition.*

JESSIE: Sing like this?

PRINCE GEORGE: Yes, please. That would be nice. Especially as Mr Lester has deserted us.

JESSIE: Well, of course, Your Royal Highness.

JESSIE *stands directly in front of him, the water still glistening on her face.*

She begins to sing.

INT. RECORDING STUDIO. DAY

We cut from the unaccompanied singing to the sound of the full band and to JESSIE, *in a different costume, singing the second verse of the same song. This time she is singing in a recording studio with a huge microphone in front of her and a red light above her on the wall. The camera is moving round her to reveal she is being watched by* BOXLEY *and some shadowy figures.* BOXLEY's *moon-shaped face is totally impassive.*

EXT. BACK ENTRANCE. IMPERIAL HOTEL. DAY

The music continues over the cut, its syncopated pulse building all the time linking the following scenes. We cut to CARLA *and* JESSIE *coming out of the back entrance of the Imperial. In the distance* JULIAN *is standing by a brand-new two-seater sports car which is shining in the sun. He calls out to them exuberantly. They run over to reach him.*

As they approach, JULIAN *holds out a record in a sleeve that announces* 'THE LOUIS LESTER BAND'.

JULIAN: Jessie, Carla, it's in the shops now! Have you
    seen it?
    JESSIE *takes the record, smiling delightedly.* CARLA *is*
    surprised to see a very big pile of the records on the
    passenger seat.
JULIAN: Oh yes, I just thought I'd help it along a bit! Not
    that it'll need it of course. I'll put them in the boot
    now! (*Turns to* JESSIE.) And then will you come for
    a spin?
JESSIE *looks at* CARLA, *hesitates, not wishing to exclude her.*
CARLA: Go on Jessie!

EXT. COUNTRY ROADS AND RIVER. DAY
We cut to JULIAN *and* JESSIE *driving in the sports car along country roads, exuberant travelling shots. The music pulsing all the time. We see them drive along a road next to a river. We then see them pull up in a picturesque spot right next to the water. We see* JULIAN *carrying a picnic basket and a large box, moving with* JESSIE *to start picnicking under the trees. We then see* JULIAN *and* JESSIE *sitting opposite each other eating, while the record plays on a wind-up gramophone that has emerged from the box, the pulsing score eliding with the thin sound of the real record.*

JULIAN: Don't laugh, but I've being imagining for a long time playing your record for the first time in this spot, with you sitting opposite me.
JESSIE: Why would I laugh? I'd never laugh at that.
JULIAN: Good . . . so don't laugh at this either. You have to say yes! (*He points at the car.*) That car is a present, I bought it for you.
JESSIE: Mr Luscombe! You didn't?! But I can't drive!
JULIAN: I'll teach you. And Louis can use it too when he wants. Say you'll keep it?! Please say yes!

INT. MUSIC EXPRESS OFFICE. DAY
The music is still pulsing, getting louder. We see STANLEY *with* MR WAX *in the* Music Express *office.* MR WAX *is staring at the latest edition of the magazine; on the cover is a picture of* LOUIS *and* JESSIE, 'LOUIS LESTER BAND DEBUT RECORD SENSATION'.

MR WAX: I like this edition . . . I had a feeling about this Louis Lester Band . . . I always said put them on the cover, didn't I? . . . I knew they'd become a big news story.

INT. THE IMPERIAL. LOUIS' HOTEL BEDROOM. LATE
AFTERNOON

The music is reaching its climax. We cut to LOUIS *lying on his
bed in his hotel bedroom, smoking. We track back: he is
surrounded by copies of the* Music Express *edition with him on
the cover and the inside spread where we see the photograph of
him sitting looking dazzlingly glamorous at a grand piano.
We cut close to* LOUIS' *eyes. We see a flash cut of* WESLEY
*looking at him and then yelling warnings at him during their
quarrel on the hotel staircase.*

The music suddenly cuts out.

INT. IMPERIAL BALLROOM. NIGHT

HARDIMAN, *his thin face looking very tense and solemn, is
standing staring straight out at us. In front of him is a
microphone labelled BBC. We cut wide, we see he has the band
behind him.* LOUIS *is at the piano,* JESSIE *and* CARLA *in
shimmering dresses are standing poised.* HARDIMAN *is on stage
with the band in the Imperial ballroom.*

HARDIMAN: And now coming directly from the Imperial
    Hotel, London, for the first time ever on the wireless,
    we are delighted to present the Louis Lester Band!
    LOUIS *starts to play. We see the real pleasure in his eyes as*
    HARDIMAN *is forced to introduce them.* JESSIE *begins to
    sing; she looks dazzling in her glittering dress. The camera
    swirls round to reveal the tables and diners in the Imperial
    ballroom, with* JESSIE *in the foreground singing a slow
    sultry number. A montage begins of the broadcast reaching
    its audience. We first see the young chefs listening to the
    wireless in the bowels of the Imperial's kitchens.*

EXT. VILLAGE STREET. NIGHT
We then cut to the main street of the mining village near LADY
CREMONE*'s estate. We see the lights glowing in the small houses,
the sound of* JESSIE*'s singing pouring out of those houses with
wirelesses all the way down the main street.*

*We see other villagers gathered round a wireless in the village
hall.*

INT. LADY CREMONE'S DRAWING ROOM. NIGHT
We see LADY CREMONE *listening to* JESSIE *singing through the
large wireless in her dining room. Her butler is standing at the
other end of the room.*

LADY CREMONE: William, stay for this, she's such a good
young singer, take a seat please, and listen.

INT. MRS MITCHELL'S HOUSE. NIGHT
We cut to STANLEY *sitting with his mother in her parlour
listening to* JESSIE *singing on the wireless. He is eating a hearty
home-cooked meal.*

STANLEY: What do you think, Mum? You think she can
sing?
MRS MITCHELL: Very nice, dear . . . they always manage to
find such good new singers on the wireless, don't they.
STANLEY: When they listen to me they do! I've been trying
everything to get this band on the wireless.
MRS MITCHELL: Of course, dear, but they do know best in
the end, don't they.

INT. DONALDSON'S STUDY. NIGHT
We cut to DONALDSON *sitting in his study listening to* JESSIE
*coming out of his wireless. He is smoking a cigar and drinking
some port.*

INT. IMPERIAL HOTEL. THE BAR. NIGHT

PAMELA, SARAH *and* JULIAN *are sitting in the bar of the Imperial on the night of the broadcast.* JESSIE*'s song elides with the score as* JESSIE *appears at the door of the bar.* PAMELA *and* JULIAN *and* SARAH *leap to their feet and start applauding. Many of the other bar members follow their example, giving her a standing ovation. Even the old dowagers look on with benign interest.* LOUIS *is standing with* JESSIE *in the doorway acknowledging the applause,* CARLA *is hovering a little way behind.* HARDIMAN *pokes his head round the door to have a look, but thinks better of sharing the moment. We see a close-up of* JESSIE, *her eyes gleaming; she is thrilled at the reception.* PAMELA *approaches her and kisses her and leads her,* LOUIS *and* CARLA *to their table.*

PAMELA: That was wonderful, darling, the best you've ever sung.

JULIAN: A sensation! We have the champagne waiting!

SARAH *greets* LOUIS *rather formally, the dowagers are watching beadily as these black people actually advance from the door and are invited into the bar.*

SARAH: Well done, Mr Lester, that was excellent, really excellent. Do come and sit and have a drink with us, please.

Eyes flash all round the bar as LOUIS, JESSIE *and* CARLA *sit with them, close and intimate. A strange hush suddenly descends on the bar.*

PAMELA: Go on, shock them Sarah, give Louis a kiss!

SARAH *smiles demurely.*

If you don't, I will.

PAMELA *leans over and kisses* LOUIS *on the cheek.*

What a fabulous broadcast, Mr Lester.

INT. IMPERIAL HOTEL. BACK STAIRCASE. DAY
Morning light. JESSIE *and* CARLA *are going down the back staircase at the Imperial.* SCHLESINGER*'s face suddenly appears above them.*

SCHLESINGER: Ladies, are you about to leave the hotel for the day?

CARLA (*nervous, thinking they might have done something wrong*): Yes, Mr Schlesinger.

SCHLESINGER: If you wish to, and only if you wish it, you may use the front entrance from now on.

EXT. IMPERIAL HOTEL. FRONT ENTRANCE. DAY
JESSIE *and* CARLA *boldly strut out of the front entrance of the Imperial. They are astonished to see a group of about fifteen men of different shapes and sizes waiting for their autograph on the pavement. They start calling out to* JESSIE. *We cut to* JESSIE *signing autographs, some of the men want* CARLA*'s too.* JESSIE *is thrilled at the attention. We see the delight in her eyes. A voice says:*

JULIAN: Will you sign mine?
JESSIE *takes the book and then sees it is* JULIAN *who is asking. She laughs in surprise.*
I am jealous of all these people wanting your signature . . . didn't I tell you this would happen! These are just the first . . . Now can I take you out to lunch? And let's talk about movies and the possibilities for you there, because I've been hearing some interesting things, I have one or two contacts . . .

INT. IMPERIAL. KITCHEN PASSAGE/PARLOUR. LATE
AFTERNOON

LOUIS *is moving along the kitchen passage at the Imperial and
into the parlour. He is startled to see* SCHLESINGER *sitting all
alone at the long table.*

In front of him is an envelope.

LOUIS: Mr Schlesinger?!

SCHLESINGER: Nathan, it's time you started calling me
Nathan, Mr Lester.

LOUIS: Of course, Nathan. (*Amused.*) And do call me
Louis.

SCHLESINGER: I've just been reading another article about
you, Louis, this time in *Melody Maker*. I'm beginning
to lose count of how many there've been.

LOUIS (*lightly*): I'm not.

SCHLESINGER: I have some good news. (*He pushes the
envelope across the table.*) You've received another
Royal summons, this time from the Prince of Wales.
LOUIS *takes the envelope.*

And it is a most surprising invitation Louis – it is for
you to play at an RAF dinner which he's attending in
his role as Air Marshal.

LOUIS: Air Marshal?

SCHLESINGER: Yes, he's a bit of a pilot, bit of a flyer. (*Sharp
smile.*) It'll certainly stir up all those Air Commodores
and bigwigs, you playing there! I almost wish I could
come . . .

At that moment JESSIE *passes the door.* LOUIS *calls out to
her, moves into the passage.*

LOUIS: Jessie!

She stops some distance away, LOUIS *waves the letter.*
Interesting news – the Prince of Wales wants us to
play for him again!

JESSIE: That's nice.

LOUIS (*smiling at her casual reaction*): That's nice! That's all?

JESSIE: Yes, well he liked us before, so he'll like us again, won't he? (*She suddenly looks more excited.*) Do you want to go for a spin in the new car, Louis?

> LOUIS *stares at her down the passage, this much more confident young woman.*

LOUIS: Not now, Jessie, no.

INT. IMPERIAL. BEDROOM PASSAGE/JESSIE AND CARLA'S ROOM. DAY

CARLA is running towards us urgently along the long staff bedroom passage. She is carrying a red spangly dress and looking very upset. She bursts through the door of the bedroom she shares with JESSIE. She is on the verge of tears.

CARLA: Jessie! Jessie! Something awful's happened. I had this cleaned for the Prince of Wales tonight but they've made a mark on it, and it won't come out! And now I can't wear it. I don't have anything else good enough – I don't know what to do!

> JESSIE *is sitting very still at her dressing table staring into the mirror.*

CARLA: What's the matter with you?

JESSIE: I'm not feeling well. (*She turns towards* CARLA.) I'm not going to be able to sing tonight.

CARLA: What?! You have to! It's for the Prince of Wales. You've got to!

JESSIE: I can't. I'm not well. You can do it instead. (*Looking straight at her.*) You know you're able to, Carla.

> CARLA, *despite the dress, can't stop herself looking excited.*

CARLA: You better tell Louis.

> JESSIE *doesn't move.*

Right now, Jessie!

JESSIE: I will. (*Staring at herself in the mirror.*) When I'm
ready to . . .

INT. IMPERIAL. MAIN PASSAGE/BAR. AFTERNOON
STANLEY *is moving along the main passage at the Imperial
towards the bar. He is smartly dressed and is holding a magazine.
The passage is dotted with Christmas decorations, piano music
is drifting from the bar.* STANLEY *passes through the double
doors and into the bar. Right in front of him, sitting next to an
enormous Christmas tree which is covered in white decorations,
is* LADY CREMONE. *An elderly woman is playing the piano,
waltzes and jolly little tunes. Some of the dowagers are sitting
having coffee after lunch.* LADY CREMONE *smiles as soon as
she sees* STANLEY.

LADY CREMONE: Stanley, you are marvellously on time.
STANLEY: Of course I am, I'm so excited.
LADY CREMONE: Excited by what, Stanley?
STANLEY: At having tea with you of course.
     LADY CREMONE *laughs at his flattery.*
     And seeing you here in London again.
LADY CREMONE: Well, you made me come up once, so
     now I find I'm doing it again. I'm here to see the
     opening of a play I've put money into. Mr Masterson is
     accompanying me, he's an interesting fellow isn't he?
STANLEY: He is indeed.
LADY CREMONE: And I thought I'd wish the band good
     luck for tonight, for their evening with the Prince of
     Wales and the Royal Air Force! (*She laughs.*) What an
     extraordinary occasion that's going to be . . .
STANLEY: Yes, even I couldn't have predicted that invitation!
     (*He hands her the magazine.*) Talking of which, I've
     brought you the Christmas edition of *Music Express.*
     (*He smiles warmly.*) It's hot off the press.

LADY CREMONE: Well, thank you very much for that. A perfect present.

STANLEY: It's tremendous what you've made happen, you know.

LADY CREMONE: What I've made happen, Stanley?

STANLEY: Yes, with the band, the success they're having.

LADY CREMONE: Well, it really helped that everybody was trapped in the club by the storm, didn't it, Stanley?! (*She smiles.*) That's what made the difference.

STANLEY: But you laid that on too, didn't you? (*He smiles.*) You can do anything!

LADY CREMONE: Stanley! (*She laughs.*) You flatterer!

STANLEY: I know I've had something to do with their success too –

LADY CREMONE: You most certainly have.

STANLEY: But I couldn't have done it without you. (*With feeling.*) So thank you.

LADY CREMONE: Well, I'm glad it's worked. (*She sips her tea.*) I feel my sons would have loved their music very much. You know, Stanley, I think all my energy for seeking out new things, for discovering the next exciting new voice . . . is still all about me dealing with grief, really. (*Her voice is calm but there are tears in her eyes.*) Even after fifteen years it doesn't seem to be getting any less. And obviously at Christmas, one feels . . . (*She stops.*)

STANLEY (*gently*): I'm sorry . . .

LADY CREMONE: Thank you, my dear, but we mustn't be sorrowful. (*Her voice lightens.*) After all, the Louis Lester Band may be only the first of many joint projects between us . . .

STANLEY: Really? Absolutely! Perhaps we should start at once . . . (*Lightly.*) You could become a guest columnist on the magazine.

LADY CREMONE: That's not quite what I had in mind! . . .

But I agree we shouldn't waste any time, not with the
world in such a mess, and everything so uncertain . . .
(*She looks straight at him.*) Have you thought about
the United States and the Louis Lester Band? That's
an interesting idea don't you think, Stanley?
A voice calls 'Lavinia'. LADY CREMONE *and* STANLEY
look up. DONALDSON, JULIAN, PAMELA *and* SARAH *are
standing in the entrance to the bar.*

DONALDSON: Here we all are . . . to wish you Happy
Christmas.

JULIAN: And of course to wave the band off on their big
day!

INT. IMPERIAL. LOUIS' BEDROOM/PASSAGE. AFTERNOON
We cut inside LOUIS' *bedroom,* JESSIE *is standing in the
doorway.*
    LOUIS *is sitting staring at her. He is coldly furious.*

LOUIS: What do you mean, you can't sing?

JESSIE: I'm not well. Carla can easily do all the songs
instead of me . . . They won't notice the difference.

LOUIS: Don't be stupid, don't be ridiculous, of course they
will. This is for the Prince of Wales.

JESSIE: I told you I'm not well.

LOUIS: Jessie, all the time you've been with the band you
know how professional we've been, nobody's ever
missed a performance.

JESSIE: Well, I can't sing tonight . . . I have a fever. I have
to go to bed now.
    She turns and walks out into the passage. LOUIS *follows
her out.* THORNTON *is at the other end of the passage; he
witnesses the scene between* LOUIS *and* JESSIE.
    LOUIS *shouts out at her.*

LOUIS: Where do you think you're going? I haven't
finished with you yet.

JESSIE *turns.*

Have you seen a doctor?

JESSIE: They've called a doctor for me. I have a
temperature. They told me to go to bed. And that's
what I'm doing.

LOUIS: If I find out, Jessie . . .

JESSIE: Find out what?

LOUIS: If I find out you're going out tonight –

JESSIE: I'm not going out tonight! Of course I'm not!

LOUIS: If you're going out with Mr Luscombe tonight or
with anybody else for that matter –

JESSIE: I wouldn't do that! Why would I do that?! I'm ill,
I'm going straight to bed. I can't sing. That's all it is!

LOUIS: Is it? (*He stares at her.*) You start getting a little
attention and this happens! I'm really disappointed in
you, Jessie . . .

JESSIE: You're disappointed in me! Because I'm ill?!

CARLA (*appearing in the passage*): She is ill, Louis, I promise!

LOUIS: You better be . . . because if I discover you left the
hotel for a single moment tonight – if I find that out –
you may not have a job with the band in the morning.

THORNTON: Mr Lester . . . Mr Donaldson and his party
are downstairs. (*He looks alarmed.*) And it's not so
long now till the time of departure . . .

LOUIS (*his tone very steely*): Do you understand what I'm
saying?

JESSIE: Of course I do. You won't find that I've left the
hotel, or even left my room. I promise you I won't,
Louis! (*She stares straight at him.*) Why don't you take
our car to the air base? Have a good spin in that, and
all your anger will go away! You won't be angry with
me any more . . .

EXT. IMPERIAL. FRONT ENTRANCE. AFTERNOON

We cut to the front entrance of the Imperial. LOUIS, CARLA *and the band are moving towards a small convoy of vehicles lined up to take them to the air base. There is a single-decker bus, a lorry with their large drum kit strapped on to it, and the two-seater sports car. Standing on the steps of the hotel watching their departure are* STANLEY, JULIAN *and* PAMELA. DONALDSON *is a few paces away, leaning against a wall smoking. Hotel porters and commissionaires are watching with a detached interest.* SARAH *is standing closer, taking pictures. A Rolls-Royce has just drawn up and is disgorging its wealthy occupants, who see the phalanx of people waiting on the steps and assume they are waiting for them.*

DONALDSON: They think we're their reception party!

STANLEY (*calling out to the band*): Make sure you send our love to His Royal Highness!

> *The wealthy guests stare in bewilderment at such a fuss being made over a group of black musicians.* SARAH *touches* LOUIS' *arm as he reaches the sports car.*

SARAH: Good luck, Louis (*Their eyes meet.*) I would give anything to be there too, to take pictures of you playing to all those military types.

LOUIS: Yes, well, let's hope we get away with it without Jessie.

SARAH: You will.

> LOUIS *gets into the sports car with* CARLA. *He looks very preoccupied. The rest of the band board the bus, looking very nervous.* LOUIS *drives off in the open-top sports car, leading the convoy down the street.* SARAH *takes pictures as they disappear from view.*

STANLEY: I really hope they manage without Jessie.

JULIAN (*very breezily*): Yes, it's such a pity she can't go, isn't it?

> STANLEY *turns sharply, very surprised at* JULIAN's *casual tone.*

INT. IMPERIAL. MAIN LOBBY. AFTERNOON
*We cut to a subjective track across the Imperial's lobby. In front
of us is* MASTERSON, *wearing a dark coat and sitting very still.*
JULIAN, PAMELA, STANLEY, SARAH *and* DONALDSON *are just
coming back into the lobby having watched the band leave.
They stop as they see the dark solitary figure of* MASTERSON.

MASTERSON: I wondered where everybody was. Nobody
　　seemed able to tell me. I'm waiting for Lady Cremone.
LADY CREMONE: And here she is.
　　*She emerges from the other side of the lobby and moves
　　towards* MASTERSON.
　　I'm so sorry to keep you waiting, we need to go don't
　　we? (*Turning to the others.*) We have rather a lot of
　　people to meet before the show tonight, so regrettably
　　we have to be on our way.
JULIAN: Yes, off you go, Walter, you mustn't be late for all
　　your meetings!
　　DONALDSON *and the others are surprised by his
　　dismissive tone.*
MASTERSON: Are you still going to Paris, Julian?
JULIAN: I am. I'm catching the train tonight.
MASTERSON (*his brooding manner seems to change*): You will
　　telephone me when you get there?
JULIAN: I don't know. I hope I'll have time. I will only be
　　gone for three days, you'll hardly notice I'm not here.
MASTERSON: Did you give me the telephone number for
　　the apartment in Paris? (*He looks at him anxiously.*)
　　I don't think you did?
JULIAN: Go, Walter, go!
　　MASTERSON *stands. His manner is becoming increasingly
　　agitated.* STANLEY *watches, fascinated.* MASTERSON *seems
　　to be shrinking in front of them.*
MASTERSON: If it was a hotel I wouldn't need the number
　　of course, but it isn't a hotel and I don't have the

address. I would like to take the number, if I may.
I need it . . .

JULIAN: Walter, don't be silly. You are being absurd. You
must go now, off you go!

MASTERSON (*he suddenly shouts*): I must have the number!
Give me the number! (*He stares at* JULIAN.) Please . . .
(*Heartfelt.*) I have to have it.

There is a stunned silence. PAMELA *looks alarmed.*

PAMELA: I'm sure Julian will telephone you – and I will
find out the number myself and give it to you, Walter.
Julian's always so vague about these things, he's
hopeless with numbers.

LADY CREMONE: What a good plan . . . Now off we go,
Walter. (*As she moves.*) I will of course expect a full
report, Stanley, about how the band got on.

MASTERSON (*turning in the exit towards* JULIAN): I will see
you in three days.

JULIAN (*as soon as* MASTERSON *has left*): Long face! He's
always got such a long face, sometimes it drives me
mad. (*He smiles.*) When you're that rich, why have
such a long face?!

STANLEY: I thought you were working for Mr Masterson,
Julian?

JULIAN: I am, but he's only given me the smallest scraps so
far, I know I can do more . . . and now he doesn't
even trust me to telephone him! (*Breezily.*) So maybe
I won't.

EXT. ROAD AND RAF AIR BASE. EVENING
The band's convoy led by LOUIS *and* CARLA *in the sports car
are driving down a long straight road towards the RAF base.*

*The lights of the buildings are glowing ahead, darkness is just
falling. As they approach, the gates are opened for them and*

*they are waved through by impassive-looking guards. We cut to
the band emerging from the bus next to a long military building.*
LOUIS *and* CARLA *are already out of the sports car.*
A SERGEANT *yells out across the yard.*

SERGEANT: Musicians this way! In here!
> LOUIS *and* CARLA *turn.*
>> *We see headlights on the long straight road; some cars
>> are bearing down on the air base.*
> You better hurry, that's some of the top brass arriving!
> CARLA *stares at the advancing cars. She suddenly looks
> very frightened.*
LOUIS: You will be fine, Carla . . .

INT. IMPERIAL BAR. NIGHT
*We cut to the bar of the Imperial. It is night, all the Christmas
lights are on, not just round the tree but all round the bar,
transforming the atmosphere in the room: it is now a place of
shadows and rather beautiful.* DONALDSON *is presiding over
a table, drinking brandy, smoking a cigar, holding forth.* SARAH
is laughing and drinking a lot. STANLEY *is also smoking a
cigar.* JULIAN *is sitting very straight, his eyes sparkling; he is
watching the door.* PAMELA's *attention is fixed on her brother;
she looks concerned. During the scene we keep cutting back to*
PAMELA *and* JULIAN.

DONALDSON: Well, the wireless has spread so fast, faster
> than anybody could have imagined, millions more
> each year! So what will the next thing be? Come on,
> Stanley, the next trend that will spread like wildfire?!
STANLEY: Cinemas on trains! Every train will have a
> cinema carriage, a movie while you move.
DONALDSON: No, with cinema I think it will be in the sky.
SARAH: In the sky?

DONALDSON: Yes, I went to a demonstration the other day, a little man, I think he's called Grindle, he's going to project images on to clouds, cinema in the sky at night hanging over the whole city.

SARAH: That'd be fantastic, imagine Greta Garbo over the whole city, her gigantic face!

STANLEY: Or Farquhar and Tonk in a cartoon jumping about over the Houses of Parliament –

SARAH: But if you could do that, of course, somebody could also have fascists goose-stepping in the sky, that would be pretty terrifying!

DONALDSON: Well, you clearly would have to have a limit, you couldn't allow that!

SARAH: Who would stop them though?

DONALDSON: People would find a way . . . but my point is we have no idea what is coming next, what new invention is going to change all our lives, it's happening so fast. I have to admit I find it very intoxicating, the uncertainty of it all.

PAMELA (*watching* JULIAN*'s intense silence*): When is your train darling? You don't want to miss it.

JULIAN: No, I won't miss it. Don't worry, I have all the time in the world. (*He grins.*) And then more on top of that. (*He looks towards the door.*)

INT. THE AIR BASE. NIGHT
We cut back to the air base. The band is lined up in the passage, just about to go on. They are nervous. JOE *the trumpeter plays a few notes.* CARLA *is wearing the red dress despite the mark. She is taking deep breaths, trying to calm her terror.* LOUIS *is standing at the front ready to lead the band on.*

There are two large Christmas cakes on trolleys, decorated with an airfield made out of icing sugar complete with little aeroplanes on it. The SERGEANT *suddenly calls out.*

SERGEANT: That's for His Royal Highness. He likes his
fucking Christmas cakes with their little planes. We
hate them!

*There is a signal from one of the royal flunkies at the other
end of the passage.*

SERGEANT: In you go now! (*Jocular smile.*) Give them hell,
I'm sure you will.

LOUIS *leads the band on to the stage, which is at one end
of a very large room. They are confronted by the sight of
a sea of blue uniforms and gold braid, the officers sitting
around an L-shaped table. Nearly all the guests are men,
Air Commodores, only about four women in among them.
One of the women is the very beautiful wife of the Air
Vice-Marshal; she is sitting next to the* PRINCE OF
WALES. *There is a tremendous hubbub in the room, the*
PRINCE *talking loudly, all the RAF officers full of drink
chatting at the tops of their voices. The* PRINCE OF WALES
*is flirting with the Air Vice-Marshal's wife. The band
begins to play, the conversation continues but the* PRINCE
*looks up. As soon as people see him paying attention the
noise tails away.* CARLA *is absolutely transfixed with
nerves as she waits for her cue.*

PRINCE OF WALES: Ah yes . . . she's an absolutely spiffing
singer, this one.

CARLA *begins to sing, a strong sound comes out of her.
She's desperately trying not to look directly at the* PRINCE
OF WALES. *But he is watching her with a quizzical
expression as if trying to work out if something is wrong.*

INT. IMPERIAL BAR. NIGHT

We cut to JULIAN's *head turning sharply in the bar at the
Imperial. Standing in the doorway, framed by the Christmas
lights, is* JESSIE. *She is wearing a stylish evening dress. She
moves slowly across the bar, turning heads as she goes.* JULIAN's

whole being seems to change; looking febrile, excited, he leaps up
and pulls out a chair for her. PAMELA *watching him closely.*

JULIAN: Here she is . . . doesn't she look beautiful! At last
    she's here!

JESSIE: I just thought I'd say hello. (*She smiles demurely; she*
    doesn't look very ill.) These lights are so lovely . . .

STANLEY: Should you be out of bed, Jessie?

JESSIE: I thought one drink might make me feel better.

JULIAN: Of course it will. Of course she's right.
    He beckons to the bar staff.

PAMELA: You must be feeling very unwell to miss singing
    to the Prince of Wales?

JESSIE: I am. I'm not feeling well at all.

DONALDSON: Your voice has gone, has it?

JESSIE: It's quite gone, when I sing, yes, it has.

STANLEY: Louis loves performing in front of royalty. I'm
    sure he can't be very pleased . . .

JESSIE: He understood. (*She smiles sweetly, looking poised*
    and glamorous.)

STANLEY: Let's hope Carla manages to bring it off.

INT. AIR BASE. DINING ROOM. NIGHT
We cut back to CARLA *singing the last lines of the song. She is*
putting everything into it. The song has a big finish. It is greeted
with momentary silence, everybody looking at the PRINCE OF
WALES. *He doesn't react immediately, as if he is still working*
out whether this is the singer he saw before. Then he beams and
starts to clap.

PRINCE OF WALES: What did I tell you! She is a splendid
    little singer, is she not?!
    Everybody follows the PRINCE*'s example and claps.*
    LOUIS *moves to the microphone full of confidence now.*

He is a commanding figure on stage.

LOUIS: Thank you. We're very pleased and honoured to be here playing to Your Royal Highness again, and to the Royal Air Force. I have to admit to you I've never been in an aeroplane myself. (*He smiles broadly.*) But maybe that'll change after tonight. This next number is about being alone in the city and hoping to meet the girl of your dreams. (*He grins at the Air Commodores.*) I'm sure we all know what that feels like!

LOUIS *returns to the piano, begins to play.*

PRINCE OF WALES: No, no, no. (*He holds his hand up.*) Forgive me for interrupting, but I just remembered something. (CARLA *looks alarmed.*) Can you play that splendid jiffy number you played last time? That was marvellous to dance to! You know which one I mean?

LOUIS (*taking a guess, begins to play*): Was it this, Your Royal Highness?

PRINCE OF WALES: That's the one! Absolutely!

He turns to the Air Vice-Marshal's wife with a very flirtatious smile.

Would you like to dance? I would love to have this dance with you . . .

He gets up with the Air Vice-Marshal's wife and begins to dance as everybody watches. The Air Vice-Marshal looks distinctly uncomfortable about the PRINCE*'s blatantly amorous manner towards his wife.*

INT. IMPERIAL BAR. NIGHT
We cut to JESSIE *finishing the last drops of her drink.* JULIAN *is sitting very close.*

JULIAN: Have another one.

JESSIE *hesitates.*

PAMELA: Maybe that's enough, Julian. Too much drink
doesn't mix well with a fever.

JESSIE: Yes. I ought to go. (*She looks at* JULIAN.) That's
best, isn't it?

DONALDSON: Rest is what you need.

JESSIE: Of course, yes. I need a beautiful sleep and then
everything will be all right, I'll be back on my feet.
She gets up, looking glowing.

JULIAN: Let me see you upstairs. I must see you to your
room.
They watch JULIAN *move off with* JESSIE *across the bar,
his hand touching her back.*

SARAH: They didn't arrange this between them, did they?
She didn't miss the concert –

PAMELA: To be with my brother? I hope that's not the case!

DONALDSON: No, I'm sure she really couldn't sing. Of
course she's ill.

STANLEY: You reckon? You know a little bit of fame . . .
He watches them disappear through the double doors.
. . . can make an awful lot of difference.

INT. IMPERIAL MAIN HOTEL PASSAGE. NIGHT
JESSIE *is moving in front of* JULIAN *down the main passage
which is full of twinkling Christmas lights.* JESSIE *is walking
dreamily among the lights. She spins around.*

JESSIE: Isn't this magical?

JULIAN: It is. (*Watching her.*) Absolutely magical!

JESSIE: So this Hollywood producer . . . where are we
seeing him tonight?

JULIAN: He's upstairs.

JESSIE: Oh, he's in the hotel, that's all right then . . . (*She
smiles a delighted smile.*) I don't need to break any
rules . . . !

JULIAN *watches her as she moves in front of him among all the Christmas lights.*

For a split moment the image of her slows as she turns towards us.

INT. AIR BASE. DINING ROOM. NIGHT
We cut back to the band playing a slow dance. The PRINCE *is dancing with the Air Vice-Marshal's wife holding her very close, his manner blatantly sexual, staring into her eyes. The Air Vice-Marshal looks intensely discomforted, helpless to do anything.* LOUIS *is watching the scene as he plays. An unsettling atmosphere has descended on the room, with the other diners trying to carry on normally, as if the behaviour of the* PRINCE OF WALES *was perfectly natural and the torment of the Air Vice-Marshal is nothing to do with them. The music stops, the Air Vice-Marshal springs to his feet in relief to allow his wife to reclaim her seat next to him. But the* PRINCE *calls out.*

PRINCE OF WALES: No, no, no, one more please. I know
     we have the speeches to come, but they can wait can't
     they! The future of the RAF? We know it's jolly bright!
     We can take on any air force in the world! So – give
     us another slow number please . . .
     He holds the Air Vice-Marshal's wife.
     The slow numbers are much the best don't you
     think . . . ?!
     The band starts to play again and the PRINCE *resumes
     dancing with the Air Vice-Marshal's wife, holding her
     tight. Initially she had seemed a little reluctant, but now
     she is allowing the* PRINCE OF WALES *to hold her so close
     and is staring back into his eyes as if she knows what's
     expected of her. The* SERGEANT *is standing near* LOUIS.
SERGEANT (*whispers*): She'll be in his bed tonight.
     LOUIS *glances in surprise.*

Of course she will! That's what's expected – if you catch his eye that's what has to happen. Doesn't matter who you're married to!

LOUIS *and the band continue to play, but* LOUIS *can feel the tension in the room. A shot of the Air Vice-Marshal desperately trying to mask his distress. The atmosphere has become very distasteful, all the other guests pretending they can't see what is happening.*

INT. IMPERIAL BAR. NIGHT

PAMELA *suddenly looks up sharply as she drinks. Across the bar, standing in the double doors is* JULIAN. *He has changed into a dark suit and is wearing a coat and carrying a suitcase. For a moment he stands stock still, looking at them. He then approaches. He looks very subdued and preoccupied compared to when he left them.*

JULIAN: Here I am . . . ready to go.

PAMELA: You've changed your clothes.

JULIAN: Yes, I used Walter's suite. (*He throws himself down in a chair.*) Maybe I'll have something to eat now. I think that will be good.

PAMELA: Don't be silly, your train is in half an hour.

DONALDSON: And it leaves absolutely on the dot – sometimes thirty seconds early! I've been caught out once or twice myself.

PAMELA: You'll miss your train, Julian!

JULIAN: Maybe that would be best . . . what's meant to happen. (*His manner suddenly very intense.*) Disappoint my friends in Paris, make Walter even more angry, maybe I'm good for absolutely nothing.

PAMELA: Don't be ridiculous, go and get your train right now.

For a moment JULIAN *sits hunched in the chair, his head*

tucked down. Then he leaps up, stares at them, his manner
suddenly febrile.

JULIAN: I've gone!

    JULIAN *darts across the bar and disappears through the*
double doors.

    We cut to PAMELA, *there are tears in her eyes.*

SARAH: What is it, darling?

PAMELA: My little brother . . . when he's like this, I worry
about him.

    There are tears pouring down her cheeks. She gets up and
leaves the table. STANLEY *gets up and follows her.* PAMELA
has retreated into a corner of the bar. STANLEY *catches*
up with her. She is really crying, her head turned away
from him.

    STANLEY *puts his arms round her, gently turning her*
towards him.

PAMELA: I worry about him so much! He is so young, so
young for his age – and I can't be there for him all the
time, I just can't . . . but when I'm not, I can't stop
thinking . . . (*She cries.*) He could be so brilliant if he
wanted, do so much, but something always stops him.

    STANLEY *touches her face, and she leans against him. He*
holds her close as people glance towards them from the bar.

STANLEY: He can look after himself I'm sure. I'm certain
he can.

PAMELA: Do you think?

    She looks at him, her eyes glistening.

    Oh I do hope you're right Stanley, please be right!

STANLEY: I know I'm right. He will be fine. Of course he
will.

INT. AIR BASE. NIGHT

We cut back to the air base, the band have just come off stage
and are in a passage which leads to a room where food has been

laid out. CARLA *is very excited she has managed to get through the performance.* LOUIS *is still affected by the atmosphere of the dinner. The* SERGEANT *turns to* LOUIS, *indicating the cake.*

SERGEANT: You want a bit to take home? It's pretty disgusting cake. It's funny how they can't tell the difference . . . You can have a plane! Want a little aeroplane?

He picks the toy plane off the cake.

LOUIS: No thanks.

SERGEANT: The real ones aren't much bigger. (*He indicates the toy planes.*) That's what we've got to take on Germany or the French, or whoever we fight next. And everybody thinks they're absolutely marvellous. That they're all we need!

He turns and disappears down the passage. LOUIS *turns to* CARLA.

LOUIS: You did well, Carla.

CARLA: I did, didn't I! (*She laughs excitedly.*) And Jessie was right, they didn't really notice anything wrong!

LOUIS: They didn't . . . (*He moves, preoccupied.*) It's been a strange evening, not what I was expecting. I think I need to go, you don't mind? I feel like a fast drive . . . If I go really fast I might make it to London in less than an hour. See if I can do it . . .

CARLA: I don't mind, Louis! You go now, I'm so happy!

EXT. AIR BASE. NIGHT

LOUIS *walks across the concourse at the air base to the sports car. The* SERGEANT *calls out to him.*

SERGEANT: You off then?! I quite liked your music as it happens.

LOUIS: Thank you.

INT. IMPERIAL BAR. NIGHT
We cut to STANLEY, PAMELA, DONALDSON *and* SARAH *leaving the bar. They are all rather drunk.* SARAH *and* DONALDSON *are laughing together.* PAMELA *seems to have recovered her poise,* STANLEY *is close to her, touching her arm.*

There is the sound of an orchestra and singing from the ballroom.

SARAH: If I wasn't so drunk I'd go and join in, the Imperial Christmas concert! Not to be missed apparently, all of the dowagers staying up really late for a singsong.
STANLEY: Yes, the Duchess of Northampton singing 'Once in Royal David's City' is meant to be an absolute highlight. She does it every year!
DONALDSON: Some things never change do they! (*He smiles.*) A few.
They are moving away from us down the passage which is lit by the twinkling Christmas lights, as the singing gets louder.
PAMELA: Well, I don't change. I intend to sleep till well past midday, just like I always do. Escape into a dream, something glorious . . .

EXT. COUNTRY ROAD. NIGHT
We cut to a shot of LOUIS *driving really fast in the open-top sports car along night country roads. We see a close-up of him through the windscreen.*

INT. IMPERIAL. MAIN PASSAGE. NIGHT
A subjective track moving along the main hotel passage through the Christmas lights. The passage is empty, music leaking up from the ballroom.

EXT. LONDON STREET/IMPERIAL BACK ENTRANCE. NIGHT
We see LOUIS *driving down a London street and then turning into the back entrance of the Imperial.*

INT. IMPERIAL. PASSAGES AND STAIRCASE. NIGHT
We see LOUIS *moving through the empty kitchen passages of the Imperial. We hear the sound of the Christmas concert from somewhere above us. We see* LOUIS *go up the back stairs of the hotel. On the first landing he stops by a door that has a window that looks on to the first-floor bedroom passage. He thinks he sees something. He goes through the door into the main passage. Right at the far end, in the shadows, he can just make out* JULIAN. *He calls out to him. The figure stops stock still for a moment in the shadows in the distance. Then he waves to him.*

JULIAN: I'm just off now, my dear friend . . . Got to run . . .
Must have missed the train, but I'm still going to
Paris.
He moves away in the shadows.
We'll see each other soon.
LOUIS *watches him go for a second, then he turns and moves purposefully up the main stairs, suspecting* JESSIE *may have spent the night out after all. We cut to him walking fast along the staff bedroom passage and stopping by her bedroom door. It is half open. He looks into the bedroom: the bed is all ruffled up, there is no sign of* JESSIE. *He turns, he calls out to her, he starts moving back along the passage. Suddenly he hears a sound, a low moan. He stops by a linen cupboard and pushes open a door.*
JESSIE *is lying sprawled in the corner of the cupboard. She is covered in blood and is barely conscious. There is blood pouring from her.* LOUIS *cries out; he goes over to her, he cradles her.*

LOUIS: Jessie, Jessie, it's Louis, look at me, look at me . . .
Come on Jessie, look at me.

Her eyes flicker open and then shut.

Jessie!!

*She opens her eyes again for a moment, breathing with
real difficulty.*

LOUIS *yells for help. He leaves her for a second, yells again
for help. The passage is completely empty. He smashes the
fire alarm, an old bell starts ringing loudly.*

We cut to chambermaids, THORNTON *and other hotel
staff swirling around in the passage. A nurse is bending
over* JESSIE *in the cupboard,* JESSIE *is now unconscious.*
LOUIS *is standing, his dinner jacket covered in blood. He
is completely dazed.* THORNTON *comes up to him.*

THORNTON: An ambulance is coming . . . (*Staring at*
LOUIS.) What on earth happened, Mr Lester?

LOUIS: I don't know . . . I found her . . . I don't know what
happened.

*He turns and stares towards the stairs. We see the image
of* JULIAN *we saw earlier, this time it is slowed.* JULIAN
waves goodbye to LOUIS *down the length of the passage.
And then* JULIAN *vanishes into darkness.*

PART THREE

EXT. LONDON STREET. NIGHT

The camera is moving at night just a few inches above the surface of the road, past the wheels of a parked car and over a drain cover with water gurgling along the gutter. It tilts to the right and moves on to the pavement, arriving at a basement window. Just as it reaches the window, a light flicks on and we see STANLEY *enter the basement kitchen.*

A caption appears:

LONDON 1933

INT. BASEMENT KITCHEN. MUSIC EXPRESS BUILDING. NIGHT

We cut inside. In a series of fast cuts, we see STANLEY *looking for food, opening drawers, the bread bin which is empty, trying to prise the lid off a jar of pickled onions. He opens the larder door to find it is totally empty, except for three rather shrivelled tomatoes and a chunk of cheddar cheese.*

INT. MAIN MUSIC EXPRESS OFFICE. NIGHT

We cut to STANLEY *crossing the main* Music Express *office with the plate of cheese and the shrivelled tomatoes.* LOUIS *is standing in the doorway of the small inner office which has a bed in the corner. He is wearing evening dress and his hand is bandaged. He watches calmly as* STANLEY *approaches.*

STANLEY: Some old cheese! It is the only edible thing the bastard has left down there –
LOUIS: Better than nothing though.
   Time cut.
   LOUIS *is sitting at* STANLEY*'s desk, eating the cheese ravenously, a large chunk in his hand, and then biting into the tomatoes.* STANLEY *is watching him closely.* LOUIS *looks up.*

LOUIS: I haven't eaten for twenty-four hours . . . so you'll have to forgive me. When do they arrive for work?

STANLEY: Eric arrives really early, always! We haven't got long, it'll be dawn soon . . .

As he is saying this, LOUIS *looks through the door into the small office, a photograph of* JULIAN *is staring directly at him. As we move in on his eyes, a strong pulsing montage begins of the story so far –* JULIAN's *head appearing round the door in the basement of the Imperial, the band playing in the ballroom with* JESSIE *singing,* LOUIS *moving round* MASTERSON's *wrecked hotel suite and then carrying the drugged girl* HANNAH *out of the hotel,* MASTERSON *presiding over the picnic in the meadow by the train,* STANLEY *and* LOUIS *spying on the Freemasons through a hole in the wall in the basement, the exuberant joy of the characters in the hailstorm outside the club as* LADY CREMONE *watches them all,* LOUIS *and* SARAH *kissing passionately in the empty* Music Express *office,* JESSIE *poised in the doorway of the bar surrounded by Christmas lights,* LOUIS *driving really fast in the sports car along night country roads. And then the shot of* JULIAN *in the shadows, right at the end of the hotel passage, waving goodbye to* LOUIS, *the image slowed.*

We cut back to LOUIS *close.* STANLEY *is calling his name.*

STANLEY: Louis, I still have no idea how to get you out of the country.

LOUIS: I know . . . neither do I.

He glances up at the photo of himself on the wall looking dazzling at the piano, and then at a picture of JESSIE *singing on the cover of the magazine. On the soundtrack, we hear the sound of people shouting, and there is a sudden violent cut to:*

INT. IMPERIAL HOTEL PASSAGE. NIGHT
*We are in the Imperial staff bedroom passage. There is a
cacophony of noise and movement around the linen cupboard
where* JESSIE *has been found stabbed. There are chambermaids,*
THORNTON, *a nurse and suddenly a doctor rushing down the
passage, yelling to everybody to keep out of the way.*

A caption appears:

SEVEN WEEKS EARLIER

We see everything through LOUIS' *eyes: the terrified faces of the
chambermaids, the blood-spattered clean linen in the cupboard,*
JESSIE'*s body being lifted up and put on a stretcher, blood
pouring from her head. The shots are jagged, our view half-
obscured, as* JESSIE *is carried away from us along the passage.*

INT. HOSPITAL. NIGHT
SCHLESINGER *and* LOUIS *are standing opposite each other in
a long tiled corridor in a big hospital. In front of them, about
twenty feet away, is a desk with a middle-aged nurse* (POLLOCK)
*guarding the entrance to the rest of the hospital. Behind them is
the reception hall where there are five upper-class revellers who
are waiting to be seen, having been involved in some sort of
fight – they are larking around drunkenly, calling out to any
passing nurse.* SCHLESINGER *has an unlit cigar clamped in
his teeth. He keeps pulling it out and putting it back.*

SCHLESINGER: This is a bad business.
LOUIS: Yes. (*He is deeply shocked but maintaining his calm
  exterior.*) Thank you for being here, Nathan.
SCHLESINGER: Least I could do. Nothing like this has ever
  happened at the Imperial before . . . not in my time.
LOUIS: No, it can't have.

He glances past NURSE POLLOCK *to the shadowy interior
of the hospital where silhouetted figures are criss-crossing
in the distance.*

SCHLESINGER: And heaven knows what'll happen to the
band now. (*He looks up.*) I – shouldn't have said that,
I'm sorry – I'm sure she'll be all right.
He calls out to the impassive nurse.
Any news yet?

NURSE POLLOCK: We'll tell you as soon as we have any.

INT. OPERATING THEATRE. NIGHT
We see across a darkened room to an operating theatre where
JESSIE *is being operated on. Initially we only see this from afar,
through a glass partition, a group of figures clustered around her.*

INT. HOSPITAL CORRIDOR. NIGHT
We cut back to the hospital corridor. STANLEY, PAMELA *and*
SARAH *are coming towards us; they are still in evening dress.
They pass the drunken revellers.* STANLEY *calls out to* LOUIS:

STANLEY: We've only just heard, how is she? Is she all right?!
PAMELA: What a shock . . .! What a dreadful thing to
happen . . .
SARAH: Have you seen her yet? (*Touching* LOUIS' *arm.*) How
is she? What are they saying?
SCHLESINGER: They won't tell us!
LOUIS: They were going to operate on her . . . I don't
know if it's finished.
STANLEY (*immediately approaching* NURSE POLLOCK): We
are close friends of Miss Jessie Taylor. We need to talk
to a doctor.
NURSE POLLOCK: As soon as there's some news, a doctor
will come down and explain the situation.

STANLEY (*staring straight at her*): No, we need to see
somebody now. (*Pointedly.*) There are some important
people – very important people – who want to know
how she is doing.

NURSE POLLOCK (*meeting his gaze*): I'm sure there are.

INT. OPERATING THEATRE. NIGHT
*We cut back to the operating theatre; this time we are on the
other side of the glass partition, in among the masked figures
that surround* JESSIE. *We move in on the unconscious* JESSIE.
An oxygen mask suddenly covers her face.

INT. HOSPITAL CORRIDOR. NIGHT
SARAH *is close to* LOUIS *as the others stand waiting.* STANLEY
is pacing impatiently.

SARAH: What happened? (*Her voice is soft.*) Has anybody
got any idea what on earth happened?

LOUIS: No, I found her lying in a cupboard . . . she was
bleeding so badly, I don't know how long she'd been
there –
*Suddenly a barrage of flash bulbs go off at the front of the
hospital; they can see the flash photography through the
windows of the reception hall.*

SCHLESINGER: They're here already, the press! How did
they get to know about it so quickly?!

EXT. HOSPITAL ENTRANCE. NIGHT
*We cut outside the hospital, a large imposing building with
columns. Some press photographers are waiting at the entrance,
their big flash bulbs popping as they photograph the police
arriving and going up the hospital steps. There is a detective,*

GUNSON, *a middle-aged man with a moon-shaped face, a second detective, and two uniformed police.* GUNSON *doesn't break his stride.*

GUNSON: Nothing to say gentlemen, absolutely nothing to say.

INT. HOSPITAL PASSAGE. NIGHT
We cut into the hospital corridor. The police are approaching LOUIS *and the others.*

PAMELA: Why are they here now? Couldn't they wait until morning?!
STANLEY: They're the ones that tipped off the press, almost certainly! (*Watching them approach.*) They knew there'd be photographers, so they've come in force!

INT. OPERATING THEATRE. NIGHT
We cut back to the operating theatre; all is in semi-darkness now. JESSIE, *lying unconscious, is being lifted on to a stretcher and then wheeled away from us.*

INT. HOSPITAL CORRIDOR. NIGHT
We cut back to the hospital corridor. The images start dissolving into each other as we see the shocked faces of the characters and their feeling of dislocation . . . PAMELA *and* STANLEY *are in the middle of talking to the police about seeing* JESSIE *in the hotel bar earlier that night. We only half hear what they are saying. We see* LOUIS *leaning against the white tiles of the corridor,* SCHLESINGER *chewing on his unlit cigar, the revellers in the background shouting and singing drunkenly. We hear a fragment of* PAMELA's *statement.*

PAMELA: My brother caught the train to Paris . . . the
9:30 . . . He will still be on it . . . He should be
reaching Paris first thing this morning . . .
The sound begins to cut out as we move in on LOUIS.
Suddenly GUNSON'*s face appears in front of him, really*
close, his voice quiet, his tone polite.

GUNSON: If you wouldn't mind, sir, giving me a statement,
I believe you were the one that found the lady . . .
At that moment we see a young nurse approaching NURSE
POLLOCK, *her footsteps ringing out. As she gets close,*
LOUIS *watches with apprehension, wondering what news*
she brings. The nurse bends down and whispers to NURSE
POLLOCK. LOUIS *cannot concentrate on the policeman;*
he watches the two nurses talking but is unable to hear
what they are saying.

GUNSON: We could do this in the morning if you prefer,
sir . . .
LOUIS, *still staring at the nurses, nods.* SCHLESINGER,
unable to contain himself, yells out to NURSE POLLOCK.

SCHLESINGER: So how is she? You can tell us now surely?!

NURSE POLLOCK: She has still not come round after the
anaesthetic. I'm afraid it's too early to say how exactly
she is.
In the distance, the doors to the reception hall burst open,
accompanied by a barrage of flash photography, and
CARLA *appears at the other end of the corridor. She is still*
in her show costume but is wearing a fine winter coat
and hat.

CARLA: There you all are! What terrible news! How is she,
tell me how she is?! Can I see her, I must see her?!
As she comes down the corridor towards them, a
photographer is following her, determined to get a picture
of her and LOUIS *together. He calls out 'Carla!' and she*
instinctively turns and looks at him. He takes the photo,
the flash bulb going off like a gunshot. SCHLESINGER

turns, enraged, his huge figure advancing on the
photographer.
SCHLESINGER: How dare you do that! Get out of here
now!
  SCHLESINGER's *fleshy face is staring into the photographer's*
  lens, his eyes blazing.

EXT. LONDON STREET. MORNING
Brilliant early morning sun flares straight into the camera as
STANLEY *crosses the street into the* Music Express *building.*
It is very early, the street is deserted. STANLEY *is still in his*
dinner jacket.

INT. MUSIC EXPRESS STAIRCASE/OFFICE. MORNING
STANLEY *is going up the stairs, the walls lined by framed covers*
of the magazine. One of them features LOUIS *and* JESSIE
together. The sun is streaming in. STANLEY *is looking*
particularly dishevelled having been up all night. He opens the
door of his office and stops in surprise. Sitting at his desk is a
tall, gangly man in his early thirties, ERIC, *who is wearing a*
tweed suit that seems a little too tight for him. He has a public-
school voice, and a slightly obsessive, distracted manner. He has
a mass of papers spread out in front of him and is peering at
them closely. He looks up absent-mindedly as STANLEY *enters.*

ERIC: Oh yes, do come in by all means.
STANLEY: What do you mean, 'Do come in'?! This is my
office.
ERIC (*deeply preoccupied by his papers*): I thought it was the
deputy editor's office.
STANLEY: It is, yes. That's me.
ERIC: And I believe it's me too now. (*Glancing up.*)
STANLEY: You're deputy editor?! (*Staring, astonished.*)

ERIC: Joint deputy editor, yes. Didn't Mr Wax speak to
    you?

STANLEY: He didn't, no.

ERIC: I'm sure he means to have a word. (*He returns to his
    papers.*)

STANLEY: He'll be having more than a word! (*Moving
    closer.*) I've been up all night and I find there's a new
    deputy editor? That's brilliant! And you're sitting at
    my desk.

ERIC: Oh, am I? . . . In which case, I'll try to move.
    *He picks up a large fistful of his papers, some of which
    scatter to the floor.*
    I may have to do this in stages . . .
    *STANLEY scoops up one of ERIC's papers and glances at it
    sceptically.*

STANLEY: What is this then – 'Next Exciting Step for the
    Televisor'?

ERIC: Oh, that's from three weeks ago, that article, it's
    already out of date. (*He searches through his papers as
    he unloads them on to a smaller desk.*) I've got a better
    one here somewhere . . .

STANLEY: Out of date in three weeks?

ERIC: Absolutely. (*Pouring more papers on to his new desk.*)
    One has to keep up.

STANLEY: Is that why you're here? (*Really sharp.*) Why
    you're the new deputy editor?

ERIC (*settling into his new desk, deep in his papers again*):
    I think it might be . . . (*Then he looks straight at
    STANLEY.*) to help you keep up.

INT. MUSIC EXPRESS STAIRS/HALLWAY. MORNING
MR WAX *and* ROSIE *have arrived at the same moment in the
hall.* MR WAX *holds the front door open for her. His tone is
bright and cheerful.*

MR WAX: Ah, Rosie, you're here too!

He looks up and sees STANLEY *at the top of the stairs staring down at them.*

It seems we're all early today!

STANLEY (*coldly furious*): What the hell do you think you're doing?!

MR WAX stares back at him; for the first time he seems steely and formidable.

MR WAX: And what do you mean by that, Stanley?

STANLEY: You know bloody well what I mean.

MR WAX: Stanley, you will not use that tone with me.

I suggest you calm down.

STANLEY: I have no intention of calming down.

ROSIE: You look dreadful. (*Her tone concerned.*) You haven't been up all night again, have you?! (*She starts to move towards him, anxious to diffuse the row.*) Why don't we go up to the office?

STANLEY: Did you know about this?

ROSIE: Know about what?

MR WAX: No, she didn't. I've been meaning to tell you both. (*A sharp complacent smile.*) But it seems Eric has beaten me to it . . .

INT. POLICE INTERROGATION ROOM. MORNING

A door swings open and a uniformed policeman leads LOUIS *into a large basement room with windows looking up towards the pavement outside. We can see people passing in the street above, just their legs moving past the window. Facing* LOUIS *is an empty desk with three chairs. Beyond the desk,* GUNSON *is pacing in the shadows. A typist is sitting at a smaller desk deeper in the room.*

GUNSON: Thank you, Mr Lester, for coming this morning . . . The senior officer on this case is about to join us.

(*He indicates to* LOUIS *to sit.*) Would you like a cup of tea?

LOUIS: No tea, thanks, no.

GUNSON (*stops pacing, glances at* LOUIS): You don't drink tea?

LOUIS (*surprised*): Yes . . . sometimes, yes.

> LOUIS' *manner is contained, authoritative. He appears an elegantly glamorous figure in the middle of this stark functional room.* GUNSON *watches* LOUIS *for a moment, then he glances up at the legs moving along the pavement. A woman's legs walking a small white dog are just passing.*

GUNSON: It's an interesting view we have here. (*Watching the legs disappear.*) It often helps us get through the day.

> *At that moment, a sharp-faced man,* HORTON, *very much younger than* GUNSON, *about* LOUIS' *age, enters the room briskly and moves to the desk.*

HORTON: Hello Mr Lester, I am Detective Inspector Horton. I am handling this case.

> *He sits opposite* LOUIS.

Thank you for being here so promptly.

> LOUIS *momentarily startled by* HORTON's *youth.*

We just need a statement from you about everything that happened last night, from when you left the air base, where I believe you were playing at a concert attended by the Prince of Wales, until you found Miss Taylor.

> *He gives* LOUIS *a shrewd but not unfriendly look.*

Absolutely everything that happened.

INT. MUSIC EXPRESS OFFICE. MORNING

We cut to MR WAX *staring down at one of the early morning papers. On the side of the front page there is a box, 'Stop Press: Singer Badly Injured in Incident at Imperial Hotel'.* ROSIE, STANLEY *and* ERIC *are watching* MR WAX.

MR WAX: I'm sorry, Stanley, I had no idea at all that this had happened last night, and to the very band you've championed, an awful business! You must be upset of course –

STANLEY: Yes, but it hasn't got anything to do with this. I'm angry because I was told absolutely nothing about the appointment –

ERIC *is standing solemnly in his tight suit.*

– of this gentleman here.

MR WAX: I understand it's a surprise. You're used to ruling the roost alone here, Stanley, I know.

STANLEY: During which time, let's not forget, I've more than doubled the circulation –

MR WAX (*ignoring this*): But I'm sure Eric and you will work well together. (ROSIE*'s head turns sharply.*) Not forgetting you, Rosie, of course.

STANLEY (*straight back at* MR WAX): I don't know what he's going to do . . . ? What on earth is there for him to do?!

MR WAX: Ah, tell him what you're going to do, Eric.

They all look at the gangling figure of ERIC.

ERIC: I will be concentrating – principally – on the latest news . . .

ROSIE: The latest news? I thought we did that already!

ERIC: By which I mean the latest gramophone designs, the newest wireless sets, the best buys –

STANLEY: Oh for heaven's sake, we'll be down to three readers a week in no time! We're a music magazine!

ERIC (*totally undeterred*): And of course there'll be other things as well, like what happened in New York last week . . . (*He pauses for a second for emphasis.*) When a singer's voice was carried by a beam of light – purely by a beam of light – from one tall building in Manhattan to another. And simultaneously broadcast to fifty radio stations – and there were no wires of any kind to be seen anywhere!

ROSIE: Just with a beam of light?! Did that really happen last week? I had no idea, that's rather exciting!

    STANLEY*'s eyes flash.*

INT. POLICE INTERROGATION ROOM. MORNING
We cut back to the interrogation room. The typist is typing vigorously as LOUIS *is finishing his statement.* GUNSON *is standing in the shadows just behind* HORTON, *who is watching* LOUIS *intently.*

LOUIS: . . . And I heard a noise coming from the cupboard, I looked in, and there she was, bleeding really badly . . . (*He stops momentarily, shaken by the memory.*) I called for help, then I broke the glass of the fire alarm –

GUNSON: That was good thinking sir.

LOUIS: Because nobody was coming. (*He stops.*)

HORTON: Thank you, Mr Lester.

    The typing stops, there is silence.

LOUIS: Is that all?

HORTON: I think so, almost all, yes.

    LOUIS *looks up.*

    In case you were wondering – (*A slight smile.*) The thought may not have occurred to you, but in case it has – you are not a suspect Mr Lester, for the simple reason you were seen arriving at the hotel in the two-seater at a couple of minutes before 11:30, and there would not have been enough time for you to have assaulted Miss Taylor before you were found with her.

GUNSON: We judge she'd been in that cupboard some time.

HORTON: For a good number of minutes anyway.

    LOUIS *meets* HORTON*'s beady look. It had not seriously occurred to him he might be treated as a suspect, but now he looks back, poised, reassured.*

LOUIS: Right.

HORTON (*still watching him*): There is just one other matter
. . . you say you saw Julian Luscombe on one of the
first-floor passages, immediately before you found
Miss Taylor, and he said he'd missed his train?

LOUIS: Yes.

HORTON: But we've been told by his sister he definitely
caught the 9:30 sleeper to Paris.

LOUIS (*calmly*): I can only repeat I did see him and he did
speak to me.

HORTON: Thank you Mr Lester, that's all we need to know.
LOUIS *stands.*
It's very important of course that you keep that last
piece of information to yourself. (*Their eyes meet.*)
Completely to yourself, for obvious reasons.

GUNSON: Until we've had a chance to talk to Mr Luscombe.

INT. POLICE BASEMENT PASSAGE. MORNING

LOUIS *is moving along the basement passage of the police station,
heading for the stairs. He turns a corner into a waiting area, lined
by a long wooden bench.* DONALDSON *is sitting there, smoking
a small cigar, alone in the room.* LOUIS *is taken by surprise.*

LOUIS: What are you doing here?

DONALDSON: I'm here to give a statement about last night.
What an awful business, Louis!

LOUIS: Yes, I'm going straight to the hospital now, to find
out how she is –

DONALDSON: I've already rung the hospital.
LOUIS *turns.*
Jessie is still unconscious, but stable they think. (*He
looks straight at* LOUIS.) Stay a moment and have
breakfast with me – after I've been in there. (*Indicating
the interrogation room.*) It won't take long, then we'll

go to the hospital together. (*He smiles warmly.*) What do you say?

INT. CAFÉ. MORNING
We cut to the interior of a greasy-spoon café, but one with fine tiled walls. There are a few scattered customers, lorry drivers and a couple of secretaries having breakfast together on the way to work. DONALDSON, *looking incongruous in his beautiful tailored suit, is sitting opposite* LOUIS, *and is watching with approval as a waitress approaches with two plates of steaming sausages.*

DONALDSON: Ah, here they come! The sausages are surprisingly edible here . . .
LOUIS (*surveying his plate*): I can't say I'm hungry.
DONALDSON: It's good to eat, Louis, even on a day like this, it helps one think. I got to know this café when standing bail for one of my protégés, a rather wild painter who'd got into a little bother. (*Seeing* LOUIS *not eating.*) I must tell you about all my projects one day.
LOUIS: Yes . . . you must.
DONALDSON: I know you must be terribly shocked still. (*Gently.*) You probably didn't sleep at all, did you?
LOUIS: No.
DONALDSON: What do you think happened to Jessie?
LOUIS (*hesitating for a split second*): I have no idea.
DONALDSON: Well, I'm sure they'll be able to find out quite soon. What a young detective he was, but rather efficient!
DONALDSON *is eating slowly and elegantly as if anything faster would be insensitive.*
And of course as soon as Jessie gets better, she will be able to tell us herself.

LOUIS: If she gets better, she must have lost a lot of blood –

DONALDSON: She will get better, Louis – I know I'm a
natural optimist, but even allowing for that, she has to
get better. She's a strong young woman and she has
such spirit.

LOUIS: That's true.

DONALDSON: She will come back to us, and the success of
the band will continue and grow –

LOUIS: I'm not even thinking that far ahead, I just want
her to wake up.

DONALDSON: All my life I've looked on the bright side,
Louis, and it's worked so far – especially recently and
it will again. (*He smiles.*) I know you wonder all the
time why I take such an interest in you and your
music –

LOUIS: No, I don't, I'm grateful for that.

DONALDSON: And I certainly can't claim any credit for
what an impression the band has made, but I like to
count you as one of my discoveries. (*He smiles.*) Even
if it's only half true. (*He looks down on* LOUIS' *plate.*)
I can see I'm not going to persuade you about the
excellence of these sausages. (*He looks at* LOUIS
warmly.) Let's go and see Jessie, shall we?

INT. FIRST FLOOR HOSPITAL PASSAGE. DAY

DONALDSON *and* LOUIS *are walking along a passage on the
first floor of the hospital. In the distance, they can see a door
being guarded by uniformed police.*

LOUIS: They've got police up here as well?! What are they
expecting to happen?

DONALDSON: It's because of the press, Louis, and the
newsreel cameras too, they'll stop at nothing to try to

get a picture. (*He smiles gently as they approach.*) Let
me handle the police.
LOUIS *holds back as* DONALDSON *talks to the police
officer.*
He's letting us in . . .

INT. JESSIE'S HOSPITAL ROOM. DAY
DONALDSON *and* LOUIS *enter* JESSIE'*s hospital room. She is
lying unconscious, heavily bandaged, especially her head.* LADY
CREMONE *is sitting on one side of the bed and* CARLA *on the
other. A nurse is also in the room. There are already quite a few
vases of flowers.* LADY CREMONE'*s tone is immediately crisp
and formidable.*

LADY CREMONE: Oh, hello you two, I've had her moved
       into this room because the other wasn't at all
       satisfactory.
CARLA: They put her into a much smaller room, but Lady
       Cremone got them to change it at once.
DONALDSON (*softly*): I'm sure Lavinia has taken complete
       charge of the hospital already.
LOUIS: She's still not woken?
       He stares down at JESSIE.
LADY CREMONE: Not yet, no, but her breathing is fine.
       Carla and I have been discussing how we might contact
       somebody from her family . . .
CARLA: I've never met any of Jessie's family, even at
       school. I think her dad's dead . . .
DONALDSON: With her picture, everywhere, in all the
       magazines, you'd have thought they'd be in touch
       before now . . .
       LOUIS *is now very close to* JESSIE'*s face.*
LADY CREMONE: Talk to her, Louis.

LOUIS: Talk to her?

LADY CREMONE: Yes, the doctor said we should talk to her, the sound of a familiar voice . . . Of course mine isn't that familiar.

CARLA: I've been chattering away, haven't I, Jessie?!

LADY CREMONE: It isn't easy to talk to somebody who isn't saying anything, and starting is particularly difficult, but one gets used to it.

LOUIS: Jessie, it's Louis . . . (*They all look at him.*) Jessie, this is me, Louis . . . I was there . . . I was the one who found you . . .

We move in on JESSIE*'s face, we can hear the sound of her breathing.*

LADY CREMONE (*to* LOUIS): It would be much easier if we weren't all watching I know. We'll take it in turns until she wakes. I can do quite a lot more now –

CARLA: That's very good of you, Your Ladyship. You must have many things you have to do . . .

LADY CREMONE: Nonsense, I certainly do not. The only thing I have to do is fuss about the play I saw last night – (*Sharply.*) And this is just a little more important than that.

She leans towards JESSIE.

Maybe I should get them to bring me an artichoke, Jessie, and then start eating it. What do you think of that? The dear child was so astonished before to see me eating one. (*Back to* JESSIE.) Maybe that would really surprise you all over again?

INT. MAIN HOSPITAL CORRIDOR. DAY

LOUIS *is moving back along the main hospital corridor towards the entrance. A voice calls his name.* SARAH *is standing by a side door that leads into a small courtyard.*

SARAH: They wouldn't let me up, they said she had too
many visitors. Is she still asleep?

LOUIS: She hasn't woken up after the operation, not yet.

The main entrance door opens as somebody leaves and
LOUIS *glimpses the press photographers clustered outside*
in the street.

They're still here?!

SARAH: Of course they are. Jessie's the singer who should
have been singing to the Prince of Wales when it
happened . . . so naturally it's a very big story. (*She*
moves to the side door.) There's a little garden, we'll be
safe from them here.

EXT. COURTYARD GARDEN. DAY

LOUIS *and* SARAH *are in a small courtyard garden which has*
some shrubs, a tree and some benches. SARAH *turns to* LOUIS,
her tone intense.

SARAH: I was so worried about you, Louis.

LOUIS: Why? Don't worry about me.

SARAH: It's such a shock for all of us, but especially for
you. It's worse this morning for some reason, last
night I was numb. (*She takes his hand.*) Do the police
have any idea yet what happened?

LOUIS (*pausing momentarily*): Not yet, no. I don't think.

SARAH: I was there with her in the bar last night. Julian
escorted her to her room, and then he came back and
caught his train. But that was hours before! She must
have arranged to meet someone else . . .

LOUIS: Yes, that's possible.

SARAH (*putting her arms around* LOUIS): We'll know soon
anyway, when she's able to tell us.

She hugs him tight. There's a sudden flash, a photographer
has got into the garden and snatched a picture. He scuttles

away. LOUIS *is too preoccupied to be outraged, but* SARAH
is furious.

SARAH: They're everywhere! I should have my camera with
me and turn it on them!

INT. MUSIC EXPRESS OFFICE. DAY

ERIC *and* STANLEY *are alone together in the* Music Express
office, sitting at their desks. STANLEY *stares across at* ERIC, *who
is now typing something with scholarly concentration.* STANLEY's
mood is mercurial, he decides to stir things.

STANLEY: What else have you got?

ERIC: How do you mean? (*He looks up vaguely as he types.*)

STANLEY: The latest news? The wonderful machines which
have now got to be put in the magazine apparently.

ERIC: Well, there's a lot to choose from . . .

STANLEY: I was afraid you might say that.

ERIC: But to pluck just one at random – which happens to
be the one I've chosen to write about today – there is
for instance, the music without instruments.

STANLEY: Right?! (*Staring at* ERIC *in disbelief.*) Silence, in
other words.

ERIC: No, absolutely not, quite the contrary. Or to put the
idea another way, the orchestra without musicians as
demonstrated recently in Germany by Herr Pfenninger
using an electrical current.

STANLEY: Herr Pfenninger?! Some mad German professor?!
You're making this up.

ERIC: I am most certainly not making this up, I have never
exaggerated or invented anything. One doesn't need to.
(*He looks straight at* STANLEY.) Herr Pfenninger and
his electronic music . . .

ROSIE (*putting her head round the door*): There's a visitor for
you, Stanley –

PAMELA *sweeps into the room. Her face is flushed, but she is exquisitely dressed.*

PAMELA: Oh Stanley, thank God you're here!

STANLEY: Pamela, are you all right?

PAMELA: Nobody can be all right on a day like this, can they?!

ERIC *is staring at* PAMELA, *her fragile beauty among the piles of paper in the office.*

STANLEY: This is Eric Stillman, this is Pamela Luscombe.

PAMELA: I'm sorry to burst in, but I need your help, Stanley. (*She hardly acknowledges* ERIC). I have to get in touch with Julian, he's in Paris, I rang the apartment – he arrived as planned earlier this morning, but he has gone out already. Of course I've sent a telegram, but I need to tell him about what's happened as soon as possible, he'll be so upset –

STANLEY (*puzzled*): What do you want me to do?

PAMELA: Julian will be lunching at a fashionable restaurant, and I want to telephone that restaurant, so I need to know what's the most fashionable place to eat in Paris at the moment because that is where he will be. And you always know everything Stanley – (*To* ERIC.) He'll deny it, but he does –

STANLEY: You want me to guess what Paris restaurant Julian is having lunch in? That's impossible!

PAMELA: No, it's not, he'll never be at the fuddy-duddy places I go to in Paris like Le Meurice – it'll be the place that everybody's talking about. You see it's not quite as stupid as it seems.

STANLEY: It may surprise you, but I don't have a list of all the fashionable restaurants in Paris in my head –

PAMELA: I'm sure you could have a try, Stanley, I was so certain you'd know. (*Her tone more intimate.*) And of course I wanted an excuse to see you, rather badly, because I need calming down –

STANLEY: I can't help you at the moment, Pamela, I've
been up all night –

PAMELA: You're not the only one who's been up all night.
(*She moves to the window.*) I have no idea what Julian
will do when he hears the news about Jessie, and I
would hate for him to find out about it from the press.
It's going to be all over the papers.

ERIC: I'm afraid it will be, and we have to decide how
we're going to cover it because this magazine helped
launch the band, isn't that right? So it's a big story
for us.

STANLEY: I do realise that, Eric –

ERIC: And of course who knows how long the band will
last now – it may be difficult for them to get bookings
after this.

STANLEY (*suddenly realising something, he turns*): You're right
of course, thank you.

ERIC: For what?

STANLEY: I need to get down to the Imperial right this
minute, I should already be there.

PAMELA: Not yet. Don't go.

STANLEY: Here . . .

He scribbles fast on a piece of paper and hands it to
PAMELA.

Start with these, and if that fails Eric will phone every
restaurant – above a certain price – in Paris.

INT. IMPERIAL LOBBY/PASSAGE/BAR. DAY

STANLEY *moves across the lobby of the Imperial. The Christmas
lights are off, there is a pall hanging over the building. An old
dowager is sitting in the shadows, a harassed-looking bellboy
scurries by.*

STANLEY *moves on down the main passage. Two uniformed
policemen walk briskly past him.* STANLEY *reaches the bar.*

MASTERSON *is standing in the empty bar reading the*
newspapers, which have been laid out on a round table. Behind
him there are silhouetted hotel staff standing on tall ladders
working on the Christmas lights, which are off. The atmosphere
is sepulchral. MASTERSON, *sensing somebody is watching him,*
suddenly looks up. His tone is very measured.

MASTERSON: Mr Mitchell . . . what a business this is.

STANLEY: Yes, it's horrible.

MASTERSON: There are police everywhere. (*Indicating the*
men on the ladders.) They even switched off the
Christmas lights, and now they won't work for some
reason.

STANLEY: That's too bad.
He watches him, fascinated, from the doorway.

MASTERSON: I've been looking at the papers, overnight
the story is just a stop press, too late for the main
editions . . . but now look at this –
He holds up the Evening News *with a front-page*
headline, 'Singer Fighting for Her Life After Attack at the
Imperial Hotel', underneath in slightly smaller letters, 'Due
to Perform for the Prince of Wales'.
This is just the start of course. It'll grow, Mr Mitchell.

STANLEY: It will, yes.

MASTERSON: And when this was happening . . . (*He studies*
the paper for a moment.) I was sitting in the theatre
watching such a dull play, and a very noisy one as
well. I will of course lose every cent I invested in it.

STANLEY: It was that awful, was it?

MASTERSON: It was, Mr Mitchell. Yes.

STANLEY: You'll excuse me, I've got to see Mr Schlesinger.

MASTERSON: You'll keep me posted on how the lady is?
Because your information will probably be more up to
the minute than mine.

STANLEY: I will. (*He begins to move off.*)

MASTERSON: Twice a day.

STANLEY (*surprised*): Twice a day?

MASTERSON: Yes, if you could be so kind. (*Suddenly with feeling.*) I pray she gets better.

INT. IMPERIAL PASSAGE/SCHLESINGER'S OFFICE. DAY
STANLEY *is walking straight towards* SCHLESINGER'*s office. The door is open,* SCHLESINGER *is on the phone. Outside the door is a police officer. A small dapper man with a bald head is just leaving the office,* STANLEY *turns and calls after him.*

STANLEY: Jack . . . !
  The shiny man turns and gives him a tiny wave while hardly breaking his stride. STANLEY *walks past the police officer and into the office.* SCHLESINGER *looks up, his manner angry and flustered.*

SCHLESINGER: Go away! I'm not in the mood for you today. (*Into the phone.*) And I'm not in the mood for you either, Harold, we'll try to settle this later, goodbye! (*Rings off.*)

STANLEY: What is Jack Paynton doing here?!

SCHLESINGER: Stanley, not now! (*He covers his face with his hands.*) The place is overrun with police, everything I've tried to do with this hotel looks like it's in ruins! Everybody told me not to have a Negro band here – everybody but you – I didn't listen, and now they're involved in a knife attack!

STANLEY: The band wasn't involved, for heaven's sake! They weren't even here, they were playing for the fucking Prince of Wales!

SCHLESINGER: And that makes it even worse! (*He waves the* Evening News.) Even more newsworthy. We are already getting cancellations this morning! When there

was that murder at the Savoy, it took nearly two years
for their business to recover!

STANLEY: Well, one way to make absolutely sure business
collapses is to book Jack Paynton now!

SCHLESINGER: That's not true – he's still quite popular as
it happens. Anyway I've got to have somebody to play
here, it's one of our biggest weeks, Christmas week!
And it's clearly impossible for Mr Lester's band to
continue in these circumstances –

STANLEY: Why? Why is it? If you stop them playing now,
you turn a bad incident into something that looks far
worse – like they never should have been here in the
first place . . .

SCHLESINGER: Stanley, I know you backed this band early
and naturally you're trying to protect your investment.
(*Sharp look.*) After all this is not good for your
magazine either, is it?!

STANLEY: I'm not sure about that. (*Straight back at him.*)
We've got a unique angle on the story remember?!
I was here last night, I was a witness – our next issue
will sell an extra forty thousand copies, minimum!

SCHLESINGER: Then what are you doing here?! Go away
and write about it!

STANLEY: I will. (*His tone suddenly quieter.*) I was right before
wasn't I – we've started to transform this bloody
hotel?! It's fashionable now. If you let the band keep
playing, people will still come – definitely – because of
their notoriety. That's how show business works.

SCHLESINGER: Don't try to teach me about show business,
Stanley.

STANLEY: But I'm not wrong, am I?

SCHLESINGER (*suddenly*): They won't play anyway. They
won't go on.

STANLEY: Who says?

SCHLESINGER: Mr Lester says.

INT. IMPERIAL KITCHEN PASSAGE. DAY

At the far end of the kitchen passage LOUIS *is sitting smoking, he watches* STANLEY *approach past the trolleys of food. In the tiled parlour* JOE *the trumpeter is sitting looking shattered, his head bent.* STANLEY *reaches* LOUIS.

STANLEY: I look terrible this morning and you don't. How is that possible?

LOUIS (*smoking*): Is that any different from most mornings?

> STANLEY *smiles at this. A bell rings above their heads. They are beneath a large box, where room numbers light up when people call down . . .*

STANLEY: And you're as calm as always.

LOUIS: Not really, no.

> THORNTON *appears suddenly as the bell rings.*

THORNTON: Room 27, come on, 27!

> *Two young men scurry off down the passage to take the order as* THORNTON *shouts after them. One of them is the boy who saw* LOUIS *carrying* HANNAH *out of the hotel in Part One. He gives* LOUIS *an urgent look before he moves off.* THORNTON *turns to* STANLEY *and* LOUIS.

THORNTON: So slow, they get slower and slower! (*Another room lights up, 39.*) Room 39 as well – make sure you do both!

> *He yells after the boys who disappear round the corner.*
>
> THORNTON *retreats back to his room.*

STANLEY: Well, he's just the same today . . .

> *He sits next to* LOUIS *and lights a cigarette.*

I'm about to stir things up a bit, Louis. (*He looks at him.*) You've got to go on performing.

LOUIS: That's not possible. Not until Jessie is much better.

STANLEY: Mr Schlesinger wants you to.

LOUIS: The band won't do it. It's out of the question.

STANLEY: Louis, shall I tell you what's going to happen if the band stops playing? If you do that, Schlesinger

won't be paying you naturally, other bookings will
prove difficult. If you're unemployed, the immigration
authorities will start chasing all your musicians that
don't have residency here.

LOUIS: I don't believe that, not right away, not after what's
happened.

STANLEY: Especially after what's happened! Your lead
singer nearly gets killed in a knife attack when she
should have been singing to the Prince of Wales! All
sorts of stories will start appearing about the band –

LOUIS: I'm not bothered about that, I don't read the press.

The number 39 starts flashing again above their heads.

STANLEY: All kinds of rubbish . . . ! And the authorities
will immediately feel they've got to take an interest in
you again. You want that to happen?

LOUIS: Of course not, but I'll see to it. It won't happen.

STANLEY: There's only one way it won't happen – if you've
still got your monthly contract here. If everybody's
employed, they can't touch you. (*He smiles.*) Nathan's
already got you booked for the 25th, and this place is
unforgettable on Christmas Day apparently!

The YOUNG WAITER *who looked at* LOUIS *suddenly
appears again at the end of the passage.*

YOUNG WAITER: Number 39 was not room service, it was
for you.

STANLEY *and* LOUIS *stare back at the* WAITER, *who
points at* STANLEY.

For you!

INT. IMPERIAL PASSAGE/LADY CREMONE'S SUITE. DAY
We cut to LADY CREMONE *opening the door to her suite and
allowing* STANLEY *to enter. It is a fine room, echoing her
elegance.* STANLEY *greets her with a humorous glint in his eye,
despite his lack of sleep. His tone is mock formal.*

STANLEY: You rang, Your Ladyship?

LADY CREMONE: I'm sorry to have you called like that,
Stanley, I heard you were in the hotel from Mr
Masterson.

STANLEY: Don't worry, I don't mind being summoned.
(*He smiles.*) By you, at least. (*He moves further into the
room.*) They've got a new deputy editor at the
magazine, so I might be doing room service for real
quite soon.

LADY CREMONE: I'm sure that's not possible! (*Then, her
tone more serious.*) I just wanted to see you Stanley,
I have no other excuse . . .

STANLEY: That's a good excuse isn't it?! (*He smiles.*) I'm
sorry I look like this, I'm feeling a little rough today . . .

LADY CREMONE: Aren't we all?

STANLEY (*can't stop himself*): But you look wonderful.

LADY CREMONE (*rather sharply*): Flattery even today! (*She
moves.*) It's been such an awful few hours . . . she's
such a lovely girl, who would do something like that
to her?

STANLEY: I don't know. I was here yesterday, I saw her.
Julian was with her, but he was on the sleeper to Paris
when it happened. All sorts of people use this hotel of
course, goodness knows who was staying here last
night . . .

LADY CREMONE: That's true. (*She looks at* STANLEY.) I've
just come from the hospital, I hate to see her lying
unconscious, not reacting at all . . .

STANLEY: She will get better. (*Then more serious, not wishing
to sound facile.*) All being well she will.

LADY CREMONE: Let's hope so. It's such a cruel thing to
happen when everything was going so well with the
band. (*She turns.*) You know I was just about to hold
my first party for heaven knows how many years, my
first since my sons . . . (*She stops.*) Just a small party

for New Year, for the band and a few friends, and of
course I was going to invite you, Stanley. But now
none of that can happen, it's not possible –
STANLEY: It might be. (*He looks straight at her.*) If the news
from the hospital gets better.

EXT. HOSPITAL. AFTERNOON
SARAH *and* LOUIS *are approaching the exterior of the hospital.*
LOUIS *is carrying a large box, the photographers crowd round,
their bulbs flashing.* LOUIS *puts the box down and poses for the
pictures. He is reluctant, but he still looks like a star, an imposing
figure on the steps. They are about to move on when* SARAH
suddenly pulls out her own camera.

SARAH: Hang on a moment! I want to try this!
     SARAH *starts photographing the photographers as they yell
     at her to get out of the way so they can get more shots of*
     LOUIS. *She calls back at them, mimicking them, asking
     them to look at the lens.*
LOUIS: Well, you've certainly had an effect!
     *He is watching from the doorway. He notices a small
     group of fans are waiting politely with their autograph
     books, keeping vigil on the pavement, sad, moon-shaped
     faces. There is a particularly strange-looking woman who
     stares back at* LOUIS. *An alarming, memorable face.*

INT. JESSIE'S HOSPITAL ROOM. AFTERNOON
*We cut to a gramophone needle being lowered on to a record. We
cut wide to see a wind-up gramophone has come out of the box*
LOUIS *was carrying; the record is Jessie's successful debut song.*
SARAH *and* LOUIS *are standing staring down at* JESSIE's
unconscious face. The stern young nurse is sitting in the corner.
LOUIS, *his voice soft, bends close to* JESSIE.

LOUIS: Jessie, it's your record! . . . Can you hear it? . . .
Hear your voice? . . . Can you hear it, Jessie?
We stay on JESSIE*'s eyes which are tightly shut.* SARAH
kneels by the bed, so her face is very close to JESSIE.
SARAH: It's Sarah, Jessie, and we're listening to your
wonderful voice . . .

INT. HOSPITAL PASSAGE. AFTERNOON
The song continues over the cut as we see LOUIS *and* SARAH
moving along the ground-floor passage past a police constable.
They suddenly see MASTERSON *is approaching them down the*
length of the passage, carrying a very small bunch of flowers.
He pauses for just a second as he reaches them.

MASTERSON: I just thought I'd bring the lady these . . .
He continues on his way.
SARAH (*staring after his receding figure*): That man's so
strange, why bring such a tiny bouquet?
LOUIS (*watching him disappear*): Maybe the string is gold.

EXT. HOSPITAL. AFTERNOON
The photographers cluster round again as LOUIS *and* SARAH
leave the hospital.

LOUIS: Come on gentlemen, you got your pictures the first
time . . .
LOUIS *suddenly looks around in surprise: the small knot of*
fans and onlookers has already doubled in size while
they've been inside.
LOUIS: So many more already . . . I had no idea.
SARAH: That she was a little bit famous?
LOUIS: Not to this extent, no . . .

SARAH *and* LOUIS *cross the road, and then pause to look back at the fans.* SARAH *lifts her camera and starts taking some photographs of the vivid faces, especially the peculiar-looking woman who stares straight down the lens at her.*

SARAH: Some truly odd faces here, aren't there?! . . . I hadn't thought of this till now, but maybe it was somebody like them who attacked Jessie?

LOUIS *looks at* SARAH. *He is about to say something but stops himself. He looks back at the unsettling woman as* SARAH *takes another picture.*

SARAH: They can be very fanatical some of these people . . .

LOUIS: They'll go away soon, they won't be here on Christmas Day!

SARAH: Oh, don't mention that, I'm dreading Christmas, alone with my father . . .

LOUIS: I'm dreading it too . . . the Imperial ballroom at lunchtime!

SARAH (*heartfelt, kissing him*): I so wish I could be with you on Christmas Day!

INT. IMPERIAL BALLROOM. DAY

We cut to Christmas lunch at the Imperial. The ballroom is decorated with wreaths of holly and berries and the round tables are occupied mostly by the resident dowagers, one or two of whom are sitting completely alone at their tables. There is a spattering of elderly men lunching together and in a corner a contingent of Germans, mostly young and mostly men, but there are a couple of women with them. As we cut into the scene the helpings of Christmas puddings are being served, and the old dowagers are beginning to eat them with extreme concentration. At the edge of the room in the doorway, CARLA *and* LOUIS *are waiting with the rest of the band to make their entrance.*

SCHLESINGER *is at the microphone about to introduce them.*

SCHLESINGER: And as we watch the Christmas puddings appear, we know it must be time for some music . . . Do be careful ladies and gentleman by the way, the traditional sixpence is hidden in some of the helpings of the pudding, so be on the lookout . . .

The old ladies are very interested to see whether their portion has a sixpence.

And now here is the Louis Lester Band to give you a real Christmas treat . . . !

SCHLESINGER *moves off the stage and whispers to* LOUIS *in the doorway.*

The crowd tonight will be a little more exciting!

LOUIS *smiles as he stares at the old dowagers.*

But there are some Germans here from their Embassy . . .

He glances over to the Germans and then back to LOUIS.

So this could prove interesting, Louis . . .

The band walks on, CARLA *moves to the microphone.*

CARLA: Happy Christmas, everybody! Hope you're having a wonderful time!

The dowagers are deep in their puddings. LOUIS *can see from the piano some of the German contingent are very unsettled at the sight of these black musicians. The band start their first number, loud and full of energy.*

Immediately four of the Germans stand up noisily, throwing down their napkins and walking out very ostentatiously, making their disapproval plain, although the dowagers are oblivious. The other members of the German contingent remain; they appear more sophisticated and tolerant. We cut to SCHLESINGER, *who is standing with* THORNTON *and watching the Germans walk out. We move in close on* SCHLESINGER.

SCHLESINGER: Fuck 'em!

LOUIS *watches the Germans walk out as he plays.*

A montage begins of this particular Christmas Day with the music pulsing strongly underneath and building.

INT. PAMELA AND JULIAN'S HOME. DAY
We cut inside the dining room of PAMELA *and* JULIAN's *parents' house.* PAMELA *is sitting having lunch with her parents. There is an empty chair for* JULIAN. *The parents have sharp aristocratic faces. The mother has an alabaster, mask-like expression, seemingly locked in her own world. They are eating soup in silence. There is tension on* PAMELA's *face, as the music plays underneath.*

INT. JESSIE'S HOSPITAL ROOM. DAY
We cut to DONALDSON *entering* JESSIE's *hospital room, carrying flowers and a small basket with a bottle of brandy in it.* JESSIE *is still unconscious. The young nurse is sitting in the shadows.* DONALDSON *addresses* JESSIE.

DONALDSON: My dear girl, I thought I might visit you, since I have no pressing need to be anywhere else this Christmas Day, and we could talk together.
He unpacks some cigars, a glass, the bottle of brandy.
I've brought my own supplies. (*He smiles charmingly at the nurse.*) Which I'm sure I'll be allowed to use today of all days . . .

INT. IMPERIAL BALLROOM. DAY
We cut back to the ballroom, the number is building strongly. A couple more from the German contingent decide maybe they ought to leave, as they see they are being watched by the group that did walk out, staring at them from the lobby.

INT. SARAH'S FATHER'S HOUSE. DAY
We cut to SARAH *and her* FATHER *having lunch alone together.*
Her FATHER *is sitting at the head of the table; he has a book*
open in front of him, his portion of Christmas pudding is half
eaten.

SARAH'S FATHER: Not too bad a meal this year, but I
    always hate the pudding . . . we can relax now . . .
    (*He starts reading his book.*) You may get down if you
    wish . . .
    A close-up of SARAH *longing to be somewhere else.*

INT. MRS MITCHELL'S HOUSE. DAY
We cut to Stanley's mother's house. They are sitting in the
parlour with a very large turkey on the table. MRS MITCHELL
is about to carve it.

STANLEY: How are we ever going to eat this bird, Mum?
MRS MITCHELL: Well, Christmas is a time to celebrate,
    isn't it?!
    The turkey looks very over-cooked, its legs slightly singed.
    I do hope it's cooked? Do you think I should put it
    back in?
    The song on the soundtrack is building in intensity.

INT. JESSIE'S HOSPITAL ROOM. DAY
We cut to DONALDSON, *glass of brandy in hand, talking to the*
unconscious JESSIE.

DONALDSON: Jessie, I want you to know . . . I live a life of
    indulgence – well, I think you know that already
    probably – and that is in some ways rather unforgive-
    able . . . Well, maybe in many ways . . . and I expect

you find it difficult to understand how I can just
afford to do 'nothing', not have a proper job of any
description . . . but it does allow me to help people
I admire, and I want you to know . . . (*Softly, leaning
forward.*) You have an extraordinary talent . . .

INT. LADY CREMONE'S DINING ROOM. DAY
We cut to LADY CREMONE *sitting alone at her long dining-
room table, eating a rather austere portion of turkey. Her butler
is standing waiting to attend to her.*

EXT./INT. MRS MITCHELL'S HOUSE. DAY
The doorbell is ringing loudly in STANLEY's *mother's house.*
CARLA *is singing a different melody on the soundtrack.* STANLEY
opens the front door. PAMELA *is standing in the doorway.*

PAMELA: I couldn't stand it a moment longer at home!
I had to see you Stanley!
She throws her arms around him. STANLEY, *though very
surprised, embraces her, touches her face. We cut to* PAMELA
appearing in the parlour, where MRS MITCHELL *is sitting
with a large portion of turkey on her plate.*
PAMELA: Forgive me inviting myself, Mrs Mitchell! . . .
I am Pamela Luscombe . . . I just had to come here . . .
I know it's unforgivable on Christmas Day, but my
brother Julian appeared for just one night and now
he's gone back to Paris on business. (*To* STANLEY.) He
was so distraught about Jessie he's trying to distract
himself!
She turns back to MRS MITCHELL.
So I was all alone with Mummy and Daddy, and if
you knew my parents, Mrs Mitchell, that's not a fate
you'd wish on anybody!

INT. JESSIE'S HOSPITAL ROOM. DAY
DONALDSON *is leaning forward next to* JESSIE*'s hospital bed,*
his face very close.

DONALDSON: Jessie, the garden, the garden Jessie, remember
how you played for the Prince in the garden?
We move in on her face, the shots getting more and more
intense.
It must have seemed so strange to you . . . well for me
too really! You and the Prince, and all of us amongst
the flowers, on that day . . .
We see a slightly de-saturated image of JESSIE *singing in*
DONALDSON*'s garden and* PRINCE GEORGE *sitting in*
among the band. Her song from the garden mingles with
the song on the soundtrack as if for a moment she and
CARLA *are performing a duet. We cut back to* DONALDSON
by her bed.
I don't think I am exaggerating when I say that was
one of the best afternoons I've ever spent . . . (*He*
smiles.) and I don't say that lightly, considering the
charmed life I've led . . .
The shots are getting closer and closer on JESSIE*'s eyes,*
DONALDSON*'s tone is intense.*
You remember that day, don't you, Jessie? Just blink if
you remember it, blink, Jessie . . .
The music hangs for a moment, JESSIE*'s eyes shut.*
He played the drums! (DONALDSON *taps the palms of*
his hands on the bedside table.) The Prince on the
drums! . . . The Prince and the jazz band! . . . He was
drunk, wasn't he?! . . . That was quite a moment,
wasn't it, Jessie?! You can picture that again, can't you,
Jessie . . . ?
The song is getting louder and louder, the camera tight on
her face. JESSIE*'s eyes flicker for a moment. The nurse*
stands up. DONALDSON*'s face close.*

Picture that Jessie, yes . . .
Suddenly JESSIE*'s eyes open, a tiny glance, taking in*
DONALDSON *and the room.*
That's right, dear girl . . .

INT. IMPERIAL BALLROOM. DAY
We cut to the band playing the last chords of the song as the
dowagers finish their meal. On the German table there are just
two people left now. There is a polite ripple of applause as the
band finishes. We see a member of the hotel staff come on stage
and whisper something to CARLA. *She shrieks with excitement*
and immediately runs across to tell LOUIS, *who grins broadly*
and turns and breaks the news to SCHLESINGER. *One of the*
dowagers is watching this with detached interest through hooded
eyes.

   We cut to LOUIS *approaching the microphone; he is smiling,*
elated.

LOUIS: We have just had some news which I really feel I
        must immediately share with all of you . . . Miss Jessie
        Taylor, who has sung from this stage so often, and
        who as many of you will be aware, has been in
        hospital in a coma . . . she has just woken up, she is
        back with us!
        There is a rustle of conversation among the dowagers, a
        pleased buzz at the news. SCHLESINGER *is now standing*
        next to LOUIS, *he takes the microphone.*
SCHLESINGER: What a perfect Christmas present that is,
        for all of us . . . and the hotel of course! (*He grins.*)
        Especially . . . Come on, everybody, a round of
        applause, ladies and gentlemen, for Miss Jessie Taylor!
        The dowagers start clapping; one of them even struggles to
        her feet to applaud the news.

INT. JESSIE'S HOSPITAL ROOM. MORNING
We cut to JESSIE*'s bedside, morning light.* LOUIS, CARLA,
STANLEY, PAMELA *and* SARAH *are staring down at* JESSIE, *as
she lies swathed in bandages. Her eyes are open, she recognises
them, a warm dreamy smile. She stretches out her hand and
touches* CARLA*'s fingers.* NURSE POLLOCK *is watching.*

CARLA: Darling?! How are you feeling?
   JESSIE *smiles back, her eyes are full of medication. She
   holds* CARLA*'s hand.*
NURSE POLLOCK: She is still very sedated of course,
   because of the wounds she has received. It'll be a little
   while before she is sitting up and chatting – with a
   head injury like she has had, it is very difficult to tell
   how long that'll be, and it is vital she has enough rest,
   so visiting times will be very strictly limited.
   LOUIS *smiles down at* JESSIE *as* NURSE POLLOCK*'s
   officious voice rings out.*

INT. HOSPITAL CORRIDOR. MORNING
We cut to LOUIS, CARLA, STANLEY, PAMELA *and* SARAH
*walking along the main hospital corridor towards the entrance.
The detectives,* HORTON *and* GUNSON, *are standing near the
entrance watching them approach.*
   STANLEY, *in ebullient mood, yells out to them.*

STANLEY: She's not well enough to be talked to yet,
   gentlemen . . . Your interrogation will have to wait.
HORTON: We have just been informed of that, Mr Mitchell,
   yes. (*He turns to* LOUIS.) Mr Lester, is it possible to
   have one very quick word?
   LOUIS *nods and moves into a corner of the passage with
   them. The others wait near the entrance, chattering
   excitedly about* JESSIE*'s recovery.*

HORTON: We have spoken to Mr Luscombe, who says he
   caught the 9:30 sleeper to Paris and he claims there
   are quite a few witnesses who must have seen him on
   the train.

LOUIS: I definitely saw him at 11:30 that night at the
   Imperial.

HORTON: Yes, I thought you were absolutely clear about
   that. (*Sharply, watching him.*) Very good. We haven't
   been able to talk to these witnesses yet, Mr Lester, or
   the passport officer, it being Christmas . . .

GUNSON: And trains are trains, aren't they?!

HORTON: Yes . . . People are not always certain what they
   see on them. (*Slight smile.*) Especially at night. We will
   check the journey, Mr Lester.

   LOUIS *looks reassured.*

INT. MUSIC EXPRESS OFFICE. DAY
We cut to a chart being pinned to the wall of the Music
Express *office by* ERIC.
   We cut wide to see he is being watched by STANLEY, *who is
leaning against the wall, and* ROSIE, *who is sitting at a desk.
All around the walls are pinned pieces of paper with section
headings, diagrams, arrows and question marks, forming a
collage.*

ERIC: So what do you think? Our first edition of the New
   Year, I thought we should see it all planned out!

STANLEY: It looks scintillating.

ERIC: We've got the four sections now, first the 'Music
   Section', of course, then the 'Best Buy' section,
   including gramophones, wirelesses, and probably very
   soon televisors as well, then the 'Latest News' section,
   all the news from the entertainment world, which
   naturally this week includes the progress of Miss

Jessie Taylor . . . (*He turns.*) I think the way you've
written about that, Stanley, is rather tasteful actually,
and quite vivid . . .
STANLEY *smiles a small smile at this. He is biding his
time.*
And then lastly, the 'Further Afield' section, where we
can have developments from around the world, things
like the electronic music, maybe accompanied by a
good photograph of the equipment! (*He smiles
enthusiastically.*) What do you think?

ROSIE: It's very thorough Eric.

STANLEY (*suddenly*): Where the hell is the Farquhar and
Tonk cartoon?

ERIC: Oh that's still here . . . down here somewhere . . .
He peers at the skirting near the floor.

STANLEY: By the wastepaper basket?!

ERIC: Yes that's right, near the back of the magazine.
*We see images of Farquhar and Tonk at a New Year's Eve
party running up a huge staircase.* ERIC *turns to*
STANLEY.

ERIC: I think on balance we should keep it, some weeks
it's quite funny – their anarchic adventures, coming
face to face with the powerful and being rude to them,
allowing the readership a little wish fulfilment, I can
see the point of it. But maybe the settings should be a
little more modern? This week for instance, they cause
mischief at a New Year's Eve party at a grand house,
but maybe it should be a little more normal for the
readers? Like Trafalgar Square?

ROSIE: You mean among the crowds? Meeting different
sorts of characters from all walks of life?

STANLEY: Blimey, what is it?! I'm being told by a public
schoolboy to be more a man of the people! (*Turning to*
ROSIE.) Is this something you've been hatching
together, you two?!

ROSIE: Certainly not, no.

ERIC: No, it's just a suggestion. (*He surveys his diagrams.*) Change can be exciting you know . . . and bring in new readers!

STANLEY: New readers will be good, Eric, and rather necessary – because when our present readership sees all your sections they'll be leaving us in droves.

ROSIE: We don't know that, Stanley, a new layout may be good, take people by surprise . . .

STANLEY: Well, let's find out shall we? (*Sharp grin.*) Let's try it and see who's right! (*He moves towards the door.*) I'd hate to stand in the way of change, me of all people . . . And now I've got to be somewhere! (*He turns in the doorway.*) Where are you seeing in the New Year, Eric?

ERIC: Oh I've some modest plans, nothing out of the ordinary. How about you?

STANLEY: Oh, I've got something rather special planned . . .

EXT. LADY CREMONE'S HOUSE / OUTBUILDINGS. LATE AFTERNOON

We see a series of quick cuts of atmospheric party decorations moving in the wind. Lanterns, lights in the trees, flowers arranged along the courtyard walls, modern sculptures, bronze heads staring out expectantly. We cut wide and we see we are on LADY CREMONE*'s estate. The stable-block courtyard has been transformed. Hanging from the trees in the mouth of the courtyard is another sculpture made of long metal tubes and seashells, moving in the wind making a shimmering noise.* LADY CREMONE *is standing in the middle of the stable block with* STANLEY. *Three servants are finishing arranging the decorations and are just turning on the lights in the trees.*

LADY CREMONE *smiles and turns to* STANLEY.

LADY CREMONE: What do you think?

STANLEY: It's splendid, elegant – naturally. (*Smiles.*) But original too.

LADY CREMONE (*laughs*): When will you ever tell me the truth Stanley?

STANLEY: I always do!

LADY CREMONE: Well I want to tell you something.
(*She opens the door in the central building of the courtyard.*) This building here hasn't been used since the war, since my sons died. My son Ralph used this as a studio . . . He was an artist, I think he was quite talented . . . (*She smiles to herself.*) I like to think so anyway . . . (*She indicates the sculpture moving in the wind.*) That's one of his . . .

STANLEY: I thought it must be. I like the noise it makes . . .

LADY CREMONE (*stares at it for a moment*): And those figures over there, those are his too. I've decided why not have them on display tonight?

STANLEY: Of course, he was talented, you are right.

LADY CREMONE: Yes, so this place has been shut up all this time, but that couldn't go on for ever . . . (*She looks at* STANLEY *with feeling.*) Could it?

STANLEY (*firmly*): It could not, no.

LADY CREMONE: No. (*There is sadness in her eyes, then it lifts.*) I thought it would be good to have the party here rather than in the house. (*She smiles.*) More fun . . .
A convey of three cars is heading up the drive in the distance.

Good Lord, our first guests are arriving already! I must change, Stanley!

STANLEY (*staring at her elegant dress, genuinely surprised*): I thought you were changed already!

LADY CREMONE *laughs.*

EXT. STABLE BLOCK. NIGHT

It is night now. We cut to the sound of laughter. The camera is snaking its way through the central door of the barnlike building in the courtyard. Inside there is one long L-shaped table groaning with food and candles. The barn is decorated with flowers and garlands. Three servants stand along the walls attending to the party. At the table, are LADY CREMONE, DONALDSON, MASTERSON, LOUIS, STANLEY, PAMELA *and* SARAH, CARLA *and about five members of the band including* JOE *the trumpeter. There are about seven other guests, friends of* LADY CREMONE. *They are eating the fish course of the giant meal. Everybody's filled with drink and New Year spirit.*

DONALDSON: Fabulous fish . . . I don't think I've ever been at a banquet – and I've been at a few in my time – but I don't think I've been at one held in a cowshed before!

LADY CREMONE: Well, in fact this building was originally used for pigs.

PAMELA: What a perfect place to guzzle then!

LOUIS (*to* SARAH): It would make a tremendous photo . . .

SARAH: I know! But I've been forbidden to take any at all –

LADY CREMONE: Yes, nobody's allowed to work this evening, absolutely not. Sarah's not to take any photographs, and the band is not going to have to play, total escape from all work is called for . . . This is my first party for fifteen years, so I think I'm allowed to make the rules . . .

We suddenly see LOUIS *look up and stare through the open door of the barn. For a moment he is the only one that notices, the others are eating and laughing. Through the open door, at first glimpsed from a distance and framed by the lanterns,* JULIAN *is walking straight towards us. He is in evening dress, with a white scarf dashingly thrown over his shoulder. He is carrying a large box which is done up in colourful wrapping paper.* PAMELA *sees him next, and*

then the others. MASTERSON *smiles a small smile,* LADY
CREMONE *beams.*

JULIAN *calls out to them as he nears the barn door.*

JULIAN: My dear friends, here I am and I come bearing
gifts! But more of that later – I've had a terrific notion
which I'm dying to tell you about . . . (*He stops in the
doorway.*) Oh how wonderful to see you all!

EXT. THE STABLE BLOCK. NIGHT

*There is an expectant hush. They are all standing outside after
the dinner in a semicircle, watching* JULIAN *open his large
parcel which he has placed on a trestle table. There are excited
laughs and* STANLEY *calls out to* JULIAN *to get a move on.*
LOUIS *is standing a little apart, watching* JULIAN *carrying on
as if he hasn't a care in the world.* JULIAN *smiles ebulliently,
and produces out of the main parcel a series of smaller parcels
all done up in different-coloured paper.* JULIAN *shoves them to
one side.*

JULIAN: Of course there are Christmas presents for
everybody, little things I've chosen for you from Paris,
but I've also brought this – (*He produces a small basket
covered in wrapping paper.*) Now nobody laugh at this,
promise! (*He looks up at them all.*) Promise not to
laugh at this . . .

They murmur that they promise.

Because I've had a business notion while I was out
there, my first ever business idea . . .

*Somebody shouts 'No work, can't talk about work
tonight!', but everybody else is fascinated at what* JULIAN
is going to produce. He is in full flow.

JULIAN: Because it is high time I earned my keep . . . and
Mr Masterson – and he's the only one who's heard

about this so far – Mr Masterson thinks it might have
possibilities . . . !

MASTERSON *smiles a small smile.*

So I've had this idea – nobody giggle, promise – (*He
takes a deep breath.*) Why not export English cheese to
the French?!

*He pulls the wrapping off the basket, which contains little
gift-wrapped pieces of cheese.*

Because they're surprisingly interested in our cheeses.
No, they are! And I don't think anybody has realised
that before! Our local cheeses, and I've got some
scrumptious examples here, for us to eat tonight! (*He
looks up with his boyish smile.*) Have I gone mad? Is it
ridiculous? Tell me if it's ridiculous?!

There are cries of 'No!' and applause, PAMELA *smiling
warmly, pleased he has found something to engage his
energy.*

PAMELA: It's not ridiculous, no, Julian.

DONALDSON: The future is made of cheese, is it?!

MASTERSON: It has possibilities . . . I can confirm it is a
business idea I can approve of . . .

JULIAN: That's so tremendous! (*He beams at all of them.*)
You approve!

*There is a sharp cut to a radio set standing on a table in
the middle of the courtyard surrounded by candles. The
characters are grouped around it staring intently, as the
announcer solemnly proclaims:*

RADIO ANNOUNCER: It is eleven o'clock, and we are now –
for the first time ever – going to broadcast New Year's
greetings from a variety of cities around the world . . .
Berlin, Milan, Warsaw, Prague, and a little later, we
are even going to New York. But the first city we are
going to visit is Vienna . . . We are going to Vienna
now . . . Hello Vienna, hello! . . .

PAMELA: But they're too early . . . ! It's not New Year yet –

LADY CREMONE: It is there! All the cities of Europe linked together . . .

DONALDSON: And what a satisfying thought that is . . . All of us drinking together, raising a toast at the same time.

STANLEY: The power of the wireless, it's amazing, isn't it?! (*He grins.*) Somebody should start a music magazine . . . !

LADY CREMONE: Ah yes, I've been meaning to talk to you about that, Stanley . . . (*He turns surprised.*) You should begin to have more of Europe in your magazine – and America too, like *Time* magazine . . .

STANLEY: Don't you start! You sound like Eric – except not even he wants me to be like *Time* magazine . . . !

LADY CREMONE: Well, why not? Why shouldn't you be? Why can't you be ambitious for your magazine?

STANLEY: I am ambitious for it, probably too much!

LADY CREMONE: All sorts of great publications started as small lighthearted magazines and then grew. (*She looks straight at him.*) You mustn't be afraid of being serious once in a while, Stanley. (*Warmly.*) Using that mind of yours . . .

The sculpture in the tree is making its shimmering noise near them.

STANLEY: I think I am serious. (*He grins.*) I can be surprisingly serious, underneath everything –

LADY CREMONE (*she smiles*): You must prove it to me, Stanley!

STANLEY: I most certainly will, at the first opportunity! I put you on the cover of the magazine, remember. I think I can be –

LADY CREMONE: We'll speak about this further but not tonight – I've broken my own rule already, talking about work!

*She stares at the guests laughing and drinking together
and listening to the wireless from across Europe.*

But they're not, thank goodness! They really do seem
to be having fun, don't they?

STANLEY: Of course they are. (*He helps himself to more
champagne.*) And I intend to have a wonderful time,
Lavinia, tonight – (*He smiles.*) while being serious of
course . . .

We cut to JULIAN *coming up to* LOUIS, CARLA *and*
SARAH, *who are standing surrounded by lanterns.*

JULIAN*'s mood is so happy after his idea has gone down
well.*

JULIAN: It's so tremendous to be back in England, my
friends, and Jessie is getting better too . . . ! I went to
the hospital but they said she was sleeping and I
couldn't see her . . .

LOUIS *is watching him carefully.*

CARLA: She's smiling a lot more now and saying a few
words more to me each day . . .

JULIAN: I brought her flowers, of course, but I suddenly
realised I should have brought her something more
special, like a songbird in a cage, so she could wake
up to this lovely sound each morning – just think how
happy that would make you feel!

CARLA: That would be wonderful.

They move off together. LOUIS *watches* JULIAN*'s sunny,
untroubled manner.*

SARAH *notices* LOUIS' *tense expression.*

SARAH: What's the matter?

LOUIS: Julian seems so happy.

SARAH: But of course he would be. He loves Jessie, he
really does . . . and now she's getting better. He's in
love with her, you must know that?!

Suddenly a large bell is rung by one of the servants.

DONALDSON *calls out.*

DONALDSON: The time is nigh! Everybody, we're off! It'll
      soon be midnight.

LADY CREMONE: Yes, it's time to join the villagers, to see
      in the New Year.

EXT. MAIN STREET VILLAGE. NIGHT

*We cut to a crane shot of the main street of the village at two
minutes before midnight. There's a street party, with tables of
refreshments, light pouring from the village hall, a loudspeaker
tied to a lamppost broadcasting the radio. Some of the villagers
are watching from their front rooms, the small cottages that line
the stark main street, but there is a group of them standing with
the main characters staring up at the loudspeaker.* JOE *the
trumpeter is improvising a fanfare on his trumpet, the
announcer on the radio is intoning as the crane shot sweeps over
the street and moves towards* PAMELA *and* STANLEY, *who are
drinking together.*

RADIO ANNOUNCER: Any moment we will be crossing over
      to Westminster to hear Big Ben strike in the New Year,
      it is now two minutes to midnight, and immediately
      after that the Archbishop of Canterbury will give his
      address.

      JULIAN *is filling people's glasses with champagne and
      chatting and joking with members of the crowd.* PAMELA
      whispers to STANLEY.

PAMELA: Could anything feel more like it was meant to
      happen than all of us together on this little street to
      see in the New Year? Isn't it perfect?!

STANLEY: Yes, maybe a little strange too. (*He indicates*
      MASTERSON.) I never expected to be seeing in the
      New Year with him, for instance, but now you
      mention it, it is kind of perfect.

      We cut to LOUIS *and* SARAH *together.* SARAH *is studying*

the faces of the villagers as they look up towards the
loudspeaker, waiting for Big Ben to strike.

SARAH: Because I can't take any photos – I have to
remember what I see! It's a long time since I've had
to rely on my memory! Normally I just click away . . .

She sees LOUIS *watching* MASTERSON *and* JULIAN
together. JULIAN *is talking animatedly,* MASTERSON, *his*
tall impassive figure towering over the crowd, is nodding
and listening, bending his head as if to catch everything
JULIAN *is saying.*

SARAH: Why do you keep watching Julian?

LOUIS: Don't you think it's odd . . .

He stares at MASTERSON *and* JULIAN, *unable to take his*
eyes off them.

Since the attack on Jessie nobody has mentioned about
Mr Masterson and what happened in his hotel suite,
the night Julian took me there . . . The girl Hannah
and everything?

SARAH: Mr Masterson was at the theatre with Lady
Cremone when it happened! And then at a first-night
party! Come on, Louis, he can't have been involved . . .

LOUIS *suddenly turns, his face close to hers.*

LOUIS: Just before I found Jessie, I saw Julian in the hotel
passage.

SARAH: You can't have done! He was on the train to Paris!

LOUIS: I did see him, and I spoke to him.

We see JULIAN *starting a countdown towards midnight,*
calling out the seconds.

SARAH: But he arrived in Paris when he was meant to –

LOUIS: I don't know how he did that, but he was in the
hotel . . .

SARAH: You've told the police?

LOUIS: Of course I have.

SARAH: Well, they'll be able to find out if he was on the
train, there'll be the passport control –

LOUIS: Yes. (*Watching* JULIAN.) That's right.

SARAH: And Jessie will tell us what happened anyway. (*She is watching* JULIAN.) There'll be an explanation about Julian, Louis, look at him! He wouldn't be here if anything had happened involving him . . . (*Watching* JULIAN's *exuberant mood*.) Not like this!

JULIAN is now standing next to LADY CREMONE *and* DONALDSON, *calling out the last few seconds of the year.* LOUIS *watches him,* JULIAN's *boyish innocent face.*

We hear the sound of Big Ben striking over the loudspeaker, the villagers and the characters let out cheers and applause. DONALDSON *gives* LADY CREMONE *a polite hug. We see* STANLEY *borrow* JOE's *trumpet, and to everybody's surprise he plays a little fanfare rather competently. He grins at the applause and waves delightedly at* LOUIS. *Then we hear the sound of the Archbishop of Canterbury over the loudspeaker, beginning his address.*

JULIAN: Oh, we can't listen to him tonight! Come on, everybody, find some music!

The dial on the wireless is moved to Radio Luxembourg, and dance music pours out.

That's right! Now somebody make a speech, one can't start the New Year without a speech, it's unlucky! Come on, who's it going to be?!

STANLEY leaps on to a chair holding a glass of champagne. He is pleasantly drunk, his mood totally uninhibited.

STANLEY: I'm not making a speech – (*People calling out to him.*) because I'm only a visitor here, but I will propose a toast – to tonight! A night where absolutely everything is allowed . . .

We hear some lewd shouts from somebody in the crowd.

Yes! And when no sleep is possible –

He looks at LADY CREMONE.

Before one has to be serious in the morning . . . and a night completely and utterly without Eric! Who none

of you know, but who is obsessed with machines . . .
so before we are all overrun with machines, we will
have the party of our lives! And to open this year
officially – to launch it like a ship – I give you, of
course, Lady Cremone!

LADY CREMONE, *who is a little drunk herself, smiles
graciously. She faces the villagers.*

LADY CREMONE: Well, as many of you will know, this is my
first party for such a long time, and I'm so enjoying
myself.

There's applause and cheers.

And so I hope are all of you. These have been very
difficult times I know for many of you – but I fervently
hope and believe this is going to be a hugely better
year for all of us . . . (*Self-mocking smile.*) And that
definitely applies to me too, because I've just invested
in my first ever West End flop! So – here's to a
wonderful year for everybody and God bless you all!

*We cut to the villagers and all the main characters dancing
with each other on the village street. Dance music is
pouring out of the loudspeaker and some of the band have
produced their instruments and are playing along with the
radio music, improvising on top of it, an exuberant
energised sound. We see* CARLA *dancing with one of the
villagers.* DONALDSON *and* MASTERSON *are standing
together surveying the scene.* MASTERSON *is staring at the
dancing impassively,* DONALDSON *smoking a cigar.*

DONALDSON: I like this very much – the villagers and the
band and how welcome they've made them. I always
say people are far more tolerant than they're given
credit for, far more imaginative . . .

MASTERSON: The world is changing, there's no doubt
about that . . . is that a good thing?!

*He takes a sip of his drink, his expression deadpan as he
stares out.*

I think it probably is . . . Now I really must have a dance.

We cut to LOUIS *watching* MASTERSON *dance with* LADY CREMONE, *and* JULIAN *dancing with* CARLA. *We move in on* LOUIS, *intercut with the euphoric faces and mood of the party on the street. He watches everybody celebrating together. Suddenly we see a flashback to the passage of the Imperial, the night he found* JESSIE, *the image of* JULIAN *waving goodbye. Now the image is slightly indistinct,* JULIAN *barely recognisable in the shadows.*

We hear SARAH*'s voice calling* LOUIS. *We cut back to the night street.*

SARAH *leans her head on his shoulder and whispers in his ear.*

SARAH: Come on, you're not allowed just to watch . . .
She envelops him in her arms, her body close.

LOUIS: You're right, I'm not just going to watch!
They begin to dance, he holds her very close, their bodies pressed together.

We cut to STANLEY *coming up to* PAMELA.

STANLEY: May I have the privilege of this dance?

PAMELA: You may.

They begin to dance together, PAMELA *stops.*

PAMELA: Kiss me, Stanley.

STANLEY: But of course.

PAMELA *and* STANLEY *kiss under the lamppost, as the wireless blasts out above their heads and the band plays.* PAMELA *entwines her fingers around* STANLEY*'s, her manner warm and sensual.*

PAMELA: That's better.

STANLEY: It certainly is . . .

PAMELA: I liked your speech Stanley . . . (*Her lips hover close, she touches his cheek.*) No machines, and no worries of any kind.

We cut to LADY CREMONE *dancing with* MASTERSON,
her eyes shining as she loses herself in the party.

EXT. WOOD. EARLY MORNING
We cut to the wood on the edge of LADY CREMONE*'s estate.
It is dawn.* STANLEY *and* PAMELA, SARAH *and* LOUIS, *are
moving through the trees in their evening dress,* STANLEY
carrying a champagne bottle and a glass, PAMELA *carrying one
of* JULIAN*'s little cheese parcels. They are full of adrenalin from
lack of sleep, but they're moving over-carefully among the
undergrowth in a hazy dreamlike state.* PAMELA *is moving
ahead of* STANLEY*; she turns to let him catch up.*

STANLEY: You look so beautiful this morning . . .
　　　　He takes her hand and touches her cheek.
　　　　Not a hair out of place, but of course you often never
　　　　go to bed, don't you –
PAMELA: That makes two of us, Stanley . . . (*Looking down
　　　　at the cheese parcel.*) Look, we've eaten nearly all of it,
　　　　and it was good wasn't it?! My little brother, maybe
　　　　he's right, maybe it is a wonderful plan, selling English
　　　　cheese to the French!
　　　　They watch SARAH *and* LOUIS *moving among the trees
　　　　together, holding hands, stopping and talking, standing like
　　　　lovers really close.*
STANLEY: Do you think it's becoming truly serious
　　　　between them?
PAMELA: Well, why not! Why shouldn't it? I think they
　　　　should get married! That would be wonderful,
　　　　wouldn't it – shock everybody?! It would be so
　　　　exciting . . .
　　　　*They can hear a noise, a mysterious high sound coming
　　　　from somewhere ahead of them in the wood. The four of
　　　　them move through the trees towards it, deeply curious.*

They come to a clearing, in the distance they can see
MASTERSON *sitting on his own on a log with a wind-up*
gramophone next to him. He is singing to himself, along
to the music, in a totally deadpan unmusical fashion.
A strange noise.
    MASTERSON *is unaware of them.*

PAMELA: Mr Masterson singing! I never thought I'd see
that!

LOUIS: I don't expect many people have . . .
Suddenly MASTERSON *stands up, still humming and*
singing. He takes off the record, slips it into a sleeve, and
then packs up the gramophone and walks slowly away
from them. He is holding himself very upright. He
disappears among the trees, still humming.

INT. HOSPITAL PASSAGE/JESSIE'S ROOM. DAY
We cut to the sound of a radio news bulletin, about preparations
in the US for the inauguration of the newly elected President
Roosevelt. We are tracking down the hospital corridor with
LOUIS *towards* JESSIE*'s room, the sound of the radio getting*
louder all the time. LOUIS *is holding a bouquet of red roses.*
Halfway down the passage, a police constable is sitting reading
a newspaper; he watches LOUIS *walk past with a beady stare.*
LOUIS *reaches* JESSIE*'s room and knocks, the radio bulletin has*
moved on to a parochial domestic story. LOUIS *enters the room,*
the radio is now very loud. JESSIE *is lying in bed, her head still*
bandaged. The room is absolutely swamped in flowers on every
possible surface. The young NURSE *is sitting in the corner.*
JESSIE *turns her head as* LOUIS *enters. An immediate look of*
recognition and delight comes into her eyes. The NURSE *turns*
down the radio. LOUIS *stands close to the bed.*

LOUIS: Hello Jessie . . .
JESSIE: Louis.

She stretches out her hand and touches his sleeve, and then his hand.

NURSE: She's had so many flowers. (*Indicating his red roses.*) We've had to put a lot elsewhere in the hospital. There's even been some from Buckingham Palace.

LOUIS *looks down and sees a card with the Buckingham Palace crest, HRH Prince George, and then handwritten 'Get better soon!'* LOUIS *crouches down by the bed.*

LOUIS: How are you feeling now?

JESSIE *doesn't reply, her eyes are sleepy, she's still sedated. She smiles again.* LOUIS' *voice is very soft.*

What happened to you Jessie? Can you tell me?

JESSIE (*very quietly*): Louis, it's so nice to see you.

NURSE: She's not nearly well enough yet to talk about it.

JESSIE: Sit . . .

LOUIS: I'll sit. (*He sits on the chair close.*)

JESSIE: That's right.

She smiles again at him and touches his hand.

Sit closer, and talk to me.

LOUIS (*moves the chair as close as he can*): I'm here, for as long as you need me.

INT. MUSIC EXPRESS OFFICE. DAY

MR WAX *walks into the main* Music Express *office, flourishing the new edition of the magazine.* STANLEY *and* ROSIE *look up from their desks. The messenger* MICK *is tidying papers under* ERIC's *watchful eye.*

MR WAX: Well I have to say I like it, our new look, four sections, it's so very clear now. It has authority – I always felt we needed a little more of that, just a touch. Now we know where everything is! (*He waves it at them as he leaves.*) A very good start. Keep it all going!

STANLEY: And how many copies have we sold?

MR WAX: Too early for that, Stanley . . . (*As he disappears.*)
but I'm sure it will be up, my nose tells me it is up.

ERIC: That's good, isn't it? (*To* STANLEY.) Maybe we can
start talking about next week's cover now?

ROSIE: Eric thinks we should try something daring, and
not just put another bandleader on the cover.
The phone starts to ring.

STANLEY: Quite right. Let's put a big picture of the
televisor on the cover, that will surprise people.
He answers the phone.
Yes, *Music Express*, what? Sorry . . . who did you say
you were? . . . Ah!
He looks up, grins and covers the receiver with his hand.
It is the German Embassy! (*Then back into the phone.*)
Yes, of course, I'd be delighted to help. When is it for?
Well, I will give it some thought, definitely give it a lot
of thought . . .

ERIC: Ask if they have more information about Herr
Pfenninger and his orchestra without musicians?!
Maybe he's going to do a demonstration over here?
(*He moves closer.*) Go on, ask them about Herr
Pfenninger . . .

STANLEY (*waving his arms at* ERIC *to shut up*): I will ring
you back as soon as I've had an idea. Yes, that is a
firm undertaking. (*He rings off.*) Well it must be your
new look, Eric, we've never had a call from an embassy
before. They're having an important function and they
want us to recommend a band to play there.

ROSIE: Not jazz, of course!

A close-up of STANLEY, *a glint in his eye.*

STANLEY: But of course not.

INT. IMPERIAL BASEMENT/TILED PARLOUR. EVENING
We cut to LOUIS *stretched out, reading a book in the tiled*
parlour in the basement. JOE *and a couple of other band*
members are also in the room, getting ready for the evening
performance. STANLEY *bangs through the door.*

STANLEY: You're here, splendid!
LOUIS: Stanley?
STANLEY: I'd like a word in private.

INT. IMPERIAL PASSAGE/CUPBOARD ROOM. EVENING
LOUIS *and* STANLEY *are walking along the kitchen passage.*
THORNTON *is busy checking room service orders.*

STANLEY: Where can we go?
LOUIS: What's this about?
STANLEY: Ah . . . !
LOUIS: Will this do?
    They go into a cupboard room full of silver dishes, silver
    teapots and soup tureens. STANLEY *closes the door.*
STANLEY: This is perfect. (*He lifts up a silver cloche.*) I
    never know what these things are called?
    He turns sharply to face LOUIS.
    Nathan told me when you played here on Christmas
    Day some Germans from the Embassy walked out as
    soon as you came on . . .
LOUIS: Well, that was to be expected, wasn't it?
STANLEY (*suddenly flaring, his mood surprisingly serious*):
    What do you mean, 'that's to be expected'? Does
    nothing make you angry, Louis?!
LOUIS: Of course it does. But from what I've heard about
    this new lot in Germany, these National Socialists,
    they want to –

STANLEY: String you all up?! Can't wait to do it? Yes, that's precisely what they want!

LOUIS: Let's just say they don't like jazz music quite a lot! So it was to be expected. But that doesn't mean I'm happy about it . . .

STANLEY: Not happy about it? Is that all?

LOUIS (*thoughtfully*): No, it's not all no. But it's not clear what one can do about it right this moment.

He looks straight at STANLEY.

Why are you suddenly so interested anyway?

STANLEY: What do you mean, 'suddenly'? It's not 'suddenly'! Believe it or not, I think when one sees intolerance like that, as crude as that, you have to do something to expose it . . .

LOUIS: And that's going to make a difference?!

He smiles despite himself at STANLEY*'s exuberant confidence.*

You, Stanley Mitchell – music journalist – are going to make a difference! Get rid of prejudice all by yourself?

STANLEY: I didn't say I'd make a difference. (*Sharp, self-mocking smile.*) Not right away!

LOUIS: So?

STANLEY *turns.*

What's your idea?

STANLEY: The German Embassy are having a little do because they have a new Chancellor in Berlin. Goodbye to old Hindenburg, hello to Herr Hitler – they've asked me to choose a band for them. (*He grins.*) What if we had a little fun?

LOUIS: That would be terrific – but they'd never book my band, they wouldn't let us anywhere near the building even . . .

STANLEY: No, of course not. But I thought I might hand pick some musicians I know and take it from there. (*He grins.*) I haven't conducted in years.

LOUIS: You? You conducting?!

STANLEY: Yes.

LOUIS (*grins*): So that's the reason you're doing it?!

STANLEY (*unabashed*): I had my own band at school
    remember, it was very successful. (*He smiles.*) We won
    a competition . . .

INT. IMPERIAL BASEMENT PASSAGE. EVENING
We cut to JULIAN *in the basement passage talking to* CARLA
through her open dressing-room door. CARLA *is in her show
costume and looking at herself in the mirror. Her dressing room
is still in one of the rooms off the kitchen passage, but it has
been converted into a proper space with bulbs around the mirror
and a carpet.*

JULIAN: No, it's going to take off, my business, people
    don't laugh when I mention it . . . I expected them
    to, but they don't. You thought it was a good idea,
    didn't you?

CARLA: Oh yes, but I've never eaten French food, so I
    don't know what they think . . . and I've never been
    to France . . .

JULIAN: You'll be having your own tour there with your
    own band very soon.

    CARLA *laughs.*

    And you'll open our first store in Paris!

    LOUIS *and* STANLEY *are approaching down the passage,*
    JULIAN *calls out to them.*

    Hello you two! Here we are, all in the basement
    together, just like old times . . .

LOUIS (*staring straight at him*): Except for Jessie, of course.

JULIAN: Yes, she's getting better all the time they say. I went
    to see her, but they said she was sleeping again . . .

and of course they said I couldn't bring pets into the
hospital . . .
He smiles at them, he seems so uninhibited and full of life.
Which is a pity, because what I really think I should
take her is a parrot – just think how wonderful it
would be to wake up and the first thing that happens
is, you are talked to by a bird! It would give you such
delight, don't you think? (*His boyish smile.*) Make you
feel you have to get better!

INT. GERMAN EMBASSY. EARLY EVENING
*We cut to a tracking shot going up the main staircase of the
German Embassy and through the door into a large reception
room, as we follow* SARAH, *dressed in an evening gown, entering
the Embassy drinks party. We see everything first through* SARAH'*s
eyes: the select gathering of guests, English society women mixing
with the Ambassador and his staff. The German Embassy staff
are divided between three older men surrounding the silver-
haired Ambassador, and a new contingent of about seven younger
National Socialist staff, who are moving, smiling charmingly,
among the guests. There's also a group of important-looking
British men, among them* DONALDSON *and* MASTERSON.
PAMELA *is standing talking to some of the younger Germans
when she sees* SARAH *enter. She smiles delightedly and waves.*
 DONALDSON *is peering at the books on the shelves.*

DONALDSON: They're absolutely stuffed full of Sherlock
    Holmes, Tennyson and Dickens here!
MASTERSON: Well they're right – it's all they need to know
    about British life isn't it? (*He smiles dryly.*)
    *We cut to the group of white musicians filing in at the end
    of the room.* STANLEY *comes on with them and stands in
    front of them. He is dressed in a white dinner jacket,
    looking every inch the bandleader. He gives a little nod*

to the assembled company and then starts conducting,
a languid foxtrot.

    SARAH *is standing with* PAMELA.

SARAH: Stanley as a bandleader, it's so funny, I didn't
    expect to see that! He's not bad either . . .

We see a close-up of PAMELA, *her eyes shining, as if she is*
expecting something else to happen.

PAMELA: He really thinks he is living one of his cartoons,
    he is being Farquhar and Tonk . . . inside one of their
    adventures . . .

PAMELA glances sideways, watching the new Germans as
they tuck into canapes. She watches the younger National
Socialists.

Maybe Julian ought to try selling cheese to this lot
too! (*She smiles.*) He really is taking it seriously, he's
back in Paris now launching the business.

The old silver-haired Ambassador is looking a little uneasy
as he hosts the party, surrounded by his new staff.

    We cut to DONALDSON *and* MASTERSON *surveying the*
throng.

DONALDSON: The new and the old Germany . . . all in the
    same room.

MASTERSON: Yes, I need to find out more about this new
    lot and if they can possibly last . . .

EXT. LONDON STREET. NIGHT
We cut outside, on to a London street. The street lighting is now
on. LOUIS *is leaning against a lamppost. He is in evening dress*
and wearing a coat. He is calmly smoking.

INT. MAIN RECEPTION ROOM GERMAN EMBASSY. EVENING
We cut back inside the German Embassy party. The band are
just finishing their number. STANLEY *is conducting very*

seriously, but with a little flourish as well. When the number
ends there is polite applause. STANLEY *gives the guests a little*
bow and is about to resume, when the pianist hunches over the
piano keys as if he has been taken ill. STANLEY *moves to the*
pianist and then turns to face the room.

STANLEY: Ladies and gentlemen excuse me a moment . . .
    (*Indicating the band.*) But they can manage without
    me for one number, as I'm sure you will see.
    He moves off the stage with the pianist.

INT. PASSAGE/KITCHEN. GERMAN EMBASSY. EVENING
We see the pianist putting on a hat and coat and scarf over his
dinner jacket in a little ante-room, STANLEY *urging him to*
hurry. Then they move through the Embassy kitchen, past a
chef preparing canapes towards the back entrance, which is
guarded by a couple of Embassy staff. The pianist is leaning on
STANLEY *for support, his head against his shoulder.*

STANLEY: He's feeling a little sick – some fresh air might
    make a difference . . .

EXT. LONDON STREET. NIGHT
We cut to LOUIS *and the pianist swapping hats, coats and*
scarves as STANLEY *urges them to hurry.* LOUIS *and* STANLEY
are laughing, almost giggling with adrenalin, not taking the
situation too seriously.

STANLEY: Come on! Come on!
LOUIS: They've got the music, have they?
STANLEY: Of course they've got the music, I've thought of
    everything! They'll follow you, they're good musicians.
    He slips the pianist a five-pound note, who then moves off
    with a wave.

More importantly, they think I'm getting them all
recording contracts –

LOUIS: You've told them you're going to make them stars,
did you, Stanley?!

STANLEY: Well let's just say they're more frightened of
Music Express and my reviews than they are of the
Germans!

INT. KITCHEN PASSAGE/GERMAN EMBASSY. NIGHT

*We see STANLEY and LOUIS, inside the Embassy, moving from
the back entrance towards the kitchen. LOUIS, wearing the
pianist's coat and hat, is keeping very close to STANLEY, his
head turned away, the scarf around him, his hands in his
pockets. They are moving fast. STANLEY calls out to the
Embassy staff in the passage.*

STANLEY: It may have worked a little we'll see – but it was
so cold out there we had to come straight back!
One of the staff steps forward to offer assistance.
No, he'll be fine, we need to get back in there for the
next number.

INT. MAIN EMBASSY RECEPTION ROOM. NIGHT

*We cut back to the musicians just finishing their foxtrot. There is
more polite applause. As this is happening, LOUIS slips on to the
stage, now just in evening dress, and sits at the piano. He looks
immaculate in his tails. He nods at the musicians and begins to
play a little intro on the piano.*

*For a moment none of the guests notices the change of pianist.
Two couples are poised to resume dancing, but then a murmur
begins to spread through the Embassy staff and people look at the
band and LOUIS. A hushed silence falls on the room. LOUIS looks
up and gives them a dazzling smile from the piano. STANLEY
walks on to the stage.*

STANLEY: Oh yes, I forgot the introduction, how careless of me. And now, we're truly privileged to have Louis Lester, from the renowned Louis Lester Band as our guest pianist tonight. Louis, who is creating such a sensation currently with his band, has broken off from his busy schedule so he can be with us tonight . . .

LOUIS (*smiles charmingly*): And it's wonderful to be here . . .

STANLEY: So – it's all yours Louis! (*Staring at the audience.*) It's Louis Lester on the piano!

LOUIS *waves to the band from the piano and they erupt into an effervescent jazz dance number. The shock in the room is truly palpable. The younger Embassy staff are staring at* LOUIS *full of disgust. The old Ambassador smiles sheepishly, not certain how he should react, torn between the representatives of the new regime and how to behave in front of his English guests.* PAMELA *is staring with delight. She gives* STANLEY *a wave.*

SARAH (*laughing excitedly*): You knew about this! Why didn't you tell me?!

PAMELA: I didn't think they'd bring it off!

We cut to DONALDSON *standing with* MASTERSON.

DONALDSON: Stanley really is an anarchist! It's rather wonderful . . .

MASTERSON (*glancing around the room*): Something's going to give any moment . . .

LOUIS *is very poised at the piano. We see the glint in his eye, as he takes his revenge really elegantly. We cut back to* SARAH *studying all the faces watching. Suddenly the younger Nazi Embassy staff ostentatiously start to leave the room. The Ambassador is left looking vulnerable, his older staff hesitate, and then one by one they follow the others out of the room. The English guests look bewildered, wondering what the correct etiquette is. And then some of them begin to leave the room too.*

DONALDSON *is watching this fascinated, as the Germans leave their own party.*

The Ambassador is now alone with the remaining small group of English guests. He mumbles some excuse about having to check on the next room and leaves. Three of the servants who are standing along the wall then leave the room too.

The music finishes. For a moment LOUIS, *the band, and* STANLEY *stare down from the stage at the small huddle of the remaining guests, including* SARAH *and* PAMELA, DONALDSON *and* MASTERSON. *There is a crowd of Germans forced on to the landing outside, but able to hear everything.*

STANLEY: Now I believe our special guest has to return to another engagement. (*He grins.*) Maybe at the Palladium . . . so thank you, Louis Lester, a big hand for him now!

INT. MAIN STAIRCASE GERMAN EMBASSY. NIGHT
We cut to STANLEY *and* LOUIS, PAMELA *and* SARAH *walking down the main staircase of the Embassy towards the front door. The Embassy staff are watching them descend with a forbidding silence, some of them staring up at them from the hall, barring their exit. We cut closer to* STANLEY *and* LOUIS; *for the first time they feel the real menace in the situation.* STANLEY *decides to brazen it out.*

STANLEY: Goodnight everybody! The rest of the band have kindly agreed to stay . . .
They reach the bottom of the stairs. We hear the sound of a reassuring foxtrot beginning to be played above them. The English guests are all crowded at the top of the stairs watching what is happening, making it difficult for the Germans to create a scene.

LOUIS *turns and gives a gracious wave. The front door is opened for them.*

EXT. LONDON STREET/DUKE OF YORK STEPS. NIGHT
We cut to a low-angle shot of STANLEY *and* PAMELA, LOUIS *and* SARAH *erupting out of the Embassy and on to the top of the Duke of York steps, the long flight of broad stone steps that runs down the side of the Embassy. The characters are outlined against the sky. Their mood is euphoric. They start to plunge down the steps, whooping with excitement.*

STANLEY: We did it, we absolutely did it!
LOUIS: I really thought we were going to get arrested! I
    thought they were going to come for us on the stairs –
PAMELA: And throw you in a dungeon!
SARAH: They couldn't believe somebody had let this
    happen, a black man playing the piano at their party!
    It could cause a major diplomatic incident . . . !
STANLEY: None of tomorrow's papers will mention it
    probably – but we will. It'll be our next cover story.
    I don't care what Mr Wax says . . .
    *They hear a voice calling after them. They look back. At
    the top of the steps* DONALDSON *is standing smoking his
    cigar, an elegant romantic silhouette against the night sky.
    Smiling, he calls down to them.*
DONALDSON: My congratulations! That was a marvellous
    thing to do –
STANLEY: It was, wasn't it?!
DONALDSON: To have the nerve to do that . . . !
LOUIS: Yes, well, I'm glad I didn't think about it more
    before I did it . . .
DONALDSON: No need to stop now! It could be the first of
    many –
SARAH: Yes, who'll be next?! Some gentlemen's club?!

STANLEY: Or maybe the Queen Charlotte's Ball?!

LOUIS: Hang on a moment, it's me that has to do it, and I definitely think we should quit while we're ahead –

PAMELA: Well, maybe not quite yet, I want you to play for my parents – and that really will be a challenge!

DONALDSON: But to see people behave like that at their own party! I'm going back in there now to hear what they're saying. They're all chattering about it at the tops of their voices. Goodnight, my friends.

They call back goodnight. DONALDSON *moves off, the cigar smoke trailing behind him.* SARAH *watches him go.*

SARAH: I've never seen him look so happy . . .

LOUIS: Oh, I don't know, he always looks happy.

STANLEY: That's because he doesn't have a worry in the world.

LOUIS: So how do we become like him, Stanley?!

SARAH *turns to* LOUIS, *puts her arms round him.*

SARAH: I was so proud watching you do that, it was so exciting!

LOUIS (*loud playfully, so* STANLEY *can hear*): Exciting but pointless.

STANLEY: Not pointless, it had a point.

LOUIS: Which was what?!

STANLEY: It embarrassed the hell out of them – they'll be talking about it for weeks.

He grins at LOUIS *and* SARAH.

And of course if they knew about you two as well . . . !

PAMELA: They'd wake up in the middle of the night screaming . . . !

SARAH *laughs, kisses* LOUIS.

STANLEY: I need some alcohol really badly!

PAMELA: Yes.

They move off down the last flight of steps. LOUIS *turns to* STANLEY.

LOUIS: Do you think they'll make an official complaint about you to Mr Wax? Try to get you dismissed?

STANLEY: Who knows?! I doubt it . . . It's difficult for them, isn't it, they won't want to make themselves look foolish and –

He suddenly stops dead, a tone of mock horror.

Oh my God! I forgot!

PAMELA: What? What is it?

STANLEY: I forgot all about it! Eric gave me firm instructions – I was meant to ask them if they knew anything about Herr Pfenninger and his machines, the orchestra without music. Eric wants to know if he's coming over here, he wants to make a big thing of it, the first electric concert in London! – And I didn't ask!

PAMELA: You'll never be forgiven!

STANLEY: He's waiting right now in the office for a report! I said I'd phone him about it immediately after I found out.

LOUIS: He's waiting in the office?!

STANLEY: Yes –

LOUIS: Well let's go and tell him about what happened –

STANLEY: No, I can't tell him I forgot! –

LOUIS: I'm dying to see this Eric – somebody that makes you nervous, Stanley, I've got to meet this person!

STANLEY: He absolutely doesn't make me nervous. You think I'm frightened of Eric?!

LOUIS: Yes.

STANLEY (*laughing*): That's absolutely not true.

SARAH: We'll soon see, let's go! What could be more lovely than walking through the city on a night like this . . .

She wraps her arms around LOUIS *tightly, holding him close.*

EXT. LONDON PARK. NIGHT
We cut to the four of them walking along a broad path on the edge of Green Park, among the plane trees. The park is deserted except for one eager young man bicycling past vigorously, sounding his bell. SARAH *and* LOUIS *are walking together, laughing, close, their mood still effervescent.* STANLEY *and* PAMELA *are walking a few paces behind them.* PAMELA *slows her pace,* STANLEY *glances at her.*

PAMELA *suddenly stops and looks straight in his eyes.*

PAMELA: I love you.

STANLEY (*as if he might not have heard*): Pamela?

PAMELA: Yes, you did hear right. You thought you'd never hear me say that.

STANLEY: No, why do you think that?

PAMELA: Because it's true, because I didn't think I'd ever hear myself say it either . . . but I love you.
She kisses him once, her tone lightens.
It must have been your conducting tonight, mustn't it?!

STANLEY: I didn't realise it was that good!

PAMELA (*her tone more serious again*): I have no idea of course how long it will last, because you know me Stanley, what a trivial person I am . . .

STANLEY: No, you're not.

PAMELA: Don't be silly, we both know.

STANLEY (*gently*): Maybe that makes two of us then . . .

PAMELA: And we also know you don't love me . . .
She lifts her fingers to his lips to stop him speaking.

STANLEY: Pamela . . .

PAMELA: Shhh . . . (*Very softly.*) Don't say anything . . . not just yet . . . I know I'm right. But for some reason I don't mind at the moment, because maybe I think . . .
She smiles into his eyes.
I can make you love me.

He stares into her eyes. STANLEY *is truly moved. He kisses her.*

The others have stopped further up the path and are watching them.

LOUIS: Come on, you two! Eric is waiting!

EXT. MUSIC EXPRESS BUILDING/STREET. NIGHT

STANLEY *and* PAMELA, LOUIS *and* SARAH *come round the corner in the street where the* Music Express *office is situated. As they approach down the road, they are surprised to see* LADY CREMONE*'s large car parked outside the offices.* LADY CREMONE *is standing next to the car, watching them come towards her. Her chauffeur is a few paces behind.* ROSIE *and* ERIC *are also on the pavement watching their approach and* MR WAX *is smoking nervously in the lighted doorway.*

STANLEY: What are they all doing here so late?

LOUIS: They must have heard already . . . The Embassy's complained immediately, obviously!

STANLEY (*delighted to see* LADY CREMONE *there*): I knew she was up in town, but I never expected her to hear about it this quickly, talk about news travelling fast –

LOUIS: That's the reason you did it, isn't it Stanley, to impress her?!

STANLEY *is staring at the serious demeanour of the group at the end of the street.*

STANLEY: Maybe a little . . . Doesn't look like they're very impressed though! (*He calls out as they reach them.*) Has the Embassy been on the phone already? Mr Wax, I can explain everything –

He stops, seeing their pale faces.

ROSIE: This isn't anything about the Embassy, Stanley.

LADY CREMONE: Louis, I need to talk to you.

STANLEY *stands and waits. He watches* LADY CREMONE
talk to LOUIS *a few paces away on the pavement.* LOUIS'
head jerks back, he moves away from her on the pavement.
His hand goes up to his face. LADY CREMONE *turns to*
STANLEY.

LADY CREMONE: Jessie's dead.

STANLEY: Oh my God . . .

SARAH: What?! What happened?

PAMELA: Jessie is dead?

ERIC *comes up to* STANLEY *not sure how to be personal*
with him. He stands awkwardly next to him and gives
him a little touch on the arm.

ERIC: I'm so sorry, Stanley, she was a fine artist.

MR WAX: Such a fine artist.

ROSIE *has tears running down her cheeks.*

ROSIE: It's so sad! (*With real feeling.*) She was so young . . .

LADY CREMONE (*to* LOUIS): I'll take you to the hospital.

INT. LADY CREMONE'S LIMOUSINE. NIGHT

LADY CREMONE *is sitting on the back seat of the limousine as*
they are driven to the hospital. She looks very dignified but
pale. LOUIS *and* STANLEY *are sitting either side of her.* LOUIS
has tears in his eyes; he is staring out of the window. We hear,
faintly at first, JESSIE*'s recording, her voice singing on the*
soundtrack, mixing with the score.

LADY CREMONE: I was just about to leave the hotel for the
theatre, and Mr Schlesinger came running into my
suite and told me the news . . . (*She looks at* STANLEY.)
We tried to phone you at the Embassy Stanley . . .
and we didn't know where you were, Louis.

STANLEY: What happened?

LADY CREMONE: She had a seizure, the poor child . . . they
were just trying to get her on her feet to take her to

the lavatory, and she just collapsed and died in their
arms . . .

LOUIS (*still staring out of the window*): What will this mean?

LADY CREMONE: I'm sure the band can find a way of
going on, Louis . . . We will all do our best to help . . .

LOUIS: No, I mean about finding out exactly what happened
to her? The attack and everything?

LADY CREMONE: The police will be able to do that, they
will find that out, Louis, of course they will, even
more so now.

STANLEY (*looking out of the window*): Look at this . . .

INT./EXT. LIMOUSINE/HOSPITAL. NIGHT
*They look out of the window, there is small crowd of fans
outside the hospital, some are holding candles, some are crying,
others are looking shocked and bewildered.*

As JESSIE'*s voice rings out on the soundtrack, we move with*
LADY CREMONE, STANLEY *and* LOUIS *from the car and
through the crowd.*

*Some press photographers are there, the flashes popping
loudly as they see* LOUIS. *Somebody in the crowd pushes forward
and presses a small bunch of violets into* LOUIS' *hand.*

LOUIS *stares around at the frightened, shocked faces of the
fans. He sees the very strange-looking woman. She watches him
go into the building with a impassive stare.*

Just as LOUIS *is about to enter the hospital, he sees the
detective,* HORTON, *standing with two uniformed police officers
a little distance away on the pavement.* LOUIS *pauses for a
moment, and looks at him.*

HORTON *stares straight back at him with a penetrating
gaze.*

The image fades to black.

PART FOUR

EXT. MUSIC EXPRESS STREET. EARLY MORNING

A wide shot of the street outside the Music Express *building in the early morning. It is entirely deserted, except for a cat that is scrabbling around a rubbish bin looking for food.*

INT. SMALL OFFICE — MONTAGE. MUSIC EXPRESS. EARLY MORNING

We cut close to LOUIS, *his eyes spring open suddenly, disorientated, uncertain where he is. We cut wide to see he is lying fully clothed on the bed in the inner office on the second floor of the* Music Express *building. The sun is stabbing brightly through a gap in the curtains.* LOUIS *looks towards the window. The curtains twitch in the breeze, the early morning sun seems dazzlingly bright; it flares straight into the camera and into* LOUIS' *eyes. Seamlessly, as if without a cut, the flare of the sun becomes the flare of the spotlight in the Imperial ballroom, as* JESSIE *is framed singing powerfully in the arc of the light.*

A surging montage begins: LOUIS *driving fast at night in the sports car,* JESSIE's *body covered in blood being lifted on to a stretcher in the hotel passage,* MASTERSON *sitting in the middle of the wood singing to himself,* JULIAN *waving goodbye to* LOUIS *in the dark hotel passage,* SARAH *pressed close to* LOUIS *as they dance together at the New Year's Eve party,* LOUIS *and* STANLEY *walking together down the staircase of the German Embassy, witnessed by a sea of hostile faces, and then* LADY CREMONE *beckoning to* LOUIS *in the street to tell him* JESSIE *is dead.*

We cut back to LOUIS. *He turns sharply on the bed. Standing silhouetted in the doorway is* STANLEY.

STANLEY: Coffee?

INT. MAIN OFFICE. MUSIC EXPRESS. EARLY MORNING
STANLEY *and* LOUIS *are standing by the window of the main office staring down at the early morning street. Both are sipping*

coffee out of chipped cups. LOUIS *is a step back from the window.*

STANLEY: Any moment Eric will be here . . .

> *As he says this a large black car appears at the edge of the street and drives towards them.*

LOUIS: That can't be Eric?

STANLEY: No.

> *The car disappears.* STANLEY *suddenly seems very tense. A smaller car appears in the street and slows for a moment below the window before moving on.*
>
> Neither is that . . .
>
> *A paper boy appears at the end of the street, moving rapidly towards them, delivering papers into letterboxes.*

STANLEY: Suddenly our street is very popular . . .

LOUIS (*taking a sip of coffee*): Yes.

> *He looks sideways at* STANLEY, *watching him closely, wondering if he can trust him.*

STANLEY (*not taking his eyes off the paper boy*): We need an idea. And quickly.

LOUIS (*sharply*): Better than the last one, Stanley.

STANLEY: It will be . . .

> *They are both staring down at the paper boy. He is now almost directly below them. They can see the papers clearly, one has a huge headline, 'WANTED' and a photograph half obscured.*
>
> *Just as we see this, there is a sudden cut, a press photographer's flash bulb on the soundtrack explodes like a gunshot.*

EXT. HOSPITAL. NIGHT

We cut to the flash bulbs of a group of photographers as LOUIS, STANLEY *and* LADY CREMONE *enter the hospital on the night of* JESSIE*'s death. Faces and cameras are crowding around* *them, as they force their way through the crowd.* LOUIS *is hemmed in by the stricken fans. As he moves away from them, he sees the detective* HORTON *with two uniformed officers staring at him as he enters the hospital.*

A caption appears:

EIGHT DAYS EARLIER

INT. SMALL HOSPITAL ROOM. NIGHT
We cut to LADY CREMONE, STANLEY *and* LOUIS *moving into a small room off the main hospital passage.* JESSIE*'s body is laid out on a trolley covered in a sheet, but her face is exposed, peaceful, her wounds almost healed.*

CARLA *is sitting in a corner, tears pouring down her face. She has lit two candles that are flickering in the draught. A* NURSE *is standing in the shadows.* CARLA*'s anguished face turns towards them.*

CARLA: Oh Louis. (*Tears pouring down her face.*) Look at
   her . . . how could this have happened?

INT. MAIN HOSPITAL PASSAGE. NIGHT
We cut back to the main corridor, the formidable figure of NURSE POLLOCK *is by the entrance, preventing the press from entering the hospital.*

INT. SMALL HOSPITAL ROOM. NIGHT
We cut back to the small room. LOUIS *is staring down at* JESSIE.

CARLA: They let me light a candle for her . . . but they said
   we couldn't put her in the hospital chapel because
   then everybody would want to do that.

LOUIS (*quietly*): I wish I had been with her when it happened.

CARLA (*suddenly beginning to cry again*): I hadn't seen her for three days, I expect she thought I'd forgotten about her . . .

LADY CREMONE: We'll help with the funeral arrangements of course, but the dear child must have some family somewhere . . .

STANLEY: Well, it'll be hard for them to miss the press coverage . . .

His voice is very quiet, moved by the sight of JESSIE*'s body, but we also see him thinking.*

It's going to be a huge story.

CARLA (*staring at* JESSIE*'s body*): Why? Why can't they leave her alone now?

LADY CREMONE: Unfortunately they won't. (*Softly but firmly.*) There'll be a lot of headlines, it may be best not to read the papers for a while.

We move in on STANLEY. *He suddenly turns.*

STANLEY: Yes – but it's not going to be just their version that people read . . .

INT./EXT. ROOF. MUSIC EXPRESS BUILDING. NIGHT

The camera is moving fast through the open window of the main Music Express *office and out on to the flat roof to reveal* STANLEY *sitting at a trestle table, typing vigorously.*

He is still wearing evening dress, but is without his bow tie. He has candles around him, and the light is spilling on to the roof from the main office. Next to him is ROSIE *at another trestle table, also typing fast, retyping his pages. She is wearing a coat. Around them, all over the roof, are pieces of discarded paper.* STANLEY *has a cigarette in the corner of his mouth and is typing with fierce concentration.*

He suddenly looks up. ERIC *is leaning through the open window, staring at him.*

ERIC: What are you doing out there, Stanley?

STANLEY: What does it look like? I always think better out here . . .

ROSIE: I don't know why, it's bloody freezing.

STANLEY *sees* PAMELA *and* SARAH *are also standing near the open window.*

STANLEY: You're all still here!

SARAH: We've been downstairs, we've been trying to find some food.

PAMELA *is looking very pale and fragile in her ball gown from the Embassy reception.*

PAMELA: Even on a night like this, one has to eat, and we did leave the German Embassy in rather a hurry . . .

ERIC *has climbed through the open window and on to the roof. He stands in front of* STANLEY *in his very tight-fitting suit.* STANLEY *has resumed typing.*

ERIC: And what are you writing, Stanley?

STANLEY (*without stopping*): You're not going to like this, Eric, but we've got to do a special edition, get the real story out to the public, how much Jessie had already achieved – (*He looks up.*) Not let it be blotted out by what's happened . . .

ERIC *opens his mouth to speak.*

No! We can't wait till our next edition, we absolutely can't let ourselves be beaten by the competition . . .

I know you won't agree to this and it will cost a lot, but this is our story! I will go to Mr Wax myself, I will make him –

ERIC: Stanley, I've talked to Mr Wax, he's agreed.

STANLEY: You have? (*Startled.*) You thought of it too?

ERIC: Yes.

ROSIE: You realise it's not just a three-page supplement
    we're doing, it's –
STANLEY: It's going to be twenty pages, with a lot of
    pictures.
ERIC: It will be a thirty-two-page edition.
    STANLEY is truly taken aback.
    That is what Mr Wax has agreed to fund.

EXT. MUSIC EXPRESS STREET. NIGHT
*A newspaper lorry rumbles towards us down the night street,
carrying the first editions. It travels straight past the Music
Express entrance.*

EXT. MUSIC EXPRESS ROOF. NIGHT
*We cut to ERIC typing at another trestle table on the roof,
having joined STANLEY and ROSIE. The three typewriters ring
out in the night air, pages all over the roof. PAMELA is sitting
smoking, watching them work.*
    SARAH steps through the open window.

SARAH: Look at this!
    She holds up the first edition of the morning paper, the
    Daily Mirror:

NOW IT'S MURDER AT THE IMPERIAL HOTEL
YOUNG SINGER DIES IN HOSPITAL,
DUE TO SING TO PRINCE OF WALES
ON NIGHT OF ATTACK

*For a moment there is silence on the roof as they are all
affected by the sight of the first headlines. STANLEY stares
at the portrait of JESSIE on the front page, a harsh
photograph of her looking awkward and dazzled by the
flash bulbs.*

He is suddenly galvanised.

STANLEY: You know, Sarah, we've got space to use quite
a lot of photographs. Why don't you get some of your
photographs, all the behind-the-scenes shots you've
taken of the band . . .

SARAH *turns.*

In fact, why don't you bring us absolutely everything
you've got . . .

SARAH: Everything I've got?!

STANLEY: Yes, go and get it now. We've got a chance to
do something very different with your pictures . . .
something nobody else will have . . .

As SARAH *leaves the roof,* PAMELA *glances down into the
street below. A tiny huddle of fans have gathered at the
entrance to the building and are staring up at them.*

PAMELA: There are one or two people keeping vigil here . . .
worrying what you're going to write about her no
doubt . . .

She stares down at the fans, their eyes meet.

We see a high shot of the roof, as STANLEY, ERIC *and*
ROSIE *resume work. We crane down on them as* STANLEY
*types feverishly. As the shot moves right into his typewriter,
we begin to hear* JESSIE *singing.*

We cut to a dynamic collage of photos and graphics.

SARAH'S PHOTOS/MAGAZINE ANIMATION
We see a series of black-and-white stills of JESSIE *caught in
informal moments, sometimes she is joined by* LOUIS *and*
CARLA. *As she sings on the soundtrack, the score merges with
the song to form a pulsating rhythm.*

The photos have a freshness and modernity; JESSIE *in her
dressing room in a cloud of cigarette smoke, running down the
kitchen passage screaming with laughter, riding one of the
hotel's food trolleys in the empty ballroom, dancing with the*

Prince of Wales in the subterranean passage, looking sideways into the camera with a humorous glint in her eyes, lounging with CARLA *in the hotel bedroom as they guzzle chocolates. And in between the photos there are some fragments of* STANLEY*'s writing, pounding out on the typewriter, and running sideways across the screen, 'A different sort of artist'* . . . *'A band unlike London had ever seen before'* . . . *'Electrifying performances in front of Princes* . . . *'*

And the drawings of ALBERT *(the magazine artist) link the photos in elegant animated lines, curling and twisting round them, showing the band causing shockwaves in the Imperial ballroom, caricatures of old dowagers wearing grotesque hats, peering at them in wonder.*

The effect is of vibrant photo-journalism bursting out across the screen, vivid and urgent. The images and music reach a climax and suddenly cut to silence.

INT. MASTERSON'S SUITE. DAY
We cut to MASTERSON *sitting in silence in his hotel suite. He is dressed in a beautiful dressing gown. He is barefoot and sipping a cup of coffee. In front of him on a small table, is the special* JESSIE *edition of* Music Express. *He flicks the pages, seemingly casually, but he is staring down at the images with intense interest.*

EXT. CEMETERY. JESSIE'S FUNERAL. DAY
We cut to LOUIS *standing by the graveside watching the funeral of* JESSIE. CARLA *is singing a lament, as she did in Part Two with* JESSIE, *but now it is for her friend. The mourners are entirely made up of the characters we know:* LADY CREMONE, MASTERSON, SARAH *and* PAMELA, DONALDSON, ERIC *who is wearing a dark suit that is too tight,* STANLEY *who is with his mother* MRS MITCHELL, *members of the band including* JOE

the trumpeter, SCHLESINGER, *and one middle-aged black
woman* (EDITH) *whom we do not recognise.*

JULIAN *is standing slightly apart, absolutely grief-stricken.*
LOUIS *watches him weep. As* CARLA *sings, he studies the faces
of the characters who have taken such an interest in the
fortunes of the band.*

LOUIS *then glances sideways, towards the gates of the
cemetery which are closed. Beyond them he can see a cluster of
press, and* HORTON *and* GUNSON, *the two detectives.*

We cut to after the funeral. LOUIS *is moving along a path
with the mourners, away from the grave.* LADY CREMONE *is
standing further down the path giving directions.*

LADY CREMONE: Everyone, it's just a little way down this
    path. Mr Masterson has arranged for the reception to
    be right here, through those trees, so we don't need to
    be bothered by the press.
    DONALDSON *accompanied by the middle-aged woman*
    EDITH *approaches* LOUIS.
DONALDSON: This is Edith, Jessie's aunt.
EDITH: Very pleased to meet you.
LOUIS: I'm delighted to meet you. (*He shakes her hand.*)
EDITH: This gentleman (*indicating* DONALDSON) has been
    so kind, so very kind. (*Suddenly she gets emotional, the
    words pouring out.*) I had no idea, no idea at all what
    Jessie had done, singing with the band and everything
    . . . I don't read the newspapers and I don't listen to
    the wireless, we've not got a wireless anyway, so I
    didn't know what our Jessie had done, not one little
    bit of it! Her mother would have been so proud!
    I wish I'd known . . . and now it's too late . . .
    She sees MASTERSON *in front of her on the path.*
    I must just thank that gentleman for his generosity,
    for making all this happen, for the arrangements . . .

DONALDSON (*watching* EDITH *leave*): Well there's a little
    reminder that there's another world out there . . .
    He sees EDITH *reach* MASTERSON, *who is looking very*
    striking all in black.
    He likes to take charge of things, doesn't he . . .
    STANLEY *is suddenly at* LOUIS' *side.*
STANLEY: We're going where prying eyes can't follow.
    He points at the cluster of press and police at the gates of
    the cemetery. HORTON *and* GUNSON *are watching them*
    walk along the path.
STANLEY: The police may start to make their presence felt
    again, Louis, if they haven't solved the case soon.
    They'll get us all to give our statements one more
    time –
LOUIS (*watching* JULIAN *up ahead on the path*): Yes . . . but
    I think they're very close to making an arrest in fact.
    At that very moment, before STANLEY *can ask more,*
    JULIAN *turns on the path and calls out loudly.*
JULIAN: This is the way everybody, down this little path
    here, there's a surprise waiting for us beyond those
    trees!
    His grief-stricken manner seems to have completely
    vanished.

INT. PALM HOUSE. DAY
We cut inside a beautiful Palm House situated next to the
cemetery, a Victorian glass house surrounded by high hedges so
that it is not visible from the path or the road. In among the
tropical plants and flowers the mourners are being waited on by
four servants in black and white uniforms. There is food and
wine on silver trays.
    STANLEY, *accompanied by his mother, approaches* LADY
CREMONE.

LADY CREMONE: Ah Stanley, I need to congratulate you.

STANLEY: On what?

LADY CREMONE: On that special edition of the magazine, it was rather remarkable.

STANLEY (*sharp grin, straight back at her*): Well it was one edition that had to be serious, wasn't it?! (*He turns.*) This is my mother, this is Lady Cremone.

MRS MITCHELL: Oh, Your Ladyship, how lovely to meet you. I was so hoping we would be introduced.

LADY CREMONE: And I'm very glad to meet you. (*She looks at* MRS MITCHELL, *fascinated.*)

MRS MITCHELL: My son never stops talking about you . . . (STANLEY *tries to interrupt.*) No, no, he does, every time I see him he mentions you, you're quite his favourite person –

STANLEY: Parents! (*Trying to laugh it off.*) They embarrass you every time, don't they!

MRS MITCHELL: He's always so interested in what you're going to say, what your opinion will be about each edition of the magazine. He asks every time, 'Do you think she'll like it, Mum?'

LADY CREMONE: Does he indeed? Well, you have a talented son Mrs Mitchell – (*She smiles.*) who ought to use his talent more –

SCHLESINGER *appears in front of them. He has already drunk a lot, his tie is askew, his manner flustered.*

SCHLESINGER: This may be the last time we ever see each other, Your Ladyship . . .

LADY CREMONE: Heavens no! I still have my apartment in the hotel, remember –

SCHLESINGER: Yes, but the Bertram family are coming to town, the owners of the Imperial – a murder in their hotel, it's something they can't tolerate . . .

LADY CREMONE: But they can hardly blame you, Mr Schlesinger?!

SCHLESINGER: On the contrary, I'm quite sure they can.

We cut to LOUIS, SARAH *and* PAMELA *standing among the tropical plants, watching* JULIAN *refill people's glasses, acting as if he is the host of the wake.*

PAMELA: I do hope my brother doesn't feel the need to make a speech, he might completely break down while he's doing it.

LOUIS *watches* JULIAN. *He doesn't look like he is about to break down; he is at his most charming and seemingly relaxed.*

We cut to STANLEY *and* MRS MITCHELL *passing close to* MASTERSON.

STANLEY: This is my mother, Mr Masterson.

MASTERSON (*an enigmatic smile*): Mrs Mitchell . . .

MRS MITCHELL: How do you do?

MASTERSON: I'm going to say an extremely obvious thing to your son now, Mrs Mitchell.

She smiles bewildered at this.

STANLEY: And what is that?

MASTERSON: I'm going to say, when something finishes, often – not always – but frequently, something else begins.

MRS MITCHELL: I'm sure that's right, oh yes! Though it's such a sad day today, she was so young . . .

MASTERSON: And I expect your son may wonder what I mean by that . . .

STANLEY: And what do you mean?

MASTERSON (*staring straight at him*): Well, maybe we should make an appointment, Stanley, you and I, and see if we can figure out what I mean.

At that moment there is the sound of cutlery against glass, and JULIAN *leaps on to a chair. We cut to* LOUIS *watching him closely.*

JULIAN: I just want to say something, nobody be alarmed – I'm not making a speech at all! But I just want to say,

the flowers, some of these flowers, were brought here
specially by Mr Masterson. (*He indicates the tropical
blooms.*) I know they look like they live here all the
time but they don't – and I want to thank him and
say what an appropriate gesture that was, because
Jessie's life was such a short life, so full of colour, so
vivid . . . (*Tears fill his eyes.*) It brought such joy into
my life, into many of our lives here I think, and I want
to pay tribute –

*There is movement and a surprised murmur among the
mourners, because suddenly they see there are faces pressed
right against the glass of the Palm House watching them.
The faces of several fans, disquieting faces, staring at them
with hostility as if saying 'Why are we out here and you in
there?'*

*We see the mourners staring back at the faces in alarm,
and then a shot from the fans' point of view of the curious
collection of mourners: the wealthy guests,* STANLEY *and
his* MOTHER, *and* LOUIS *and the band, all mingled
together among the flowers.*

SARAH *is standing by* LOUIS.

SARAH: Even Mr Masterson couldn't stop them finding us.

DONALDSON (*to* PAMELA): It's probably not a good idea
after all to hold a wake in a glass house!

JULIAN*'s manner is suddenly more withdrawn, his
confident speech interrupted. He stares back at the fans.*

JULIAN: We seem to have company.

SARAH (*to* LOUIS): We ought to get away from here.

LOUIS: Yes.

SARAH (*softly*): We could go to my house . . .

LOUIS (*surprised*): Your house?

SARAH (*looking straight into his eyes*): My father is away for
a few days . . .

INT. SARAH'S FATHER'S HOUSE. DAY
A high shot of the hall as SARAH *and* LOUIS *enter the house, and begin to move up the stairs. A maid (*LUCY*) is standing in the doorway of the living room watching them go up the stairs. At first they don't notice her, then* SARAH *calls down to her.*

SARAH: Just showing Mr Lester my latest photographs
   Lucy . . . If there are any callers, I don't want to be
   disturbed.

INT. SARAH'S DARK ROOM. DAY
A light flicks on abruptly. LOUIS *and* SARAH *are standing in the corner of the dark room. All around the walls are hanging her photographs of the fans as they waited outside the hospital. Unsettling faces, especially the strange gaunt woman.* SARAH *has blown up the photos quite big and hung them close together so they form a large disturbing panoramic shot, an eerie chorus of characters clustering round the walls of the dark room.*

LOUIS: We leave them at the funeral, and here they are
   again!
SARAH: That's right. (*She smiles.*) They're following you!
   (*She shuts the door.*) I haven't quite finished developing
   them all . . .
   We cut to a photograph floating in the developing tray, another rather manic face beginning to appear in ghostly outline in front of them.
LOUIS: That is a spooky sight, certainly!
SARAH: Yes. (*She lifts the image up.*) This one looks rather
   hungry. (*She glances at the other faces.*) I think a few
   of them look as if they haven't had enough to eat . . .
   We see sharp cuts of the photographs, the faces watching them from the wall. LOUIS *stares at one of the fans who is holding up Jessie's record sleeve, her hit song.*

LOUIS: How dedicated they were to Jessie already, after
such a short time . . .

SARAH *is hanging up the new photograph.*

SARAH: Exactly . . . (*She turns.*) I think one of them
attacked Jessie in the hotel.

LOUIS (*unconvinced*): One of these?

SARAH (*staring at the faces*): It doesn't necessarily have to
be one of these in this room. (*She looks at the strange
woman's face.*) Though it could be! (*She turns to face
him.*) Stanley thinks this too – they wanted Jessie all
to themselves . . . People become so obsessed with
their favourite performers, they want power over
them, to own them –

LOUIS: Yes, but I never saw any of them inside the hotel,
ever.

SARAH: They could have got in! (*She is close to him.*) I
haven't told anybody what you've told me, I promise –
but it can't have been Julian, I really believe it can't
have been him –

LOUIS: I did see him that night in the hotel –

SARAH: But there will be an explanation for that, there
really will!

SARAH*'s face is very close to his, just like the first time
they were alone in the dark room. But this time* LOUIS
puts his arms around her.

We don't need to think about it now.

LOUIS: No we don't . . .

SARAH (*kisses him, a long kiss*): Why do funerals . . . ? (*She
stops.*)

LOUIS: . . . always make one want to . . .

INT. SARAH'S BEDROOM. DAY
We cut to SARAH *and* LOUIS *naked under the sheets, making
love in* SARAH*'s bedroom. We see a wide shot of the room which*

is decorated with her photographs, including a discreet one of
LOUIS *at the piano which is near the bed. It is raining heavily,*
the sound of the rain pouring down the large window. We cut
close to SARAH, *kissing* LOUIS *passionately, as they make love.*

INT. SARAH'S HOUSE/HALL. DAY
We cut to LUCY, *the maid, polishing the table in the hall and*
glancing up the stairs towards the bedroom.

INT. SARAH'S BEDROOM. DAY
We cut back to LOUIS *and* SARAH *making love. Suddenly*
LOUIS *catches sight of himself on the wall and begins to laugh.*
SARAH *is startled.*

SARAH: What's the matter?
LOUIS: I don't think I've ever done this, watched by myself
before . . . !
SARAH (*softly*): Don't you like it? I do, it means I've got
two of you . . .
She wraps her arms around him and kisses him.
Suddenly we hear LUCY*'s voice calling: 'Miss Sarah,*
Miss Sarah!'
LOUIS: You're wanted.
SARAH: Ignore it . . .
But LUCY*'s voice is really loud: 'Miss Sarah, there's*
somebody at the door, Miss Sarah!'
SARAH: That girl! I told her!

INT. SARAH'S HOUSE/HALL. DAY
SARAH *is standing at the front door. It is open, the rain is*
bucketing down. GUNSON *and a young detective are on the*
doorstep. SARAH *is bare-legged, her clothes obviously just*
thrown on.

LOUIS *appears on the landing above; he is in shirt and
trousers, but barefoot.*

SARAH: It's the police, Louis.
>   GUNSON *takes in* LOUIS' *state of undress. There is a glint
>   in his eye, but his manner is courteous.*
GUNSON: Ah, Mr Lester, I wonder if you can help us with
>   some identification?
LOUIS: Identification?
>   *He moves towards them down the stairs.*
GUNSON: Yes we need to make an identification, and we
>   believe you, as a witness, can help us. Are you willing
>   to do that?
LOUIS: Of course.

INT. POLICE STATION/BASEMENT PASSAGE. AFTERNOON
*The long basement passage at the police station. It is still
raining heavily.* GUNSON *is escorting* LOUIS *towards the
interrogation room. As they draw near, the door opens and*
THORNTON *comes out. He moves briskly towards them, his
glasses glinting in the light.*

LOUIS: Hello, Harry.
THORNTON (*without breaking his stride*): Good afternoon,
>   Mr Lester . . .
>   LOUIS *turns and watches* THORNTON *disappear down
>   the passage.* GUNSON *indicates* LOUIS *should enter the
>   interrogation room. He does not follow but shuts the door.*

INT. POLICE INTERROGATION ROOM. AFTERNOON
We cut to a wide shot of the interrogation room. LOUIS *is now
seated in front of the desk, a young detective is standing in the
shadows, a typist is in the corner.* HORTON *is sitting opposite*

LOUIS, *the rain is pouring down the window of the basement room, and we see the occasional legs of passers-by scurrying past.* LOUIS *is sitting calmly, ready to assist the police. He looks immaculate again, in the suit he wore for the funeral.*

HORTON: You saw Mr Luscombe in the hotel passage when he maintains he was on the train to Paris?

LOUIS: I did, yes.

HORTON: And how many feet away from him were you when you saw him?

LOUIS: I don't know, it was the length of the passage, sixty feet . . . seventy feet . . .

HORTON: It would be at least that, wouldn't it? Turn round, if you could, Mr Lester.

> LOUIS *turns in his chair. The door of the interrogation room has been opened again without him noticing. Now he can see down the length of the passage; a figure is standing right at the far end in the shadows.*

HORTON: Who is that at the end of the passage Mr Lester? Can you tell me?

> LOUIS *stares at the figure, trying to make it out.*

Is it Mr Gunson, who you know? . . . Can you tell me for sure that it is Mr Gunson? . . . Or is it Sergeant Thomas, who you don't know? . . . Or could it even be Mr Thornton from the Imperial Hotel, who was here just a short while ago? . . . Which one is it, Mr Lester?

> *The sound of the rain is really loud.* LOUIS *tries to make out who the figure is. It waves at him from the shadows and then calls out, 'Louis . . . ' The voice is very distant.* LOUIS *cannot tell who it is.*

LOUIS: This is nothing like it was, there is more light in the hotel . . .

> LOUIS *turns back to* HORTON. *He is determined to try to remain calm, not to be browbeaten.*

HORTON: You can't tell me, can you?

LOUIS: Is this why I was brought here? Is this the 'identification' I was supposed to make?! It's a completely meaningless test, Mr Horton.

HORTON drops a British passport down in front of LOUIS on the table.

He leans forward, his young face level with LOUIS.

HORTON: This is Mr Julian Luscombe's passport, he gave it to us entirely voluntarily. Please have a look . . .

LOUIS stares at the various stamps on the passport from different borders, Julian's trips.

It bears the correct stamp of the French passport control for the night train in question, the right date – and of course there is only one night train. We also have witnesses, a Mr Leopold Fitzmaurice and Mr Horace Verney, who both saw Mr Luscombe in their first-class compartment and then saw him embark with them on the ferry. Neither Mr Fitzmaurice nor Mr Verney are friends or acquaintances of Mr Luscombe, but they identified him at once. He apparently never stopped talking the whole journey.

HORTON becomes less terse, suddenly reasonable and persuasive.

Is it possible, Mr Lester, that it was someone else who you saw at the hotel that night? Someone else who called your name?

The typist has stopped. There is only the sound of the intense rain.

Is it possible you can't be absolutely sure you saw Mr Luscombe?

LOUIS looks up from the passport back at HORTON. The reflection of the heavy rain is running down the walls.

For one second he sees the hotel passage again, the figure now totally indistinct, waving at the end of the passage.

LOUIS: If you're asking me if I'm absolutely sure . . .

HORTON: I am.

LOUIS: Then I suppose it's possible I'm not . . .

The loud sound of the typist typing this rings out.

HORTON: Thank you. That is extremely helpful, Mr Lester.

INT. JULIAN AND PAMELA'S PARENTS' HOUSE/MAIN
RECEPTION ROOM. LATE AFTERNOON

JULIAN *and* PAMELA *are playing chess sitting on the floor of
the reception room of their parents' house. They are still in their
clothes from the funeral. The torrential rain is running down the
windows. The chess set they are playing with is a Victorian one,
made from celluloid ivory, frogs against mice; the squat chess
pieces are holding swords and daggers as they go into battle.*
PAMELA *has just moved one of her bishop mice.*

JULIAN: Why have you done that?

PAMELA: Is it very stupid?

JULIAN: No, I just don't know why you've done it.

PAMELA: Well you taught me how to play, so it's all your
fault!

JULIAN: You're better than you think.

PAMELA (*laughs*): Well only sometimes . . . (*Suddenly, very
fondly.*) All the wonderful battles we've had, I used to
want them never to finish . . .

JULIAN: Yes, and sometimes they lasted for days . . .

PAMELA: We saved our lives with games. (*She looks down.*)
Especially with these mice and frogs, and I still need
them!

*Their mother appears in the doorway giving instructions to
a maid.* JULIAN *sees her first, a troubled look comes into
his eyes.*

JULIAN: Hello, Mummy, how was your little holiday? Was
it a success?

MRS LUSCOMBE: No, not really. The hotel was horrible.

A glint comes into JULIAN*'s eyes; he deliberately draws his mother out.*

JULIAN: Some guests you didn't like, Mummy?

MRS LUSCOMBE: There were some guests I couldn't abide, yes, nor could your father, we had to move rooms twice in fact, to get far enough away from them.

JULIAN (*innocently*): There were some Jews in the hotel? Is that what you mean, Mummy?

MRS LUSCOMBE: Unfortunately yes, the hotel seemed to be crawling with them . . . and you really wouldn't expect that in Cornwall, would you?

She disappears down the passage. JULIAN *watches her go. He then turns to* PAMELA.

JULIAN: How could we have come out of that person? Don't you ever think that, darling, how on earth are we part of her?

PAMELA: I think about it all the time . . . (*Staring after where her mother has gone. She laughs bitterly.*) Nearly every morning . . . (*She turns back to* JULIAN.) You won't leave me here alone with them? Promise?! You're away so much now, you won't go away for good?

JULIAN: I'll never leave you, darling, I promise. I have plans of course, great plans at the moment! Mr Masterson has been so encouraging. But wherever I go, I will always come back.

PAMELA: You're not going soon?

JULIAN: No, absolutely not! And I've decided – I'm going to fill this house with Jews and Negroes, maybe that's what we should do for Mummy's next birthday in fact! (*His face clouds.*) Although of course Jessie can't sing for her now.

PAMELA: I know you're so upset about Jessie. (*She takes his hand.*) You can talk to me about it darling, how much you miss her . . . you can tell me all about it.

JULIAN: I know, I know I can. (*He holds her hand tightly.*)
I loved her, I loved her so very much . . .

INT. THE IMPERIAL/THE MINOTAUR SUITE. MORNING
It is morning. The door of the Minotaur Suite opens; MASTERSON
is dressed in a beautiful suit. He stares at STANLEY, *who is in
his rather worn working clothes.*

MASTERSON: Come in, Mr Mitchell, come in. I was
wondering where you were.
STANLEY: I'm not late, am I?
MASTERSON *doesn't reply; he indicates* STANLEY *to enter.
The curtains are half drawn in the suite, the morning sun
is making all the gold ornaments, that seem to be on every
surface, glisten. There are gold cigarette cases, clocks,
ornamental boxes, a gold music box.*
MASTERSON: You've not been here before?
STANLEY: No, I haven't . . . (*He smiles, feeling just a little
nervous.*) There's a lot to look at!
MASTERSON (*watching* STANLEY *stare at the ornaments*):
Everybody runs to gold when times get hard . . .
He lifts the lid of the gold music box; it plays a little tune.
But I didn't get where I am now by doing the
obvious, Mr Mitchell.
STANLEY: No, I'm sure you didn't.
MASTERSON *is staring at him with a penetrating look.*
STANLEY *has no idea what he wants.*
MASTERSON: Stanley . . . You don't mind if I call you
Stanley?
STANLEY: Of course not . . . Mr Masterson.
MASTERSON: You caused quite a rumpus at the German
Embassy the other night, didn't you, Stanley . . .
STANLEY *leaps to his own defence, thinking this is why he
has been summoned.*

STANLEY: Well, that was a joke, and I thought a good joke, as it happens – I just wanted to give them –

MASTERSON: No, no, no need to explain.

He is still staring straight at STANLEY *as if forming a judgement on him.*

A little mischief may well do them some good . . . (*He shuts the music box.*) You probably don't know much about the business I'm in, do you, Stanley?

STANLEY: More than one business isn't it, Mr Masterson?

MASTERSON: That's correct. It's mainly real estate in the US, a little coal of course, and quite a lot of oil . . . The financial crash affected me, naturally, but only in the mildest of ways . . .

STANLEY: I'm glad to hear it.

MASTERSON: In a depression like we're in now, there are certain things people always still want – food of course, soap, a little entertainment and news. At the moment I don't own any of those.

STANLEY: Except for Julian's English cheese business of course!

MASTERSON (*a faint smile*): Yes, except for that.

He sits near the coffee table, the light behind him. His matter-of-fact demeanour gives him great power.

STANLEY *is left still standing in front of him, not knowing what to expect.*

MASTERSON: I don't want you to say anything to what I'm about to put to you.

STANLEY: Not at all? Whatever it is?!

MASTERSON: That is correct.

MASTERSON *moves the newspaper that is lying on the coffee table.* STANLEY *catches a glimpse of a story halfway down the front page:*

POLICE LOOK FOR LEADS IN HOTEL MURDER

Underneath the newspaper is the JESSIE *edition of* Music
Express. MASTERSON *pushes it carefully towards* STANLEY.

MASTERSON: I was impressed with this edition of your
magazine, Stanley. I have just written to Mr Wax to
propose that I buy *Music Express* off him. I intend to
find a new larger premises for the magazine and to
expand it greatly.

He opens the magazine to reveal SARAH's *behind-the-
scenes photographs.*

I am extremely interested in the possibilities of
photographic journalism – I don't think anybody has
grasped its full potential. I intend to make *Music
Express* the foremost entertainment magazine in
Europe . . . I further intend to found a news magazine
in a year or so which will rival *Time* magazine, and
then overtake it . . . (*He looks at* STANLEY.) I propose
to make you Editor-in-Chief of *Music Express*, Stanley.
That is if you would like to be, of course.

STANLEY *looks stunned. He is about to reply.*

MASTERSON: No, I don't want you to say anything
for the moment . . . (*His tone formidable.*) Anything at
all . . . I just want you to consider it, silently, for a
few days.

There is excitement in STANLEY's *eyes, but he manages to
just stop himself saying anything.*

INT. IMPERIAL/SERVICE STAIRCASE. NIGHT

LOUIS *and one other member of the band are moving across the
lower landing of the service staircase at the Imperial when
suddenly a voice shouts down to them.*

LOUIS *looks up,* SCHLESINGER *is several floors above him,
staring down, his shoulders hunched, his massive face tense.*

SCHLESINGER: Harry wants to see you, Louis.

LOUIS: What's it about?

SCHLESINGER: He will tell you . . .

> LOUIS *begins to move back the way he came.* SCHLESINGER *calls after him.*

I'm not going to be able to sleep Louis, and the one thing I dread is not being able to sleep.

INT. IMPERIAL/THORNTON'S OFFICE. NIGHT
LOUIS *knocks on the door of* THORNTON*'s little office in the basement of the Imperial and then enters.* THORNTON *is surrounded by ledgers, one of which he immediately shuts on seeing* LOUIS. *The room is lit by just one bare light bulb.*

LOUIS: You wanted to see me?

> THORNTON *looks at* LOUIS *with a penetrating glance. There is a new confidence about him.*

THORNTON: Yes, a request has come up . . . the Freemasons are having their annual dinner for their new worshipful master in the rooms they have here, and rather surprisingly – surprising to me anyway – they have requested you play at it.

LOUIS: The Masons? That'll be interesting . . .

THORNTON (*sharply*): You will be limited to seven musicians and your singer Carla. I just wanted to check you can manage to do it, to play at all – in the circumstances.

LOUIS: Yes. We're going to go on performing, that's already been decided.

> THORNTON *stares at him with a cold and meaningful look.*

THORNTON: For the time being . . .

LOUIS: What's that mean?

THORNTON: Until it's decided otherwise . . .

> *There's a malevolent feeling inside* THORNTON*'s little office.*

LOUIS: It is up to Mr Schlesinger who plays at this hotel.
THORNTON: At the moment it is . . .
> *There's a sudden crash from outside, in the hotel's backyard.*
> THORNTON *is galvanised.*
THORNTON: I don't believe it. Will they never stop! I will
not stand for it!

INT. IMPERIAL/BASEMENT PASSAGE. NIGHT
We see THORNTON *careering down the length of the passage.*
Suddenly possessed with almost demonic energy, he is bellowing
as he goes.

THORNTON: Stop that right now! At once!
LOUIS *is following him, watching his manic run.*

EXT. IMPERIAL/BACKYARD. NIGHT
THORNTON *emerges into the backyard of the Imperial. It is*
a foggy night, some beggars are scavenging among the dustbins.
THORNTON *screams at them.*

THORNTON: Get out of here . . . NOW! . . . OR I'LL
HAVE YOU ALL ARRESTED!
> *We see young faces look up from the dustbins, young people*
> *in their twenties. They all appear badly malnourished.* LOUIS
> *joins* THORNTON *in the yard as* THORNTON *continues to*
> *yell at the beggars, some of whom are determined to go on*
> *scavenging.*
I don't care how hungry you are, you're not stealing
food from here! I'll get you all locked up!
> THORNTON *watches them scurry off.*
I do not understand how people can have so little
pride, let themselves fall so low.
LOUIS: People have to eat . . .
THORNTON: Not out of my dustbins they don't.

He moves to check his dustbins. LOUIS *begins to leave.*
    THORNTON *calls after him across the foggy deserted yard.*

THORNTON: Oh by the way, Mr Lester . . .

    LOUIS *stops.*

The police came and asked if they could take away the sports car that belonged to Miss Taylor. I said of course they could.

LOUIS: Why did they want that?

THORNTON: I believe they've got it into their heads they need to have a thorough look at it.

INT. MUSIC EXPRESS OFFICE. DAY
We cut to ERIC *and* ROSIE *staring in disbelief at* STANLEY *in the* Music Express *office. Sharp winter sunlight is illuminating the room.*

ROSIE: Mr Wax is selling the magazine?!

STANLEY: It's not happened yet, no.

ERIC: To this American millionaire?

ROSIE: He's one of the richest men in the world – why does he want our little magazine?!

STANLEY: He sees possibilities in it, that it'll grow enormously.

ERIC: And he's offered to make you captain of the team, has he?

STANLEY (*for a moment surprised by* ERIC): Nothing was finalised at all . . .

ERIC: But it was discussed wasn't it?! You opening the batting?

STANLEY (*getting exasperated*): I told you absolutely nothing was finalised – I'm not supposed to be breathing a word about it to anyone, but I thought you ought to know . . .

ROSIE (*sharply*): Thank you Stanley, for not keeping it a
total secret. (*She moves.*) Maybe Mr Wax won't sell
after all.

ERIC: For the right price, most people will sell anything.

STANLEY: Mr Masterson has great plans for the magazine.

ROSIE (*urgently*): He'll never give you any freedom,
Stanley, you realise. It will all change completely here.

STANLEY: I'm not sure about that. And if he suggests
things we don't like, we won't do them.

ROSIE: How?! You won't be able to control what's
happening, Stanley –

There is a brief knock on the door and then it opens. MR
WAX *is standing in the doorway with* LADY CREMONE.
MR WAX*'s manner is complacent, his eyes glinting.*

MR WAX: Excuse us for a moment, but I'm sure you won't
mind the interruption, Her Ladyship just wanted to
see in here . . .

LADY CREMONE *takes in the walls of the office,* STANLEY*'s
chaos of drawings and photographs and* ERIC*'s tidy
charts.*

LADY CREMONE: So this is your lair Stanley?! . . . I've only
ever seen it from the outside.

STANLEY *is very taken aback by her unexpected visit.*

STANLEY: Well, it's usually a fraction tidier than this . . .

LADY CREMONE (*disbelieving smile*): Is it Stanley? (*She
glances round the room.*) I always wondered what it
would look like.

ROSIE (*pointedly*): Well it may not look like this for much
longer.

LADY CREMONE *smiles at this. They can't tell if she
knows something or not.*

LADY CREMONE: That sounds interesting . . .

MR WAX: Maybe Your Ladyship would like to see the
collection of back copies we have? I have them in my
office.

He steers LADY CREMONE *out of the room.*

LADY CREMONE: I would love that. I have in fact quite a
few bound copies of your magazine in my library . . .
Not many people can say that I expect!

MR WAX (*laughing sycophantically*): And you are on the
cover of one of our editions of course, one of our very
best covers I always say . . .

STANLEY *watches them disappear together.*

INT. IMPERIAL/SCHLESINGER'S OFFICE/PASSAGE. EVENING
*Two gaunt-looking men in dinner jackets, the Bertram brothers,
are moving down the passage together.* SCHLESINGER *is standing
with* THORNTON *in the doorway of his office, watching them
from a distance. One of the Bertram brothers looks back at
them just as he disappears, an unnerving look.*

SCHLESINGER: Have you ever seen the Bertram brothers
before, Harry?

THORNTON: I have not.

SCHLESINGER: They never ever come here. (*He watches
them vanish at the end of the passage.*) They could stop
me getting another job anywhere in the hotel business.
A few weeks ago, this was one of the most fashionable
hotels in London . . . and now . . .

The fog is swirling outside the window of SCHLESINGER'*s
office.*

And they've brought this filthy weather with them . . .
I have a terrible feeling about this week.

THORNTON: Have they said anything to you?

SCHLESINGER: No . . .

Suddenly looks at THORNTON, *his glinting glasses.*

Have they spoken to you though, Harry?

THORNTON: Just a few words, as I showed them to their
suite . . .

SCHLESINGER: What did they tell you, Harry?

THORNTON (*calmly*): That a murder at this hotel was one of the worst things they could ever imagine happening.

SCHLESINGER: Yes, and unsolved of course too . . . !

THORNTON (*carefully*): So far, yes.

INT. IMPERIAL LOBBY AND MAIN STAIRCASE. NIGHT
We cut to DONALDSON *and* STANLEY *standing in the lobby watching a group of dark-coated men carrying special small briefcases at the other end of the lobby.*

The men disappear down the main staircase towards the basement.

DONALDSON: Every time I see them gather, I can't help being fascinated.

STANLEY: Me too.

DONALDSON *moves towards the staircase, followed by* STANLEY. *They stare down the stairwell at the men in dark coats descending towards the basement.*

DONALDSON: There'll be a few dukes and marquises down there tonight, some minor royals perhaps, and some senior politicians of course – all sorts of surprising people belong to the Central London Lodge.

STANLEY: Yes . . . I thought now the band is playing at the dinner –

DONALDSON: Isn't that so unexpected?!

STANLEY: Yes, I'm quite jealous, I'd love to be there! But now that's happening, I thought maybe I can do an article about the Masons, in this hotel –

DONALDSON (*breezily*): If you did, you'd never work again! (*He watches another figure disappear.*) Of course, this could be the very last time they're here . . .

STANLEY: Because of the murder?

DONALDSON: I suppose we have to call it that, the 'murder' – but yes, they may be moving on, colonising another hotel. I hear they've been scurrying around looking at all sorts of basements!

STANLEY (*peering down the stairwell*): But if they're having the band play for them tonight, why do they feel they have to move?

DONALDSON (*watching the last Mason disappear down into the basement*): Well , I don't think they like being connected to a building that's becoming notorious . . . I have no idea who arranged for the band to play to them tonight. (*He smiles.*) God knows what will happen . . . ?! (*He turns.*) You look surprisingly smart today.

STANLEY *is wearing a white tie with his dinner jacket, and has a carnation in his buttonhole.*

STANLEY: I have an important dinner appointment, that's why –

DONALDSON: In the new Atlantic Bar?

STANLEY: That's right.

DONALDSON: So do I . . . As you know, Stanley, I always have to try out anything new.

As they move off, we stay for a second staring down into the stairwell; one last Mason is making his way down to the basement.

INT. IMPERIAL/ATLANTIC BAR. NIGHT

We cut to a new area of the hotel, a gleaming Art Deco bar with tables for light meals. It looks like an elegant bar on an ocean liner. But it is almost deserted; there are two old dowagers sitting in a corner eating a pudding each, two young couples sitting at the bar, and a beautiful young woman at one of the tables. In a discreet corner, wearing a splendid evening dress, is LADY CREMONE.

DONALDSON *and* STANLEY *appear in the entrance to the bar.*

STANLEY: There's practically nobody here!

DONALDSON: It's not the best day of course to try to open
a new bar . . . but what a lovely room! (*He surveys the
scene.*) I collect beautiful rooms round London
Stanley, I don't see why one shouldn't spend as much
of one's life as possible in them . . . (*Glancing across at*
LADY CREMONE.) Well, you must join Her Ladyship,
you mustn't keep her waiting.
He then moves to greet LADY CREMONE *himself.*
Lavinia, you look magnificent as always . . .
He kisses her, then indicates the beautiful young woman
sitting on her own.
I must join that wonderful young artist over there,
I'm hoping to help her get her first exhibition, she's
exquisitely talented . . .
He moves off and greets the beautiful young woman.

LADY CREMONE: Arthur has a new project it seems! (*She
smiles as she watches him with the young woman.*) To go
with all the others! (*She turns back.*) Now, Stanley, we
have a great deal to talk about . . .

STANLEY: I know.

INT. IMPERIAL/SUBTERRANEAN PASSAGE LEADING TO
MASONIC TEMPLE. NIGHT
We cut to MASTERSON *moving along the basement passage*
towards the Masonic temple. He is moving at a very deliberate
pace, not rushing at all. THORNTON *is watching from the*
shadows. MASTERSON *gives the attendant in the passage a brief*
nod before he disappears into robing room.

INT. ATLANTIC BAR. NIGHT
We cut back to STANLEY, *who is sitting opposite* LADY CREMONE, *surrounded by the glowing new decor of the bar.*

STANLEY: What do you know about Mr Masterson?
LADY CREMONE *looks up.*
What's he really like?
LADY CREMONE: I wish I knew . . . Some people are completely unknowable, aren't they?
STANLEY: Even to you?
LADY CREMONE (*smiles at this*): Certain people use mystery to suggest huge things are going on inside their heads, but in fact underneath they're really quite dull. My dear late husband was a little like that, though I miss him enormously of course . . . (*She looks straight at* STANLEY.) But Mr Masterson is different . . . I love his mystery.
STANLEY: You do?
LADY CREMONE: Yes, he makes all sorts of things happen. He is one of the few people I've ever met who seems always to be ahead of events.
STANLEY: Can one trust him?
LADY CREMONE: Funnily enough, I think one can.
STANLEY: So you are involved with his acquisition of the magazine?!
LADY CREMONE: I could be, yes . . . (*She laughs.*) Of course he doesn't need my money, but he needs a proprietor who lives here, who can be on the spot, while he travels the world.
STANLEY: So I'll be working for you?
LADY CREMONE: Is that such a terrible prospect?
STANLEY (*grins*): I'm not even going to reply to that!
LADY CREMONE: If all this happens, we will both be working for Mr Masterson ultimately, but yes, you will be working for me in a way.

STANLEY: I knew somehow this might happen . . . For
some reason I always felt it might!

LADY CREMONE: Well, I don't know how that's possible
Stanley, because I didn't until yesterday! Suddenly
I realised the way I was living was absurd – you can't
be half a recluse, who's ever heard of that?! (*She
laughs.*) Half a hermit! (*She sips her wine.*) Living like
that was never going to bring my sons back, it was
pointless . . . (*She leans forward.*) Now I know I want
to do something with the rest of my life, get involved
Stanley, get really involved . . .

INT. IMPERIAL/SUBTERRANEAN BASEMENT. NIGHT
Several members of the band and LOUIS *are standing waiting
in the dark subterranean passage that lead towards the Masonic
temple and Masonic dining room.* THORNTON *is standing a
few feet ahead of them in the passage, watching the door of the
robing room.*

THORNTON: Where's your singer?

LOUIS: Carla? She'll be coming, don't worry.
He steps closer to THORNTON, *watching him closely.*
Are you usually down here with them, Harry, when
they have their dinners?

THORNTON: Sometimes, yes.

LOUIS: I thought they had their own people.

THORNTON: They do, but once or twice I help them with
their arrangements.
He stares down the passage.
Of course I'm never allowed into the temple.
*Suddenly the door of the robing room opens, and figures
spill out. They are all the dark-coated men, now dressed
in evening dress. They head towards the Masonic dining-
room door.*

THORNTON: I never see them in their robes . . .

JULIAN *is among the figures coming out of the robing room. He calls down the passage.*

JULIAN: There you are, Louis! This is going to be so good . . . such fun! You will get your cue in just a moment . . .

MASTERSON *appears out of the robing room and the two of them walk towards the dining room deep in conversation.* LOUIS *is watching* JULIAN, *wondering about him.* JULIAN *turns again and gives him a little wave.*

THORNTON *is watching* MASTERSON.

THORNTON: He is the best tipper in the hotel, a very generous man, Mr Masterson.

LOUIS: Well, I suppose he needs to be doesn't he?

THORNTON (*turns sharply, his glasses glinting*): Why does he need to be?

LOUIS: If you smash up your hotel suite the way he does, you rather need to leave good tips don't you?!

THORNTON: I have no idea what you mean?

LOUIS *and* THORNTON *are now standing a few yards down the passage, a little distance from the rest of the band.* THORNTON *is staring at* LOUIS.

LOUIS: Oh, come on Harry . . . ! I saw his suite completely smashed up, you must have had to arrange to get it all cleaned up . . . You've probably had to do that several times, haven't you?!

THORNTON (*his voice rising*): I have absolutely no idea what you are talking about . . . !

LOUIS *stares back at him, his sharp little face. Suddenly, he has had enough of* THORNTON'*s malevolence. There is a dangerous calm about him as he faces* THORNTON.

LOUIS: What are you so frightened of, Harry?

THORNTON: Frightened? You think I'm the one that's frightened?!

LOUIS: Oh yes, I think you're extremely frightened, Harry.
(LOUIS' *face is close.*) What is it you're afraid of?
*THORNTON's voice falls to a hoarse whisper, but his tone
is viperish.*

THORNTON: You really think you're clever don't you, that
you can strut about with your musicians and get away
with anything. You even think you're different from all
the other minstrel bands, don't you?! Well, let me tell
you, this hotel will be destroyed because of what
you've done!

LOUIS: What have I done Harry?
Close to him, THORNTON *shrinks slightly against the wall.*
Go on, tell me what I have done?
But THORNTON *meets his gaze.*

THORNTON: Ever since you've been here I saw this coming,
how it was going to lead to disaster!
At that moment CARLA *appears on the stairs, wearing a
dazzling show costume.*

CARLA: Here I am, and I'm early, aren't I?!

LOUIS (*smiles, to* THORNTON): I told you there was nothing
to worry about!
*The attendant at the far end of the passage, in front of the
door of the Masonic dining room, beckons for the band to
enter.*
Perfect timing, Carla!
The band move off down the passage. Suddenly THORNTON
calls after LOUIS.

THORNTON: Remember I saw you with her! I saw you with
Jessie Taylor . . . I saw you arguing the night she was
attacked!
LOUIS *stops, the rest of the band have already entered the
dining room.*
For one moment, LOUIS *is alone with* THORNTON, *who
is right at the other end of the passage.* LOUIS *calmly calls
back to him.*

LOUIS: Everybody knows I had nothing to do with Jessie's
death, Harry . . . Remember I was playing to the
Prince of Wales! (*He gives* THORNTON *a little wave.*)
Now I think the Masons are waiting for me . . .
*LOUIS enters the dining room. For a moment we stay on
THORNTON as he watches the doors shut.*
THORNTON: Just wait till tomorrow . . .

INT. MASONIC DINING ROOM. NIGHT
*LOUIS enters the Masonic dining room, a long basement room
decorated with symbols of the lodge and portraits of past
Worshipful Masters. There is a select group of about twenty
men, mostly middle-aged and older but with one or two younger
men. As LOUIS enters the room, a warden is calling out:*

WARDEN: The Worshipful Master will now take wine with
his personal guests.
*LOUIS sees that MASTERSON is standing next to the
Worshipful Master at the head of the table. The band are
at the far end of the room where their drum kit and piano
have been set up. LOUIS moves to join the band. The
toast has finished and the men are sitting down to begin
their meal.*
JULIAN comes bounding up to greet the band.
JULIAN: Don't worry, I know it all looks a little strange,
but it's just an ordinary meal really! They can be
surprisingly jolly occasions, not much mumbo-jumbo
once we all get eating!
CARLA (*quite excited*): Have they ever had a singer in here
before?
JULIAN: No, I don't think so. It was my idea of course to
invite you . . . I don't know how it's all going to go
down! We'll see!
At that moment a young man appears at JULIAN's side.

JULIAN: Ah, this is my friend Leopold Fitzmaurice, we
joined the lodge together on the same day! He very
much wanted to say hello to the band, didn't you,
Leopold?

LEOPOLD *is smiling admiringly at* CARLA. LOUIS *is
immediately startled. He remembers* LEOPOLD *'s name
from the police.*

LEOPOLD (*addressing* LOUIS *and* CARLA): I know you're
going to liven up our dinner no end!

LOUIS: Leopold Fitzmaurice?

JULIAN: Yes, that's his name . . . it's a grand name isn't it?!

LOUIS: He was on the train with you was he, on the night
train to Paris?

LEOPOLD *immediately disappears among the diners, but*
JULIAN *'s manner is totally unabashed.*

JULIAN: Leopold and I always bump into each other on
trains!

LOUIS *is staring straight at him, but* JULIAN *looks
completely unconcerned.*

Oh yes, so it was Leopold who saw me on the train . . .

He waves across to another young man.

As did Horace over there, Horace Verney, he always
seems to be in my compartment! Now I must join the
others.

*He begins to move off, then suddenly comes back and
whispers to* LOUIS.

There's a first time for everything, and this is an
absolute first . . . I'm so interested to see how it goes!

LOUIS *sits at the piano. He is trying not to show how
deeply affected he is by* JULIAN *'s brazen behaviour, the
sight of his 'witnesses' sitting among their fellow Masons.
We see shots of their faces as* LOUIS *watches them, this
completely male gathering sitting closely together in this
strange dining room.* JULIAN *has now joined them, taking
his place at the table, and he laughs and jokes with them.*

We see everything through LOUIS' *eyes. The effect is overpowering, the strength of all these people, their blatant confidence.*

JULIAN *suddenly calls out.*

JULIAN: The Louis Lester Band are going to give us their first number!

We are very close to LOUIS *as he sits there at the piano staring at the diners. The sound is starting to cut out, the people begin to look very disconcerting, the camera angles become more extreme. The atmosphere in the room is rapidly growing more and more claustrophobic. The faces of the Masons stare at* LOUIS, *the sense of an extremely exclusive gentlemen's club, with all its power, all its mutual links, at one end of the room, and the band at the other.*

We see MASTERSON *presiding next to the Worshipful Master, who is a much less impressive-looking individual.* MASTERSON *dwarfs him.*

There is a sound beating in LOUIS' *head, a mixture of a heartbeat and the amplified sound of police typewriters. It is getting louder and louder, until suddenly it stops. For a moment, there is hushed hovering silence on the soundtrack.* LOUIS *is watching the faces of the Masons, who one by one are turning to stare at him, but he can hear nothing.* CARLA's *face suddenly appears in front of him.*

CARLA: Louis . . . ?

The sound comes rushing back.

Louis, what are you doing?!

The ambient sound in the room is back. Together with laughter and interjections being called out by the diners, 'Where's the bloody music?'

LOUIS *stares down at the piano keys, and slowly begins to play an intro.*

LOUIS: The first song we're going to play, the first song is . . .

CARLA: 'Dancing on the Moon'.

LOUIS: Yes . . . 'Dancing on the Moon'.

> CARLA *begins the first verse, but as soon as she begins singing, a man appears through the door at the far end of the room and moves towards* MASTERSON *and the Worshipful Master. He whispers in the Worshipful Master's ear and then into* MASTERSON*'s.*
>
> *The Worshipful Master holds up his hand and* LOUIS *stops playing.*

INT. IMPERIAL/ATLANTIC BAR. NIGHT
PAMELA *is standing in the entrance to the Atlantic Bar in a lilac dress. She looks very pale and tense.* STANLEY *glances up.*

STANLEY: Pamela . . . ? You're a little early aren't you?

> *He turns to* LADY CREMONE.

We're going on somewhere later. If you wanted to join us, of course, that would be delightful.

> PAMELA *is nearing them.*

PAMELA: Haven't you heard the news?

STANLEY: What news?

LADY CREMONE (*sharply*): What's happened?

> PAMELA *turns and addresses the whole bar.*

PAMELA: Somebody has tried to shoot the American President.

DONALDSON: What?!

> *There is a shocked murmur in the bar.*

PAMELA: Somebody has tried to assassinate Mr Roosevelt.

INT. IMPERIAL/PASSAGE OUTSIDE MASONIC DINING ROOM. NIGHT
The subterranean passage is swirling with the news, the Masons are standing in the doorway of the dining room or pacing the passage, their dinner interrupted. There are all talking at the tops of their voices.

We see LOUIS *emerge into the passage, watching the agitated faces. The Worshipful Master is moving in a bewildered state.*

MASTERSON *is standing just a few feet away. He bends towards* JULIAN *and whispers.*

MASTERSON: They're all worried how this will affect the stock market.

JULIAN (*his tone breezily unconcerned*): Will there be another Crash again, Walter?

MASTERSON: We need some more news, some reliable news . . .

JULIAN *sees* LOUIS *watching.*

JULIAN: Oh Louis, what a massive pity this is! I so wanted to see what they thought of the music!

INT. IMPERIAL/ATLANTIC BAR. NIGHT

We cut back to the Atlantic Bar. Everybody is standing crowded round a radio set which is behind the bar. DONALDSON, STANLEY, LADY CREMONE, PAMELA *and the other occupants of the bar staring at the radio, all except one of the dowagers who is sitting in the corner drinking coffee.*

Light orchestral music is coming out of the radio.

PAMELA: They're only playing music!

STANLEY: That's ridiculous! . . . An enormous story like this . . . they've got to do an extra news bulletin surely?!

LADY CREMONE: Instead they're just playing Strauss waltzes like they always seem to at this time of night. (*She smiles.*) Nothing can stop that.

DONALDSON: Well, I definitely don't think we'll get some more news from the BBC tonight, maybe we could try to find some other station from abroad . . . ?

The barman moves the dial, there are squeaks and hisses
from the radio, but it is picking up no other station.

STANLEY: That's useless! The reception is not good enough
in here –

LADY CREMONE: Well we'll just have to wait till the
morning and the newspapers.

INT. IMPERIAL /HOTEL LOBBY. NIGHT
The group from the Atlantic Bar are crossing the main lobby.
They see MASTERSON *standing there.* MASTERSON *addresses*
them as they approach.

MASTERSON: Have you heard the news from the US?

DONALDSON: We have, we're trying to find out more.

MASTERSON: I think I know where we can find out more.
I suggest you come with me . . .

STANLEY: To where?

MASTERSON: Ah . . . it's really quite walkable.

INT. IMPERIAL/HOTEL LOBBY. NIGHT
We cut to LOUIS *and* CARLA *coming up the main staircase and*
reaching the hotel lobby just as MASTERSON *is leading his*
party – JULIAN, STANLEY, LADY CREMONE *and* PAMELA *–*
towards the front entrance. The lobby is quite dark, big shadows
falling across it from the lamps glowing at the side. In the
corner, LEOPOLD FITZMAURICE, *Horace Verney and one other*
Mason are talking together. JULIAN *goes up to them to bid them*
farewell. LOUIS *sees him laughing and joking with them.*
LOUIS begins to move across the lobby. He calls.

LOUIS: Stanley! . . .

STANLEY *turns. His mood is excited, eager to know where*
he is being led by MASTERSON.

STANLEY: Ah, Louis, how were the Masons? You must tell
me about it some time . . .

LOUIS: I will, but I need to talk to you right now about
something else –

STANLEY: Not now, Louis . . . Haven't you heard the news
from America?!

LOUIS: I have, they tried to kill the President –

STANLEY: Yes, we don't know if he's badly injured or dying
even, we don't know what's happened . . . (*Indicating
the group ahead.*) But Mr Masterson is taking us
somewhere to find out . . .

*The group ahead are now disappearing through the main
entrance into the night.*

It's one of his mystery tours, like his picnics! I can't
lose him, or I won't know where they've gone . . . Why
don't you come too. Louis?

INT. IMPERIAL/ATLANTIC BAR. NIGHT

DONALDSON *is now back in the bar with the beautiful young
woman, the barman and the solitary dowager in the corner. He
is smoking a cigar, as over the radio the announcer is telling the
nation the station is closing down for the night, and the national
anthem begins to play.* CARLA *appears in the doorway and calls
across to* DONALDSON.

CARLA: What a terrible thing to happen, isn't it, Mr
Donaldson?!

DONALDSON: Indeed, it is quite awful of course.

CARLA (*glancing towards the radio*): Somebody will probably
try to kill the King next! . . . And all this after Jessie!

DONALDSON: Please, come and join us, Carla. (*He fills
another glass for her.*) Come on, and let us three drown
out all the bad news together.

EXT. LONDON STREETS. NIGHT

We cut to LOUIS *moving with the group down a London street lined by big commercial buildings. It is very foggy now. Ahead of them* MASTERSON'S *tall figure is leading them towards a large Victorian building. It is the only building glowing with some light, making it stand out vividly in the dark foggy street.*

LADY CREMONE: We seem to be the only people mad enough to be out on a night like this!

> LOUIS *is a few steps behind the group, watching* JULIAN.

STANLEY: Keep up, Louis, or you'll lose us.

JULIAN (*calling out in the fog*): So where are we going, Walter? Is it another party you haven't told us about?!

> MASTERSON *doesn't reply. He is walking purposefully ahead in the fog.*

> STANLEY *suddenly sees a figure ahead on the steps of the lighted building. It is* SARAH, *watching them approach.*

STANLEY: How does she know about this?!

> MASTERSON *moves up the steps and into the lighted building without looking back. The others follow him up the steep steps towards the imposing entrance.*

> LOUIS *reaches* SARAH.

LOUIS: Sarah, do you know why we're here?

SARAH: No, I got a telephone call from Mr Masterson just as I was going to bed . . . He said I had to come, he had something to show me . . . I leapt into a taxi and –

> *Their heads turn. The sound of dance music suddenly starts pouring out of the lighted building.*

INT. LARGE BUILDING, FOYER. NIGHT

STANLEY, LOUIS *and* SARAH *enter the large building. It has a grand foyer, as if it was once the office of a shipping company. Now the foyer is totally empty. An impressive staircase leads off it and light is spilling down from the landing.*

The dance music is loud and coming from upstairs.
They begin to climb the stairs.

INT. LARGE BUILDING, FIRST FLOOR. NIGHT
SARAH *is slightly ahead of* LOUIS *and* STANLEY *as they enter*
a large, completely empty room; it has no carpet and no chairs.
It is lit entirely by a large standard lamp in the corner.
　　Dominating the room, sitting on a table, is an enormous
radio set, the largest the characters have ever seen.
　　Standing by it is MASTERSON. LADY CREMONE *and* PAMELA
are already in the room, and standing right in the corner, in the
shadows, is the tall figure of ERIC.
　　STANLEY *is startled by the sight of him.*

STANLEY: What is Eric doing here?
SARAH: What an incredible wireless!
PAMELA: It's fit for an emperor!
MASTERSON: Come in, come in . . . this set here should be
　　able to get us every station in Europe . . . (*He begins to*
　　move the dial.) Let's see what we can find . . .
　　We go in close on the dial, it is glowing out very brightly in
　　the dark room. We hear fragments of German and Dutch,
　　and suddenly we hear an authoritative voice speaking
　　French.
MASTERSON: This is Radio Luxembourg . . . they at least
　　have news right into the night.
LADY CREMONE (*staring down at the dial, translating*):
　　They're saying the President-Elect Mr Roosevelt is
　　not injured, but the Mayor of Chicago has been shot
　　and his condition is very serious . . . and several other
　　people are shot.
　　The voice changes tone, moving on to another item.
　　　LADY CREMONE *is suddenly riveted.*
　　Good heavens!

STANLEY: What? What is it? What are they saying?!

LOUIS (*translating effortlessly*): They are talking about the murder that happened in a London hotel . . . The young coloured singer, Jessie Taylor, who had sung for royalty . . . (*He looks up.*) They say the police are now following new leads . . .

They begin to hear JESSIE's *voice, as the news item starts to play her hit song.*

STANLEY: I knew it would be a huge story – but I didn't know they'd be talking about it across Europe . . . ! (*He looks across at* LOUIS.) And I didn't realise you could speak French . . .

SARAH: You don't know everything about him!

JULIAN: Oh. I can't bear this! (*His voice very emotional.*) It's so sad hearing her voice, it's too upsetting!

MASTERSON *switches the radio off. For a moment there's a silence, the characters are disturbed at hearing* JESSIE *coming out of the radio unexpectedly.*

STANLEY *looks around.*

STANLEY: What is this place anyway?

MASTERSON: Don't you know?

ERIC: This is going to be our new home, Stanley.

INT. THE BUILDING, SECOND LARGE ROOM. NIGHT
We cut to a huge empty room, next to the room with the wireless. It has large windows outside which the fog is swirling. There are no curtains and no tables. The room is lit by a series of practicals that are sitting on the floor.

We are with LOUIS, *as he watches* STANLEY, ERIC *and* SARAH *excitedly exploring the vast space.*

STANLEY: This is extraordinary . . . this is our new office?! This room here – ?!

MASTERSON: Not just this room . . .

ERIC: It is the whole building, Stanley.

> STANLEY *is stunned but exhilarated; he is moving round the space.*

STANLEY: Not the whole building, that can't be right?! (*He turns.*) When did you buy it, Mr Masterson?

MASTERSON: Oh only the other day . . . (*Dryly.*) I bought the wireless first, and then had to have somewhere big enough to house it . . .

ERIC (*to* STANLEY, *out of the corner of his mouth*): He approached me just today, could I be so kind, would I look at the new premises . . . and see if I approved?!

> JULIAN *is whooping round the huge room with excitement, letting out bellowing calls to test the echo.*

JULIAN: What an office this is!

PAMELA: Even *The Times* would be so jealous of this!

> *The camera is travelling fast with the characters as they realise there are even more empty rooms off the huge central one.* LOUIS *watches them giddy with excitement, completely wrapped up with the sudden possibilities of everything.*

MASTERSON: You will of course have space for rather more staff . . . (*To* SARAH.) And a large photographic department, where all your photographs can be . . . and the other photographers working with you . . . or I should say for you. (*He stares straight at* SARAH.) The use of photography is the future . . .

SARAH: It is the future, yes.

> MASTERSON *is moving on.*

Am I being offered a job?

> MASTERSON *has left the room.* SARAH *turns to* STANLEY.

Was that a job offer?!

STANLEY: I rather think it was.

SARAH (*stares around her*): This is just so very exciting . . . wonderful . . .

We are moving with LADY CREMONE *into a smaller room
which has an impressive window. In this room there are a
desk and a chair.* STANLEY *follows her.*

LADY CREMONE: Maybe this would be an appropriate
room?

STANLEY: This is your room of course . . . After all, it is
the only one with furniture!

LADY CREMONE *sits on the only chair, at the desk. She
leans across the desk.*

LADY CREMONE: It will be the first regular job I've ever had
in my life Stanley . . . ! (*She laughs.*) With an office!

STANLEY: The proprietor's office!

LADY CREMONE: Is it absurd to start this sort of thing at
my age?!

STANLEY: No there's nothing absurd about it, it's the
obvious thing to do in fact. (*Very serious.*) I really
believe that, Lavinia.

We move in on LOUIS *as he watches the characters'
excitement, their voices exuberantly ringing out through
the empty rooms. He turns and sees at the other side of the
central room, in the shadows,* JULIAN *and* MASTERSON
deep in conversation.

JULIAN: Of course, I might wish to be part of this too,
Walter. I think we should forget all about the silly
cheese idea –

MASTERSON (*patiently*): Julian, the plans are decided . . .

JULIAN *suddenly erupts really loudly. We see he still has
the power to hurt* MASTERSON.

JULIAN: I will decide my own future thank you. I absolutely
refuse to be told what to do. I'm not a child, Walter.
(*Viciously.*) You have to stop treating me like one, or
I will go and work somewhere else . . .

MASTERSON *remains impassive but we can sense he has
been affected by* JULIAN*'s outburst. Suddenly they both see
they are being watched by* LOUIS.

JULIAN's *manner immediately becomes sunny again.*
What do you think Louis? (*Indicating the rooms.*) Isn't
this all so divine?

MASTERSON: We live in the age of the magazine, Mr Lester
. . . They have the power to influence many things.

LOUIS: Yes, I'm sure it will soon become the most talked-
about magazine in London . . .

JULIAN: In London?! (*His voice rising.*) Walter is not just
interested in London! Don't be silly, Louis, how could
he be interested in that?! His plans are much greater!
The two of them both look across at LOUIS, *who sees the
closeness of their relationship demonstrated in that instant.
One moment* JULIAN *is punishing* MASTERSON, *the next
he is springing to his defence.*

LOUIS: Of course. My mistake. (*To* MASTERSON.) I'm sure
you will conquer the world with it.

JULIAN (*laughs*): After all who's to stop him?!

LOUIS: Excuse me a moment.

LOUIS *walks back into the room that is dominated by the
huge radio set.* SARAH, STANLEY *and* ERIC *are standing
on the other side of the room casting shadows.*

ERIC: If only I had a tape measure with me, I could start
planning the layout of the offices immediately. But
maybe I can make some rough estimates.
He starts to measure the room with his big stride.
Here goes!

SARAH (*seeing* LOUIS *approach*): Louis, I've got a new job –
at least I think I have!

LOUIS: Yes, I heard.

SARAH *sees his preoccupation.*

I need to talk to you.

STANLEY (*calling out to* ERIC): We can have a room each,
remember! (*Exuberantly.*) And you can have a whole
department dedicated to electrical music!

LOUIS (*to* STANLEY): I think you should hear this too.

INT. THE BUILDING, LARGE CENTRAL ROOM. NIGHT
We cut to PAMELA *walking into the room where* MASTERSON
is standing with JULIAN. MASTERSON *is talking to* JULIAN
intensely, as if trying to persuade him about something.

PAMELA: Oh, I'm sorry, I didn't mean to interrupt.

JULIAN: No darling, you weren't interrupting. What Walter
was saying wasn't that important at all, not in the
slightest. Just a little trip we might be taking . . .
MASTERSON *doesn't reply, he is half turned away.*

PAMELA: It's very cold don't you think . . . ? Maybe I'll try
to light a fire . . .

INT. THE BUILDING, ROOM WITH WIRELESS. NIGHT
We cut back to STANLEY, LOUIS *and* SARAH. STANLEY*'s head
turns sharply on the cut, he looks shocked.*

STANLEY: What on earth have you been doing, Louis?

LOUIS: I told the police what I thought I'd seen –

STANLEY (*his voice incredulous*): You told the police that
you saw Julian in the hotel when he couldn't possibly
have been there – when he was on the train to Paris?!

LOUIS: He got his friends to lie for him –

STANLEY: That's ridiculous. You think all the passport
controls are lying?! But then what do you do?! You
change your story?!

LOUIS: I didn't change my story, I told them I couldn't be
certain . . .

SARAH: I wish you hadn't told them about Julian –

STANLEY: Don't you realise what a stupid thing that is to
have done, to *change your story*, what could have
possessed you? The police will have been wanting to
include you as a suspect all along –

LOUIS: They can't, I was playing at the air base. They cannot make me a suspect.

STANLEY: Why not?! They can try to prove you could have got back in time –

PAMELA enters at the end of the room and starts lighting a fire in the grate with old newspapers. She is kneeling on the floor with her lilac dress spread round her. STANLEY *has to lower his voice to an intense whisper.*

STANLEY: You changed your story, Louis, when you realised Julian couldn't possibly have been there . . . What do you think a jury will make of that?!

LOUIS: A jury?! It's not going to come to a jury?!

SARAH (*very agitated*): I'm sure it won't, there won't be a trial or –

STANLEY (*to* LOUIS, *in a furious whisper*): I told you to be careful of the police, I warned you, Louis, that they would start again . . . .

The fire is beginning to flicker. We cut to PAMELA *on the other side of the huge room. She seems to be oblivious to them, she is staring into the flames.*

We cut back to STANLEY, *his voice very tense.*

STANLEY: You need a lawyer, and very quickly –

LOUIS: Right, I will get one. I will go straight back to the hotel now and go through –

STANLEY: No you won't –

LOUIS *turns.*

You stay away from the hotel. Listen to me, Louis, I know what I am talking about, the police may well come for you in the morning. You have to try to be with a lawyer when they arrest you.

LOUIS: Arrest me? They can't arrest me. There's no evidence.

SARAH: He's right, they can't arrest him –

STANLEY: We've got to find you a lawyer. Maybe Mr Masterson will help –

LOUIS (*powerfully*): I'm not taking any 'help' from Mr
   Masterson, I promise you, that's the last thing I'll do.
   STANLEY *is startled by his vehemence and then very*
   angry.

STANLEY: You've got to stop thinking he's involved in
   some way, and Julian too, for goodness' sake Louis,
   that's only going to make things worse for you! (*He is*
   furious with LOUIS.) You can't say those things about
   them, don't you realise, you just can't! You have to
   stop. And they're just through there in the next room
   for Christ's sake!

LOUIS: So? Maybe it's time they heard it.

SARAH: Mr Donaldson will find Louis a lawyer, he will
   know somebody . . .

STANLEY (*seizing on the idea*): Yes, of course he will,
   that's perfect. (*Sharply.*) Except he never gets up till
   midday . . .

EXT. IMPERIAL, BACKYARD. MORNING
We cut to a high shot of a police officer driving JESSIE's *sports*
car into the backyard of the Imperial. GUNSON *and another*
detective are standing with a stopwatch, carefully watching the
car as it approaches.

   From a window above them we see THORNTON *watching.*

EXT. DONALDSON'S HOUSE. DAY
LOUIS *and* SARAH, *both still in their evening dress from the*
night before, walk up to the entrance to Donaldson's house, a
large London villa set back from the road with its spacious
walled garden where the band first played for the Prince.

   SARAH *rings the doorbell and the door opens almost*
immediately. They are greeted by two small girls of about eight,
VIOLETTA *and* EMILY.

SARAH: Hello? Who are you?

VIOLETTA: What do you want? (*She sees* LOUIS.) If you're selling something, you've got to go to the back entrance.

DONALDSON *appears behind them in the hall.*

DONALDSON: No, no, Violetta, these are friends. (*He smiles at* SARAH *and* LOUIS.) Welcome to you both, come in, come in. (*The little girls watching.*) This is Violetta, my niece, and her friend Emily, they're staying with me for a couple of days. (*To* LOUIS.) What a nice surprise to see you both!

LOUIS: We did telephone . . .

SARAH: But your housekeeper –

DONALDSON: Said I was still in bed . . . (*He smiles charmingly.*) The day has only just begun, hasn't it? (*He looks at their evening dress.*) You two obviously don't worry about sleep . . .

SARAH: We need your help, Arthur.

DONALDSON: Of course, whatever I can do.

LOUIS: How quickly can you get me a lawyer?

DONALDSON: A lawyer? How quick? Let me think . . . Maybe forty-five minutes. No, I don't want to exaggerate, let's say fifty.

INT. DONALDSON'S HOUSE. RECEPTION ROOM. DAY
We cut to DONALDSON *on the phone in the main reception room. There's a framed Farquhar and Tonk cartoon just by the telephone, showing both cartoon characters screaming at each other on the phone.* SARAH *and* LOUIS *are standing watching* DONALDSON. VIOLETTA *and* EMILY *are sitting together on a small sofa, staring expressionlessly at* LOUIS.

DONALDSON: So, Neville, how quickly can you come? Yes, to see a friend of mine Mr Louis Lester, that's right,

he needs your advice rather urgently. An hour? No,
that's excellent, thank you. If you can make it fifty
minutes, that would be even better . . . (*He rings off.*)
Neville is one of the best lawyers in London.

LOUIS: Thank you . . . I appreciate it.

SARAH *glances across at the clock: it is twenty to two.*

SARAH: I said I'd meet my father at St Pancras, he's
coming back today. His train is in half an hour, and
he'll worry if I'm not there to meet him . . . and of
course I haven't been home since last night, but
maybe I can get Lucy to –

LOUIS: No, you must go. I will be fine here.

DONALDSON: He will be. I will make sure nobody enters
this house until Louis has had time with his lawyer.

INT. IMPERIAL, SCHLESINGER'S OFFICE. AFTERNOON
GUNSON *and two uniformed officers are approaching*
SCHLESINGER'*s office, seen through a half-open door.*
SCHLESINGER *is sitting slumped at his desk; all his blustery*
confidence seems to have drained out of him.

GUNSON: We have a warrant for the arrest of Mr Louis
Lester on suspicion of murder.

SCHLESINGER *lifts his head slowly.*

SCHLESINGER: Well, what are you telling me about it for?
Arrest him!

GUNSON: He is not in his room.

SCHLESINGER: Well, he must have heard you coming,
mustn't he?!

INT. DONALDSON'S HOUSE, RECEPTION ROOM. AFTERNOON
We cut back to LOUIS *and* DONALDSON *in the reception room.*
A clock is ticking loudly, it is now ten past two.

Masterson at the German Embassy.
'I need to find out more about this new lot.'

Donaldson at the New Year's Eve party.

Louis and Sarah, Stanley and Pamela walk in the woods.

The reception at the German Embassy..

Stanley introduces Louis and causes outrage at the German Embassy.

Lady Cremone tells Louis Jessie is dead.

Stanley preparing the edition of *Music Express* dedicated to Jessie.

The Masonic dinner at which Louis has been invited to play.

Julian finds the loaded gun among the toys.

Louis approaching the *Music Express*
office on the night he goes on the run.

The band about to board the night train to Paris

Pamela at the Imperial, her first day out after her brother's death.

Carla sings Jessie's lament at the end of the story.

DONALDSON *is placing a needle on a gramophone record,*
some light classical music. VIOLETTA, *now by herself on the*
sofa, is staring at LOUIS *with a piercing stare.*

DONALDSON: I thought some music might help . . . (*He*
smiles.) Stop us getting too tense.

LOUIS: Yes, don't you get tense.

DONALDSON (*self-deprecating laugh*): Of course I won't . . .
He sees LOUIS *taking in the room, the photos on the*
mantelpiece of European vistas and palaces.

DONALDSON: I'm afraid those are all of my travels . . .
very egotistical, having them on display I know. It
was a wonderful time then, Louis, and Europe was a
wonderful place, you could go absolutely wherever
you fancied without a passport, stroll across any
border, it was heavenly to be young . . . (*With feeling.*)
Before the war . . .

LOUIS: Yes, it must have been.

DONALDSON (*sitting opposite* LOUIS): Louis, you're always
so marvellously calm.

LOUIS: Not today, I'm certainly not today.

DONALDSON: Well you've been up all night my friend.
VIOLETTA *is still staring at* LOUIS.
I admire you so much, how you conduct yourself – if
I'm allowed to say that – how you don't allow yourself
to be cowered.

LOUIS: No I don't like to be 'cowered', Mr Donaldson.
And I refuse to panic now . . .

DONALDSON: That's right. There's no reason to panic.

LOUIS: But just realising you're going to be accused of a
crime, and a very serious crime, and probably you can
do nothing to stop that happening and somehow the
evidence is going to be 'adjusted' in a way so it points
straight at you – that is just a little alarming, Mr
Donaldson.

DONALDSON: Of course that's alarming Louis, but the English police, they may not be as efficient as they claim to be, but they never wilfully hang the wrong man.

LOUIS *looks up sharply. The word sends a chill through him.* VIOLETTA *is staring unflinchingly.*

DONALDSON: I'm sorry, that was quite the wrong thing to say! Quite hopeless of me . . . Don't worry, any moment Neville will be here.

EMILY *is standing in the doorway. She is wearing* LOUIS' *top hat and cape. She beams at them.*

EMILY: It's time for tea!

DONALDSON: It's not nearly time for tea, my dear.

EMILY: But we've made some cakes! And we're going to eat them in the kitchen!

INT. DONALDSON'S HOUSE. KITCHEN. AFTERNOON

We cut to LOUIS *standing in the kitchen watching* VIOLETTA *and* EMILY *proudly take their cakes out of the oven, watched over by* DONALDSON *and the cook, Mrs Courtney.* EMILY *is still wearing* LOUIS' *top hat and cape.*

DONALDSON: Marvellous-looking cakes, you two! I congratulate you, they look irresistible.

VIOLETTA: There are three each. (*She looks across at* LOUIS.) Oh, I forgot about him.

DONALDSON: I'm sure there's plenty for all of us . . . Have a seat, Louis, I think we're going to be eating these cakes whether we like it or not for quite some time . . . Certainly till Neville is here . . .

LOUIS *sits on the other side of the kitchen and watches Mrs Courtney bustle around with the girls. The kettle is on the stove, just beginning to whistle gently.*

DONALDSON: Mrs Courtney will make us all some tea . . .
I see no reason why we shouldn't have two or even
three teas today . . . There's no law against that, is
there girls?!

VIOLETTA *has stood on a chair and reached for a large*
bread knife which is hanging with the other knives.
But Violetta, leave the knives alone, Mrs Courtney
will cut the bread . . .

DONALDSON*'s voice is fading away. We stay close on*
LOUIS, *watching the scene in the kitchen. There is a tabby*
cat sitting in the corner, the little girls with the cakes, the
sound of the kettle whistling.

We move in on his eyes, the sound of the kettle is
increasing all the time. We are getting closer still on his eyes
and then back to the scene in the kitchen.

Suddenly the sound of the kettle slides into the whistle of
a steam train.

EXT./INT. FLASHBACK

We see the steam pouring out of the train's engine. We are in the
field, having the picnic in Part One, with MASTERSON *presiding,*
as his private train stands waiting. The scene is idyllic, except
for WESLEY, *the band's manager, who is watching it all with*
suspicion. LOUIS *ignores him.* SARAH *is beckoning to* LOUIS.
She is holding her camera and calling to him.

SARAH: I really want to take your picture, just need to find
the right spot! Come on, Louis . . .

They are moving into the wood, above the picnic site,
away from the train.

LOUIS *is following* SARAH, *who is making her way*
through the trees.

Suddenly the trees form a much darker tunnel in the
woods, the foliage thicker. For a moment SARAH *is hardly*

visible; she is obscured by the undergrowth and overhanging branches. LOUIS *is after her, calling on her to slow down. She does not slow down. The wood is getting truly dark.*

A door suddenly swings open and LOUIS *finds himself moving along an institutional passage, with bars on its windows.* SARAH *is walking ahead of him, dressed in the same dress.*

LOUIS *is being guided along the passage very firmly but he cannot see the person's face, just the arm clamped to him and the shape of a figure pushing him forward.* MASTERSON *is standing in the passage with* JULIAN *watching* LOUIS *go past.*

SARAH *does not look back at him. She is walking very fast, her footsteps ringing out loudly.*

Suddenly she steps aside, in the distance a door is opening and LOUIS *can see two figures. One looks like* THORNTON, *the other is in dark clothes, lurking in the shadows.*

LOUIS *turns sharply round, trying to retreat, but the figure who has got hold of him stops him moving. He cannot see his face. The figure lunges towards him, trying to put a hood on* LOUIS' *face. The hood goes over him.*

INT. DONALDSON'S HOUSE, KITCHEN. NIGHT
LOUIS *awakes with a terrible start as somebody seems to lurch at him.*

He sees he is staring down into the eyes of the cat that has jumped on to his lap.

We move in on LOUIS' *eyes and then cut wide.*

LOUIS *is alone in the kitchen. He is startled to realise it is now dark outside.*

LOUIS *stands up. There is no sign of the cakes and the tea.*

He touches the stove, it is completely cold. His clothes EMILY *was wearing are lying on the table.*

He walks over to the kitchen door, which is half glass. It is locked. He calls out.

LOUIS: Hello? Anybody there?
He tries the door again. He sees a figure approach. It is the little girl VIOLETTA. *She stares at him through the glass door with a look of total hostility.*
LOUIS: Please, would you open this door?
The child stares back at him. She shakes her head, while not taking her eyes off him.
Mrs Courtney suddenly appears and bustles the child away. She avoids looking at LOUIS *as she does so, except for one quick frightened look.* LOUIS *watches her retreat with the child into the rest of the house.* LOUIS *puts on his coat.*
He turns and walks across the kitchen to the back door. It is also locked. He looks up at one of the kitchen windows that overlooks the garden. He can hear a doorbell and loud knocking. He then hears DONALDSON*'s voice in the hall.*
LOUIS looks round the kitchen for something to break the window with. He suddenly sees the bread knife that Violetta tried to get and all the other knives have been removed from the kitchen. Now he can hear men's voices talking to DONALDSON *in the hall.*
He turns and grabs the first thing he can to break the window, a small saucepan. He smashes the glass of the side window and pulls himself up, cutting himself on the jagged glass as he goes.

EXT. DONALDSON'S GARDEN. NIGHT
We cut to LOUIS *moving across the large walled garden, away from the house. The only light is spilling from the back of the house.* LOUIS *is trying to find the small door he entered the garden with, when he was with the band and played for the*

*Prince. He lurches among the flowerbeds. He is bleeding very
badly from the cut.*

*He reaches the small door in the wall and pulls and pulls at
it, but it won't open.*

*A voice calls out, he turns and sees the two small girls are
standing on the veranda. One of them is pointing at him.*

VIOLETTA: He's there! He's over there!

*He sees movement from inside the house, men moving
towards the veranda.*

*He pulls on the door with all his strength, it finally
comes open and* LOUIS *emerges into the side street. He can
see there are two police cars parked in front of the house.*

He runs off down the side street and into the night.

INT. IMPERIAL, BALLROOM. NIGHT

We cut to STANLEY *entering the ballroom at the Imperial. It is
entirely empty except for a central T-shaped table arranged in
the middle of the room for a private banquet. There are only ten
places laid. The table glows out in the middle of the surrounding
darkness.* PAMELA *is standing in the evening dress she wore
when she saw the band for the very first time. She is alone in
the room.* STANLEY *is in a dinner jacket, his manner is
preoccupied, businesslike.*

PAMELA: Stanley!

STANLEY: Hello, you look beautiful . . .

PAMELA: I'm surprised you noticed, but then this is such a
rare thing.

STANLEY: What do you mean?

PAMELA: You and I alone . . .

STANLEY: Ah. (*Sharp grin.*) We'll soon have plenty of
chances for that. (*He moves to take her arm.*) You're
here very early.

He tries to touch her but PAMELA *moves out of reach.*

PAMELA: So are you. But then I don't want to miss a moment of Mr Masterson's farewell meal –

STANLEY: It's not farewell, he's just visiting the USA for business reasons –

PAMELA: You're very well informed about his movements all of a sudden.

STANLEY: Well, I've been in meetings with him all day . . . ! You know Julian is going to have a job in his office in America, for a few months at least.

PAMELA: Yes, I heard that, my brother is going to be an American businessman . . . and suddenly you're his partner too, aren't you? Mr Masterson's?

STANLEY: Not a partner, no, but definitely a colleague. This is such an enormous chance for me Pamela . . .

PAMELA *looks at him across the width of the room.*

PAMELA: It certainly appears to be Stanley, yes.

EXT. PARK. NIGHT

We cut to LOUIS *hurrying along a path in a park. It is very dark. He is bleeding profusely; he stops underneath a lamp and starts tearing at a hankerchief with his teeth, trying to tear it in two so he can make a tourniquet out of it. Two old men are walking towards him down the path, one of them with a stick. They are bearing down on him, the old man's stick ringing out on the path.* LOUIS *can't tear the hankerchief, instead he twists it round his hand in a crude bandage. It soaks with blood immediately.*

He turns to get away from the old men and walks straight into a young boy on a bicycle. The bicycle and the boy go over on the grass; the boy is shouting curses. LOUIS *stops, and reaches with his other hand to help the boy up. The boy sees the blood pouring out of his bandaged hand.* LOUIS *follows his gaze, he tries to make light of it.*

LOUIS: It's just been a very clumsy day . . .

The boy's eyes staring at him. LOUIS *turns and moves off into the night.*

INT. IMPERIAL, BALLROOM. NIGHT

We cut back to the ballroom. The meal has started. MASTERSON *and* LADY CREMONE *are sitting at the head of the table.* JULIAN, STANLEY, ERIC, PAMELA, SARAH *and* CARLA *are sitting round the table. There are two empty places. Candles are flickering along the table. The food hasn't been served yet, the waiters are pouring wine for the guests.* LADY CREMONE *clinks her glass and stands.*

LADY CREMONE: I thought we'd get rid of the the speeches before the serious eating has begun. (*She smiles.*) It's always so much more relaxing that way! So even though we're missing one or two people –

MASTERSON: I'm sure our missing guests will be here soon.

JULIAN: He likes everything to be so orderly, always! (*His manner towards* MASTERSON, *loud and assertive.*)

LADY CREMONE: Yes, I just wanted to thank Walter, or should I say Mr Masterson, since he's my 'boss' now –

MASTERSON *smiles at this.*

– for not only laying on this meal –

MASTERSON: I thought we'd have the ballroom to ourselves for once, as we've spent so much time here.

LADY CREMONE: Yes, and it's a charming gesture, I think we'd all agree!

We see PAMELA *watching* LADY CREMONE, *how she's embracing her new role almost too effusively.* PAMELA*'s look moves from* LADY CREMONE *to* MASTERSON, *to* STANLEY *and then to* JULIAN.

LADY CREMONE: So this meal is not only to bid farewell to Mr Masterson on his trip to the United States – (*She smiles.*) where hopefully he will keep the President quite safe, and hopefully too, where he will not spend too much time.

JULIAN: Oh, he'll be back, don't worry! He's only happy when he's travelling!

LADY CREMONE: But also this is to celebrate the great new venture we're embarking on together, under Stanley and Eric's editorship. (*To* MASTERSON.) We understand of course, we're just a corner of your empire –

MASTERSON: Not a corner, never just a corner . . .

LADY CREMONE: But we hope, in our own way, to make many waves –

The door opens at the end of the ballroom and DONALDSON *hurries in.*

DONALDSON: I'm so sorry I'm late . . . I got unavoidably held up! Please forgive me.

As he sits, he looks across at SARAH.

I'll explain everything in a minute . . .

EXT. CHURCH SQUARE. NIGHT

LOUIS *is approaching a garden square, dominated by a church. The door of the church is open and light is spilling out. We can hear organ music. There is a telephone box by the railings near the entrance to the church.* LOUIS *stands in the shadows, still bleeding badly. A woman is on the phone.*

INT. IMPERIAL, BALLROOM. NIGHT

We cut back to the dinner in the shadowy ballroom. The guests are eating their main course. JULIAN *is watching* MASTERSON *presiding at the head of the table. There is a glint in his eyes as if he wants to cause a little trouble. He suddenly stands up.*

JULIAN: Carla has agreed to sing!

CARLA, *in the middle of her food, looks up surprised.*
Come on, you want to, don't you?!

PAMELA (*watching her febrile brother*): Julian, it's the middle of the meal . . .

JULIAN: When better?!

He takes CARLA's *hand and leads her towards the grand piano in the corner.*

Until Louis turns up, you will have to put up with me accompanying you . . .

CARLA: Well then we'll do one very simple song, shall we?!

JULIAN, *oblivious to the commotion he is causing, sits at the piano and nonchalantly plays a few notes. The doors at the far end of the ballroom open again, this time they bang open.* SCHLESINGER *is standing there, he looks across at* SARAH.

SCHLESINGER: There's a telephone call for you, apparently it's urgent . . .

SARAH *gets up and crosses the ballroom.*

MASTERSON *looks at* SCHLESINGER *from the head of the table.*

MASTERSON: You must join us, Mr Schlesinger, no, please . . . I was just thinking in fact what I might do for this hotel . . . (*Dryly.*) I've always liked it here.

INT. IMPERIAL, ROOM NEXT TO BALLROOM/CHURCH SQUARE

SARAH *is in a booth in the lobby area, outside the ballroom. The door of the ballroom is open and we can hear* CARLA *begin to sing.*

We intercut between SARAH *and* LOUIS, *who is in the phone box outside the church. While he is on the phone, some elderly members of the congregation are entering the church for evensong. One or two old ladies glance at him with idle curiosity.*

SARAH: Louis?! Where are you?

LOUIS: Near a church.

SARAH: Where is the church?

LOUIS: You don't need to know that.

SARAH: You can tell me where you are! You don't trust me suddenly?! Why did you telephone me if you don't trust me?

LOUIS: I need somewhere to go.

SARAH: Come here and we will work out the best plan –

LOUIS: Come back to the hotel?! I'm not that stupid, Sarah!

SARAH: What are you saying? That you don't trust any of us? You think we've all turned against you in two days?! Just like that?! I can't believe you'd think that, Louis . . .

LOUIS: Donaldson called the police.

SARAH: He did not call the police! They appeared at his house, he's just told me what happened –

LOUIS: They 'appeared' at his house?!

SARAH: Yes – of course they were going to visit everybody you know, they're looking for you . . . !

LOUIS: And no lawyer ever turned up –

SARAH: He got delayed . . .

LOUIS: Do you know what they did? They locked me in, as if I was –

SARAH (*passionately*): They wanted to let you sleep, they wanted to stop the children disturbing you – you've got to believe me! Come here Louis, please. This is where people can help you . . .

An elderly lady accompanied by a portly young man in his twenties have seen LOUIS *in the phone box and how badly he is bleeding. They stand staring at him.*

LOUIS: How many times do I have to tell you I'm not coming back to the hotel?!

SARAH: Then I'll meet you somewhere else, wherever you
     like! The police are going to arrest you . . .

LOUIS: They've got to find me first –

SARAH: You can't run away from them!

LOUIS: I can get out of the country –

SARAH: You'll never manage that on your own! (*Tears are
     pouring down her cheeks but she is passionate, her tone
     has power.*) I would hate something to happen to you!
     You must meet me, Louis, I can't bear the idea that
     you don't trust me, you have to trust somebody
     Louis, you have to!
     *The elderly lady and the portly young man are moving
     closer to the phone booth. The portly man has sharp little
     eyes.*

LOUIS: Maybe I don't . . . I think this will be a lot easier
     if I don't trust anyone.

SARAH: Louis, you have to remember –

LOUIS: What do I have to remember? 'Who' I am? Is that
     what you mean?!

SARAH: Yes, that is what I mean! But not in that way . . .
     (*Crying.*) *Please listen to me*, not everybody thinks like
     me or Stanley, not everybody wants to help you –

LOUIS: No, Sarah, that's where you're wrong, that's what
     I've just found out. You think just the same as
     everybody else.
     LOUIS *rings off. The portly young man is very close to the
     box and both he and the elderly woman are looking at
     how much* LOUIS *is bleeding; it is all over his hands.*
     LOUIS *decides to brazen it out.*

     Thank you for being so patient. (*Indicating that the
     phone is now free.*) And don't be concerned, I'm going
     to see a doctor now . . .

INT. IMPERIAL, BALLROOM. NIGHT

SARAH *is re-entering the ballroom looking very pale.* CARLA *is singing,* JULIAN *is accompanying her quite competently on the piano,* DONALDSON *is smoking a cigar,* SCHLESINGER *is standing in the shadows,* PAMELA *is watching them all closely.*

STANLEY: Was that Louis? Is he on his way . . . ?

SARAH: That was Louis. He's not on his way.

MASTERSON: That's a disappointment, a real pity, we won't have a proper chance to say goodbye.

LADY CREMONE (*smiles vaguely, she's talking plans with* MASTERSON): How strange Louis's not here, I wouldn't have thought he'd want to miss this.
Suddenly PAMELA *interrupts, her voice cutting through with sharp intensity.*

PAMELA: Stop playing, Julian! Julian, will you stop playing!
JULIAN *stops. They are all looking at* PAMELA. *She stands up holding her glass, she looks fragile and pale, she is a little drunk but her voice has authority.*

PAMELA: I have my own toast to propose . . . to pay tribute to how everybody seems to be working for you now, Mr Masterson.

DONALDSON: I'm not. (*He smiles at* CARLA.) Carla isn't . . .

PAMELA: Everybody, that is, except for me, and I'm sure that is how it should be, because I have no speciality of any kind and I'm quite unqualified for regular work, but I'm sure it is a wonderful thing –
She looks straight at SARAH *and then* STANLEY.
– to be working for Mr Masterson . . . and he will take care of my brother I am sure, too, in his career over the ocean –

JULIAN: I'm only going to be there a while, a short while.

PAMELA: Because my brother is a very sensitive person . . .
(*She stares at* JULIAN *for a moment.*) So my toast –

what is my toast? – (*They are all staring at her fragile figure.*) My toast is to you . . . (*Pointedly.*) You will all prosper I am sure, in the ways you want, in what you've set your hearts on . . . by working for Mr Masterson.

She looks at them all, then raises her glass.

And to our benefactor, Mr Masterson!

They all join in the toast. We cut close to STANLEY. *He's been watching* PAMELA*'s speech intensely, he suddenly makes a decision and gets up.*

STANLEY: Well, it's copy night back at the magazine, our last edition in the old place, and though it has been put to bed, I think I'll go back there.

ERIC *looks up.*

No, Eric, I'll do this, I just feel the need . . .

STANLEY *leaves. We cut back to* MASTERSON.

MASTERSON: Thank you, Pamela, for your generous speech.

For a second he stares at them all, especially JULIAN.

And I'd just like to add, because there's an empty chair, I'm sure before this meal is through, Mr Lester will be joining us . . .

There is a high shot of the banquet, glowing out in the middle of the shadowy ballroom, with the characters sitting round the lavish table presided over by MASTERSON.

INT. MUSIC EXPRESS OFFICE. NIGHT

We cut to STANLEY *banging through the door of his office,* ROSIE *turns.*

STANLEY: Our last edition here, Rosie! I thought I'd have one more look.

ROSIE: That is just what Mr Wax is doing too.

STANLEY: Really! I had no idea he was that sentimental . . .

ROSIE: Are you sure you're doing the right thing, Stanley?
Letting Mr Masterson buy our magazine and –
STANLEY: Absolutely, without a doubt . . .
ROSIE: We'll have no control at all . . .
STANLEY: We've got to grow! Don't you see?! (*He turns.*)
Rosie, this is going to change all our lives. (*He smiles
excitedly.*) And not just for a few months, for ever.

EXT. LONDON STREET. NIGHT
We cut to the Music Express *street. A figure is approaching the
lighted building. It is* LOUIS. *We see him from behind, just as we
did at the beginning of Part One. It is the same sequences of
shots:* LOUIS *waiting for the messenger to leave and then
entering the building. But then just as he slips through the door,
the camera moves back, turns, and stares down the night street.
We see something we didn't see before.*

*Coming round the corner of the street is the portly young
man from the church.*

He pauses and stares up at the lighted window.

PART FIVE

EXT. MUSIC EXPRESS STREET. EARLY MORNING

The paper boy is nearing the Music Express *building. We are moving with him along the street as he delivers papers fast. We can see clearly now the picture and headline on the front of the paper: a large photo of Louis under the headline:* WANTED, HOTEL MURDER SUSPECT. *As the boy reaches the front door of the* Music Express *office, he glances up after delivering the paper.* STANLEY *is standing at the second-floor window,* LOUIS *is behind him in the shadows. For a fleeting moment,* STANLEY *and the paper boy stare at each other.*

INT. MUSIC EXPRESS OFFICE. EARLY MORNING

We cut inside the Music Express *office, the jumble of boxes, paper and typewriters.*

STANLEY: He didn't see you, pretty sure he didn't.

LOUIS: He's holding a picture of me. (*Watching the boy move off down the street.*) So he'd better not have . . .

STANLEY: Did I tell you I spoke to Eric?

LOUIS (*his head turned sharply*): No you didn't. When did you do that?

STANLEY: When you first arrived last night. (*Indicating* LOUIS' *bandaged hand.*) Bleeding all over the place . . .

LOUIS: And what did you say to him?

STANLEY: I said bring a car first thing in the morning – we need to move Louis. (*He looks at him.*) I didn't know who else to call . . .

LOUIS: And he can be trusted?

STANLEY: Not sure, we'll soon see. If the police turn up now –

Just as STANLEY *says this, a very large black saloon car appears at the end of the street and drives slowly towards the* Music Express *office.*

LOUIS: Who's this?

STANLEY: I don't know . . . It's like Mr Masterson has sent
it for you.

*They stare down through the window. The large car stops
in front of the building and the gangling figure of* ERIC
gets out.

STANLEY: Eric?! What on earth is he doing bringing
something that size!

INT./EXT. MUSIC EXPRESS STAIRCASE/FRONT DOOR.
EARLY MORNING

We move with LOUIS *as he walks down the staircase in the*
Music Express *building. In front of him he can see* STANLEY
and ERIC *framed in the front door which is open; beyond them
is the large saloon car.* LOUIS *is still in full evening dress, but
carrying his jacket.* ERIC *is in vigorous discussion with* STANLEY.
LOUIS *can half hear what they are saying.*

ERIC: It's the only thing I could get my hands on! It's my
uncle's car . . . I said I needed it to help us move
premises.

STANLEY: It's not exactly inconspicuous, Eric, is it?!

ERIC: I was lucky to get anything at such short notice –

STANLEY: We're going to get stopped immediately in that.

ERIC: I don't think so, not this early, not if we drive
straight there. (*He looks round.*) Louis! Come on,
I think I have somewhere we can go!

STANLEY (*to* LOUIS): Put your jacket on. If you're half-
dressed you're even more noticeable –

LOUIS: You've managed to change from last night and
I haven't . . .

STANLEY: We'll see to that, somehow.

EXT. STREET/INT. CAR. EARLY MORNING

We cut wide, STANLEY, LOUIS *and* ERIC *emerge from the building into the empty street. The paper boy has gone, the street is eerily quiet.*

STANLEY: Get in the car, Louis.

LOUIS: Not until I know where we're going.

ERIC: We're going west, about six miles.

LOUIS: Why are we going west?

STANLEY (*urgently*): We can't stand around having a discussion! Get in the car!

LOUIS *gets in the back of the large saloon car,* STANLEY *and* ERIC *in the front.*

LOUIS: Everybody's going to look at this car . . .

STANLEY: Yes, so you've got to keep your head down –

LOUIS: And not see where you're taking me?

STANLEY: That's right . . . the whole way. You've got to lie right down on the seat – go on, lie down.

LOUIS *hesitates. Right at that moment another smaller car appears in the street and stops about twenty feet from them.*

STANLEY: Maybe it's already too late . . .

SARAH *gets out of the smaller car and walks towards them.* LOUIS *watches her approach.*

LOUIS: Don't let her get in this car.

STANLEY: What?

LOUIS: You heard me, don't let her get in.

SARAH *reaches them.* STANLEY *winds down his window a few inches.*

STANLEY: Sarah, what are you doing here?

SARAH (*to* LOUIS): I thought this was the only place you could come . . . (*To* STANLEY.) I wanted to say something to Louis –

STANLEY: Were you followed here?

SARAH: No, I wasn't.

ERIC: How do you know?

SARAH: That's Pamela's car. (*Indicating her car.*) I stayed
with her last night, nobody's going to follow her . . .
I need a word with Louis, just for a moment . . .
She opens the back door of their car, to get in.

STANLEY: We've got to go, Sarah . . .

SARAH: I have to have a word with Louis . . .

LOUIS: Some other time, Sarah . . .
He closes the door, but SARAH *is still leaning against the
car.*

STANLEY: We can't wait around like this, we're going to
be seen!

ERIC: She can follow us. (*To* SARAH.) You can follow us.

SARAH: Right! –

STANLEY: But keep your eyes open!
ERIC *accelerates down the street; we see everything from
inside the car, from* LOUIS' *point of view;* SARAH *running
back to her car, getting in and starting to follow them.*

LOUIS: Why on earth did you do that?

ERIC: She was going to follow us anyway, so why not put
her to use? It makes it much more difficult for anybody
else to follow us –

STANLEY: Does it? We're in convoy now . . . (*Suddenly
erupting.*) Get down Louis for God's sake! GET
RIGHT DOWN! If you sit like that, we won't even
get a hundred yards . . .
LOUIS *ducks down on the back seat.*

ERIC: Stretch out, it's very comfortable, I went to the
seaside a few weeks ago in this car . . .
LOUIS *stretches out flat on the back seat. He can only see
the tops of the buildings, the trees, the high walls, church
towers, everything seen from his point of view lying in the
back. The car is picking up speed, the outside is becoming
more blurred, the sun stabs straight into his eyes.*

We cut abruptly to what has led LOUIS *to be lying, hunted, on this back seat. We see* JESSIE*'s body in the hospital,* MASTERSON *and* JULIAN *among the Masons in the basement dining room as* LOUIS *and the band begin to play,* THORNTON *calling down the passage at* LOUIS *that he knows what happened to* JESSIE, STANLEY *arguing with* LOUIS *in the magazine's new empty offices, the police turning up at* DONALDSON*'s house, the portly man and his mother watching* LOUIS *bleed in the phone booth,* MASTERSON *presiding over the ghostly banquet in the ballroom, and then the portly man appearing in the night street and staring up at the lighted window of the* Music Express *building.*

We cut back to the present with a jarring cut. The interior of the car is full of smoke, STANLEY *is chain-smoking. A car is careering towards them, with a bell ringing loudly, it roars past the saloon car coming very close to it. We see this all from inside the car, from the windscreen and the side window.*

LOUIS *can't stop himself sitting up, to watch where the police car has gone. He sees it disappear down the street,* STANLEY *shouts at him.*

STANLEY: Get down, Louis! For Christ's sake! I told you to keep down . . .

ERIC: The police have probably worked out what Sarah worked out, where you are most likely to be . . .

LOUIS *lies back down, staring at the back of* STANLEY*'s head through the smoke.*

LOUIS: Why won't you tell me where you're taking me?

STANLEY: We have told you, we're going west.

LOUIS: I don't know why on earth we're going out to the suburbs –

STANLEY: Because we need somewhere to put you . . .

LOUIS: I don't believe they'll be watching every station yet . . . the obvious thing for us to do is to get to

Victoria, you buy a ticket, you give it to me, and I get
on the boat train. We should be doing the simplest
plan –

STANLEY: Really?! You've done this before, have you?!

LOUIS: The longer we leave it, the more places they'll be
watching, going in the opposite direction is plain
stupid –

STANLEY: Pull in! Pull in here, Eric!

ERIC *turns, startled.*

Pull up, Eric, right now!

EXT. INDUSTRIAL BUILDING. DAY

*The car pulls up in a side road, dominated by very high walls
of an industrial building. The road is a track leading to a dead
end and waste ground.* SARAH*'s car pulls up in the mouth of
the side road, and keeps its distance. We see in a wide shot*
STANLEY *and* LOUIS *getting out of their car and* STANLEY
indicating that LOUIS *follow him along the track. We cut closer,*
STANLEY *turns and confronts* LOUIS *by the huge industrial wall.*

STANLEY: You want to do that? Go and catch the boat-
train?!

LOUIS: Yes. I think I should go straight there.

STANLEY: Then we'll turn right round, and drop you at
the front of Victoria Station, and watch you being
arrested within twenty seconds.

LOUIS: We don't need to do it like that, of course, I –

STANLEY: And you have your passport on you, do you,
Louis?

LOUIS: No, because it's at the hotel, and you told me not
on any account to go back there, but one of the band
could get it from my room and meet me –

STANLEY: While you sit in a restaurant on Victoria Station
drinking coffee, I suppose?! Listen to me, Louis –

Donaldson told all of us last night the police have
Harry Thornton saying he saw you screaming at Jessie
the night she was attacked . . . then they've got
another witness too, some waiter saying he saw you
carrying an unconscious girl out of the hotel when
you first started playing at the Imperial. They have
timed the drive from the air base where you were
playing when it happened and worked out you could
have easily got back in time to knife her –

LOUIS (*coming right back at him*): And then after I had
attacked her, I got back in the car did I?! Covered
in blood, because I would have been totally covered in
blood, and drove up again to the hotel so I could be
seen arriving, as relaxed as could be?! And then I rang
the fire alarm, and woke up the whole hotel, so I
could be discovered with her? Is that what they're
suggesting I did . . . ?!

STANLEY: Yes, they think you could have done that –

LOUIS: How?

STANLEY: Because you're a clever Negro . . . 'He thinks
he's a clever Negro, everybody knows what an opinion
he has of himself!' That's what they've decided you
did – So if you want to take your chance with the
English legal system then I'm not going to stop you,
I promise you, I'm not . . .

SARAH *has got out of the car and is walking towards
them.* ERIC *is close by, watching.*

Because I don't have to do any of this you realise,
carrying you around London . . . while the whole
police force –

LOUIS: Why are you doing it then?

Their eyes meet.

I'd like to know that, Stanley.

STANLEY *is infuriated by* LOUIS' *apparent lack of trust in
him. He meets his gaze.*

STANLEY: Maybe because the last ever interview you give
will make quite a good story –

*There is the sound of a car horn, they look around startled.
Some children are playing around* SARAH*'s car, a couple
of them have actually got into the car and are sounding
the horn repeatedly, shrieking with laughter.* SARAH *runs
back towards the car.*

SARAH: Stop that at once! Get out of the car! . . . All of
you get away from the car!

*The children continue to laugh and shout and thump the
bonnet of the car.*

LOUIS: I don't trust her . . .

STANLEY: Well, she's here, so there's not a lot of choice,
you've got to trust her.

EXT. SUBURBAN STREETS AND HOUSES. DAY

ERIC*'s large car driving through a suburban housing estate,
mock-Tudor buildings built around a duck pond. There are two
large apartment buildings surrounded by smaller houses. It is an
idyllic-seeming suburban spot. We see the approach through the
windscreen: the black and white buildings, all surreally uniform,
the neat gardens, a net curtain twitching, two old ladies walking
together with a dog. We cut wide: the large black car standing
out among the mock-Tudor buildings and neat hedgerows.*

STANLEY *and* ERIC *get out of the car.* SARAH *parks a little
distance away and walks towards them.* LOUIS *gets out of the
car standing in his dinner jacket in the morning light. He is
moving slowly, unhurried, as if he is the owner of the car.*

STANLEY (*under his breath*): Come on, come on!

LOUIS: There's no hurry . . .

LOUIS*' tone is as if to an employee. He forces himself to
walk as nonchalantly as he can towards the large mock-
Tudor block. Another net curtain twitches. They move inside.*

INT. STAIRCASE. APARTMENT BLOCK. DAY
STANLEY, ERIC, LOUIS *and* SARAH *are going up the staircase
inside the block of flats.*

STANLEY: What were you doing out there?
LOUIS: If I run, people will notice.
> ERIC *is opening the door of an apartment, jangling a large
> bunch of keys.*

INT. SUBURBAN APARTMENT. DAY
*The door swings open to reveal a cramped little apartment,
which is full of boxes, dismembered radios, gramophones and
bits of film projectors. It is like a workshop where somebody is
hoarding machines. In the corner there is an almost complete
projector.*

STANLEY: Eric, what is this place?!
ERIC: It's my brother's . . . He's even more interested in
     taking things apart than I am.
LOUIS: Where is he?
ERIC: He won't be back till later . . . he works in a film
     studio, I have a key because I work with him
     sometimes. We're building a projector together . . .
STANLEY (*suddenly to* LOUIS): Keep away from the
     window!
> *They are all very tense, adrenalised with nerves, talking
> across each other fast, not able to sit, criss-crossing the
> small flat. The shots are jagged and close.* SARAH *is opening
> drawers; she finds a pair of scissors. They can hear voices
> from the flat above.*
LOUIS: And how long am I going to be here for?
STANLEY: We need a few hours.
ERIC: Till it's dark.

STANLEY: There's a meeting with Mr Masterson in just
    under two hours . . .

LOUIS: Are you going to go to that?

STANLEY: Eric and I have to . . . Sarah too, but she can
    join later – Mr Wax is signing away the magazine, we
    need to be there for that, if we're not . . .

ERIC: They may think we're holding a fugitive, which we
    are – (*Turns to* LOUIS.) First time I've ever broken the
    law . . .

    SARAH *is by* LOUIS; *she has cut up a pillowcase.*

LOUIS: What are you doing?

SARAH: I need to change your bandage.

LOUIS: It's all right, it's stopped bleeding –

SARAH: You need a new bandage, it'll get infected
    otherwise. I'm going to do this, keep still.

LOUIS (*reluctantly keeping still, straight at* STANLEY): You
    want me to stay here all day, till it's dark?!

STANLEY: Yes.

ERIC: If you don't move, you're quite safe, nobody's going
    to come in here . . .

LOUIS: What if somebody wants your brother?

STANLEY: Don't answer the door, whatever you do –

SARAH: Keep still, please. (*She is fixing the bandage.*) I'm
    going to do this properly.

STANLEY: I think I will get your passport, it's much easier
    for me than for anybody else – I've got just enough
    time before the meeting . . .

LOUIS: You know what the most important thing is –
    (*Indicating his clothes.*) I need to get out of these,
    wearing this in the middle of the day is –

STANLEY: By the time it's night, it won't matter.

SARAH: I'll get you a change of clothes, I'll do that –

LOUIS: You're expected at the meeting –

SARAH: They won't worry if I'm late, I'll get them and
    come straight back.

STANLEY: We can't both go to the hotel . . .

SARAH: I won't go to the hotel –

LOUIS: When I've got a change of clothes, I can do the rest
on my own . . . Thanks for the help, but I don't want
you all to take risks, so –

STANLEY: Louis, hard as it is, you've got to stay in this
room. When it's dark we'll move you. Maybe we can
find somewhere out of London for a couple of days
and then you can try to reach a port. (*Very sharp.*)
Promise me you won't be stupid and try to move.

INT. THE MAGAZINE'S NEW OFFICES. DAY
*We cut to the suite of large empty rooms in the central London
building which is now the new office of* Music Express. *There
is hardly any furniture, but the largest room is dominated by
the great radio set. There is one large desk at the far end of the
central room. Through the double doors is another almost totally
empty room in which* ROSIE *is working at a temporary desk,
a trestle table. She is typing. She looks up,* MASTERSON *is
standing by the desk in the far room. He is holding a slim
briefcase with a golden catch.*

ROSIE: Mr Masterson . . . !
She gets up, MASTERSON *gives a little nod of greeting,*
ROSIE *moves towards him.*
Is there anything I can get you, sir?

MASTERSON: No, no, quite unnecessary. Please carry on.
He sits at his large desk in the empty room. ROSIE *goes
back to her desk, they talk over the huge distance.*
You're even earlier than I am . . .

ROSIE: Well, it's a big day, the signing of the agreement,
so I thought I should be early, days don't get much
bigger than this, do they? Well, for me anyway!

MASTERSON (*studying papers on his desk*): Nor for me . . .

After the signing I'm leaving the country with Mr
Luscombe.

ROSIE (*surprised*): You're going today, sir?

MASTERSON: Indeed, it's a very interesting trip in prospect.
We're flying to Cherbourg tonight, then crossing to
New York on a brand-new liner, which is kind of
appropriate, don't you agree?
He looks at ROSIE *across the empty office.*
How all new ventures ought to begin . . .

INT. PAMELA AND JULIAN'S HOUSE. BEDROOM. DAY
We cut to a bedroom in PAMELA *and* JULIAN'*s house. Large
suitcases are spread out on the bed and a thin-faced valet is
packing* JULIAN'*s beautiful clothes.* JULIAN *is sitting on a chair,
smoking, watching his clothes being packed.* PAMELA *is
standing in a corner.*

JULIAN: I don't think I should take too many clothes,
because I will get a whole new wardrobe out there,
won't I?

PAMELA: I'm not sure you need a whole new wardrobe,
darling . . .

JULIAN: I need to look like an important businessman,
who can impress New York . . . stun them! I'll have to
have some very serious shoes especially, so people
look at me and say, 'My God, this young man is
someone!'

PAMELA: I'm sure they'll find you some extremely serious
shoes.

JULIAN: Oh God, darling . . . ! (*He gets up.*) A day of
goodbyes, what a terrible prospect. I will cry so much.

PAMELA: And I will miss you so much . . . ! You will do
most of your goodbyes on the telephone won't you?
That way you won't get delayed –

JULIAN: Marvellous idea, that'll be so much easier! Then I
can just say, 'This goodbye has gone on long enough,
so goodbye!'
He mimes ringing off the phone. He moves to PAMELA.
You'll be here?
PAMELA: Of course I'll be here, nearly all the time.
JULIAN: You'll stay close by me? (*Intensely.*) Really close?
PAMELA: I'll stick very close. (*She kisses him.*) Almost all
the time.

INT. IMPERIAL HOTEL LOBBY. DAY
STANLEY *is crossing the lobby of the Imperial Hotel. There are
two uniformed police officers by the main desk.* STANLEY *walks
purposefully towards the lifts. A voice suddenly says 'Mr
Mitchell'.* STANLEY *turns. The detective,* GUNSON, *is standing
in the shadows.*

GUNSON: Why are you here this morning, Mr Mitchell?
STANLEY *is momentarily surprised. He decides to sound
affronted.*
STANLEY: Why am I here? Is that your business Mr
Gunson?
GUNSON: Yes. I believe it is.
STANLEY: I've come to see how Lady Cremone is this
morning. (*Pointedly.*) We're going to be working
together, from now on. (*He moves to go on.*) May I . . . ?
(*He walks past* GUNSON.)

INT. IMPERIAL, MAIN PASSAGE/BACK STAIRCASE. DAY
We cut to STANLEY *moving through a side door of the hotel and
on to the back staircase. He glances up the stairs; there seems to
be nobody around, just the sound of maids' voices. He starts to
climb the stairs, suddenly two uniformed police appear above*

him on one of the landings. They are talking loudly to each
other. STANLEY *retreats down the stairs, and re-enters the main*
part of the hotel.

INT. IMPERIAL PASSAGE/LADY CREMONE'S SUITE. DAY
STANLEY *knocks on* LADY CREMONE's *hotel suite door and a*
maid lets him in. He moves into the reception room of the suite,
to be confronted by LADY CREMONE *holding a little coffee*
party. DONALDSON *is sitting in a fine chair drinking coffee out*
of beautiful china, and there are three of the old dowagers in their
Edwardian dresses drinking coffee too, their lined aristocratic
faces staring out of the gloom. It is very dark outside, and the
suite is in deep shadow.

LADY CREMONE: Stanley, good morning! We've all decided
    to have a final cup of coffee together.
STANLEY: A final cup of coffee?
DONALDSON: Well, the old hotel is going up in smoke
    apparently – it may well be closing down. This cake is
    delicious by the way . . .
LADY CREMONE: We're all giving up our apartments here,
    it's very definitely time to move on, we've all agreed
    on that . . . I myself am leaving here for ever
    tomorrow . . . (*She turns to her guests.*) This is Virginia,
    Lady Altringham, Maud Hartingdon and Sybill
    Thirstwood – they've been here for absolute ages, far
    longer than me!
    The dowagers nod and grunt, as STANLEY *greets them.*
    They are very impassive.
DONALDSON: And if one thinks back to the great things
    that have happened, to the wonderful artists that have
    played here! It is all a little heartbreaking. Ivor Novello
    was here regularly when I first came, in its glory days.

I thought those days were coming back, I really did, when the Prince of Wales came to hear the Louis Lester Band play. But then a fight among musicians, a fatal stabbing, a young singer dies – and it's the end of the place, certainly the hotel we knew . . .

STANLEY: Was there a fight among musicians?

LADY CREMONE: Well, that is what the police seem to believe . . .

DONALDSON: Mr Lester does appear to be the culprit, does he not? Which is tremendously sad of course, but until the court has pronounced, we certainly mustn't –

LADY ALTRINGHAM: Guilty! Guilty! Guilty!

The old lady stares stonily out of the shadows. STANLEY *is unnerved for a second.*

LADY CREMONE: It's so dark in here. (*She switches on a side light.*) It looks like there's going to be a thunderstorm . . . We must get to work shortly, mustn't we, Stanley? Mr Masterson awaits!

STANLEY: He does. (*He stares at the dowagers.*) He was a neighbour of yours in this passage of course . . .

The dowagers peer back at STANLEY.

He is a bit of a man of mystery, isn't he? Did any of you ever see who he entertained in his suite?

The dowagers looks back at STANLEY *very coldly, giving him nothing.*

DONALDSON: Walter is unknowable, Stanley, just when one thinks one has got his measure, he seems to change completely – becomes interested in all sorts of new things . . .

LADY CREMONE: And we'd better not be late for him today. You can come in my car, Stanley.

STANLEY: We need to go already?

LADY CREMONE: I think so, yes. Have to be early on our first day.

INT./EXT. IMPERIAL PASSAGE AND BACKYARD. DAY
We cut to LADY CREMONE *and* STANLEY *moving down the
main hotel passage towards the back entrance of the Imperial.
The rain is bucketing down as they stand in the doorway,
staring across the backyard, where* LADY CREMONE*'s limousine
is parked. Her chauffeur is hurrying towards them across the
yard with a large umbrella.*

LADY CREMONE: Here he comes! I told him to bring the
     car round here to the back, because there's so many
     taxis out the front! Everybody's trying to get away –
     STANLEY *is glancing behind him, thinking about the
     passport.*
     What is it Stanley?
STANLEY: I have to do something . . .
LADY CREMONE: There isn't time now.
     We move with LADY CREMONE *and* STANLEY *as the
     chauffeur guides them towards the car. They get in the
     back as the rain pours down.*

INT. LADY CREMONE'S CAR. DAY
LADY CREMONE *and* STANLEY *are together on the back seat of
the limousine. The rain is hurtling down outside; all they can see
is the back of the hotel, where huge vats of rubbish are being
moved in the rain.*

LADY CREMONE: My goodness, suddenly it is black as
     night almost! (*Turns to* STANLEY.) This is exciting,
     isn't it, our first day?!
STANLEY: It is . . .
     He leans forward, starts winding up the glass partition.
LADY CREMONE: What are you doing that for . . . ? I have
     no secrets in front of Pardoe.

The car has started; it is slowly manoeuvring round the
yard and towards the exit, as the rubbish vats are moved
in front of it. It has to pause for a moment.

STANLEY: I want you to consider something.

LADY CREMONE: What is that?

STANLEY: That Louis isn't guilty.

LADY CREMONE: Well of course one hopes that might be
the case, but the evidence is rather damning –

STANLEY: There is no evidence. Of course there isn't. But
we need a little time –

LADY CREMONE: We? What do you mean, 'we'?

STANLEY: He needs somewhere to go while things calm
down . . . I wondered if you could help?

LADY CREMONE: If I could help . . . ?

The car is about to leave the backyard of the hotel. LADY
CREMONE *is staring straight at* STANLEY.

STANLEY: If we could use your house in the country for
a couple of days? Nobody will look for him there . . .

LADY CREMONE: Stop the car, Pardoe! (*She turns to*
STANLEY.) I'm amazed you should ask that, Stanley,
when the police are looking for him right at this
moment!

STANLEY: I don't know why you're amazed . . . We
encouraged the band, we got to know them, we helped
create some of their success –

LADY CREMONE: I don't see how that changes anything . . .
I'm stunned you should ask me, Stanley, truly
stunned –

STANLEY: But I am asking you, because I know in a way
you will understand, and want to do something . . .

LADY CREMONE *stares at him.*

Just for two days, we use your house – you could say
you knew nothing about it – after all, I've been to the
house, I could have suggested it to Louis, there's the
stable block –

LADY CREMONE: There was a knifing in this hotel, Stanley, and the girl died. Louis is a very intelligent man, of course, but that mustn't blind one. It was always the most likely outcome . . . a Negro band in the hotel, a fight, a stabbing-

STANLEY: Do you really believe that, Lavinia?

LADY CREMONE: Yes . . . I do.

STANLEY (*passionately*): What if Mr Masterson is involved?! What if he's protecting Julian . . . ?

LADY CREMONE: That's impossible, quite impossible. And you know that.

STANLEY: Do I? I thought it was impossible, but maybe it isn't –

LADY CREMONE: Stanley, if you're helping Louis –

STANLEY: I didn't say that, I didn't say I was.

LADY CREMONE: You could go to prison for a long time.

STANLEY: I know that, Lavinia.

LADY CREMONE (*powerfully*): Are you helping him? You'd better tell me. (*Straight at him.*) Are you?

STANLEY: No, I'm not. Not yet.

LADY CREMONE (*suddenly getting very emotional*): We had a plan, we have a plan, I'm going to be the proprietor of the magazine, this is the first day . . . and I was looking forward to it, us working together, really looking forward to it, and you bring me this . . . !

STANLEY: What do I bring you, Lavinia?

LADY CREMONE: You bring me chaos.

She has tears in her eyes, she is furious and upset.

And I can't have any more of that. God knows I've had enough of that in my life, with what happened to my sons –

STANLEY: I know that, Lavinia, of course –

LADY CREMONE: And I will not have any more, not one minute more. You can't even begin to understand! Every single day I've been nervous of the telephone

when it rings, dreading it might bring me bad news,
I've been terrified of telegrams, absolutely terrified,
and I can't go back to that. I won't. For a moment I
thought it had stopped . . . but now this . . . ! (*Her eyes
are full of tears.*) I don't know what you thought you
were doing, Stanley?! Talking to me like this . . . ?!
You've ruined everything, you've ruined our day,
totally ruined it. I don't know what's going to happen
now . . .

*She opens the door and gets out into the pouring rain. She
is crying. The chauffeur is calling 'Your Ladyship' and
moves after her with the umbrella, across the yard, back
towards the hotel.*

INT. IMPERIAL. MAIN PASSAGE. DAY
We cut to STANLEY *emerging out of the rain back into the
hotel. In the distance he can see* LADY CREMONE *being escorted
by her chauffeur down the passage.*

   STANLEY *calls after her . . .*

STANLEY: Lavinia . . . !

   But LADY CREMONE *disappears round the corner without
   looking back.*
   STANLEY *moves further down the passage. He is shaken
   and upset by what's happened. For a moment he is
   undecided what to do, whether to go after her. Then he
   realises he is totally alone in the passage. He decides to
   try again to reach* LOUIS' *room.*

INT. IMPERIAL, BACK STAIRCASE/STAFF BEDROOM
PASSAGE. DAY
We cut to STANLEY *running up the back staircase and then
emerging in the staff bedroom passage. There is a maid sorting*

linen outside the rooms, but seemingly nobody else around. A
subjective shot, as STANLEY *approaches* LOUIS' *room. He passes*
a bedroom with the door open; JOE *the trumpeter is packing up*
his belongings.

INT. LOUIS' BEDROOM/PASSAGE. DAY
We cut to STANLEY *going through drawers in Louis' room,*
pulling things out in a series of fast cuts, looking for the passport.

STANLEY: Where the hell is it? He said the bottom
  drawer . . .
  The bottom drawer is full of old copies of Music Express.
  He starts throwing them across the floor. He hears maids'
  voices and laughter in the passage. He finds the passport
  right at the bottom of the drawer. He slips it into his pocket
  and walks out of the bedroom.
      THORNTON *is standing at the other end of the passage.*
THORNTON: What are you doing?
STANLEY: I'm looking for Carla . . . I'm doing an article
  about the break-up of the band.
THORNTON: Are you indeed?!
STANLEY: Yes.
THORNTON: You think anybody wants to read that now?!
STANLEY: Maybe, we'll see. Do you know where she is?
THORNTON: I do not . . .
  STANLEY *is moving off down the passage.*
  You've brought the roof down on all of us, Stanley,
  you realise?
STANLEY: I have?!
THORNTON: Yes, you brought the band here, and so you
  helped bring the roof down!

INT. SUBURBAN APARTMENT. DAY

We cut to LOUIS *alone in the suburban apartment, surrounded by boxes and dismembered radios and gramophones. The nearly completed cinema projector is staring back at him from across the room as if it is about to spring into life.* LOUIS *moves to get another cigarette from his jacket; he is keeping well away from the window. The thunderstorm has just finished, the last drops of rain running down the window pane.*

Suddenly there is some shouting: an old woman's voice yelling outside on the staircase, the words are unintelligible but he can hear the anger in her voice. LOUIS *moves to the door, the shouting gets even louder. He then moves to the window, keeping right to the edge, in the shadows.*

Exactly as he reaches the window, he sees SARAH*'s car draw up outside. The shouting is continuing on the stairs.* LOUIS *is startled to see* SARAH *is not alone in the car.* PAMELA *gets out with her. She is dressed, as always, in a beautiful dress and coat as if she was going to the races.*

INT. ROOM/STAIRCASE. DAY

We cut to LOUIS *opening the apartment door to* SARAH*; he is keeping well inside the room. As he opens the door, the shouting begins again, we see an old woman is yelling down from above:* 'It happens all the time! Every week! And they don't do anything about it! They think we'll put up with it, but we're not going to!'

SARAH *closes the door behind her. They are alone in the flat.*

SARAH: I don't know what she's shouting about. Did she
    see you, do you think?

LOUIS: No she can't have, I've not been out of the room.
    (*Sharply.*) Why is Pamela here?

SARAH: She insisted on coming! I couldn't stop her.

    We see a shot through the window of PAMELA *standing by the car, lighting a cigarette.*

Don't worry about it, though, Louis, she wants to
help . . . I really believe she does. (*She turns from the
window.*) I've brought the clothes with me, they're in
the car –

LOUIS: Why are they in the car?

SARAH: I wanted to check first that you were still here –
*At that very moment she stops by the window, having
glanced out again. Her face is in shock. She turns to look
at* LOUIS. *He moves over to the window. He sees a police
car is drawing up outside the apartment block. It pulls up
next to where* PAMELA *is standing and two uniformed
police officers get out.* LOUIS *is watching from the shadows,
he glances urgently towards* SARAH.

SARAH: Nobody followed us here I promise! I was keeping
an eye out all the way . . . nobody could have
followed us!

LOUIS: So how do they know I'm here?
Their eyes meet.

SARAH (*really upset*): I don't know . . . !
We see the police talking to PAMELA *for a moment and
then moving off towards the other apartment block.* LOUIS
watches them for a second.

LOUIS: We've got to move . . .
SARAH's *head turns.*
I'm not just going to sit here waiting for them . . . !

EXT. SUBURBAN APARTMENT BUILDING. DAY
We cut to LOUIS *and* SARAH *in the main doorway of the
apartment building.* PAMELA *has her back to them, smoking by
the car. The front door of the apartment block is slightly open
and they can see through the crack, the police have come out of
the other apartment block and are heading straight towards
them.* PAMELA, *still with her back to* LOUIS *and* SARAH, *moves
towards the police and engages them in conversation.*

For a second the police are looking at PAMELA *and away from the entrance, and* LOUIS *seizes the moment to come out of the apartment block,* SARAH *right behind him. They move along the wall of the building, and then round the corner and down a footpath that runs along the side of the apartment block towards some trees.*

We cut to a wide shot of PAMELA *standing with the police. The old woman is yelling something unintelligible out of her apartment block window. The police look up at her.*

EXT. PATH/SUBURBAN PARK

We cut to LOUIS *and* SARAH *moving fast along the narrow path which runs between the mock-Tudor houses. Ahead of them they can see trees and hear the sound of distant voices. They glance behind them; for a moment they are alone on the path, nobody is following.*

They round a corner on the path and they can see ahead of them an opening in the trees. A curtain moves in one of the windows of the houses that overlook the path.

LOUIS *and* SARAH *move on.*

Suddenly there is a sound behind them. They turn and see PAMELA *is coming towards them, carrying a suitcase. She is moving very determinedly. For a moment they watch her bearing down on them, she is waving her arm at them.*

LOUIS: What's she doing? What does she want?!
PAMELA: Keep going! Keep going! (*She is calling down the length of the path.*) I'll catch you up . . . !
We cut to LOUIS *and* SARAH *reaching the gap in the trees. They can see a stretch of park leading towards a clubhouse and a bowling green. On the green some elderly bowlers are moving in an untroubled way, seemingly totally concentrated on their game.* PAMELA *reaches* LOUIS *and* SARAH.

PAMELA: I've got the clothes . . .

LOUIS: And what did you say to the police?

PAMELA: As little as I could . . . They said they were investigating a burglary . . . I don't know if somebody saw you in that room, or it was just a coincidence –

LOUIS: It's not likely to be a coincidence –

SARAH: Where are they now?

PAMELA: I don't know . . . I think they were about to drive off! I didn't wait to see . . .

SARAH: Better not go back to the car yet!

They are moving along the path on the edge of the park, watching through the trees, the members of the bowling club in their white clothes and white shoes playing bowls on the immaculate green.

Behind them along the path, a woman with a dog is approaching.

PAMELA: We've got to get you changed, Louis . . . (*Staring at his evening dress.*) Because looking like that everybody notices you!

LOUIS *looks at the two of them. He is suspicious of both women:* PAMELA*'s febrile manner, as if this was some sort of game, and* SARAH*'s intensity.*

LOUIS: And where do you suggest I change?

PAMELA (*pointing at the clubhouse*): We'll do it in there.

SARAH *stares across at the clubhouse, and the expanse of grass they have to cross to reach it.*

SARAH: And how do we get there?

PAMELA *moves through the trees into the park, in full view of the bowlers, and turns.*

PAMELA: We act as if it's the most natural thing in the world . . . You carry the suitcase Louis, after all why shouldn't you be my servant? That's what they'll think –

We cut wide, the women cross the stretch of the park towards the clubhouse and LOUIS *follows carrying the case.*

*We cut close; they reach the edge of the bowling green
and skirt it. The bowlers glance up at the strange sight: two
well-dressed women, one exquisitely fashionable, the other
dressed for the office, and a black man in a dinner jacket
carrying their suitcase.*

*As they reach closer to the clubhouse, they see two
elderly men are standing watching the bowlers and
guarding the entrance.*

PAMELA *indicates that* SARAH *and* LOUIS *wait for her.*

PAMELA: Sit there. (*She indicates a low wall.*) And I'll go
and find out if I can get us in . . .

SARAH (*under her breath*): Sit here? In full view of everybody?

PAMELA: Of course, the police won't look for him here –
Got to hold your nerve, Sarah, and sit here . . .

She turns to LOUIS *and addresses him as if he was her
servant.*

Bernard, you and your friends are going to provide
the music are you not . . . ? I will see how big the
space is, and if it'll suit.

PAMELA *approaches the clubhouse, and addresses the
elderly men with total confidence.*

I just wanted to see inside . . . I hear there was a room
for hire . . . ?

The elderly men mumble back.

There is? Then you must show me, lead the way . . .

The elderly men shepherd PAMELA *into the clubhouse. The
bowlers are glancing up at* SARAH *and* LOUIS *sitting on
the low wall.*

SARAH, *while staring ahead, talks to* LOUIS *with an
intense intimate tone.*

SARAH: I didn't bring them here – the police – I promise!
They didn't follow me . . . I know they didn't!

LOUIS: It doesn't matter.

SARAH: What doesn't matter?! It matters to me what you
think more than anything . . . (*She turns her face away.*)

LOUIS: Sarah, you can't cry.

SARAH: I'm not crying . . . I'm not going to cry.

Her head is turned away from him but then she looks back, forcing back the tears.

LOUIS: If I'm your servant, I ought to stand . . . I shouldn't be sitting here.

SARAH: Don't stand, please don't stand, talk to me. I won't cry, I promise . . .

LOUIS *remains seated, but with a respectful distance between him and* SARAH.

LOUIS: Look as if you're giving me orders, about the party . . .

SARAH: What party?

LOUIS: The party you've hired me and my friends to play at.

SARAH: That's not easy, to pretend, right at this moment –

LOUIS: Pamela's not finding it so difficult –

SARAH (*her tone hushed but very intense*): Well, there's an obvious reason for that isn't there?! She doesn't care about you the way I do . . .

LOUIS *turns to look at her and then back at the bowlers.* No, don't say anything to that or I will break down. You've got to trust me, Louis, it hurts so much you don't trust me.

LOUIS: You're right, we shouldn't talk about this now.

SARAH: But that doesn't mean we never should, Louis . . . when the chance comes . . .

LOUIS *is staring at the bowlers.*

LOUIS: Give me orders, about what you require, for the entertainment at your party.

SARAH: Yes, yes. (*Louder.*) How many of you will there be, providing the music?

LOUIS: About ten, ma'am.

SARAH (*staring anxiously at the clubhouse*): Where is Pamela? Why is she taking so long?! (*She looks at* LOUIS.) I've

got to go to this meeting, the signing of the magazine's
future, and we need to get you changed and away
from here before that, and –

PAMELA *is now approaching them. She addresses* LOUIS
in a loud voice.

PAMELA: I think it might do. It might well be what I am
looking for.

LOUIS (*indicating* SARAH): The lady's got to go.

PAMELA: Yes, you go, Sarah, take the car.

SARAH (*very startled*): Take the car?!

PAMELA: Yes.

She leans forward to adjust the buttons on SARAH's *coat,
allowing her to be very close.*

If they're following the car, it's best Louis isn't in it . . .

SARAH: But where will you go?

PAMELA: We'll find somewhere back in town, maybe that
funny little club where Louis played for the Prince
and there was that hailstorm . . .

She kisses SARAH *and says loudly:*

Go to your meeting, darling, we will do all the
arrangements . . . Go! Go!

We cut to SARAH *moving off across the park. She turns to
look back at* LOUIS *for a moment.*

We cut back to LOUIS, *watching her go. He turns to
look at* PAMELA, *her pale upper-class face, her seemingly
lighthearted manner.*

PAMELA *meets his gaze, as if she is reading his
thoughts.*

PAMELA: Now you've just got me, for the moment anyway.
(*Then in her public voice, turning towards the clubhouse.*)
Let's see if this could possibly work, Bernard, or
whether it's far too pokey!

INT. CLUBHOUSE. DAY
We cut inside the clubhouse. It is dark inside, with the elderly bowlers moving about, eating sandwiches. They are staring fascinated at this elegant white woman with a black servant in a dinner jacket.

PAMELA (*whispers*): In a minute, we'll find somewhere for
    you to change. (*Watching the elderly people move slowly
    across the room.*) This may take a little while . . .
LOUIS (*suddenly*): Why are you here?
    PAMELA *turns and stares straight at him.*
PAMELA: I'm not sure you should worry about that right at
    this moment, Louis.

INT. THE MAGAZINE'S NEW OFFICE. DAY
We cut to STANLEY *walking into the main room of the
magazine's new office, which is dominated by* MASTERSON's
desk and the radio set. As STANLEY *comes into the room,* ERIC
*is doing a presentation. All over the floor are big pieces of paper
with section headings on them, forming a large visual map of
the new shape of the magazine.*

    MR WAX *is sitting in the middle of the room smoking and
staring at the display,* MASTERSON *is at his desk, flanked by
two legal representatives who have the documents ready to be
signed.* ROSIE *is watching from a corner, and so is the
magazine's artist,* ALBERT.

MR WAX: Where on earth have you been, Stanley?
    They all look at him.
STANLEY: I've been with Lavinia, with Lady Cremone.
    She's going to be a little late . . .
MASTERSON: Almost everyone seems to be late today –
MR WAX: Just when their future's being decided!
STANLEY: And Sarah will be with us very soon, I think . . .

MASTERSON (*dryly*): Yes, we have something for her.

MR WAX: Eric was just showing us the new magazine, quite a transformation!

ERIC: Yes, I was just explaining the blueprint, it's only a suggestion of course, Stanley – but we're going to have the chance for so many more pages, so much more space, I thought we needed to expand boldly. So our biggest new section is our cinema section, which will have at least three particular subdivisions – the USA, Hollywood of course, Europe, and naturally us, our native movies! And equally exciting I think – (*The camera is exploring all the new headings and shapes.*) is this: a special section on censorship, on movies that can't be shown here – at least not yet – like this amazing new erotic film from Czechoslovakia, *Extasy*, it is quite poetic but it does have full nakedness . . . !

MR WAX: A few photos from that will move a hell of a lot of copies!

ERIC: So it's not just going to be music, Stanley, that is of course if you agree . . .

STANLEY *stares at all the sections spread on the floor, including the cinema section, in the middle of which there's a big ink drawing of Farquhar and Tonk, the cartoon characters, going to the movies. They are scrambling up a giant staircase towards a blank cinema screen and then dancing exuberantly inside the screen holding champagne bottles while watched by an audience.*

ERIC: Albert has just knocked that up, this morning. Isn't it fun? What do you think Stanley . . . ?

ERIC*'s manner is so enthusiastic, as if he has totally put out of his mind the early morning journey with* LOUIS. *His mood is infectious.* STANLEY *is immediately intrigued and excited by what he sees spread out on the floor.*

STANLEY: It's rather terrific, you've done very well, Eric, lots of possibilities here . . .

MR WAX: And to think I'm about to sell the bloody thing!

MASTERSON (*dryly*): Of course it's not too late to change your mind . . .

MR WAX: No, no, I won't do that . . . (*Slightly nervous laugh.*) I don't think I will!

ROSIE: And there are going to be so many photographs, about ten times more than we had –

ERIC: Yes, Mr Masterson has bought a brand-new camera for Sarah, this fast-speed camera has only just come out!

ERIC *lifts it out of its box.*

MASTERSON: I think it will cause quite a revolution in the use of photographs. And we will show the way.

STANLEY (*picking the camera up*): A new camera . . . Sarah will love that . . .

MASTERSON (*stands*): Stanley, I need a word with you.

STANLEY: A word with me?

MASTERSON: In private. If you could be so kind, before we sign.

Without waiting for STANLEY *to reply,* MASTERSON *moves into the large empty room next door.*

INT. MAGAZINE OFFICE, SECOND LARGE ROOM. DAY
We cut to STANLEY *and* MASTERSON *facing each other in a completely empty room. The door is closed.*

STANLEY: What is it, Mr Masterson?

MASTERSON: You must call me Walter.

STANLEY: Walter, what is it?

MASTERSON (*taking a piece of paper out of his pocket*): I just wanted you to check your new salary . . .

He gives STANLEY *the piece of paper.*

It seemed to me to be a fair number, to start with . . .

STANLEY *looks up, truly startled at the size of the figure.*

*He tries not to look too excited, but doesn't completely
succeed.*

MASTERSON: Do you agree to that figure?

STANLEY: Yes, it's very generous, of course I do!

MASTERSON: Good . . . as we expand further, it will go up.
(*He is standing in the shadows across the room.*) I just
need to ask you, Stanley, have you seen Louis Lester
in the last few hours?

STANLEY: I have not.

MASTERSON: Where have you been this morning?

STANLEY: I've been with Lavinia, with Lady Cremone. She
knew she might be late, so we had a discussion, so her
views could be represented –

MASTERSON: You don't know where Mr Lester currently is?

STANLEY: I do not . . . what has this got to do with the
signing?

MASTERSON: This is the first magazine I have owned . . .
I think people would feel it is rather sensible of me
to make sure my editor is not about to go to gaol.

STANLEY: That certainly isn't going to happen. (*Their eyes
meet.*)

MASTERSON: Good. I'm reassured. You've had no contact?

He is still staring at STANLEY.

STANLEY: No.

MASTERSON*'s gaze is unflinching.*

Of course when the police do arrest him, I'm going to
see if I can get his last interview . . .

MASTERSON: That would be a scoop, certainly, yes. And in
fact Mr Lester is about to be found.

STANLEY: He is . . . ?

MASTERSON: I fully expect him to be found before
midnight tonight, because I have offered a reward of
ten thousand pounds for information leading to his
capture. It is about to be announced.

We move in on STANLEY, *he is stunned.*

STANLEY: You have offered a reward?! Ten thousand
　　　　pounds?!

MASTERSON: Yes, why is that so surprising?

STANLEY: Because we all knew Louis, we all did . . . It's one
　　　　thing not to actually help him, it's a little different
　　　　isn't it offering a huge reward for his arrest?

MASTERSON: Is it . . . ?

　　　　He stares at STANLEY.

　　　　I think we have to disagree about that, Stanley, it
　　　　seemed to me to be the right thing to do, because
　　　　although I wasn't responsible for the band being at
　　　　the Imperial, I am a resident there, I've seen what's
　　　　happened to the hotel. (*He turns.*) In any case it's
　　　　done now – it will be out in the first edition of the
　　　　evening newspapers which is in under an hour.
　　　　(*Dryly.*) And we'll see what effect that has . . . (*He
　　　　moves across the room.*) Now I don't think we should
　　　　keep Mr Wax waiting any longer, do you?

INT. MAGAZINE OFFICE. MAIN ROOM. DAY

We cut to MR WAX*'s pen hovering over the legal document. He
looks up, a sharp beady smile.* MASTERSON, STANLEY, ERIC,
ROSIE, ALBERT *and the legal representatives are all watching.*

MR WAX: Do I take the plunge . . . ? (*He smiles.*) Or do
　　　　I have a change of heart?! (*He hovers over the paper
　　　　again and then signs.*) No change of heart, the price
　　　　was too good!

INT. IMPERIAL LOBBY. DAY

LADY CREMONE *is sitting on the edge of the grand lobby in the
Imperial, drinking coffee. She looks very shaken, her surface
confidence seems to have gone. She is watching two old dowagers*

moving with their entourage of servants and luggage as they leave the hotel.

She looks across to the corner of the lobby, where two young men of leisure are laughing and chatting together; they are joined by a fashionable young woman. LADY CREMONE *watches these images of society people blithely going about their business. She suddenly sees* JULIAN *walking towards her.*

JULIAN: Lavinia, all alone? Why're you all alone?!

LADY CREMONE (*trying to appear in control*): Oh I'm just perching here for a moment –

JULIAN (*sitting opposite her*): You mustn't ever drink alone, even coffee, it's such a bad idea!

LADY CREMONE: I was just a little early for a meeting – and now I may be a little late . . .

JULIAN: For Walter's meeting?

LADY CREMONE: Yes.

JULIAN: Oh, your life will be full of Walter from now on, his calls, his telegrams, his commands! So will mine – he's taking me away, you know . . .

LADY CREMONE: I do know that, yes.

JULIAN: He has a finger in every pie, it is quite amazing isn't it, because he doesn't say much, does he, you don't ever hear any deep thoughts from him – but suddenly he is in every pie! (*He looks across at her.*) Come on, Lavinia, why are you so sad? You can smile at that!

LADY CREMONE: I'm a little upset, of course, about what has happened to Louis Lester, it's a terrible business –

JULIAN: It is! It is utterly shocking, quite awful! (*Blithely.*) And something new seems to be happening every minute too, doesn't it? Walter told me this morning he is offering a reward, and actually a really big reward, for any information that leads to his arrest!

LADY CREMONE *looks up. She is startled by this news.*
LADY CREMONE: He is offering a reward? Are you sure?
JULIAN: Oh yes, it's going to be in the paper!

INT. SUBURBAN CLUBHOUSE. DAY
We cut to PAMELA's *head turning sharply in the dark interior
of the bowling green clubhouse.*
  *We see the elderly members of the clubhouse watching beadily
as* LOUIS, *now dressed in working clothes, moves with the
suitcase up to* PAMELA. *She looks at his clothes, adjusting one
of his buttons, as if she is making him smarter, conscious they
are being watched by everybody.*

PAMELA: That took long enough. (*She whispers.*) They
    nearly fit . . .
LOUIS (*under his breath*): Where do they come from, one of
    your servants?
PAMELA: Yes. (*Then loudly in her public voice.*) But that's
    much better . . . he thought this place was going to be
    much grander than it was, isn't that touching?! (*She
    turns to the club members.*) But of course it's lovely and
    perfect for what I'm looking for! (*She moves across the
    room.*) Come on, Bernard, over here, the taxi will be
    here any moment.
    She indicates LOUIS *should stand next to her, where she is
    sitting. She talks to* LOUIS *in her public voice.*
PAMELA: When the taxi arrives, Bernard, I want you to tell
    the driver to go to Fortnum and Mason's in
    Piccadilly, I need a couple of items from there.
LOUIS: Yes, ma'am.
    *The bowlers on the other side of the clubhouse room are
    moving around, coming in and out of the room. For just
    a moment,* LOUIS *and* PAMELA *are alone.*

PAMELA: Maybe we should stay here? (*She lowers her voice.*) I don't think anybody recognised you, it looks like people who bowl don't read the newspapers.

LOUIS: We're not going to Fortnum and Mason's are we?

PAMELA: Of course not, when we're back in town we'll head for that little music club, don't you think?
Some bowlers appear again in the room, talking among themselves at the far end. PAMELA *glances at them and continues in her lowered voice.*

PAMELA: It's funny what people choose to do with their lives isn't it?! (*Suddenly.*) I expect my mother would like this place – I don't think bowls is very popular with Jews, so she wouldn't find many here. (*Her tone sharp.*) And that would make her so happy!
LOUIS *looks at her, surprised by her tone, trying to work out how seriously she is taking the situation.* PAMELA *meets his gaze, she whispers.*

PAMELA (*whispers*): Don't worry, the taxi will be here at any moment.
The bowlers are across the room and through the curtain which divides the lounge area. They can't hear what they are saying. LOUIS *turns to* PAMELA.

LOUIS (*leaning forward, his voice hushed*): As soon as it's dark, I am going to get out of London, to Bristol or Cardiff, and get a ship.

PAMELA: Well, let's hope it's that easy.

LOUIS: It'll be easier on my own . . . (*Then as one of the bowlers looks across at them.*) Ma'am.

PAMELA: Maybe.
She looks back at LOUIS *and whispers.*
Or maybe you are less easy to spot when you're being a servant, Louis.
A bowler steps forward across the lounge and announces.

BOWLER: Your taxi is here, Miss.

PAMELA: Thank you so much, and thank you for your
hospitality.

She gets up and commands LOUIS.

Come on Bernard, bring the luggage.

INT. IMPERIAL KITCHEN/SMALL ROOM. DAY

We cut to JULIAN *moving along the tiled kitchen passage, lined
with its trays of desserts. He comes to a door in the passage and
knocks. Without waiting for an answer he enters.*

  CARLA *is sitting in her dressing room, the small basement
room that she has transformed over her time in the hotel. It has
glowing light bulbs next to a big mirror, and a stylish little sofa.
It is full of personal touches and gifts she has been given.*

JULIAN: There you are!

CARLA: Mr Luscombe . . . what a surprise!

JULIAN: I'm saying goodbye all over town, and of course
one of my first, and one of my biggest, had to be you,
Carla –

CARLA: Well it's been such a terrible day hasn't it? With
these awful things in the paper about Louis. It's not
possible, it's just not possible he did anything to
Jessie! I know he can't have!

JULIAN: Of course not, of course he didn't. And I'm quite
sure that will come out in the end –

CARLA: Will it?

JULIAN: Oh yes, it usually does, doesn't it?

CARLA: I don't know, Mr Luscombe . . .

JULIAN: Always so formal. (*He takes her hand.*)

CARLA: Am I?

  JULIAN *sits close to her. The door is open on to the passage
but* JULIAN *is oblivious of anybody passing, his manner is
intense and sexual.*

CARLA: I miss Jessie awfully! . . . I find myself saying things
to her still, because there's so much I wish I had said
to her, when I had a chance –

JULIAN: That is absolutely right, so do I . . . I often feel
that way with so many people – that I wished I'd
said things to them, or I could find a way of saying
certain things, because often I can't . . .
He touches her hair.
It's especially true today because my sister's gone
missing, for a little while at least, and I've got all these
goodbyes to do in just a few hours –

CARLA: You're going away today?

JULIAN: Tonight, yes! (*He reaches up and closes the door.*)
I really don't want to go, I hate the idea of a business
job, of belonging to someone, of not being able to do
what I want, like you can, Carla –

CARLA: I won't be any more, we're all having to leave here,
the band is breaking up.

JULIAN (*so close to her*): That is probably the worst thing of
all. When I get to America . . . I'm going to look after
you, Carla, bring you over there for a holiday, tell
everybody what a wonderful talent you have . . .
His face is so close, it is almost touching her.
And how much you mean to me . . .

CARLA (*very disconcerted*): Mean to you?

JULIAN: How unforgettable you are, and our times
together, you and Jessie and me, it will always be, it
is the highlight of my life . . .
He is gripping her arm.

CARLA: You're holding me too tight Mr Luscombe,
please . . .

JULIAN: How would you like us to say goodbye then?

CARLA: I don't know, maybe we shake hands, like a
proper –

JULIAN: Like a proper what? Like a proper gentleman?!
   I don't know, Carla, if I ever will be a proper
   gentleman, and shall I tell you something? (*Very
   intense.*) Nobody I know is, absolutely nobody!
   He turns. SCHLESINGER *is standing in the doorway.*
   Except Mr Schlesinger of course.
MR SCHLESINGER: Mr Luscombe, good morning.
   He turns to CARLA, *his voice is tentative, he looks a
   broken man.*
   Carla, I have to tell you this now, I'm afraid, tonight is
   the last night you can use your bedroom here . . .
CARLA: That's our notice, is it? Just one night!
JULIAN (*outraged*): That is so unjust!

INT. MAGAZINE'S NEW OFFICE. DAY
STANLEY *is standing by the window in the new offices, staring
down into the street. He can see a news vendor on the other side
of the road; a van draws up and bundles of the first edition of
the evening papers are delivered.* STANLEY *can't quite see the
front of the paper.*
   *There is the sound of voices through the open double doors
from the central room.* SARAH *has just arrived and has been
given the new camera.* STANLEY *sees her smile in delight as*
MASTERSON *hands it to her.* ERIC *is explaining the new
mechanism to her, all the possibilities of the new camera.*
STANLEY *turns back to the window and watches a bowler-
hatted man buy an evening paper and stare at the front page.*
STANLEY *still can't get a glimpse of the headline.*
   SARAH *is standing in the doorway, she calls across.*

SARAH: Did you see what I've been given?
STANLEY: Yes, I did . . .
   SARAH *is holding the camera.*

SARAH: I will be able to capture all sorts of things with this I couldn't before . . .

She moves up to STANLEY *at the window.*

And Mr Wax has sold the magazine!

STANLEY: He has.

SARAH: So there's no going back.

STANLEY: No, there isn't . . .

SARAH is staring down at the news vendor, she lowers her voice to an intense whisper.

SARAH: Louis had to move . . .

STANLEY: What? I told him –

SARAH: He had to, the police turned up –

STANLEY: Where is he now?

Before she can reply ERIC *enters the room, supervising* ROSIE *and the messenger,* MICK. *Both are carrying large boards.* ERIC *is carrying sheets of his blueprint.*

ERIC (*waving his sheets*): I think if we start by putting this all up around the walls, so we can see the magazine at a glance! But first the boards must go up . . . I'm so glad I had those delivered – one can do without chairs, but not noticeboards!

STANLEY (*hushed, watching* ERIC): It's like this morning never happened . . .

SARAH: Yes . . .

STANLEY: I'm not sure we should involve him any further –

SARAH (*whispers*): I left Louis with Pamela –

STANLEY: Pamela?! What was she doing there?

SARAH: I couldn't stop her coming . . . she said they might try to get to the club in Lyle Lane, you know, the one you first found Louis in –

ERIC: No, no! (*Supervising* ROSIE *and* MICK.) Put them closer together!

SARAH (*staring out of the window next to* STANLEY): I'm going to go home in a moment . . . because Pamela can contact me there –

STANLEY: Yes, they've got to be able to find us . . . (*Staring down at the news vendor.*) He's offered a reward, you know, right now people are reading about it . . .

SARAH (*glancing at* MASTERSON *through the doors*): I know, he's just told me.

STANLEY (*watching two women buy a paper*): It's the first time I've found myself wishing something terrible has happened in the news, a liner has sunk, or an airship has crashed – so his reward doesn't get much space in the paper.

We see the news vendor beginning to read the evening newspaper for himself.

I've got to find out . . .

STANLEY *moves out of the room sharply. At that exact moment* ERIC *calls to* SARAH.

ERIC: Can you help us with these boards, Sarah? We're going to put them right around the room, a complete panorama of what we're doing, all the nineteen sections. (*Pointedly to* SARAH.) And all of those will need photographs, of course!

INT. LOBBY OF NEW OFFICES. DAY
We cut to STANLEY *entering the lobby of the offices from the street. He has just bought an evening paper and is reading the front page as he walks. A voice says:*

MASTERSON: Good position, is it?

STANLEY *looks up.* MASTERSON *is standing on the stairs, watching him.*

STANLEY: What?

MASTERSON: The reward? Has it got a good position?

STANLEY (*holding up the paper so he can see*): Yes, I think you can call it that.

There is a picture of Louis on the front page, and a large
headline: £10,000 REWARD!

MASTERSON: So do you think it will work, Stanley?

STANLEY (*hesitates for a split second*): I'm sure it will.

MASTERSON: So am I.

He beckons to STANLEY *to follow him.*

Now come up and chair your first editorial meeting . . .
We have to decide how many new staff you're going
to have – you need to be head of a powerful team,
Stanley.

STANLEY (*following him back up the stairs*): Yes, and I will
be . . .

INT. IMPERIAL. PASSAGE/ATLANTIC BAR. DAY

We cut to SCHLESINGER *moving along the main passage of the*
Imperial, his shoulders hunched, his eyes sunk. He stares
through the door of the new Atlantic Bar.

He sees DONALDSON *drinking on his own. The bar is almost*
empty, an old dowager and a young couple in the corner.

SCHLESINGER (*approaching*): Mr Donaldson . . .

DONALDSON: Nathan, this must be horrible for you, all the
rumours about what's going to happen to the hotel . . .

SCHLESINGER: Yes, unless something extraordinary
happens the Bertram brothers are going to sell the
place and it's going to be demolished and an office
block put up . . .

DONALDSON: Knocked down for an office block, the final
insult! So it really is the last days of the place . . .

SCHLESINGER: Yes.

DONALDSON (*blowing smoke*): You never know, Nathan,
something extraordinary might happen.

SCHLESINGER: Like what?

DONALDSON: Another buyer will ride to the rescue!

SCHLESINGER: No, not even Mr Masterson would want this old pile.

DONALDSON: We'll see. That man is very unpredictable. (*He drains his glass.*) While I'm the complete opposite, of course.

INT. POLICE STATION, INTERROGATION ROOM. DAY
We see the interrogation room at the end of the long passage in the basement of the police station. The older detective, GUNSON, *is sitting at the desk, the* PORTLY YOUNG MAN *whom we saw at the end of Part Four is coming through the door.*

GUNSON: Take a seat.

PORTLY MAN (*remaining standing in front of the desk*): I have information about the whereabouts of Louis Lester, the bandleader.

GUNSON: Oh yes?

PORTLY MAN: I didn't know whether to go to the newspapers or come here.

GUNSON: You made the right decision . . . So?

PORTLY MAN: I followed Mr Lester to the offices of the magazine *Music Express*.

GUNSON: You're not going to get ten thousand pounds for that.

PORTLY MAN: No? I saw him go inside.

GUNSON: You're still not going to get ten thousand for that . . .

PORTLY MAN: I bet that's better information than anybody else has given you!

GUNSON: We've been to those offices, there's nobody there.

The PORTLY MAN *stares at him with his beady eyes.*

PORTLY MAN: They're helping him though, aren't they? They must be.

GUNSON's *moon-shaped face is impassive.*

GUNSON: We've visited all Mr Lester's friends – and will continue to do so.

EXT. ALLEY AND ENTRANCE TO BASEMENT CLUB. DAY
We see PAMELA *and* LOUIS *emerge from the taxi and walk down the alley towards the basement club. Two young women walk past them in the opposite direction, glancing at* LOUIS *as they go.* PAMELA *addresses* LOUIS *sharply, as if to a servant.*

PAMELA: Mind that bag, there are fragile things in there!
They reach the metal steps that lead down to the entrance of the basement club. PAMELA *stops* LOUIS *halfway down the stairs.*

PAMELA: You'd better wait . . . we don't want to give them too much of a surprise do we . . . ?!
PAMELA *rings the bell. As* LOUIS *waits on the steps, an old man walks past on the pavement above. He slows his walk and peers at* LOUIS *as he passes.*
The door of the club is opened by a very small shrimp-like man.

PAMELA: Is Deirdre here?
The small man stares at her for a second. He then peers up and sees LOUIS *waiting on the steps, dressed in servant's clothes; the small man doesn't recognise him. He disappears into the darkness without saying anything. A moment later* DEIRDRE *is at the door.*

PAMELA: I have a visitor for you.

DEIRDRE (*very startled at seeing him*): You've bought Louis here?!

PAMELA: I have. Can we come in?

INT. BASEMENT CLUB. FOYER/INNER OFFICE. DAY
LOUIS *and* PAMELA *are standing in the foyer of the basement club. It is very dark inside, the lights are not on in the foyer. The door into the yard where the hailstorm happened is ajar and sunlight is spilling into the darkened foyer. The door of the auditorium is also half open, and we see a glimpse of a large white woman rehearsing a jazz number accompanied by the shrimp-like man on the piano.*

DEIRDRE *is looking very nervous.*

LOUIS: Hello, Deirdre . . .
DEIRDRE: You can't be here long, Louis, not long at all!
PAMELA: We won't be long . . . I just need to make a
    telephone call . . . May I use your office?
    She goes into the inner office. The walls of the office are encrusted by years of posters and flyers. PAMELA *picks up the phone. She is deep in the shadows, and* LOUIS *can only half see her.*
DEIRDRE: What has happened to you, Louis? Why are they
    saying these things about you and Jessie Taylor?!
    LOUIS *is disconcerted to see how frightened* DEIRDRE *is.*
LOUIS: Why do you think?
DEIRDRE: What do you mean?
LOUIS: Because they think I must have done it . . . Excuse
    me . . .
    He moves to the door of the inner office. PAMELA *has just finished dialling.* LOUIS *is watching her very closely; she meets his gaze.*
PAMELA: This won't take a moment.

INT. JULIAN'S PARENTS' HOUSE/BASEMENT CLUB. DAY
The phone is ringing in the empty reception room in PAMELA *and* JULIAN'S *parents' house.* JULIAN *comes running into the room, his manner flustered and intense. He grabs the phone.*

JULIAN: Yes?!

PAMELA: Darling, it's me.

JULIAN: There you are! I've been looking for you . . . Where have you been . . . ?

PAMELA: Oh, I just had to pop out.

JULIAN: But where are you now?

PAMELA: I just had to do a little shopping, I've been to Swan and Edgar, I'm coming home . . .

We cut to LOUIS *watching her lie and then back to* JULIAN.

JULIAN: But I need you here! You said you wouldn't leave me . . . I've got so much to arrange before tonight –

PAMELA: I'll be back very soon darling –

JULIAN: Promise?!

PAMELA: I promise.

JULIAN: I went to the hotel, to try to do some proper farewells but everybody was so busy and so depressed – it was very upsetting!

PAMELA: It must have been . . . Concentrate on getting everything packed darling, making sure you've got everything you want to take. You've got to be ready for when Mr Masterson comes to pick you up because you can't keep him waiting –

JULIAN: Oh, I'll be ready, more than ready to assist Walter – to help him buy all sorts of things! . . . Magazines, skyscrapers! From now on, I will do everything he says.

PAMELA: That's good. I will see you very soon, darling.

JULIAN: Come quickly . . . !

We cut to PAMELA *ringing off.*

LOUIS: Why did you lie to him about where you were?

PAMELA: Why do you think? Because he's the most indiscreet person in London. You'd rather I'd told him, would you?!

LOUIS *is giving her a very searching look. His tone is forceful.*

LOUIS: What do you know about your brother and Jessie?

PAMELA *doesn't flinch from his gaze.*

PAMELA: What are you trying to say?

LOUIS: I'm saying – what happened between Julian and Jessie?

A momentary pause. PAMELA *looks straight back at him.*

PAMELA: My brother didn't kill Jessie Taylor, if that's what you mean, of course he didn't. (*Calmly.*) If you think that's the reason I'm here, out of guilt, because Julian attacked Jessie, then you're quite wrong.

LOUIS: Then why are you here?

PAMELA: Because neither did you . . . attack Jessie. (*She resumes her normal blithe tone.*) And naturally, I don't want to see you swing for it, is that so strange? After all, we have spent rather a lot of time with you and the band haven't we?

LOUIS *is staring at* PAMELA, *trying to work out what she is really thinking.*

PAMELA: It would be a pity if that all went to waste, wouldn't it?!

INT. JULIAN AND PAMELA'S PARENTS' HOUSE, PASSAGE. DAY
We cut to objects being thrown across the passage floor from the bottom drawer of a cupboard. JULIAN *is sitting cross-legged on the floor, just outside the reception room in his parents' house. His mother passes.*

MRS LUSCOMBE: Don't make a mess please, dear, this house always seems to get untidy –

JULIAN: I won't make a mess, Mummy . . . (*He calls after his mother.*) You know I'm going off tonight?!

MRS LUSCOMBE (*her tone distant*): Yes, and I'm sure it will be thrilling working for Mr Masterson, he is such a capable man, and there are so few capable men

nowadays. (*She moves off down the passage.*) When he
arrives, we'll say a proper goodbye.

JULIAN *stares after his mother for a moment, then returns
to the drawer. There are old toys, a travelling clock and a
mahogany box. He lifts the lid of the box; there is a
revolver inside. A maid passes just as* JULIAN *is looking
inside the box.*

JULIAN: This house is full of guns, isn't it?

The maid smiles vaguely. JULIAN *spins the gun and sees it
is loaded. He looks up.*

It would be a shame to leave this behind . . .

INT. MAGAZINE'S NEW OFFICE. DAY

We cut to STANLEY *sitting at his temporary desk, a trestle table
in the large empty room which is now his office. The boards are
now all up on the wall. Through the half-open double doors he
can see* MASTERSON *sitting at his desk, as* ERIC *is showing him
some papers. Nobody is looking at* STANLEY.

STANLEY *slips* LOUIS' *passport out on to the desk in front of
him. He flicks through the pages, seeing the different stamps, all
the ports* LOUIS *has visited. He flicks another page and sees*
LOUIS' *occupation is described as 'Merchant Seaman'.*

A thought strikes him, he looks up sharply.

*Suddenly the double doors are opening wide and workmen
are bringing in a large impressive desk, stumbling under its
weight.*

MASTERSON (*calling out across the two rooms*): Your desk has
arrived, Stanley . . .

STANLEY: So I see.

STANLEY *glances at* ROSIE, *who is working on the other
side of the room. He beckons to her to come over and
whispers to her.*

Do you think he is trying to bribe us all . . . ?

ROSIE: If he is, he has left me out.

> STANLEY *looks at his splendid desk which is being placed at the far end of the room. Then he watches* ERIC *deep in conversation with* MASTERSON.

STANLEY: It seems to be working doesn't it . . .

> *Suddenly* STANLEY *makes a decision, he stands up.*

I've got to go, Rosie . . . Tell him I've gone to talk to the police, see if I can encourage them to let me have a few minutes with Louis after they've arrested him –

ROSIE: Where are you really going?

STANLEY: Best you don't know . . .

> STANLEY *moves off into the passage and along towards the stairs. Just before he reaches the landing, he sees two detectives and two uniformed police coming up the stairs directly towards him. They are being shown the way by the messenger* MICK.

> STANLEY *stands in the shadows and watches them move into the suite of offices and walk towards* MASTERSON.

> *We stay on* STANLEY *for a moment. He watches* MASTERSON *greet the police.* STANLEY *then moves off abruptly. He walks fast down the stairs and into the lobby.*

EXT. STREET. DAY

We cut to STANLEY *in the street, moving along the large dark wall of the building that now houses their offices. We are very close on him, on a long lens. A couple of passers-by move between him and us, blurred shapes as we stay on* STANLEY. *His face is taut.*

A hand suddenly lands on his shoulder, he spins round in surprise. ERIC *is standing there.* STANLEY *has no idea if he has come after him because of the police.*

STANLEY: Eric?!

ERIC: I think I should come too . . .

STANLEY: You don't know where I'm going.

ERIC: I've got a pretty good idea.

Their eyes meet.

You're going to help Louis move somewhere . . .

STANLEY *stares at* ERIC, *his tall earnest figure in his too-tight suit.*

STANLEY: How did you do that anyway?! You were showing him your diagrams a minute ago?!

ERIC: He is still looking at the diagrams, he is probably showing them to the police now . . .

STANLEY: You've got to go back, we can't both disappear!

ERIC: If it looks odd, I can't help it! I'm not a very good liar, Stanley, so when I saw the police, I thought I'd better pop out . . .

INT. BASEMENT CLUB. DAY

We cut to the front door of the basement club being opened and another singer arriving, a white woman in a very flowery hat.

DEIRDRE *is watching from the doorway of her office; behind her* PAMELA *and* LOUIS *are sitting in the shadows.*

DEIRDRE *is extremely tense.*

DEIRDRE: That's another singer, in a minute there will be twelve more arriving . . . I won't be able to stop them coming in here! One of them is going to recognise you, Louis!

LOUIS: There must be another room we can go to, Deirdre?

PAMELA: Just for a moment . . .

DEIRDRE: We haven't got anywhere down here!

The doorbell rings again.

They're early . . . I told you they'd be here! You'd better go upstairs while they're arriving. We don't own upstairs, but it's the only place.

She bustles them up the stairs.

I want to help of course, but this is too difficult! It
really is!

INT. ROOM ABOVE BASEMENT CLUB. DAY
We can hear a piano being played. DEIRDRE *knocks very
sharply on the door of the room upstairs, and then without
waiting enters.*

*There is a ballet class in progress, six rather large teenage
girls in ballet costume being accompanied by a sharp-faced
woman on the piano.* DEIRDRE *addresses the woman.*

DEIRDRE: These people are – (*She is totally flustered.*) Are
waiting –
PAMELA: For a taxi.
DEIRDRE: Yes, for a taxi, and just wondered if they could
watch while they are waiting.
The woman and the girls look very startled.
LOUIS *is watching* PAMELA*'s breezy confidence.*
PAMELA (*to the woman*): I really hope you don't mind . . .
She indicates sharply to LOUIS *to bring her a chair.*
But I simply love dance . . .

EXT. SARAH'S FATHER'S HOUSE. DAY
SARAH *is approaching her house, carrying her new camera in
a box. As she reaches the front door, a voice calls her name. She
turns. The senior detective,* HORTON, *is standing with another
detective by a car a little further down the street.*

HORTON: Miss Peters, you've been a difficult person to
find.
SARAH: Have I?
HORTON: We'd just like a word with you if we may?

INT. SARAH'S FATHER'S HOUSE, HALL. DAY
We cut to SARAH*'s* FATHER, *watching as* SARAH *enters the hall accompanied by the police.*

SARAH: It's all right, Father, the police just want a word.

HORTON: That's right, we just wanted to ask your daughter if she knew the whereabouts of Mr Louis Lester?

SARAH: Louis Lester? His whereabouts? No, I don't know that.

HORTON: When did you last see him, Miss Peters?
Her father is watching them closely.

SARAH: A couple of days ago, I think, at the Imperial.

HORTON: A couple of days ago?

SARAH: Yes, that's right. Before there were all the stories in the newspapers.

HORTON: You must have been very shocked by those?

SARAH: I was.
HORTON *turns to her father, his tone respectful.*

HORTON: Sir . . . if you have no objection, could we look upstairs . . . ?

SARAH'S FATHER (*startled*): Upstairs? What do you expect to find up there?! No please, look upstairs, by all means . . .

INT. THE DARK ROOM. DAY
We cut to the door of SARAH*'s dark room opening.*

SARAH *and* HORTON *are framed in the doorway.*

SARAH: This is just my dark room, as you can see.
She begins to close the door.

HORTON: I would like to look inside, if I may.

SARAH: It's just my photographs . . .

HORTON: I'm very interested in photography, we're using it more and more ourselves . . .

He steps inside the room, indicating SARAH *to follow him.* HORTON *closes the door.*

SARAH *is surprised to find herself alone with him, in this confined space, his sharp youngish face staring at her. All around them are her photographs of the band, at the picnic, at the Imperial, the fans' faces outside the hospital,* JESSIE *singing, and above all* LOUIS: *leaning against a tree in the wood, in the ballroom playing, laughing backstage. Her photographs of him have an intimacy, a warm intense connection with the subject.*

HORTON: And this is a splendid collection of photos!

SARAH: Thank you.

HORTON: Especially of Mr Louis Lester . . .

He is standing close to one of the best portraits.

SARAH: I took a lot of pictures of his band, yes, of course.

HORTON: Yes, we've heard about how much time you've spent with the band, from Harry Thornton at the Imperial.

SARAH: Harry . . . he never liked the band.

HORTON: You were having an intimate relationship with Mr Lester, weren't you?

SARAH: He was a friend of mine.

HORTON: You were having a sexual relationship with him?

SARAH: I'm not going to answer that –

HORTON: You don't have to, I just have to look around at your photographs, they say it all.

SARAH: Where is your colleague?

HORTON: He's just outside the door, Miss Peters. Do you want him to come in?

SARAH hesitates.

It might become a little crowded . . . maybe just you and I can deal with this . . . ?

He stares straight at her.

You were having regular sexual relations with Mr
   Lester?

SARAH: That is not against the law.

HORTON: Not in this country, no, you're quite right, Miss
   Peters, in other parts of the world it would be quite
   another matter, wouldn't it . . . ?

SARAH: I didn't realise you spoke for them as well.

HORTON (*smiles at this*): Your father is Russian?

SARAH: He is.

HORTON: His real name is Petroff?

SARAH: It was, before he became a resident here.

HORTON: Let me put this simply, Miss Peters. Your father's
   had dealings with the Soviet Trade Delegation as part
   of his work –

SARAH: Has he? I don't know much about my father's
   work . . .

HORTON: Well I'm telling you that as a fact, Miss Peters.
   And anybody who's had dealings with the Soviet
   Trade Delegation and whose conduct comes under
   suspicion can be summarily deported under the
   Undesirable Aliens Act. The Home Office have those
   powers. If Mr Petroff's daughter was suspected of
   helping a fugitive escape from justice, that of course
   would be a case for deportation.

   SARAH *is startled, very shaken.*

SARAH: So you're threatening my father, Mr Horton, to
   get me to –

HORTON: No, I'm just explaining what will happen if you
   don't tell me what you know . . . (*Indicating the
   intimate photographs of* LOUIS.) What I can see you
   must know, what a talented photographer you are,
   what a future you ought to have in the professional
   world . . .

   SARAH*'s eyes fill with tears, she fights them back.*

SARAH: My father can't go back to Russia!

HORTON: No, I understand that. And I know you won't
    want to be the reason that happens. So you tell me
    what you know, where Mr Lester is . . .
    SARAH *is staring at him from the shadows.*
    Or would you rather talk over the matter with your
    father first? Talk over your dilemma with him?
    HORTON*'s sharp eyes staring back at her.*
    Although I'm not sure it is that much of a dilemma
    for you, Miss Peters . . .
    We move in on SARAH.
HORTON: You're sensible enough to put your own future
    and your father's future first.

EXT. STREET BY DONALDSON'S HOUSE. DAY
We cut to JULIAN *walking along the street, lined by substantial
stucco villas, that leads to* DONALDSON*'s house and garden. He
is carrying the mahogany box.*

EXT. DONALDSON'S GARDEN. DAY
JULIAN *pushes open the small door that is set in a high wall.
He enters the large walled garden where* JESSIE *first sang for the
Prince. There is the lawn that stretches up to the house, and the
paths that snake between the trees leading to secluded places.*
JULIAN *walks along one of these paths. We can hear* JESSIE
*singing on the soundtrack, very faintly at first, as he crunches
along the gravel.*
    He is deep in thought, as JESSIE*'s voice grows louder.*
    *He turns a corner. Two little girls of about eight are standing
in the middle of the path,* VIOLETTA *and* EMILY.

VIOLETTA: Mr Luscombe!
JULIAN: Hello you two.
VIOLETTA: We're staying with Uncle Arthur! Are you on a
    surprise visit?

JULIAN: I am on a surprise visit, yes.

EMILY: Why? Why is it a surprise?

JULIAN: Because I like surprising people . . . and I like this garden very much . . . let's explore it together shall we?
He takes VIOLETTA*'s hand and the three of them move together on the path.*
One of the best days of my life was spent in this garden . . . I like this area especially. (*He stops and looks around.*) Is Uncle Arthur in the house?

VIOLETTA: He is, yes.

JULIAN: Well, let's not. call him just yet, shall we?

VIOLETTA (*smiling, joining in the secret*): No, we won't.

EMILY: What's in the box?

VIOLETTA: Is it a present for Uncle Arthur?

JULIAN: No, but you can look inside if you want.
He opens the box, they see the gun.

EMILY: Is it a real gun?

JULIAN: Yes, but you can hold it if you like.
EMILY *takes the gun out of the box.*

VIOLETTA: Why have you brought it with you Mr Luscombe?

JULIAN: Oh, I just thought I'd go for a walk with it, in case I see something I want to shoot . . . (*He smiles.*) Like a really fat pigeon, or a particularly hideous man, or a revolting mangy dog . . .

EMILY: You wouldn't do that would you?

VIOLETTA: Shoot a dog . . . or an ugly man?
JULIAN *takes the gun off* EMILY. *He points it at a spot in the garden and then slowly sweeps the barrel across the lawn, until he reaches the girls and is pointing it at them.*

JULIAN: No I probably wouldn't.
He looks down at the gun, feels its weight in his hand.
It would be better to wait until one saw somebody really important . . .

We see a figure through the trees. DONALDSON *is standing
on the verandah of the house, smoking a cigar.*

VIOLETTA (*calling and waving her arms*): Uncle Arthur!
Uncle Arthur, look who's here!

JULIAN *slips the gun back into the box. He then steps on
to the lawn with the girls so* DONALDSON *can see him.*

DONALDSON: Julian, my dear fellow! To what do I owe this
honour?

INT. UPSTAIRS ROOM AT CLUB. DAY
We cut to PAMELA *looking up sharply. We see her in medium
close-up, her face like a mask, as the girls dance in the foreground.*

INT. SARAH'S FATHER'S HOUSE. DAY
We cut to SARAH *on the landing of her father's house, staring
down into the hall.* HORTON *is standing with her father. The
other detective is watching by the front door which is closed.*

SARAH'S FATHER'*s tone is very polite as he addresses the
police.*

SARAH'S FATHER: You've seen all you need to?

HORTON: We have, yes.

SARAH'S FATHER: And everything is satisfactory?

HORTON: Absolutely. Your daughter has been extremely
helpful, she has given us a lead to follow up . . .

SARAH'S FATHER: I knew she would give you any
information she had, she's a good girl. She saw a little
of that man, but only a very little, you understand.

HORTON: She told me that, yes.

SARAH'S FATHER: What a business this is!

We are moving in on SARAH. *Her face is ashen.*

HORTON: I'm going to stay here, Mr Peters, for just a few
moments more, until I receive a phone call. We have
passed the information on –

We are now very close on SARAH.
– and I just have to wait for the results . . .

INT. BASEMENT CLUB FOYER. DAY
We cut to STANLEY *and* ERIC *entering the dark foyer of the basement club. There is the sound of singers' voices from the auditorium rehearsing a jazz number.*
DEIRDRE *is standing in the shadows.*

DEIRDRE: They're upstairs, Stanley, but they can't stay any
    longer! If it was your idea they are here –
STANLEY: It was not my idea–
DEIRDRE: It wasn't a good plan at all! I can't have him
    here, I just can't . . .

INT. ROOM ABOVE CLUB. DAY
We cut to STANLEY *and* ERIC *going upstairs and knocking on the door. There is the sound of the piano, and the* SHARP-FACED WOMAN*'s voice calls 'Come in!' They enter the upstairs room to be confronted by the sight of* LOUIS *coolly playing the piano as the girls dance in their ballet costumes.* STANLEY *grins at the scene,* LOUIS *dominating at the piano despite the tension* DEIRDRE *has created.*
    PAMELA *is sitting regally in the corner. She looks across at him.* STANLEY *is about to say something,* PAMELA *lifts a finger to her lips.*
    LOUIS *stops playing.*

SHARP-FACED WOMAN: The gentleman was very kind . . .
    He offered to play so I could watch more easily and
    it really was a help, wasn't it, girls? And he's quite a
    good player I have to say, not bad at all . . .

INT. BASEMENT CLUB. FRONT DOOR/FOYER. DAY
*There is a loud knocking at the front door of the club. The small
man opens the door,* GUNSON *and another detective are
standing there, three other police officers are on the metal steps
above them.*

INT. STAIRS/UPSTAIRS ROOM ABOVE CLUB/PASSAGE. DAY
We cut to DEIRDRE *hurtling up the stairs, her face frightened,
panicked. She rushes into the upstairs room where the ballet
class is.*

DEIRDRE: You've got to go now!
STANLEY: Go where?!
DEIRDRE: You've got to get out! You can't be found in this
    building . . . ! (*She is stricken with indecision.*) But I
    don't know what to do . . .
    She starts herding LOUIS *and* STANLEY *across the room to
    the door away from the stairs. The shots are jagged, hurtling
    with them, there is an atmosphere of chaos, of genuine
    panic. The dialogue is escalating, overlapping.* DEIRDRE *is
    pushing them through the far door, away from the ballet
    class as the girls watch, stunned.* DEIRDRE *closes the door,*
    LOUIS, STANLEY, PAMELA *and* ERIC *are in the passage
    with her.*
DEIRDRE: The police are here! They're downstairs –
LOUIS: The police are here?!
    He looks straight at STANLEY.
STANLEY: They didn't follow us! Absolutely nobody
    followed us –
DEIRDRE: You can't go back down there, you can't be
    found in the club! They'll close me down! . . . I'll be
    finished!
    *She's trying to lower her voice but she is genuinely frightened
    and keeps raising it in panic.*

I didn't ask you to come here but they'll never believe me – why did you ever come here?! (*Her voice rising.*) I don't know why you came here of all places?!

ERIC: There must be a way out this way, another flight of stairs?

DEIRDRE: There isn't! There's no other way out!

LOUIS: No other way out to the street?

STANLEY: There's got to be another way out –

DEIRDRE: I tell you there isn't! – everybody up here has to leave through the club, we all use the same front door, there's no other way in!

They are moving along the passage. There is a warren of small rooms above the club. LOUIS *is opening doors into the other rooms.*

LOUIS: We'll use one of these rooms, we can go in here. You can lock us in?

PAMELA: Lock us in?

STANLEY: Tell them it's a store room –

DEIRDRE: I'm not doing anything like that, anything that looks like I've helped you –

PAMELA: But we are here, Deirdre, so you might as well –

DEIRDRE: You're not using these rooms! They'll find you here anyway . . . (*Her voice rising in panic.*) I don't know what to do . . . There's no way out this way . . . ! There isn't anything to do!

LOUIS: Is there a way out to the roof?

DEIRDRE: You can't get out on to the roof! They'll see you!

ERIC: There must be a cellar? Can it be reached this way? (*He turns sharply.*) Can we use the cellar?

STANLEY: The cellar?! We'll be trapped –

INT. CLUB CELLAR. DAY

We cut to a low-angled shot of the cellar door opening. The camera is inside the cellar looking up; there is a very steep short flight of stairs.

    LOUIS *and* STANLEY *are staring down the stairs into the darkness of the cellar.*

ERIC: Get down there. Come on . . . !

    LOUIS *hesitates and then goes down the stairs into the cellar.* STANLEY *follows him down.*

STANLEY: I'll join you, Louis, it might be rather obvious if they find me in the club . . .

    ERIC *is about to shut the door and seal them in the cellar, when* PAMELA *moves past him and down the stairs into the darkness.*

PAMELA: I think I'd better come too . . . I don't know how I'd explain why I'm here . . .

DEIRDRE: I know nothing about this . . . If they ask me to show them the cellar – I'm not going to refuse . . . !

ERIC: Don't talk, don't make a sound! (*Closing the door, really nervous.*) I'll stay out here and speak to them . . . they don't really know me, maybe I can lie?

    ERIC *shuts the door with a deep thud. There's a second of pitch darkness.*

INT. BASEMENT CLUB FOYER. DAY

We cut to a shot of the police moving around the foyer of the club, watched by the small man. GUNSON *starts to climb the stairs.*

INT. ROOM ABOVE CLUB. DAY

We cut to the upstairs room. The girls are huddled together looking very frightened in the corner. The SHARP-FACED WOMAN *is looking very pale.* ERIC *is addressing them.*

ERIC: It's the immigration authorities that are here . . .
You know how strict they are about musicians,
musicians of colour especially – how they often get
deported unjustly. Well, they're making enquiries
about the gentleman who was playing for you a
moment ago, so if you could just say –
GUNSON *comes through the door with two uniformed*
police officers.
GUNSON: Have you seen a Negro in this building?
The girls look terrified. The SHARP-FACED WOMAN *is*
conflicted, she stares at her girls. GUNSON*'s tone is very*
sharp.
GUNSON: Was there a Negro here? A Negro musician?
One of the girls bursts into tears.
ERIC: I'm afraid you've made her cry . . .

INT. THE CLUB CELLAR. PITCH DARKNESS
We cut to the pitch-dark cellar, a second after the cut. PAMELA
flicks her cigarette lighter. Her face is illuminated by the flame.
A moment later STANLEY *flicks his cigarette lighter; he moves*
with the light, bangs into something sharp. He looks across to
the others in the darkness, holding the flame out in front of him.

STANLEY: Louis, where's your lighter . . . ?
LOUIS: It must be in my other clothes –
PAMELA: There's got to be another light somewhere . . .
She's groping in the dark along the wall.
This is rather horrible being down here . . .
STANLEY *stares at* PAMELA, *her face glowing above the*
flame of her lighter.
STANLEY: Why on earth are you here, Pamela?
PAMELA: People keep asking me that . . . why shouldn't
I be here? Why shouldn't I help?

LOUIS *finds a light switch, he flicks it on. One bare light bulb illuminates the cellar. They see they are surrounded by junk: a rusty bicycle, rotting old theatre seats from the auditorium, a mattress covered in dirt.*

PAMELA *stares around her in disgust.*

PAMELA: What a place to be found in!

LOUIS: They're not going to find us –

They hear the sound of footsteps and voices above them.

PAMELA: They're getting nearer . . . ! (*She looks up.*) Are they nearer?

PAMELA*'s face really tense. For a moment they listen to the sound of the police.*

LOUIS: When they've gone, I'm going to get the band to come here –

STANLEY (*turns sharply*): So you've had the same idea as I've had?

LOUIS: I don't know what idea you've had, but I know what I'm going to do –

STANLEY: Try to hide yourself in the band?

PAMELA: In the band?! Don't be silly –

LOUIS: Yes, they'll be looking for me as the leader of the band, but if the band's going somewhere and I'm carrying the luggage –

STANLEY: If you're a servant –

LOUIS (*to* PAMELA): Like I've been to you . . . there's a chance they won't spot me, even if they're looking at me . . . it's the only way I've thought of . . .

STANLEY: But where can the band go?

LOUIS: I don't know . . . I've no idea.

There's a loud noise directly above their heads. The sound of many footsteps and voices, people congregrating around the entrance to the cellar.

STANLEY: If they find us now –

LOUIS: Then even you won't be able to talk your way out of it –

STANLEY: You'll need a lawyer very quickly –

LOUIS (*staring up at the cellar door*): It's too late for lawyers, I'm not sure they'd ever have helped me . . . I should've gone straight to the station, Stanley, like I said . . .

STANLEY: We'll never know that . . . ! (*Sharply.*) But if it's my fault, I'm sorry!

LOUIS: Maybe you wanted to hold on to your story . . . take me to what you thought was a safe location, get a scoop nobody else has got . . .

There is silence for a moment above them. The footsteps seem to have stopped.

STANLEY: You really think I meant that! I can't believe you think that's what I'd do –

LOUIS: I think it's part of it . . . maybe not the main part.

PAMELA: But a little part of it . . .

STANLEY turns sharply, looking at PAMELA across the cellar. At that moment there's a loud rattle at the door. It is being yanked open, but it will not open.

PAMELA stares up, her face pale and frightened.

PAMELA: Oh God, here they are . . .

The door flies open. For a moment they can't see anything except the blast of daylight.

Then they see ERIC staring down at them.

ERIC: I think they've gone . . . ! But I'll make sure, you'd better stay for a moment longer . . .

ERIC shuts the door sharply.

INT. IMPERIAL. LADY CREMONE'S SUITE. AFTERNOON
We cut to LADY CREMONE sitting alone in her suite. She is surrounded by the evening papers with their headlines about the £10,000 reward. There is a knock on the door.

LADY CREMONE: Come in . . .

THORNTON enters the suite.

THORNTON: Your Ladyship?

LADY CREMONE: Harry, thank you . . . I wondered if you could get somebody to come and do my packing, my maid has gone out for the afternoon because I thought I was leaving tomorrow and I wanted to be on my own – but now I've decided to leave at once, by tonight.

THORNTON: Of course . . . I will get someone to come immediately.

But he doesn't move, he looks across at her, eager to say something.

So many people are doing this today, leaving the sinking ship!

LADY CREMONE: So I gather . . .

THORNTON: And of course it's understandable, how could people do anything else?!

LADY CREMONE: Well, in my case it was a rather difficult decision – it was going to be a new start for me this week . . .

THORNTON (*suddenly his voice rising*): It was a terrible thing to have that band here, to have them actually staying in this hotel! And look what it's led to – everything's finished here!

LADY CREMONE: Well I'm sure you'll survive, Harry, find somewhere else –

THORNTON: Oh don't worry about me! . . . you never have to worry about me . . . (*Beadily.*) I have all sorts of plans! (*He indicates the papers.*) And that should help find him, shouldn't it?! Such a big reward . . . !

LADY CREMONE: Indeed yes, a very big reward. (*Staring down at the paper.*) Surprisingly big.

THORNTON: Very public-spirited of Mr Masterson.

LADY CREMONE: Yes, it must be mustn't it? (*Quietly.*) What other reason could there be?

We stay on her for a moment.

INT. MAGAZINE'S NEW OFFICE/JULIAN'S PARENTS' HOUSE
MASTERSON *is sitting at his desk in the large empty room.*
Strong afternoon light, creating shadows. He is on the phone,
sitting very still, very upright, but his face is tense.

MASTERSON: What do you mean, he isn't there?
> *We cut to* MRS LUSCOMBE *on the phone in the reception*
> *room of her house.*

MRS LUSCOMBE: Julian is not currently here, I thought he
> was with you.

MASTERSON: No, he is not with me . . . I was about to
> come round in my car to pick him up, so we can have
> a meal before we go to the airport . . .

MRS LUSCOMBE: Well, I'm sure he will be back any
> moment, he knows he mustn't keep you waiting –

MASTERSON: You have no idea where he's gone?

MRS LUSCOMBE: I'm sorry, I don't. We've already said
> goodbye, so I wasn't really . . . (*Her voice tailing off.*)
> looking . . .

MASTERSON: Will you ask him to telephone me at once,
> as soon as he gets back? I am about to return to the
> Imperial Hotel, he can find me there.
> *He rings off.* ROSIE, *sitting at her trestle desk, is watching*
> *through the double doors. She sees* MASTERSON *isolated at*
> *his desk.*
> *He looks up and sees her watching him.*

MASTERSON: Come here, please.
> *As* ROSIE *approaches him.*
> Everybody appears to have left except for you and
> me, Miss Williams.

ROSIE: Yes sir.

MASTERSON: Do you know why that is?

ROSIE: I don't sir, no.
> MASTERSON *indicates the evening newspapers on his*
> *desk.*

MASTERSON: You see this. (*He points at the story on the bottom of the front page which has a small dark photo.*) This is the coverage of the assassination attempt on the American President. What a terrible little picture that is, don't you agree?

ROSIE: Yes sir.

MASTERSON: If we had my news magazine full of photo journalism already out on the streets, we could have done a great job covering this major story with really dramatic pictures, couldn't we?!

ROSIE: Yes sir.

MASTERSON (*suddenly staring straight at her*): You see I'm not just playing at this, Miss Williams . . . I do have a vision of things.

ROSIE is startled, it is as if he has read her thoughts. She is very nervous of him; one moment he seems vulnerable, the next quite frightening.

ROSIE: I can see that, yes, sir.

MASTERSON: But it is important in my life that things work to schedule . . . The one thing I do not allow are changes to my travel plans. Mr Luscombe and I are going to be taking off at 8:30 tonight as arranged, without fail.

INT. DONALDSON'S HOUSE. RECEPTION ROOM. AFTERNOON
JULIAN is sitting with a glass of wine in the reception room of DONALDSON's house. DONALDSON is sitting opposite him, also with a glass of wine. The two little girls are watching from the sofa. The afternoon light is closing in.

JULIAN: How lovely to drink in the middle of the afternoon.

DONALDSON: I have to say I don't like rules about when I'm allowed to drink, or indeed when I'm allowed to do anything.

JULIAN: That's right. I couldn't agree more . . . (*He looks around.*) And what a perfect room this is, full of all the things you've collected. You have such a wonderful life, Arthur, don't you? So few worries and problems!

DONALDSON: Yes, every day I wake up and think to myself how fortunate I am compared to so many others.

JULIAN (*suddenly very intense*): Could I stay here, Arthur? Just for a few days, hide inside your wonderful life?

DONALDSON: But you're going away Julian . . .

JULIAN: Well, you know what Walter's like – he makes plans for everybody and sometimes you just have to find a way of saying no . . . Just for a few days? You'll let me stay? (*Very intense.*) Please.

DONALDSON: I will. If that's what you want.

JULIAN: And you won't tell anybody where I am? Promise me, Arthur. You won't tell?!

DONALDSON: I won't, no.

INT. IMPERIAL, PASSAGE BY BALLROOM. AFTERNOON
CARLA *is moving along the passage near the ballroom. She sees* SCHLESINGER *standing in the shadows.*

CARLA: I've just come for my last wages, I think I'm owed a week . . .

SCHLESINGER: I can't help you I'm afraid, all that's been taken out of my hands!

THORNTON *suddenly appears.*

THORNTON: There's a phone call for you, Carla . . . (*His tone is cold, dismissive.*) You can take it in that booth there – no, not that one, the other one! They'll put it through for you . . .

CARLA *goes into the booth, she picks up the phone.*

CARLA: Hello, who's there . . . ?

There is a pause.

LOUIS (*voice-over*): Hello Carla . . .

> CARLA *flinches with surprise at hearing his voice.*

CARLA: Louis!

> *She breaks into a smile, then realising* SCHLESINGER *and* THORNTON *are still standing in the passage, she turns away in the booth so they can't see her face.*
>
> *We cut to* THORNTON*'s point of view as he watches* CARLA *in the booth, her body half turned away.*

INT. BASEMENT CLUB. AFTERNOON

We cut to the foyer and office of the basement club. ERIC *is standing in the doorway of the office watching* LOUIS *as he rings off.* STANLEY *is watching from the corner of the office,* PAMELA *is stretched out on a shabby sofa, staring at the ceiling and smoking.*

ERIC: Did you tell them to bring their passports? Did you remember that?!

LOUIS: I told Carla, yes, to get them all to do that, and they will . . .

> *We see* DEIRDRE *letting out the large jazz singer and the small man. She shuts the front door firmly. She calls across to the office.*

DEIRDRE: That's the last one gone . . . but I know the police will be back soon. I want you out!

STANLEY: Give us half an hour –

DEIRDRE: Half an hour?! You won't keep to that!

INT. IMPERIAL LOBBY. AFTERNOON

We cut to the main lobby of the Imperial. We see THORNTON *in the shadows watching everything.*

> MASTERSON *is walking across the lobby towards the lifts, his tall enigmatic figure; he is holding himself very straight, but his face is extremely tense.*

We cut back to THORNTON. *He then sees* CARLA *moving into the lobby with a suitcase and joining* JOE, *who is already standing there with his suitcase.* THORNTON *moves a little closer, watching them.*

INT. BASEMENT CLUB FOYER AND OFFICE/EMPTY
AUDITORIUM. AFTERNOON
We cut back to the basement club. LOUIS *is now standing by the encrusted walls of the office, with all the years of posters on them. The posters have been pinned on top of each other, so that the walls are literally bulging with the recent history of the club, all the bands that have played there.* LOUIS *is beginning to unpin the posters, he is doing it in an intense methodical way.* STANLEY *is watching him.*

PAMELA *is just ringing off on the phone. She looks concerned.*

PAMELA: My brother's not at home . . . (*She moves.*) He
  must be at the hotel, mustn't he? Of course . . .
  STANLEY *is concentrating on* LOUIS, *he doesn't hear her.*
  We move with PAMELA *across the foyer into the empty auditorium, where* ERIC *is working, drawing up plans.*
PAMELA (*to herself*): He will be all right won't he?
  ERIC *is deep in the plans, he doesn't hear.*
  We cut back to LOUIS, *a shower of old flyers and posters are coming away from the wall.*
STANLEY: Trying to find your band underneath all that?
LOUIS: I am . . . Our first poster might still be here, they
  seem to keep everything . . .
  He is pulling away at the collage of posters, the camera catching the evocative spread of old images and flyers.
LOUIS: You lied of course that first time . . .
STANLEY: You keep saying that, I didn't lie!
LOUIS: Yes, you came in here, having missed the whole thing,
  and lied your head off about how good we were . . .

STANLEY: I didn't lie! I'd heard enough, it was enough to get you on your way, wasn't it?!

LOUIS: And look where it's led . . .

We cut back to PAMELA *in the auditorium as she writes a letter.*

PAMELA: (*voice-over*): My darling brother,

When you get this you will already be in New York, no doubt having bought your splendid new shoes and maybe talking with a little bit of an American accent – although after only a few days that would be quick!

We cut back to LOUIS *in the office, as he comes across a very early poster of them on the wall.*

LOUIS *turns back to the wall, we are close on him, his tone more intense.*

LOUIS: Every time we got more success – I told myself it's not going to last, they're going to move on, they're going to find something else they think's more exciting, and that's going to be OK – because we'll still be able to make a living . . . I was ready for that. But I never thought it would end like this, that I'd –

STANLEY: That you'd be up for murder?! Well, naturally you didn't . . . ! Just because we didn't see it coming, doesn't mean it's inevitable –

LOUIS: That they hang me . . . ?

STANLEY: Don't lose control now, Louis! You used to drive me mad how you were always in control – but now it would be really useful . . .

LOUIS: That's easy for you to say –

STANLEY: You mean I'm just here for the ride?! To do the interview . . . ?

He moves closer, trying to distract LOUIS.

What should be the first question then? 'How are you feeling right now, Mr Lester . . . ?'

We cut back to PAMELA *writing her letter to* JULIAN. *We*

*hear the voice-over as the camera gets closer and closer to
her until her eyes fill the screen.*

PAMELA (*voice-over*): I just thought I'd put down a few
thoughts about you working with Mr Masterson and
how exciting it could prove to be for you . . . and also
how much fun – because we all know how many
parties he likes to hold?! I can just imagine you
dancing at the top of the Empire State Building and
keeping half of Manhattan awake. Just try to listen
carefully to what he says and to feed him plenty of
cheese of course! I know it's going to be a gloriously
successful time for you, if only you can apply yourself
and remember to get up in the morning, because I
won't be there to badger you . . .

*There's the sudden sound of heavy rain. The doors of the
yard are open, we move towards the doors, the rain is
dancing in the yard.*

We cut back to LOUIS *and* STANLEY. *They both turn,
watching the rain pouring down.*

STANLEY: Remember the rain here . . . ?! It was like the
end of the world!

We move in on LOUIS.

LOUIS: Of course.

Flashback: we see SARAH *and* LOUIS *running to the taxi
outside the club in the rain, laughing with excitement.*

We can begin to hear the sound of JOE *playing the
trumpet and* JESSIE *singing and laughing. We cut back.
We are moving in on* STANLEY.

STANLEY: You weren't here for the hailstorm, that was
incredible! You missed that.

LOUIS: I didn't miss it completely.

Flashback: we see SARAH *and* LOUIS *collecting the
hailstones off the windowsill inside the* Music Express
office and then kissing passionately. JESSIE*'s singing is
erupting on to the soundtrack.*

*We see the yard at the club full of hailstones and then
the characters exuberantly dancing in the hail;* JESSIE *with*
PRINCE GEORGE, JOE *playing the trumpet, the anarchic
energy and joy in the storm.*

*There is a sudden loud knocking. We cut back to the
present.*

DEIRDRE *is opening the front door of the club.*

The band are standing there with CARLA *as the rain is
pouring down, silhouetted against the metal staircase.*

*They are holding their suitcases and look disorientated
and dispossessed.*

INT. DONALDSON'S HOUSE, RECEPTION ROOM. AFTERNOON
JULIAN *is writing a letter at a table by the window.* VIOLETTA,
unseen by him, is lifting the lid of the mahogany box.
DONALDSON *is putting on a record.* VIOLETTA *and* EMILY
both peer down at the gun in the box. VIOLETTA *is about to slip
her hand in to lift up the gun.*

Suddenly JULIAN *leans across and snaps the lid of the box
shut. He then lifts his finger to his lips.*

VIOLETTA (*whispering secretively*): What are you writing?
JULIAN: I'm writing a letter to explain to Walter why I'm
    not going to America with him, but hiding away with
    you instead. Of course I'm not going to post it yet –
EMILY: Because then he might know where you are!
JULIAN: Exactly, and nobody's going to know that.
DONALDSON (*moving closer, it is nearly dusk outside*): I like
    that . . . the idea of hiding away from all trouble. (*He
    is by the window.*) Sometimes I walk out into this
    garden and think I can just shut the door and live here.
    I've got everything I need, food and an occasional
    delightful companion would come through that little
    door in the wall – but I would never need to go out

again, or be bothered about what's happening on the other side of the wall.

INT. BASEMENT CLUB, AUDITORIUM. LATE AFTERNOON
We cut to the auditorium of the basement club with its mixture of round tables at the front and raked seating at the back. The auditorium is empty except for the band, who are sitting looking very tense in the raked seating, with CARLA *in the middle, and* STANLEY, ERIC *and* LOUIS *who are leaning against the round tables facing the band.* PAMELA *is sitting at one of the tables, smoking.*

ERIC: So Louis will tell you what we've got in mind, and then I'm going to pick it up. (*He flourishes some papers.*) And go into more detail . . .
    DEIRDRE *is passing in the foyer outside. She yells through the open door into the auditorium.*
DEIRDRE: I'm locking up in ten minutes! Goodness knows how I've allowed you to stay this long – but I am now about to lock up.
LOUIS (*facing the band, his voice lowered*): We're going to get a train, we're going to say Carla and the rest of you are playing in Paris, there's no more work at the Imperial so you're going there, and I will be one of two people carrying most of your luggage. If I carry the luggage they will see a servant, not a bandleader. When we get to Calais, I will disappear and get a ship somewhere, as a merchant seaman.
STANLEY: Which is what your passport says – (*He turns to the band.*) It sounds desperate, but it might work . . .
ERIC (*explaining*): Any man of colour trying to get on a train by himself will be questioned very closely at the moment –
LOUIS: That's why I can't do it on my own.

PAMELA: You'll never all manage to get on the boat-train at Victoria, they'll stop you –

ERIC: This is true . . . (*He flourishes his bit of paper.*) But I have a route, the train stops at Bromley or South Bromley to be exact, if we use a suburban station, there'll be fewer police and no press hanging around –

STANLEY: Except for me, I will be travelling with you to 'cover' the concert – (*He waves his passport.*) I've picked up my passport specially.

PAMELA: Won't that just draw attention? You being there?

STANLEY: No, we need to make it look like a real booking, when we're going through customs – as if Carla is going to make her Paris debut –

He stops himself. CARLA *has her hand in the air.*

LOUIS: Yes, Carla?

CARLA: There's a problem, Louis.

ERIC: Yes?

CARLA: I don't have a passport.

STANLEY: What?!

CARLA: I don't have a passport . . . I've never been out of the country.

INT. IMPERIAL. BEDROOM PASSAGE. LATE AFTERNOON
We cut to LADY CREMONE *walking purposefully along the main passage and stopping at the Minotaur Suite. She knocks. She is holding one of the evening papers; she glances down at the reward headline. The door opens, a valet stares at her.*

LADY CREMONE: Is Mr Masterson in?

INT. IMPERIAL. MASTERSON'S SUITE. LATE AFTERNOON
LADY CREMONE *enters the Minotaur Suite. We see through the double doors to the bedroom where* MASTERSON *has clothes spread across the bed and two suitcases open.*

He is doing his own packing, moving methodically in the
shadows. The sun has just set, and the curtains are half drawn.

MASTERSON: Lavinia . . . ?

LADY CREMONE: Walter, I apologise for the intrusion, I just
wanted to ask you something.

MASTERSON: Yes . . . I'm a little busy, as you can see,
because we're leaving very shortly, the flight is at 8:30,
so you'll have to forgive me, if I continue doing this . . .

LADY CREMONE: Of course, Walter.
She is standing watching him through the open door.
I just wanted to ask you . . . (*She pauses momentarily.*)
why you've gone to the newspapers and offered a
reward for Louis Lester's arrest?
MASTERSON *continues to move by the bed, carefully*
folding his clothes.

MASTERSON: I've always done my own packing . . . one of
the little habits I've retained from my youth. I like to
know exactly where the things that matter to me are.
(*He looks up.*) I offered a reward so he could be
apprehended quickly, why else? (*He starts laying out*
his ties.) He let us down, did he not, after we'd
encouraged him so much . . . in many places he would
never have been able to mix in the way he did . . . and
then it –

LADY CREMONE: It turned out disastrously for him.

MASTERSON: It did not turn out well, no.
He starts packing his ties.

LADY CREMONE: And what about Julian?

MASTERSON: Julian? (*He looks up sharply.*) Yes . . . I keep
ringing him.

LADY CREMONE: You do?

MASTERSON: Yes, I don't know where he is . . . (*His tone*
suddenly agitated.) He is not at his home . . . his sister

rang up just now, she doesn't know where he is either!
(*He looks at her.*) You don't know where he is, do you?

LADY CREMONE: I don't Walter, no.

MASTERSON: I have to find him in the next half hour. (*His
voice tense.*) I'm sure I will.

LADY CREMONE: You're very fond of Julian, aren't you?

MASTERSON (*looking up from his packing again*): I think he
has promise, yes.

LADY CREMONE: That's not what I meant, Walter . . .

MASTERSON: Then you'll have to tell me what you mean?
Their eyes meet.

LADY CREMONE: That you have strong feelings for him,
that you care about him deeply?

MASTERSON (*resuming his packing*): I don't have a son . . .
For some reason, I come to this country and I find a
boy who is so full of life, and is not afraid – so many
people are afraid of me but he is not . . . So I find this
young man who is like a son, as maybe you have with
Stanley Mitchell . . . ?
We see a close-up of LADY CREMONE, *affected by this.*
Of course you've lost your sons, so it's not the same
at all, and the sorrow must be immense I know.
He looks at her, suddenly formidable again.
Until maybe recently? The magazine came along, a
new life beckons, which is about to start . . .
LADY CREMONE *is not intimidated, she returns his gaze.*

LADY CREMONE: So you have a very powerful affection for
Julian?

MASTERSON (*returning to his suitcase*): The small objects
are the ones that are most difficult to find if anybody
else ever packs my luggage . . . (*He puts a small gold
travelling clock into his case.*) What are you trying to
say to me, Lavinia? Because I'm afraid you will have
to say it more clearly.

LADY CREMONE: That your love for Julian could have led you to want to protect him at all costs . . .

MASTERSON (*a pause, he continues to do his packing*): I would have thought it's natural to try to protect those we care for . . . It's not always possible of course.

There is silence in the room.

LADY CREMONE (*with urgency*): Walter . . . is there something you can do for Louis Lester? (*She stares at him from the door.*) Even at this late stage?

MASTERSON: I can't imagine what that would be . . .

The phone rings in the suite; it is answered by the servant in the reception room. MASTERSON's *manner completely changes, he looks nervous and hopeful.*

MASTERSON: Could it be? (*Suddenly louder.*) Could that be him?!

VALET: A call sir . . .

MASTERSON *picks up the phone by the bed as* LADY CREMONE *watches closely.*

MASTERSON: Yes? Yes . . . Thank you . . . No, immediately. Yes, absolutely immediately.

He replaces the receiver. He turns and suddenly smiles broadly, excitedly. His whole body has relaxed.

MASTERSON: They've found him, they've found Julian! That was Arthur calling . . . Everything is back on track, Lavinia . . .

INT. DONALDSON'S RECEPTION ROOM. DUSK

JULIAN's *head turns, his face is in shock.*

JULIAN: You told him where I was?!

DONALDSON: Yes.

JULIAN: Why?! You promised you wouldn't do that?!

JULIAN's *tone is panicked, the girls look at* DONALDSON.

DONALDSON: I thought I had to, Julian, he has been so generous to you, arranged a new career for you – if you really don't want that, you have to tell him yourself.
For a moment JULIAN *stares straight at him, then he moves and smiles.*

JULIAN: Arthur, you're quite right, forgive me. Please ring him back immediately.
DONALDSON *moves to the phone and starts dialling,* JULIAN *picks up the mahogany box, he turns to the girls.*
I was behaving like a spoilt child, don't either of you ever do that . . .
JULIAN *moves to the phone, holding the mahogany box.*

JULIAN: Walter, there you are! Yes, I went missing but I'm back now . . .

INT. IMPERIAL BALLROOM. DUSK
We cut to SCHLESINGER *opening the door of the ballroom. It is completely empty and looking ghostly in the evening light. For a moment, as he stares around, he hears the sound of laughter, the hum of conversation, and then the music of the Louis Lester Band.*

There is a noise behind him.

THORNTON: Without the smell of cigar smoke, you don't recognise the place, do you?

SCHLESINGER: The last days of a hotel are always horrible. People suddenly treat you with contempt, say things they would never have said before.

THORNTON: We have to look to the future, Nathan . . . (*His spectacles glint in the light.*) and for a start maybe we can find Louis Lester? And get some of that money?

SCHLESINGER (*taken aback*): How would we do that, Harry?

THORNTON: Just by thinking clearly . . . Where did Stanley first spot the band? What club were they playing at when he found them?

He looks straight at him.

What was it called, Nathan?

SCHLESINGER *is unnerved by* THORNTON*'s penetrating gaze.*

SCHLESINGER: I don't remember . . .

THORNTON: Are you sure about that, Nathan?

SCHLESINGER *stares back, he gives him nothing.*

As it happens, I think I remember myself . . .

He starts to move off down the passage.

Let's see if I'm right.

He disappears from view.

INT./EXT. BASEMENT CLUB. FOYER/METAL STAIRCASE.
NIGHT

We cut to the band swirling around the foyer of the basement club; they look extremely tense. They are all now dressed in their dinner jackets, LOUIS *still in his servant clothes.* ERIC *is standing by the front door, which is open.*

STANLEY: It's time to go Eric, please!

ERIC: A few minutes yet, it has to be completely dark –

STANLEY: It is dark, Eric, if we stay here any longer we're going to run out of luck –

DEIRDRE *is locking the back door.* PAMELA *is standing in a corner of the foyer looking ghostly pale and tense.*

STANLEY: Go home, Pamela.

PAMELA: Why do you want me to go?

STANLEY *moves close. He stares at her, suddenly seeing her grave expression. We stay on him for a moment, then back to her, it is as if he has realised for the first time her true seriousness.*

STANLEY: I don't want you to go, but you've done a lot,
and you should be at home, your brother's leaving.
Why aren't you at home with him?

PAMELA: I should be there, you are right . . .
*She looks straight at him, not answering for a moment, as
if making a decision.*
But I'm not going to be . . .

STANLEY: Why?

PAMELA: Because I will be needed tonight.

STANLEY: How will you be needed?

PAMELA: Well to start with, for this probably . . .
She produces a large wadge of white five-pound notes.
Somebody's got to pay for all the first-class tickets –
I like the boldness of us all going first-class . . . I
brought this money for Louis –

STANLEY: Give it to him and then you can leave . . .

PAMELA: No . . . (*She puts it back in her bag.*) Because
you're going to need me for something else,
something that might happen on the train.
She looks at him.
I just have a feeling I might be useful . . .
We cut to LOUIS *by the front door, the band around him.*
ERIC *is on the metal steps outside. A telephone is ringing
in the background.*

LOUIS: It's time isn't it, Eric?! It has to be –

ERIC: Yes, the transport is here . . . Everybody make sure
you have your luggage with you, make straight for the
vehicles – but don't run, don't rush, just walk normally.
All right – go!
They start to leave up the metal stairs. We cut to DEIRDRE
in her office; she has answered the phone.

DEIRDRE: No, he can't speak now, he can't. No, I didn't
say he was here . . . (*She looks up and calls across.*)

LOUIS *hesitates for a moment and then moves swiftly to the phone.*

We intercut between LOUIS *and* SARAH *on the landing at her home.*

SARAH: Louis . . . I've been trying and trying! This line has been engaged for ages –

LOUIS: Sarah, I can't talk now –

SARAH: I so wanted to see you, but I couldn't come myself, I might have been followed –

LOUIS: The police came anyway . . .

SARAH: But they didn't find you . . . ?! (*Then realising.*) Of course they didn't!

LOUIS: You knew they were coming then?

SARAH: I couldn't stop them . . . I was weak Louis I know, I couldn't find a way of not telling them . . . (*Her voice breaking.*) I am so sorry . . . it's not completely how you think it was – I'm sure you think that about me, maybe you have to right now, but –

LOUIS: I can't talk Sarah, a lot of people are taking risks for me, I can't make them wait –

SARAH: But we can't say goodbye like this, Louis!

LOUIS: We're going to have to Sarah . . . I can't say something that makes everything all right –

SARAH: I don't want you to do that, because I know everything's not all right, so it wouldn't mean anything . . . I just don't want to say goodbye like this, Louis –

LOUIS: It's not always possible to have the right sort of goodbyes, Sarah.

He puts the receiver down.

We cut back to SARAH. *She is distraught. She leans against the wall. She is shaking with sobs.*

We cut back to LOUIS. *He realises everybody has gone. He hurries out of the foyer and up the metal steps.*

DEIRDRE *calls after him.*

DEIRDRE: I hope you're not too late (*As he goes.*) Good
luck, Louis.

EXT. ALLEYWAY. STREETS. NIGHT
LOUIS *is walking fast down the alleyway, he is trying not to
run. A subjective shot as he nears the end of the alleyway. A
young couple walk past, the man turns and looks back at him
as if studying him for a moment.* LOUIS *reaches the mouth of
the alleyway, there is no sign of* ERIC, STANLEY *and the band.
He looks around, trying not to seem like he's panicking. He
crosses the road, the street is deserted except for the young couple
who are now standing watching him from the alley. Suddenly
out of the foggy night,* ERIC *appears in the distance, calling.*
LOUIS *starts towards him.*

ERIC: Come on quick! We had to move the transport, we
were too conspicuous.
ERIC *leads him around the corner into a small side street
where the large black saloon car is waiting and a lorry
with a covered back. In the lorry the band are sitting.*
ERIC (*indicating the lorry*): My brother arranged this. Come
on . . . get in! Quickly! And pull the flap down . . . !
LOUIS *climbs aboard the lorry. The band are sitting
uncomfortably in the back, one or two of them looking
very scared.*
LOUIS: I'm sorry, something happened . . .
*The black car accelerates away, and the lorry follows,
down the misty night street.* LOUIS *watches the road recede
from the back of the lorry; he drops the flap down.*

INT./EXT. ERIC'S CAR. NIGHT
We cut inside ERIC's *car.* STANLEY *is in the front passenger
seat, chain-smoking,* ERIC *is driving,* CARLA *and* PAMELA *are
in the back.*

STANLEY: You've got to act the star, remember, Carla, when we get out – got to order the band around, boss Louis like a servant.

CARLA (*quietly*): Just when I've lost my job, I've got to act the star . . .

PAMELA *is staring out of the window; she catches a glimpse of a young woman out walking a dog.*

PAMELA: You think everybody you see must know . . .

STANLEY: On the train, Carla, it's got to really look like the band is going to Paris. Do it with confidence and people will believe it, after all why shouldn't you have an engagement there, and be taking your servant . . . ?

CARLA: Yes . . . I'll try. I'm so sorry everything had to change!

ERIC: Half a plan is better than no plan –

STANLEY: We'll get the train to Dover and then we'll see what Louis can do. There are no passport controls before Dover –

PAMELA: Why can't we try to drive all the way?

ERIC: We will get stopped if we try to drive.

EXT. DONALDSON'S HOUSE. NIGHT
We cut to MASTERSON*'s car driving up to the front of* DONALDSON*'s house.* JULIAN *is standing ready in the porch, wearing his coat and holding the mahogany box.* DONALDSON *is by his side, the little girls are watching from a window with the housekeeper.* MASTERSON, *in the back of the car, winds down his window.*

JULIAN: Walter!

MASTERSON: I have all your luggage with me, everything is taken care of.

JULIAN: I want Arthur to come to the meal as well. (*He turns to* DONALDSON.) You will come, won't you,

Arthur, help me say goodbye to the old country?!
Please.

INT. MASTERSON'S LIMOUSINE. NIGHT
DONALDSON, JULIAN *and* MASTERSON *are sitting in the back
of the limousine as they drive along a night street. We are inside
the car.*

JULIAN: Please let me choose where we're going to eat?!
MASTERSON: I've decided already, I've booked a table at
    the Savoy, an early meal, before we drive to the
    airport –
JULIAN: No, no, I have the perfect place in mind! Please
    let me choose, I know what would be absolutely the
    right choice.

INT. GREASY SPOON. NIGHT
*We cut to the large greasy-spoon restaurant with tiled walls that
DONALDSON and LOUIS went to in Part Three. It has a series
of tables with check tablecloths, and a narrow but very long
interior, which tapers away from us. It has a mixture of people
eating there, the young and the old, pin-striped clerks and more
working-class characters mingled together, sheltering from the
cold night. Steam is pouring from the tea urns that line the
counter.* MASTERSON, JULIAN *and* DONALDSON *stand in the
doorway.* MASTERSON *looks particularly incongruous dressed in
his magnificent coat.*

JULIAN: This is the ideal place don't you think, in which to
    say goodbye to England! Good sausages, normal
    people of course, milky tea. (*He turns, his eyes shining.*)
    Doesn't it seem exactly right?!

INT. IMPERIAL HOTEL, BEDROOM PASSAGE. NIGHT
We are in the bedroom passage in the Imperial. LADY CREMONE
*is just opening the door to her suite. A door opens down the
passage and* LADY ALTRINGHAM *looks out.*

LADY ALTRINGHAM: I thought I heard somebody. I was
    worried I was completely alone up here.
LADY CREMONE: No no, I'm here . . .
LADY ALTRINGHAM: I thought you were leaving, Lavinia?
LADY CREMONE: Yes, I was, but suddenly I felt I had to
    stay, I knew I had to be here tonight.
    We move in close on her.
    I'm not sure why, but I do . . .

EXT. SUBURBAN STATION. NIGHT
We see LOUIS, STANLEY, PAMELA, ERIC, CARLA *and the band
clustered on the platform of a suburban station. There is hardly
anybody else around, a tiny huddle of other travellers in winter
coats waiting for the boat-train, two guards but no police. The
faces of the band are very tense.* LOUIS *is moving the luggage
while* CARLA *is standing confidently, demanding attention from
the band. They hear the sound of the approach, and then we see
the train steaming towards us out of the night.*

INT./EXT. TRAIN AND PLATFORM. NIGHT
We cut inside the stationary train and see CARLA *climbing
aboard with the band. The first-class carriage is divided into
different luxury compartments; two are full of young upper-class
men on a jaunt to Paris; they are already quite drunk, there is
a powerful sense of them all off for an indulgent weekend.
Another compartment is empty except for a man in a dark suit
and one is entirely empty.* CARLA *settles into the empty
compartment, ordering the band to go next door except for* JOE

who will stay with her, STANLEY *and* PAMELA. ERIC *is arranging for the heavy trunk they are carrying to be taken to the luggage carriage,* LOUIS *is heaving all their hand luggage on to the train, as* CARLA *shouts at him to be more careful with it.*

    LOUIS *stares at the faces watching him, the upper-class young men laughing at the sight of these black musicians getting into first class. We hear them shout out 'Got a lot of banjo players here, who let them on the train?!'*

    LOUIS *climbs aboard the train, one of the young men yells at him.*

YOUNG MAN: A nigger band in first class! The world's gone mad!
    LOUIS *meets the contemptuous gaze of the* YOUNG MAN *with a powerful stare.* STANLEY *is suddenly by his side.*
STANLEY: Get that luggage inside now! Carla wants that case with her . . .
ERIC: I have to say goodbye . . . (*He is calling from the platform through the open door.*) I've got to take the transport back. Have a wonderful tour! Wonderful concerts!
    The YOUNG MAN, *stirred up by* LOUIS' *insolent look, follows him down the corridor to* CARLA's *compartment, where* LOUIS *is putting the luggage up on the rack.*
YOUNG MAN: Where are you all going may I ask?
STANLEY: The lady's going to Paris.
CARLA: I am going to Paris. With my band. For some special concerts.
    The YOUNG MAN *doesn't move.*
STANLEY: Is that enough?!
YOUNG MAN: (*keeps looking at them, contemptuous*): They like your sort of music in France, don't they?!
    STANLEY *is getting angry, about to say something.*
    PAMELA *suddenly turns to* LOUIS, *ordering him in her grandest manner.*

PAMELA: Bernard, will you close that door, we want a bit
of peace and quiet on this journey!

LOUIS *slides the door across the* YOUNG MAN'*s face.*

  LOUIS *is still in the compartment putting up the
luggage. They are all very tense.*

PAMELA: Why aren't we going? Why is it still here?

STANLEY: It often waits at this stop.

PAMELA: Waiting for what?

LOUIS: Maybe for them . . .

*He can see from the window two uniform policemen on the
platform.*

PAMELA: Oh God, are they going to search the train . . . ?

*The door of the compartment opens, and a large middle-
aged woman and a young man stand wanting to enter.*

PAMELA: Please come in . . .

CARLA: Yes, my servant has just finished putting the
luggage away . . .

*The couple sit down frostily, disconcerted to find they are
sharing the compartment with black people.*

CARLA (*to* LOUIS): Be where I can see you, I want you near
me at all times, that's why you're in first class.

LOUIS: I will be just outside.

  LOUIS *stands in the passage, the young men are laughing
and shouting down the corridor at him: 'They're going to
stay at the Ritz!' There is the scream of the whistle and the
train lurches forward. We move in on* LOUIS. *He watches
the young men's faces, their shouting, their laughter.*

  *Suddenly the train explodes into sharp sunlight. We
flashback into the private train hurtling towards the picnic
and* SARAH *and* WESLEY *and* STANLEY *coming towards*
LOUIS *exuberantly down the passage, full of excitement.*

  We cut back to LOUIS *and the present, just as the train
enters a tunnel.*

INT. GREASY-SPOON RESTAURANT. NIGHT
Three plates of sausages and mash are put down in front of
DONALDSON, JULIAN *and* MASTERSON.

JULIAN: Marvellous! . . . (*He turns to the waitress.*) But
　　　maybe, do you think? (*He picks up his plate.*) You can
　　　take them back and burn them a little? I just love
　　　burnt sausages . . .

MASTERSON: I'm not sure we have time for that . . .

JULIAN: Oh, it doesn't take long to burn some sausages.
　　　He pops one on to his side plate and hands his plate back
　　　to the waitress.
　　　You take the others back . . . and burn them.
　　　The waitress goes, JULIAN *starts eating the sausage in his*
　　　fingers.

MASTERSON: You want your last meal you have in this
　　　country for a while –

JULIAN: To be burnt sausages? Yes! (*He looks around.*)
　　　Arthur loves this place, don't you, he often brings his
　　　'discoveries' here . . .

DONALDSON: I have been known to, yes.

JULIAN: Isn't it wonderful to be able to select a young
　　　person, and give them a chance, transform their lives
　　　just like that?!

DONALDSON: That's what we both try to do . . .

JULIAN: Of course, and you do it so well! (*He looks about*
　　　him, his eyes shining.) We must have more than just
　　　sausages here. We must try everything Arthur
　　　recommends –

MASTERSON: I told you, we don't have a lot of time . . .
　　　JULIAN*'s mood is building in intensity. He suddenly says*
　　　loudly:

JULIAN: I don't believe you, Walter! It is your private
　　　plane, after all, and we know now what we can do
　　　with private planes . . . ! Get them to take you to

France at very short notice, maybe even in the middle
of the night! And then get your passport stamped with
all sorts of different times and stamps . . . when a
little money changes hands . . . !
We move in on MASTERSON.

DONALDSON (*attempting to deflect* JULIAN): It is a terrible
thing isn't it, this world of passports and papers and
officialdom – how I loathe it . . .

JULIAN: Yes, but then you two can do anything you want,
can't you?! Nothing really inconveniences you . . . !
After all, these people here . . . they might lose
everything just like that tomorrow, in another crash!
We see shots of the faces of the people in the restaurant.
JULIAN's *eyes are shining.*
But you two will float above it . . . always able to float!
Nothing can touch you! And me too of course – am
I any different? No! I can float just as well as anybody
else, always come out on top. We sail above it all – us
three, together! (*He stands.*) Excuse me. (*He is holding
the box.*) I need to put this to good use.
He moves off down the restaurant.

MASTERSON: What is that, Julian? That box?

JULIAN: Nothing that special. (*Sharp smile.*) But worth a
look!

INT. TRAIN. NIGHT
*The train is moving through the night, the compartment door is
opened, the ticket inspector calls out 'Tickets please!'* STANLEY,
PAMELA, CARLA *and* JOE *offer their tickets. As they do so,
another official appears in the corridor; a border control*
IMMIGRATION OFFICER.

IMMIGRATION OFFICER: And we'll be stamping your
passports too, please have them ready!

STANLEY: Our passports?! Why do you want our passports?

IMMIGRATION OFFICER: It's our new procedure – for first-class passengers only – so they do not have to queue at Dover with the second-class and third-class passengers, they just walk on to the boat.

CARLA's face looks stricken with tension. The middle-aged woman is watching her closely. STANLEY tugs at his cigarette, he is thinking quickly.

STANLEY: You can start with him in the passage. (*He indicates* LOUIS.) We just have to find ours . . .

The ticket officer and IMMIGRATION OFFICER *look at* LOUIS.

Yes, he does have a first-class ticket! Why don't you ask him?

CARLA: I like to have my servants close . . .

The IMMIGRATION OFFICER *starts to look at* LOUIS' *passport. We see the officer hesitate for a moment when he sees the name, as if he half remembers it. He looks at the profession, 'merchant seaman', then he looks at* LOUIS' *servant clothes.* LOUIS *meets his gaze.* STANLEY *is looking incredibly tense, he lights another cigarette.* JOE *is staring at the ground. Suddenly* PAMELA *calls out to the officer with a really sharp tone.*

PAMELA: Will you hurry up! We need him – (*indicating* LOUIS) to help us find our passports. He has packed them away in our luggage, and now he has to show us where he put them!

The IMMIGRATION OFFICER *stamps* LOUIS' *passport promptly. He turns to him.*

IMMIGRATION OFFICER: Of course carrying their luggage is a lot easier than working on ships, isn't it!

The IMMIGRATION OFFICER *turns to* CARLA. PAMELA *interjects again, at her most commanding.*

PAMELA: I think, on reflection, the rest of us will have to queue with all the other people. It is regrettable, but

I don't want to keep you waiting – while he (*she points to* LOUIS) has to snuffle around in our luggage! So please, carry on!
The IMMIGRATION OFFICER *turns.*
You should have advertised your new service more clearly – and then we'd have been prepared!
The officer leaves. STANLEY *stares across at* PAMELA.
He lowers his voice.

STANLEY: You were right . . . you were needed.
PAMELA: Yes. (*She leans back, her voice quiet.*) I hate trains.
We stay on her a moment.

INT. LADY CREMONE'S SUITE. NIGHT
We cut to LADY CREMONE *sitting in her suite in her darkened reception room . . . She is alone. We move towards her, as if she senses something.*

INT. GENTLEMAN'S LAVATORY. GREASY SPOON. NIGHT
We cut to JULIAN *in the lavatory of the greasy spoon. He takes the gun out of the box. He spins the chamber to check it is fully loaded.*

INT. GREASY SPOON. NIGHT
JULIAN *walks out of the lavatory and starts surveying the main room in the restaurant. He looks sideways into the kitchen where two young cooks are frying lots of sausages, and harassed waitresses are moving back and forth. The door into the back yard is open, and it has begun to rain.* JULIAN *suddenly moves into the doorway of the kitchen. The* WAITRESS *who served him is just about to pick up two plates.* JULIAN *gives her the letter he was writing in* DONALDSON's *house.*

JULIAN: Will you keep this for a moment? It's very private. Don't let anybody have it until I say so, do you understand?

The WAITRESS *looks alarmed, the cooks have their backs to them.*

Please, just for a moment . . .

The WAITRESS *stares at him bewildered.*

WAITRESS: You mean keep it until you leave the restaurant, sir?

JULIAN: That's right . . . It explains a few things . . . why I think it happened. How she looked at me, how I wanted to love her so much, and how she fought me when I tried to show my love . . .

WAITRESS: I'll bring it back with the bill, shall I, sir?

JULIAN: Keep it until you hear from me.

The WAITRESS *takes the envelope.* JULIAN *moves out of the kitchen, and stands in the shadows staring down at the long interior of the restaurant. He takes the gun out of his pocket and aims it at a man eating on his own; he then swivels across and lines up two women eating together; and then away again at an older couple; and then across again to a mother eating with her teenage daughter. A young waiter passes, not looking at* JULIAN.

JULIAN: How many do you think I should get? They don't know what's about to hit them . . . none of us do!

We move in on JULIAN *and then back on to the people in the restaurant. For a moment the oblivious faces and the laughter slow.* JULIAN *takes aim again, this time lining up* DONALDSON *and* MASTERSON.

JULIAN: I'll take these two first, just to make sure, and then the rest.

The WAITRESS *is moving with some plates, getting closer to* JULIAN. *She can't see the gun at first.* JULIAN *turns to look at her. Now she sees the gun.*

For a split moment she is frozen with terror as they look at each other. We move in on JULIAN. *He is suddenly affected by the fear on her face, she is imploring him with her eyes. He stares back at her.*

JULIAN: You're right, you're absolutely right, I shouldn't do that. Why do that tonight? I'll leave that to somebody else to do . . . This is much better, makes much better sense . . .

JULIAN shoots himself through the temple, the blood splashing across the kitchen wall. He falls on the floor, surrounded by the cooks, food frying, and the WAITRESS *screaming.*

We move in on DONALDSON *and* MASTERSON.

DONALDSON *gets up and moves straight down the length of the restaurant, past shocked and terrified faces and into the kitchen where* JULIAN *is lying with half of his head blown off.* DONALDSON *turns.* MASTERSON *is coming down the length of the restaurant towards him, his tall figure, his face masklike, transfixed.*

DONALDSON: Walter, you must go, don't look . . . I will take care of this, you must go!

But MASTERSON *brushes past him. He stares for a second at* JULIAN, *then sinks down next to him and cradles his body as blood goes all over his clothes.*

MASTERSON: The boy . . . the boy . . . (*He cradles his head.*) He was a difficult boy . . . (*He touches his hair.*) Oh, my difficult boy, what have you done?

We cut back to the main section of the restaurant, people are crying and huddled in corners, terrified.

We cut back to the kitchen. MASTERSON *stands, his clothes covered in blood.*

DONALDSON: You must go, Walter. Go now!

MASTERSON *moves slowly, his face expressionless, out of the kitchen and through the restaurant. We watch from the doorway as he disappears. We cut back to* DONALDSON.

He moves into the doorway of the yard as the rain pours down. The WAITRESS *is crying by his side.*

DONALDSON: Has somebody called the police?

The WAITRESS *nods and continues to cry. For a moment* DONALDSON *stands beside her.*

DONALDSON: However terrible things are, they pass, this will pass, everything will carry on. (*His face is pale but his tone quite calm.*) It always does . . .

INT. MASTERSON'S LIMOUSINE. NIGHT

We cut to MASTERSON *sitting in the back of his limousine. His shirt and waistcoat are covered in blood. He is staring ahead as he is driven through the night, his eyes full of tears.*

He disappears into the shadows.

INT./EXT. TRAIN AND PLATFORM. NIGHT

The train stops with a sudden thud.

PAMELA: Are we here?

STANLEY: This is Folkestone . . . Dover is the next stop in a few minutes.

He looks out of the window, the platform seems almost deserted.

Maybe . . . ?

We cut to LOUIS *who is also staring out at the platform. There are three guards but no sign of police. He beckons to* STANLEY.

Ah yes. (*In a loud voice for the benefit of the other passengers.*) I forgot this is where we are getting off! (*To* CARLA.) We are being met here . . .

He indicates to CARLA *and the band to start getting off.* LOUIS *begins collecting all the luggage he can as they spill on to the foggy platform. The young men have all gathered*

at the window of the train to stare at the band on the
platform. We hear voices calling out 'Maybe we'll be spared
them on the boat!'

STANLEY *turns to* PAMELA *and* LOUIS *as they are*
being watched by all these faces. STANLEY *lowers his voice.*

STANLEY: How do we say goodbye with all these bastards
watching?

PAMELA: We can't . . .

LOUIS *is staring at the train and then at the others, as he*
places the luggage down at their feet.

STANLEY: You're right, we can't . . . (*To* LOUIS.) Just walk
off now . . .

LOUIS: Yes.

He moves a few feet from the luggage and then turns in
full view of the train and the young men and calls out to
STANLEY.

Thanks, travelling first-class was not too bad . . .

STANLEY: No . . . pity about the company one has to keep
though!

CARLA (*to* LOUIS): You must go and check if the car is
here.

She goes up to LOUIS, *adjusting a button on him so she*
can whisper.

Be careful . . .

LOUIS: Don't worry about me . . .

STANLEY *catches his arm just as he moves off.*

STANLEY: I never got the interview . . . (*Then whispers.*)
Don't rush . . .

LOUIS *disappears along the platform, amidst the smoke*
and the misty night. There are four other men in working
clothes moving towards the exit with him.

LOUIS *vanishes from view.*

CARLA *turns, trying not to cry, the young men are still*
watching them from the train.

CARLA: Well, what a journey!

PAMELA: Maybe it'll work . . . (*She stares along the platform.*) I'm just going to telephone home, make sure Julian has left for the airport. He should be about to get on his aeroplane.

She moves into a waiting room, which is glowing out with light amongst the surrounding darkness on the platform.

The train begins to move off, the young men shouting abuse at the band as the train disappears into the night.

CARLA: They've gone! We can celebrate!

STANLEY: Hopefully . . . (*He turns to her.*) You played the star really well . . .

CARLA: I thought so, yes.

STANLEY *turns to see* PAMELA *sitting strangely in the lighted waiting room. He moves towards her, a subjective shot as he enters the waiting room. She replaces the phone. Her voice is barely audible.*

PAMELA: Julian is dead.

STANLEY: What?!

PAMELA: He shot himself . . . (*Suddenly she cries out.*) Oh my God, what have I done, what have I done, Stanley! Why wasn't I there . . . ?! I should have been there . . .

She is crying uncontrollably. STANLEY *holds her.*

STANLEY: You had to be here, you chose to be here . . . (*He holds her tight.*) And that was very brave . . .

She weeps into his shoulder, her whole body shaking.

It was so difficult I know . . . but very brave. I love you.

We see a wide shot of the waiting room. STANLEY *is holding* PAMELA *tight as she cries. He kisses her and holds her in his arms.*

STANLEY: I love you.

EXT. IMPERIAL BACKYARD. DAY

Morning light. SARAH *is walking very purposefully across the*

*back yard of the Imperial. She is carrying her new camera. Her
face is grave but determined.*

*She passes a young waiter throwing away large trays of
uneaten desserts.*

INT. IMPERIAL. BASEMENT PASSAGE. DAY
We see SARAH *moving down the Imperial basement passage
very sharply. At the end of the passage, right in front of her,*
THORNTON *is watching her approach.*

THORNTON: Miss Peters, what can I do for you?
    SARAH *is taking pictures as she walks towards him.*
SARAH: You can just stand there, I have a new high-speed
    camera.
    *She is taking photos very fast, the camera clicking in a
    threatening fashion.*
    Which can take pictures very quickly of people who
    don't always want to be photographed.
    THORNTON *backs away, she follows him around the
    corner, photographing all the time.*
SARAH: People who prefer to live in the shadows, such as
    you, Harry!
    *She is getting closer and closer to him as he stands in a
    corner, very unnerved.*
    Now I can catch them with this . . . And shall I tell
    you something else, Harry . . . I'm going to try to find
    him. I'm going to find Louis.

INT. OLD MUSIC EXPRESS OFFICE. DAY
*We cut to her photographs of the Imperial basement and the
ballroom staring out of the pages of the latest edition of the
Music Express. We cut wide to see we are in the old Music*

Express *office and* STANLEY, ERIC *and* ROSIE *are back at their desks.*

    Stanley is examining the magazine. We see the banner headline 'THE REAL STORY OF JESSIE TAYLOR'S DEATH', *and then photographs of* JESSIE *and of* JULIAN, *and a smaller headline 'The Confession of Julian Luscombe'.*

ERIC: Don't expect it to sell thousands and thousands of copies, Stanley.

STANLEY: Why not . . . ? (*He looks up.*) You don't think people want to hear the truth?

ERIC: Not as much as when Louis was the culprit . . . The other papers reported it in a very small way, didn't they? In a few months I doubt anybody will remember the Jessie Taylor case that clearly . . . it'll slip away bit by bit.

STANLEY: I hope you're wrong, but you probably aren't, and of course we don't have Louis' side of the story, I still haven't heard a word . . .

    He looks again at the photos, this time of PAMELA *and* JULIAN.

ERIC: Do you think she knew about her brother?

STANLEY: I don't know. In a way maybe, deep down . . .

ERIC: But she spent the whole of that day with Louis?

STANLEY: She did . . . (*We move in on him, quiet.*) It was an extraordinary thing to do . . .

    MR WAX *appears in the doorway.*

MR WAX: I thought you'd like to know, I've been dealing with some colleagues of Mr Masterson, and I've held on to the magazine, he doesn't want it any more. (*He stares at them.*) But of course I may have to make some changes . . .

    He gives them a beady stare and disappears.

INT. IMPERIAL LOBBY AND BALLROOM. EVENING
*We cut to the camera moving across the Imperial lobby to the
ballroom. It picks up* PAMELA *walking on her own. She is
dressed beautifully, as always, in an evening gown. Her face is
alabaster pale, her demeanour dignified, withdrawn. She moves
past a notice that says* 'TONIGHT, THE JACK PAYNTON
ORCHESTRA'.

We move with PAMELA *into the ballroom. It is glowing with
a little of its old glamour. Some of the round tables are occupied,
there is a sprinkling of younger guests. The old dowagers are still
eating at tables on their own. There's no band on the stage at
this moment.* PAMELA *moves across the ballroom to find*
STANLEY *sitting waiting for her at a table.* STANLEY *gets up
to greet her.*

STANLEY: Aren't you surprised? For once I'm early . . . !
PAMELA: Well, I'm never on time, you should know that
      Stanley . . . and some things will never change.
      She takes a deep breath as she sits.
      This is my first night out for a long time . . .
STANLEY: It's strange being back here, isn't it?
PAMELA: It's very strange . . .
      We stay on her for a moment. STANLEY *holds her hand.*
      SCHLESINGER *is beckoning to* STANLEY *from across the
      room. He still looks a haunted figure, not the expansive
      person he once was.*
STANLEY: What does he want?
      He stands up. SCHLESINGER *calls across.*
SCHLESINGER: There's a telephone call for you.

INT. IMPERIAL. PHONE BOOTH OUTSIDE BALLROOM/BAR.
EVENING
We cut to STANLEY *taking the phone call inside the booth.*

STANLEY: Yes . . . ?

LOUIS: Hello Stanley.

STANLEY: Louis! – is it really you?!

We cut to LOUIS *in a dark bar, there are people out of focus behind him.*

LOUIS: It is me, yes . . .

STANLEY: Where are you?

LOUIS: I'm in Marseilles, trying to get a ship to America . . .

STANLEY: What are you going to do there? Start a band?!

LOUIS: Maybe . . . there's a lot more competition there . . .

STANLEY: Louis? I didn't think that –

LOUIS: You'd ever hear from me?

STANLEY: No I didn't, but I knew you must have got out of England! Have you read about Julian?

LOUIS: I did, just a few lines – best we don't talk about that . . .

STANLEY: Right. OK.

LOUIS: I have to be quick.

The line crackles really badly.

STANLEY: I can't hear you –

LOUIS: I said I have to be very quick, this is costing a fortune, but I've got to know, what are you doing back at the Imperial? I called the magazine and they said you were there –

STANLEY: Yes, it's my first time back! None of us have been here for several months –

LOUIS: So it didn't close! The old place is still there?!

STANLEY: Just . . . It's sort of holding on, week by week, getting shabbier . . . ! It's very like it was before we ever met, the old dowagers sitting in corners, maybe even the Masons have crawled back . . . If I look across the lobby now, there's Lady Cremone coming down to dinner. She and I . . .

We move with LADY CREMONE *as she sits at a table. She looks elegant but alone.*

LOUIS: Are not quite what you were before?

STANLEY: That's right, and you'll never guess this, but Jack Paynton is about to play!

LOUIS: Jack Paynton?! He's not back there playing, is he?! It really is as if we were never there.

STANLEY: Not quite . . . twice a week, for a short while . . .

The camera is beginning to move across the lobby, around the corner and towards the ballroom doors.

STANLEY (*voice-over*): Before Jack Paynton plays . . . just as the dowagers are tucking in to their salmon mousse . . . This happens –

We move through the ballroom doors, past some of the diners, and then we see the band has come on stage. JOE *the trumpeter is still out front,* CARLA *is standing at the microphone. She begins to sing one of the numbers* JESSIE *used to sing.*

We move towards her across the ballroom as she sings with heartfelt passion, staring directly at us.

The image slowly fades to black.

INTERVIEWING LOUIS

INT. DARK ROOM

A photograph of LOUIS *is developing in the chemical tray of the dark room. Its ghostly shape is slowly coming into focus as* STANLEY*'s voice plays over the image.*

STANLEY (*voice-over*): During my friendship with Louis Lester, and I think I can call it a pretty remarkable friendship, I made several attempts to interview him in my official capacity as Deputy Editor of *Music Express*. After all, I had championed his music and his band, given them a lot of publicity and rave reviews, what was more natural than to follow this up than with a really major interview?

I never got a chance to finish it, though, before the terrible events that engulfed us all happened. But I firmly believe the fragments I got are worth publishing – especially as the conversation took such an unexpected turn, one I could never have predicted. However there was a problem in interviewing Louis, as you will see. He was just far too prepared for me. *Caption on black:*

LONDON 1932

INT. INTERVIEW ROOM

LOUIS *and* STANLEY *are sitting opposite each other in the interview room. There is a trolley next to them, a genteel collection of sandwiches.* STANLEY *is holding a notebook that from time to time he writes in.*

STANLEY: Are you ready to do this?
LOUIS (*lighting a cigarette*): That depends.
STANLEY: Depends on what?
LOUIS: A few conditions.
STANLEY: Conditions? What conditions? You've done all these other interviews – why do *I* get conditions?

LOUIS (*ignoring this*): When I say something is not to be published, that means it is not to be published. (*he stares straight at* STANLEY) You understand?

STANLEY: I don't know. We'll have to see about that. (*He smiles at* LOUIS.) Depends how exciting you are *on* the record.

LOUIS: Then forget it. I've changed my mind.

STANLEY: That was a joke, Louis.

LOUIS: No it wasn't.

STANLEY: You made these conditions to all the other interviewers, did you? I don't believe you did for one moment –

LOUIS: I didn't have to, I knew I wasn't going to say anything I regretted . . .

STANLEY: You trust them, you don't trust me?!

LOUIS (*calmly smoking*): Let's just say, you may lure me, Stanley, into saying something I don't want to.

STANLEY: I will 'lure' you . . . ? After all the promotion I've given you, I will lure you into saying something disastrous? Is that what you think?!

LOUIS: Yes. (*he smiles*) So when I say – and listen to this Stanley – you are not going to print something, that's what it means and you'd better not.

STANLEY: You start by threatening me – I can't believe this!

LOUIS: We start with me making my conditions absolutely *clear*.

STANLEY: Well why don't we do it like they would on the wireless then? Is that what you want, with all the questions and answers written out beforehand, a ridiculous stilted interview?

'It must be exciting to be a well-known coloured musician in London Mr Lester'?!

LOUIS: That's a tempting idea, but we can't do that because you'd insist on writing all my replies as well.

(*he smiles*) So now you've promised not to write
anything I don't want in this article, I think you can
ask your first question.

STANLEY: Did I make that promise?

LOUIS: Yes I heard you promise it very clearly. (*lightly*) We
both know one of us is going to come out of this
interview really regretting they'd agreed to do it
(*he leans forward*) and you know it may not be me,
Stanley . . .

STANLEY: Blimey, what does that mean? You're trying to
scare me now?!

LOUIS: You think I can't?

STANLEY: I know you can't.

LOUIS: I know I can.

They stare at each other.

STANLEY: I'm not going to start with your childhood.

LOUIS: No, I agree, everybody always starts with
childhood . . .

STANLEY: On the other hand –

An abrupt cut. We see a caption on the screen with the
Music Express *logo:*

CHILDHOOD AND THE WAR

INT. INTERVIEW ROOM

LOUIS (*lighting another cigarette*): My parents were both
from Jamaica . . . They met each other in this country,
at Waterloo Station – by Platform 7 to be exact. They
had a friend in common – my mother's family had
come to England fifteen years before my father. He
was a merchant seaman, travelled all over the world.
That's what I started doing too, as you know – before
I formed the band. I got my first job at sea, when I
was seventeen –

STANLEY: You're in a bit of a hurry to leave your parents

Louis, let's just stay with them a moment. What about your mother? What happened to her?

LOUIS: My mother was in service. She was lucky. She got a job at a great house, where there had been a tradition, off and on, of having some coloured servants, going all the way back to the seventeenth century. There was a big picture apparently somewhere in the house, of one of the dukes, at the time of Charles I, with his black page standing behind him.

STANLEY: Why was she lucky to be there?

LOUIS: Because the lady of the house took a bit of an interest in her, which of course was very unusual – still is! And no, I'm not going to name her, because they are very much around at the moment, not the lady in question, but the family . . . (*lightly*) I read about their social engagements in *The Times* newspaper.

STANLEY: Maybe they are about to have a great party and they'll ask for your band to play there, and you'll return in triumph to where your mum worked –

LOUIS: That thought had occurred to me too, be funny if that happens. (*he smiles*) Maybe it will . . .

STANLEY: How did this duchess, or whoever she was, take an interest in your mother?

LOUIS: Just in small ways of course . . . she gave her books to read, she gave her *Vanity Fair* (*teasingly, as if Stanley might not know*) by William Makepeace Thackeray. My mother couldn't read, she didn't dare tell the lady of the house, so somehow she taught herself to read . . . and then read the whole of *Vanity Fair* and she gave it to me just before she died.

STANLEY: And have *you* read it?

LOUIS: I have, yes, though I have to admit I had to start it three times.

STANLEY: You've probably read more than me.

LOUIS: I'm sure that's true.

STANLEY: I find it difficult to finish books –

LOUIS: Why doesn't that surprise me?

STANLEY: Or rather I finish them but I skip, I get the initial idea and then it's usually blah blah blah . . . so you jump over all the bloody subplots, and all those unneccesary minor characters and then I skip to the end. And I've not lost a week of my life! Anyway – your mum and dad – were you close?

LOUIS: No, that's all I'm going to say about them, let's move on.

STANLEY: Hang on, that's twice you've tried not to talk about them, is that all you're going to give me, your mum and a copy of *Vanity Fair*?

LOUIS: Yes, the truth is I didn't talk much to either of them. (*he leans forward*) This is off the record now Stanley and *not to be printed* . . .

STANLEY: You're only allowed three.

LOUIS: Who says? Where did that come from?

STANLEY: I'm telling you, you're only allowed three off-the-records, *and I'm counting.* You're sure you want this to be one of them?

LOUIS: Yes.

STANLEY *stops writing in his notebook.*

My mother was – (*he stops himself*) She had problems – especially when my father was away at the war. She prayed every night for him to be saved. She was in a state of constant fear. She would often scream when she saw the postman coming down the street, or the telegraph boy –

STANLEY: Yes, the most hated boys, the telegraph boys – I nearly did that during the war. I watched them coming down our street, and I decided I was never going to be that boy, bringing news of death all the time. (*he looks at* LOUIS) You look surprised.

LOUIS: I was surprised, that's –

STANLEY: A bit serious for me?

LOUIS: I didn't say that –

STANLEY: But you thought it. (*holds up his hand*) Leave it. I was very stupid to interrupt you when you were talking about your mother.

LOUIS: My mother . . . (*he blows smoke*) Her moods got more and more frequent. (*He stops.*)

STANLEY: She went mad?

LOUIS: That is why we're off the record, yes, but I wouldn't say she went mad – she was locked inside her own world. Her fear for my father – every night she yelled out at God, had this passionate conversation with him. She thought a black soldier, for some reason, a black soldier was much more likely to be killed. Sometimes I came across her, in the kitchen, quite naked, on her knees, praying and praying . . . I have never prayed in my life, Stanley, and I certainly never intend to do so, but her prayers, it *did* bring him home. Her great love. She only had eyes for him, always just for him. But then my father, he hardly ever spoke about the war, and what he'd seen –

STANLEY: The war! Nobody wants to talk about the war.

LOUIS: I know . . . It's strange, isn't it? It's as if – at the moment – there isn't a single person who wants to remember the war –

STANLEY: We were lucky, so bloody lucky, to be just young enough to miss all that!

(*suddenly*) I remember going down to the river, one day, just after the war started, it was a very sunny afternoon, went down to the beach at Battersea where at low tide you can wade in the river. And the boats were all going past, still a lot of young men on them taking their girls out on the water.

And there was one girl on the river bank, just above the beach, and she had her young man with her, and her dog, and they tied the dog to a tree. And then they were kissing really passionately, just near me, and touching each other all over – I was only eleven, it was a tremendous free show, I watched it all. She says goodbye to him, he was in uniform, he was going to the war . . . and then he leaves her. And she turns round, and the dog was gone, it managed to get free, and she starts running all over the park looking for the dog. And I decide to help her, I mean after the wonderful show they'd given me it's the least I can do. And I remember so clearly as we looked for the dog together how joyful she was about what had just happened, because he must have said how much he truly loved her, and yet how sad she was at the same time because he'd gone. She was so full of both those things at once and I could feel it so strongly because I was right next to her.

LOUIS: And did you find the dog?

STANLEY: Yes, I found the dog for her. 'Here he is!' I said, and she gave me a little kiss on the top of my head and she was gone.

I often think about her, what happened to her and if he ever came back. (*he grins*) She was a beautiful girl . . . Sweet little story really?!

LOUIS (*sceptically*): It is.

STANLEY: So why are you looking like that?

LOUIS: You tell me a story of your own, Stanley, hoping I'll open up to you a bit more.

STANLEY: Maybe. (*smiles*) But you're going to open up to me Louis *anyway*. So, you don't have brothers or sisters, you were all alone with your deeply religious mother?

LOUIS: Yes . . . Do you have brothers or sisters?

STANLEY: I don't.

LOUIS: That's a coincidence. Both of us only children . . .

STANLEY: Yes. Might explain something of course, don't know what though!

And both your parents died in the flu epidemic. That must have been the most devastating time.

LOUIS: Are we still off the record?

STANLEY: Oh, for heaven's sake! You can tell me that! Your parents die, you're incredibly upset!

LOUIS: We are still off the record, Stanley.

STANLEY: If we have to be.

LOUIS: It was in a way, devastating of course. But in another way, I was already on my own. I had naturally seen very little of my father during the war . . . and then when he came back he never really spoke to me much. (*Blows smoke.*)

There was a time, shortly before he died, when we were walking along the street, and he stopped and bought some toffee apples for us both, though I was a little old for toffee apples I thought . . . but I realised he wanted one, and he was pretending it was for me really, why he was buying them. And we walked a little way together eating the toffee apples and I did think here is chance, a chance to ask him about the war – you've *got* to try to talk to him about it . . . So I asked him about sleep, how easy was it to sleep in the trenches? Did you ever get used to it?

STANLEY: And what did he say?

LOUIS: He said he didn't really remember . . . even though it was only less than a year after the war . . . He couldn't really remember about sleep.

And we walked along the street eating our toffee apples and that was the last time I ever spoke to him. *A sharp cut. A caption appears on black:*

BEING INVISIBLE

INT. INTERVIEW ROOM. A FEW MINUTES LATER
LOUIS' *jacket is off, he is sitting back with his feet up on the chair.*

LOUIS: Shall I tell you the brutal truth?

STANLEY: The brutal truth? That sounds promising – you must tell me the brutal truth, Louis, but only if it is on the record.

LOUIS: This is on the record, but you won't want to print it.

STANLEY: I'm sure I will.

LOUIS: I know you won't.
He leans forward and takes a sandwich.
Thanks for providing the sandwiches, by the way.

STANLEY: I also have a bottle of champagne about to appear – but at this rate, you're not going to earn it . . .

LOUIS: Don't rush to judgement, Stanley.

STANLEY: What is the brutal truth?

LOUIS: It is, people don't like the idea of me being English, not even you.

STANLEY: I don't know why you say that? What have I done to deserve that?

LOUIS: It's true . . . Everybody finds it much easier to think of me as American. The most frequent question I get asked is, 'Are you going back to America soon?'

STANLEY: Well, that only proves what a novelty you are here – an all-black band which isn't a minstrel band, playing jazz and being successful.

LOUIS: I'm not sure that's what people mean when they ask that question.

STANLEY: Of course many people are prejudiced, but I keep telling you – there are many that aren't, and those numbers are growing –

LOUIS: This is Stanley Mitchell's own research, is it?

STANLEY: In a way, yes. It is my considered opinion in my role as 'professional observer of the current scene'.

LOUIS (*lightly*): Oh is that what you are, a 'professional observer'?

STANLEY: Anyway, if you were American, and you were there now . . . in quite a few states you could be sent to jail for sleeping with a white woman.
A pause.

LOUIS: I'm just going to eat your sandwiches, Stanley, until you move on to another subject. I'm certainly not going to comment on that.

STANLEY: Of course I'm not going to write about your personal life. Do you think I'm that sort of journalist? I'm quite offended, Louis –

LOUIS: I will make one observation though. (*He inspects the sandwiches.*) You, Stanley Mitchell, have never been to America, you are deeply fascinated by it of course, but you have absolutely no idea what it is really like.

STANLEY: I haven't been to America, *not yet*, no. You know my mum had never heard an American accent until a couple of years ago when she first went to the talkies, and that was true of most of the country, they'd never heard it either. She said, 'So *that's* what they sound like!'

LOUIS: Yes. (*lightly*) Well, to state the obvious, Stanley, I have seen a lot more of the world than you.

STANLEY: That is obvious, yes, since you spent all that time criss-crossing the ocean, scrubbing decks – but then again, too much travel often shrinks the mind, as the saying goes.

LOUIS: What saying? I've never heard that saying!

STANLEY: When have you ever met somebody who's travelled the world and had anything original to say when they get back? They just spend their time staring at things – whereas I, for instance, stuck at a typewriter all day, have to *think* for a living.

LOUIS: Well, you don't do it that often judging by what's inside *Music Express* every week.

STANLEY *smiles at this.*

STANLEY: Tell me, Mr Lester, what is it like being a coloured musician in London now?

LOUIS: Well, and I haven't used this before, even though it may sound like it, it is always a mixture of being visible and invisible. And at the moment, I am more visible, the band is more visible.

STANLEY: So being invisible, you mean being out of work, not getting bookings . . . ?

LOUIS: No, that's not what I mean. This is now off the record Stanley.

STANLEY *rolls his eyes.*

When you are a coloured person, you are very visible, of course, and people make remarks all the time. You get used to it – sometimes you can't ignore them, most of the time you find a way, at least I do, of letting it slip past you. But also at the same time you are invisible. Because you are coloured, you're obviously not a person of consequence – (*he mimicks*) 'Of course how could he be!' So even if you hear something very private, they think you will never know anybody important enough to repeat it to.

And if you're a musician that is doubly true, because you're just providing the background sound to all these people's lives, so they often behave as if you don't exist and you get to hear some *very* intimate things.

For instance, on some of the big ocean crossings, just after the financial crash, when I was playing in first class, I heard people talking about killing themselves right in front of me. And I heard other people laying out all their business plans, how exactly they were going to destroy all their rivals. So I feel quite lucky in a way to have been able to eavesdrop on so many people, as part of the furniture of their lives . . . and now, of course, because I've had success they don't talk in front of me like that any more.

STANLEY: Give me some more examples of what you've heard.

LOUIS: You think I'm mad?! I'm definitely not doing that.

STANLEY: I won't print it. I'm just fucking curious.

LOUIS: I'll give you one more example, but it will disappoint you because it's not about anybody famous or aristocratic.

STANLEY (*grins*): Then don't bother.

LOUIS: But if you can tell a story about a girl, then so can I . . . I was at a bus stop, it happened just after I met you, about a year ago before we'd had any real success. There was this couple at the bus stop, just me and them. And suddenly she turns on the man and she rages at him, that she will never forgive him, that she wishes he was dead, and that she would spit on his grave – her whole love affair had turned to complete hate, and it pours out in front of me as if I am totally invisible. At one point she even seems to prop herself up on me as she cries, as if I was part of the bus stop, and not really a living thing –

STANLEY: I don't think that's a good example at all! That scene could easily have happened if you were white as well, waiting at the bus stop –

LOUIS: Not if you were wearing a top hat and had your manservant with you, she wouldn't have done that!

STANLEY: But then you wouldn't have been at a bus stop at all, if you had a manservant with you! (*He lights another cigarette.*) You know Louis, this visible and invisible stuff, it sounds a bit over-prepared to me, a bit too polished.

LOUIS (*lightly*): But isn't that who I am, Stanley? A little polish is good.

STANLEY: Right . . . the Louis Lester polish . . . of course! (*He blows smoke.*) So let me ask you, Louis Lester, would you consider yourself a radical person? Somebody with left-leaning sympathies?

LOUIS' *manner is effortless, taking this change of tack in his stride.*

LOUIS: Generally I am not a political person. Of course we live at a time when there is such a huge gap between the rich and the poor, and naturally like most reasonable people I don't believe that's right, but I'm not a communist like the wonderful Mr Robeson, Paul Robeson, who incidentally is a hero of mine. I was lucky enough to meet him after seeing his incredible performance as Othello at the Savoy Theatre, but I'm not like him.

STANLEY: No, you're too conventional for that.

LOUIS: Maybe I am. I suppose I believe there's never just *one* solution for any given problem . . .

STANLEY: Blimey, sounds like you've used that before! 'There isn't just one solution for any given problem'! God help us! You're not talking to the bloody *Daily Express*, you know.

LOUIS: I'm very aware of that, Stanley – they would have prepared for this interview a lot better!

STANLEY: So what's your conclusion then, about how things are, from all this invisibility? This position you've been in . . . which you seem to regard as quite a lucky position?

LOUIS: You're going to yell at me, because it's so obvious –

STANLEY: I probably will.

LOUIS: My conclusion is – there's a hell of a lot of ignorance about people like me.

STANLEY: From most people?

LOUIS: From everybody.

STANLEY: Everybody?! Fucking hell! Well, it's lucky we're
doing this interview then, isn't it?!

INT. THE IMPERIAL BALLROOM
We see the band playing in the Imperial Ballroom, led by LOUIS
*at the piano with his usual calm confidence. It's the concert they
gave at Christmas to the old dowagers, the faces from the hotel's
past staring at the new band as they eat their Christmas
pudding.*

We see a montage of music from this Christmas concert as
STANLEY's *voice-over begins to ride over the images.*

STANLEY (*voice-over*): The feeling in the ballroom of the
Imperial Hotel when the band played used to vary
wildly from night to night . . . from high excitement to
complete incomprehension. The performance I really
wish I'd been there for was when they played to all
the old dowagers on Christmas Day as they tucked
into their puddings, the old ladies looking to see if
they'd been lucky and got a sixpence in their portion.
Never had there been a more unlikely audience for
jazz music, and yet, I'm told, there was a feeling of
reasonable tolerance in the room, broken only by the
shocking spectacle of members of the German
Embassy walking out in protest . . . which just helps
to prove how powerful the right music can be when it
confronts the wrong audience.

A caption appears on black:

AROUSING THE ARISTOCRACY

INT. INTERVIEW ROOM
The sandwiches have all gone except one.

STANLEY: Have the last one.

LOUIS: I think I will.

He reaches for it, inspects it and then puts it back.

For some reason, you're not asking me the question you really want to ask.

STANLEY: How very idiotic of me.

Why am I not asking that question?!

LOUIS: I don't know, Stanley. I don't know why you're pussyfooting around it?

STANLEY: And what is that question?

LOUIS: This is off the record, of course.

STANLEY: That's three down now, you've had your lot.

LOUIS (*firmly*): We'll see about that.

The question you're not asking is – why are so many upper-class people – no, not so many, that's quite wrong – why are *some* upper-class people, including royalty, so interested in jazz music and black musicians?

STANLEY: I don't have to ask you that, for the simple reason I know the answer.

LOUIS: You know?

STANLEY: Yes, it's easy – they find it very sexually exciting.

LOUIS: Oh, so that's the reason, is it?!

STANLEY: You can look me in the eye can you, and tell me that's not the reason?

Go on . . . just try . . .

There is a pause.

Go on Louis, tell me I'm wrong.

LOUIS: Some of that is true . . .

STANLEY: What do you mean, 'some of that'?! It *is* the truth.

LOUIS: If you're talking about Prince George –

STANLEY: Certainly the Princes, Prince George and the Prince of Wales, find it extremely sexually arousing. But not just the Princes.

LOUIS: It is exotic for them, that is the attraction, and a change –

STANLEY: From the ghastly Jack Paynton, and all those terrible foxtrots!

LOUIS: Well, you know I agree about that! If you want my opinion . . .

STANLEY: That's why I'm here.

LOUIS: I think they find in the music a chance to escape, for a few minutes, from all the rules and codes of behaviour they have to live by, and everything they have to do in public.

STANLEY: But *you* love all that, don't you?

LOUIS: Love what?

STANLEY: Royalty. And all the rules of etiquette. And having to bow to them. And having the chance to chat to them for a few precious seconds, and play for them, and answer their dumb questions . . . I'm right, aren't I?!

There is a pause.

LOUIS: I find it an exciting challenge, putting on a performance for a royal audience, yes.

STANLEY: 'An exciting challenge'? Oh come on. Louis, I can't believe you just said that. You're not on the bloody wireless!

LOUIS (*deliberately winding him up*): And it's an honour too of course, a great honour . . .

STANLEY: Louis Lester considers it a great honour to play for the Royal Family!

Thanks so much, you've just given me the scoop of the century!

Caption:

THE INTERESTING SIDE OF FAME

INT. INTERVIEW ROOM
The air is now thick with smoke.

STANLEY: Do you consider yourself famous?

LOUIS: No.

STANLEY: But you *are* quite famous, right at the moment.

LOUIS: The band has had success. Jessie, our lead singer, has had a great success, yes.

STANLEY: So *the band* is famous?

LOUIS: The band is well-known, at the moment, yes.

STANLEY: And what is the biggest change fame has brought? What are you able to do you couldn't before?

LOUIS: Being able to use the front entrance at the Imperial Hotel . . . being able to call for a taxi . . . being introduced to royalty – I know that's the bit that really interests you. Having a little money . . . not having to worry about members of the band being deported because we have regular work . . . That sort of thing.

STANLEY: So you feel much safer, more secure?

LOUIS: Of course. As much as anybody can at the moment.

STANLEY: And do you think you've had to be quite ruthless to get where you are?

LOUIS: No, I don't think that, no.

STANLEY: But your manager, Wesley Holt, was deported over a year ago, ending a long association between you, and that didn't seem to affect you that deeply?

LOUIS: On the contrary, it was a very difficult time . . .

STANLEY: You didn't seem to be thrown off your stride at all.

LOUIS: I wouldn't put it like that . . . We had many months when I felt the band was making no progress and we were going nowhere. (*He looks at him pointedly.*) As you well know, Stanley.

STANLEY: And Wesley Holt? Do you know what happened to him?

LOUIS: I do not. We've lost touch.

STANLEY: You made no attempt to find out what happened to him?

LOUIS: Of course I have. I've made several attempts.

STANLEY: There was a serious court case pending against him in the state of Illinois, was there not?

LOUIS: I believe so. I'm sure he didn't go back there.

STANLEY: Do you know if he is alive or dead?

LOUIS: I'm sure he's alive.

STANLEY: So why haven't you heard from him?

LOUIS: Because I think he may have felt I could have done more about his situation. I don't think I could have done, but I think he may well have felt that.

STANLEY: Would you like me to find out what happened to him?

LOUIS: Of course – if you think you can.

STANLEY: Maybe I'll try my own lines of enquiry.

They stare at each other. The mood has darkened. For a moment LOUIS *looks more vulnerable, troubled.*

My point is, his loss didn't stop your single-minded approach to promoting the band – even without a manager.

LOUIS: Those are your words.

STANLEY: They are.

He lights another cigarette.

So has success changed you, Louis? Your personality? It changes most people in my experience . . . So how has it changed you?

There is a pause.

You've got to answer that.

LOUIS *doesn't respond for a moment.*

You've got to allow me to get beneath the surface, Louis – otherwise this is pointless.

So, how have you changed?

LOUIS: I *will* answer that.

STANLEY: Go on.

LOUIS: But in this way, Stanley . . .

And it's not what you're expecting.

STANLEY: Surprise me, Louis, good!

LOUIS: There has been a very interesting side to the bit
of fame we've had – something you could never guess
at – and it'll give you a story.

STANLEY: Marvellous.

LOUIS: But you'll need to do a bit of work to find it.
(*He stares straight at* STANLEY.)
You've got to talk to Carla and to Jessie . . . and then
you might know what question to ask.

STANLEY: Blimey, you're setting me tasks now, are you?!

LOUIS: I am.

STANLEY: Is this because I've started asking you awkward
questions?

LOUIS: No it's not, it's because that's all the time I can
spare you now.
He gets up.

STANLEY: Jessie's impossible to talk to. She won't talk
about herself at all – absolutely refuses to!

LOUIS: Get Carla on your side and she may.

STANLEY: Carla's a nice enough girl, but what's she going
to tell me?
LOUIS *stands in the doorway. He smiles at* STANLEY *and
then leaves.*

INT. RAF AIR BASE
We cut to CARLA *singing for the Prince of Wales at the RAF air
base. We see a montage of her dramatic performance that night,
as she sings from the minstrels' gallery above the banquet for the
Prince of Wales. As she sings, she and the band watch the Prince
seduce the Air Vice-Marshal's wife to the sound of the Louis
Lester Band.*

Over these images we hear STANLEY*'s voice-over.*

STANLEY (*voice-over*): Carla always got very nervous before she sang. She had extraordinary presence but didn't seem to realise the effect she had on people, how much they were drawn to watch her.

CARLA *reaching the ebullient finale of her song.*
Caption on black:

FOLLOWING THE TRAIL

INT. INTERVIEW ROOM
CARLA *is sitting near a window.* STANLEY *is sitting a reasonable distance away.* CARLA *looks up sharply.*

CARLA: Did Louis say this was all right?

STANLEY: He did. He said I had to talk to you.

CARLA: I can't think why. What are you going to find out from me?

STANLEY: I'm trying to do a really full interview about Louis and the band's success, Carla, much better and more serious than anybody else has done, and I think he feels strongly you should be involved in the article, and so do I of course.

CARLA (*carefully*): I see.

STANLEY: I'm interested in how success has changed you and the band . . . if it has that is?

CARLA: Well, we've been so lucky, so very lucky . . . in all sorts of ways, not having to worry about food, about being hungry for a start!
(*She turns and stares at him.*)
Have you ever been hungry?

STANLEY: On occasions, yes . . . like walking home after school!
CARLA *smiles faintly at this.*

CARLA: You've never been hungry, have you?

STANLEY: Not like you, Carla, no.

CARLA: Well, the biggest difference for me, the very biggest difference the successs has made to me, was going

into Fortnum and Mason's and having three Welsh
rarebits, one after the other, a place I could never
have gone into before in my wildest dreams! Never,
ever ever. Three Welsh rarebits! It's 'rarebits', not
'rabbits'. That's cheese on toast with some –

STANLEY: I know what Welsh rarebit is, Carla.

CARLA: Do you know why it's called that?

STANLEY: I don't know that, no.

CARLA: No, nor do I. I forgot to ask!

    So that's the biggest difference, three Welsh rarebits,
one after each other.

    There is a pause.

STANLEY: And that's it? That's why Louis wanted me to
talk to you? To hear about cheese on toast?!

CARLA: I thought *you* wanted to talk to me?

STANLEY (*hastily*): Yes, I do, of course.

CARLA: So that's the biggest difference, that's what success
has meant to me.

    She stares at him confidently. STANLEY *decides to take
another tack.*

STANLEY: And what happens if it goes? Of course I'm not
saying that will happen at all, but sometimes in show
business things don't go on for ever . . . How difficult
do you think it would be to go back?

CARLA: Go back where?

STANLEY: To your life before.

CARLA: It would be easy.

STANLEY (*doubtful*): Would it?

CARLA: Yes, and I expect it will happen. One day.

STANLEY: But before then, do you have a sort of dream
where you may end up?

    CARLA *stares straight at him.*

    Your own show in the West End?

CARLA: Ah!

STANLEY: What do you mean 'Ah!'?

CARLA: Louis said tell him about the man in your street if
  you're asked that question.

STANLEY (*startled*): Louis has been coaching you . . . how
  to answer my questions?!

CARLA: He talked to me, yes.

  He said if you wanted to know the answer to that,
  I should tell you about the man and the room. I think
  I would have anyway, because it's what I believe.
  She looks across at him.

  In the street where I grew up –

STANLEY: Which was where?

CARLA: I'm not going to tell you that.

STANLEY: Why ever not?

CARLA: Because it's private.

STANLEY (*exasperated*): But it was in London, was it? You
  can tell me that much!

CARLA: Yes, it was in London. But we didn't have any
  space. We didn't have much space at all. There were
  six of us, my brothers and sisters, and we all slept in
  the same room. So a room of your own was a very
  special thing . . . Of course I know you know that.

STANLEY: I do, yes.

CARLA: So one day across the street, a man arrives. He was
  called Mr Dunwoodie. He was from Scotland, although
  he didn't have a Scottish accent really. He was a very
  short man, but he was so full of life and energy and
  every time we passed him in the street he would call
  out 'Hello children, what a day it is today! A lovely
  day, a day for great ideas!'

  And Mr Dunwoodie had two rooms of his own
  across the street, all to himself. And soon we found
  out that Mr Dunwoodie was working on a wonderful
  invention that would make his fortune, and he said he
  would show it to us as soon as he'd finished it. That's
  what he was doing in his special rooms. And every

time we saw him, we would call out, ask him how it was going, was it finished yet? And he would always reply, 'Nearly there children, nearly there!'

He was always so happy.

But after a few months, we couldn't wait any more. You know what kids are like – we wanted to see the great invention. And so we ran across the street. It was autumn, it was nearly dark. And we ran up the stairs at No. 36, because that's where he was, Mr Dunwoodie. And we knocked on the door. 'Can we come in, Mr Dunwoodie?' And he shouted, 'Go away, children!' But we didn't go away. We tried the door handle, and it wasn't locked, and it flew open and in we went.

And all over the floor were pieces of metal, in this terrible mess . . . little pieces and big pieces. Everywhere you looked, bits of scrap metal. And Mr Dunwoodie was screaming at us, 'Go away, you terrible children, *go away right now*!' And of course we ran away.

And for days we didn't see Mr Dunwoodie. And then when he did come out in the street he was different; pale, and older-looking and his face was terribly sad. And he never smiled at us ever again, not once. A little later he went away, he disappeared, with all his bits of metal on an old cart.

And so I learnt from that a big lesson: you can have a dream, but you must never describe that dream to anyone or let them see inside it too closely, because one day they may burst in through the door and you may see your dream through somebody else's eyes, how it must seem to the world, and that can destroy it for ever.

Silence.

STANLEY: How strange.

CARLA: What's strange?

STANLEY: That Louis should coach you like this, make you tell me a kind of fable . . .

CARLA: It's not a fairy story, it happened!

STANLEY: I'm not saying it didn't happen, but I don't see who I'm meant to be in this story. I'm not going to try to destroy your dream of success for goodness' sake, quite the opposite.

CARLA looks across at him. STANLEY meets her gaze.

STANLEY: I thought this would be easy, the interview with Louis and you – it's proving quite the opposite!

CARLA (*sharply*): I'm sorry I haven't given the answers you wanted.

She moves from where she was sitting by the window.

If you want to talk about how things can change people, you should talk to Jessie, of course.

STANLEY: You think she'll talk to me?

CARLA: We'll see. (*She stares across at him.*)

If you're gentle with her . . . and don't get too impatient, Stanley.

But do you think you can do that?

INT. THE IMPERIAL BALLROOM

We cut to JESSIE singing 'Dancing on the Moon' in the Imperial Ballroom, moving and dancing with ease and sensuality and completely in her element. We see her singing in a powerful close-up, totally immersed in her song and confident about the spell she is casting in the room. As the song proceeds, we begin to hear STANLEY's voice-over over the images.

STANLEY (*voice-over*): I always found Jessie unknowable, a mysterious little creature who seemed to have emerged into the world fully formed, without parents, brothers or sisters, or any past she would talk about.

Her tragic death has only deepened the mystery of course but I knew, the morning I spoke to her, I had to try to relax her if she was going to open up to me and give me a lead. And so I encouraged her to bring some of her fan mail with her and then I tried to ask her as little as possible and be patient.

Something, as Carla said, I find it very difficult to be . . .

Caption on black:

JESSIE'S CLUE

INT. THE INTERVIEW ROOM
JESSIE *is sitting at a table with a box of letters in front of her. We move towards her as* STANLEY'*s voice-over ends.*

JESSIE *looks up sharply. She is sitting by a small table with a pile of letters in a blue box.* STANLEY *is off-camera, his voice more gentle, persuasive.* JESSIE *is sorting through the letters.*

JESSIE: The letters I get are such a mixture, such a strange mixture. Every day I wake up and think, 'What surprise will there be today in the box?'

I put them all, each new lot of letters, in this blue box – and then I go through them, without opening them, just looking at the writing on the envelope, deciding which I will open first . . . and which maybe I will never open.

She holds some of the letters up, looking at the handwriting. She peers for a moment at one or two and then puts them back.

A lot of them of course are saying nice things about me, usually very nice, about how pretty my singing is, what a good dancer I am . . . I am a good dancer I think.

She looks up sharply towards the camera.

Not many people have written about that, Stanley, you know.

She burrows into the box and produces two letters with strange handwriting on them on the envelopes. She then pushes these back in the box.

JESSIE: And then of course there are the letters which are simply disgusting, all about people thinking about me without my clothes on and that sort of thing.

STANLEY (*off-camera*): I wonder if Jack Paynton gets letters like that?

JESSIE: I expect he does.

STANLEY (*off-camera*): Not something one wants to think about, a naked Jack! I'm sure even Mrs Paynton has a problem with that!

Sorry, I interrupted –

JESSIE: Yes, well, there's one thing about these letters I really wish . . . It would be so much better if people sent pictures of themselves with the letters, because I often think, after receiving a very peculiar letter, who could have written a letter like this?! I wonder what he looks like? Or what this woman looks like – because lots of women write to me too, it's not just men . . .

I wish I had a picture of the man who sent me three boxes of peaches last week – yes, I got three boxes of peaches, they were delivered to the hotel with a note saying 'In Admiration'. And a few weeks ago I got a little dog, I got sent a puppy! I couldn't keep it of course – we can't keep pets in our rooms at the hotel. But somebody is looking after it for me, and I will get it back one day.

And sometimes you know, Stanley, people write about their lives to me in such a way, all the most private things, and asking me for advice, and you can't really help them at all. I mean *I* can't.

She looks up very sharply.

No, you *can't* read them.

STANLEY (*off-camera*): I didn't say anything, Jessie.

JESSIE: No, but I'm just making clear, nobody can read them – not even my letters from the Prince – and I have had *several* letters from the Prince, and those of course are the most special of all.

STANLEY (*off-camera*): Of course. (*gently*) And your parents? They must be very proud of you. Do they write to you often?

JESSIE: I don't talk about my parents.

She pauses for a moment.

My dad disappeared when I was three, I never knew him, I think he's dead now anyway. He was white.

I think he worked in Covent Garden, you know in the market . . .

STANLEY (*off-camera, softly*): And your mother?

JESSIE: My mother . . . I'm not talking much about my mother either. She left as well when I was little. I was about eight when she went. She was a bit of a singer too as it happens.

One of my few good memories of her is her singing to me when I was tiny as she said goodnight, but she didn't do it that often.

She had many admirers, many men, nearly all of them were white. They came and knocked on the door and gave me a little pat on the head.

She sang at Collins' Music Hall, the one in Islington, so she can't have been that bad, can she?

STANLEY (*off-camera*): Did you ever go and see her in the theatre?

JESSIE: Yes, I saw her once, I think it must have been at Collins'. There were three of them, with my mum in the middle, singing a silly song about bananas. And

I knew at once I wasn't going to be a singer like her,
I was going to be a singer, I knew that, but I was
going to be completely different.

She left us anyway, me and my aunt, she left us.
Suddenly one night she was gone, never was in touch.
I haven't seen her for years. Maybe she's dead too.
She stares across towards the camera.
You think I sound hard?

STANLEY (*off-camera*): I didn't say anything, Jessie.

JESSIE: I know you didn't say anything. I'm asking you,
do I sound hard?

STANLEY (*off-camera*): You sound like you haven't forgiven
her.

JESSIE: I haven't, no. (*quietly*) I don't think I've forgiven
either of them. But that doesn't mean I'm hard. After
all, I owe everything to one man, and I always say
that, I always make that clear . . .

STANLEY (*off-camera*): You mean Louis I take it?

JESSIE: Well, Louis too, of course, but no, I didn't mean
him. I meant before him – there was my teacher in
the East End, Mr Rabinowitz. He gave me singing
lessons. Of course I couldn't really pay him, not what
he normally charged, not what he charged the others.
My aunt paid what she could – he did a special rate
for me.

I wish he could see me now. I wish he could have
been there when I sang for the Prince of Wales, and
heard me singing on the wireless. I would've given
anything for him to be there, to be here still. But he
died three years ago.
We stay on JESSIE's *face for a moment. She seems to be
about to cry.*
His heart was broken . . .

STANLEY (*off-camera, very quiet*): Who broke his heart
Jessie?

JESSIE: Well it certainly wasn't me!   There was one girl
who had lessons with him called . . . (*she stops for a
moment*) Well, I'll call her Annie though that's not her
real name, because you'll know her real name. She
was very pretty – now she's beautiful. I don't know
where she lived, not round us anyway. She came and
had lessons with him twice a week, she was very good
and he was really taken with her. I mean he was in
love with her, but he never would do anything with
her you know, which wasn't proper, wasn't right. He
never took advantage of any of us . . . He was in love
with her talent and how amazing she was when she
sang. So he loved her.

Anyway Annie, the person I'm calling Annie, has
become very successful, she's starring in a revue right
now in the West End. I probably shouldn't have said,
now you'll probably guess her name –

STANLEY (*off-camera*): I won't guess that, Jessie.

JESSIE: Although she owed him everything, owed Mr
Rabinowitz her career, she never answered his letters.
And when he went to see her the first time she was in
a West End show, she kept him waiting for ages at the
stage door, and then she didn't even come down to
see him. Instead she sent down a small box of
chocolates, and when he opened them, half of them
had already been eaten!

Just imagine doing that to your old teacher! What a
terrible thing to do . . . ! It broke his heart.

He was my friend. I could never behave like that.
I could never change towards people in that way, no
matter what happens! People that have helped you . . .
She looks down at the letters.
However much you get your head swollen by what
people say in the letters, you mustn't believe them,
you mustn't change. (*She laughs.*) You know some of

them run down the street after me blowing kisses, just like Julian said they would! But I'm not going to change . . .

She looks across at STANLEY.

Of course just like the letters the people that wait outside the hotel for my autograph, outside the Imperial, are such a *mixture* too. But you can see their faces – so whatever they say to you, and sometimes they do whisper things that are a shock, whatever they say it isn't as strange as some of these letters. And you can smile at them and talk to them, and be friendly enough so it doesn't become anything worse. You understand what I mean?

STANLEY (*off-camera, softly*): Yes.

JESSIE (*suddenly loud*): Oh, has Louis told you about the *woman*?

STANLEY (*off-camera*): What woman? No, he hasn't.

JESSIE: He hasn't? (*suddenly very animated*) You've got to make him tell you about *the woman*! (*she stands up*) In a way, it's the most exciting thing that's happened. He hasn't told you about the woman – I can't believe that?!

Caption on black:

MEETING THE WOMAN

INT. INTERVIEW ROOM

LOUIS *is now in evening dress sitting opposite* STANLEY. *We are in the same room as before. There is a bottle of champagne in an ice bucket next to them.*

LOUIS: I'm pleased to see today we're starting with champagne – last time it never showed up, did it?

STANLEY: Well, today it's a bribe.

LOUIS: I realise that.

STANLEY: So I've been on the little mystery tour you
wanted me to – and Jessie told me to ask you about
the woman. So I'm hoping you're not going to muck
about –

LOUIS: Muck about?!

STANLEY: Yes I'm hoping you're going to tell me about her
straight away.

LOUIS: I will, in a moment.

STANLEY: In a moment? Here we go again, not the bloody
off-the-record business! What tiny minuscule bit of
this interview am I actually *allowed* to publish?!

LOUIS: I'm not saying this is off the record.

STANLEY: You're not? Why not? (*smiles*) It can't be that
exciting then.

LOUIS (*lightly*): It's just I know you won't have the guts to
publish it.

STANLEY: I'm not going to even rise to that . . .
    You know I've been very stupid, and you don't
often hear me say that –

LOUIS: That's true.

STANLEY: But I have. I forgot for a moment that you're a
musician, and you're treating this interview a bit like
your jazz music, I ought to have realised! You seem to
be improvising away, talking about this and that, but
all the time I'm being led somewhere, aren't I?

LOUIS: You are, yes.

STANLEY: To the woman?

LOUIS: To the woman, yes. What I meant by the interesting
side of fame, or being well-known, since we're not
famous –

STANLEY: Of course, yes . . . merely well-known!
    LOUIS *suddenly looks straight at* STANLEY, *his tone more*
    serious.

LOUIS: This'll *never* be in your magazine.

STANLEY: Of course it will.

LOUIS: I'll bet you a hundred pounds.

STANLEY: I don't bet, Louis. But who knows, if it's worth it, I might pay you something!

Where did you meet this woman?

LOUIS *lights a cigarette.*

LOUIS: I was dressed like this, getting ready to play in the ballroom. It was a few months ago, I was in a little room near Schlesinger's office, he lets me use it sometimes (*he smiles*) to get away from the band! I was in a rather good mood I remember –

INT. HOTEL ROOM. EVENING

We cut to LOUIS, *in evening dress, but without his jacket on in a small, rather impersonal room with a couple of chairs and a small table. There's a telephone on another small table in the corner.* LOUIS *has some of his music with him which is strewn around the room. The telephone rings, he picks it up. A sharp telephonist voice says, 'There's a telephone call for you, Mr Lester.'*

Then we hear a husky rather sexy female voice.

JOSEPHINE: Hello?

LOUIS: Hello.

JOSEPHINE: You don't know who this is, do you?

LOUIS: I have to admit I don't.

JOSEPHINE: You never noticed me then?

LOUIS: Noticed you? Where?

JOSEPHINE: If you have to be told, then you haven't noticed me.

LOUIS: If you told me your name, it might help.

JOSEPHINE: You want to know my name, how would that help if you've never noticed me?

LOUIS: Well, if you described yourself . . .

JOSEPHINE: Describe myself? Where should I begin?
　　Well, what if I told you I was naked?
　　LOUIS *hesitates, about to ring off.*
　　Does that help?
LOUIS: Excuse me, I'm just getting ready for tonight's
　　performance, so I will . . . .
JOSEPHINE: Sorry, don't ring off, I shouldn't have said
　　that . . .

INT. JOSEPHINE'S ROOM. EVENING
*We cut to a fine-looking woman wearing an evening gown. She
is talking on a white telephone in a room suggestive of a small
sitting room in a hotel suite. The lights are very low. You can
only see her, the white telephone, a small table, distant darkness
and curtains. We intercut between her and* LOUIS.

JOSEPHINE: That was plain stupid, Mr Lester. I apologise.
LOUIS: There's no need to apologise –
JOSEPHINE: No, I do apologise . . . first of all because I'm
　　not naked so it was pointless me saying that. (*she
　　smiles*) Though of course depending how long we talk
　　that situation can always change.
LOUIS: I really must go, so . . .
JOSEPHINE: Sorry, that was just a poor joke, and actually
　　I've got something quite interesting to tell you, so I
　　should stop spoiling it, shouldn't I?
　　　　The point is I'm of course a great admirer, and I've
　　sat in the ballroom at the Imperial and heard you play
　　many times . . . and maybe I was there last night . . .
　　quite close to the stage, wearing a rather revealing
　　dress, and maybe you *did* notice me?
LOUIS: When I'm playing I don't see much from the
　　stage, so –

JOSEPHINE: I'm sure you're concentrating on your music, Mr Lester, of course! I was just explaining what a devoted follower I am of your band, and perhaps at this very moment I'm telephoning from somewhere in the hotel so I'm not too far from you –

But before you reply to that, let's leave all that vague shall we? Because I don't think I should tell you too much, I think it's probably better you don't know my name, because it would be safer for you, *and a lot safer for me*, if you didn't know my name.

A close-up of LOUIS.

LOUIS: Safer? In what way safer?

JOSEPHINE: I keep saying things I oughtn't, things that make me sound bonkers, and that is precisely how I don't want to sound.

I want to congratulate you on not ringing off – but yes, it would be so much safer for both of us if I remain anonymous.

I hope that's not too cowardly – do you think it's cowardly?

LOUIS: I'm sure it isn't. But now – whoever you are – I really am in the middle of doing some work here, so intriguing as it is to talk to an anonymous lady who may or may not be naked – I am sorry, but I'm going to ring off now.

JOSEPHINE: If you ring off, you won't stop me.

LOUIS *rings off.*

INT. INTERVIEW ROOM
We cut back to LOUIS *with* STANLEY.

STANLEY: Blimey, I can't believe you did that! Why did you ring off?

LOUIS: I had work to do.

STANLEY: Of course, I forgot, you're always working!
LOUIS *smokes for a moment.*
LOUIS: The next day, at exactly the same time, about an hour before we were going to play, the telephone rings again.

INT. HOTEL ROOM. EVENING
We cut to LOUIS *with his jacket off and not wearing his bow tie, answering the phone. Just before he speaks, we cut back to the Interview Room.*

INT. INTERVIEW ROOM
LOUIS: And I warn you Stanley, you're not going to like this.
STANLEY: Why not?
LOUIS: Because it's going to affect you personally. I left this bit out when I told Jessie.
STANLEY: I'm flattered I'm getting it all.

INT. HOTEL OFFICE/JOSEPHINE'S ROOM
We intercut between the small hotel office and JOSEPHINE'S *room.*

JOSEPHINE: How very unimaginative of you to ring off last night.
LOUIS: Well I explained I had work to do.
JOSEPHINE: You sound like my husband, whom we will soon be talking about. (*suddenly, her tone intense*) Please don't ring off, it's important, promise me.
LOUIS: I won't ring off, yet.
JOSEPHINE: Good. (*her voice brightens*) Are you wondering what I'm wearing?
Pause.

That was a long pause . . . Come on, I'm rather an
attractive woman, I can't believe you aren't wondering
how much or how little I'm wearing – especially as
I hear you're rather partial to white women. So what
do you think I'm wearing?

LOUIS: Before you tell me that –

JOSEPHINE: Yes? What do you want to know, Mr Lester?

LOUIS: What do I call you, since you won't tell me your
real name?

JOSEPHINE: Oh I'm so glad you're not threatening to ring
off yet . . . Call me Josephine, as in Napoleon and
Josephine.

LOUIS: So, Josephine, what are you wearing?

JOSEPHINE: I'm sitting here in my petticoat, waiting for
my husband to come back, and take me to a very
boring dinner party.

LOUIS: Right . . . so why did you call me?

JOSEPHINE: I'm coming to that. But I realise before you
can really take me seriously you need somebody to
vouch for me – and so I'm going to hand the
telephone now to somebody who you know . . . but
on one condition –

LOUIS: What condition is that?

JOSEPHINE: You never make her tell you who I am. Do
you promise that?

LOUIS *hesitates for a moment.*

LOUIS: I promise that.

JOSEPHINE: If you break the promise, it could be fatal for
me, you understand.

LOUIS (*startled*): I understand.

INT. INTERVIEW ROOM
We cut back to a close-up of STANLEY *in the interview room.*

STANLEY: It's going to be Pamela, isn't it?! It's going to be one of her nutty, upper-class friends on the phone, isn't it?

INT. JOSEPHINE'S ROOM
We cut back to PAMELA *taking the white telephone in* JOSEPHINE's *room, standing just in a pool of light in the dark room.*

PAMELA: Hello, Louis.

INT. INTERVIEW ROOM
We cut back to LOUIS, *leaning towards* STANLEY *in the Interview Room, his tone suddenly serious.*

LOUIS: You've got to promise me, you won't try to make her tell you who this lady is.
STANLEY: Now *I've* got to promise, do I . . . ? What on earth is this all about Louis?
LOUIS: Unless you promise I won't tell you.
STANLEY: Well, I'll have to promise then, won't I?
LOUIS: And mean it?!
STANLEY (*reluctantly*): I mean it.

INT. JOSEPHINE'S ROOM
We cut back to PAMELA *on the white telephone in* JOSEPHINE's *room.*

PAMELA: Hello, Louis, this is Pamela.
LOUIS: Good evening, Pamela.
PAMELA: I'm here with the person you know as Josephine, and she has got something to tell you which she hasn't told me, and which she won't tell you until

I've left the room – but I'm letting you know she's not batty, not batty in any way . . . and I think what she has got to tell you may make you understand something . . .

LOUIS: May make me understand what, Pamela?

PAMELA: Well I'm guessing of course, because I don't know what special thing she has to tell you, but I'm sure it has something to do with the world of my parents and their friends, and their country-house parties and all the conversations they have.

And how many things they hate . . .

You know of course already how much they hate what they call niggers, my parents and their friends, because I've told you that, Louis . . . and how they hate Jews, and they hate Irish people . . . and the French of course, and they hate Americans, everything American, and they hate musicians, and they hate actors, and they hate gypsies, and they hate homosexuals even though some of them are queer themselves . . .

They have so many hates and they find new ones all the time! And the funny thing is, I mean it's funny in an awful way, they spend a lot of their time in their beautiful houses with the most wonderful gardens, but they never look properly at what they've actually got! Because they move around their lovely lovely properties with so much loathing going through them . . .

My parents for instance, and you've been to our house, Louis –

LOUIS: I have, yes –

PAMELA: So you know what I mean, our house is crammed full of the most wonderful pictures, left to them by my grandparents, but they never ever look at them, my parents, they have no idea about art at all!

And my father had a good education, better than the one he arranged for me, but what does he say?

'Too many fucking pictures! Too many fucking pictures on our fucking walls!' That's what he says . . .

Of course I know I shouldn't talk about all the families whose houses I've stayed in like this, and probably I'm being so unfair, because after all they can't all be like that, can they?!

But I want to be unfair, because I want to make you listen to Josephine.

And now I'm going to leave the room, I'm handing back the telephone, I'm leaving the room Louis . . .

INT. INTERVIEW ROOM
We cut back to STANLEY.

STANLEY: She said all that to you?

LOUIS: She did.

STANLEY: More than she's said to me!

LOUIS: I bet . . . You will keep your promise though?

STANLEY: Not got a reason to break it. (*he smiles*) Not yet.

INT. HOTEL ROOM/JOSEPHINE'S ROOM

JOSEPHINE: Are you still there?

LOUIS: Yes.

JOSEPHINE: We're alone now, just you and me, Mr Lester.

LOUIS: What do you want to tell me?

JOSEPHINE: Well, what I have to tell you is this . . . (*she whispers*) And God forgive me . . . (*her tone brightens*) I know, Mr Lester, I'm not sure that I'm meant to, but I do know that Pamela's brother Julian showed you a little hole that allowed you to spy on the Freemasons in their temple in the basement of the Imperial Hotel. Is that true?

Pause.

Oh, come on, Louis, you can tell me, because obviously I do know . . . Is it true?

LOUIS: Yes. It was in a linen cupboard.

JOSEPHINE: A linen cupboard . . . how wonderful. You in a linen cupboard, spying on the Masons! And it's all right, I think I can assure you, they're not going to come and slit your throat for that, for spying through a hole, not today anyway.

So this is what I've got to tell you Louis – my husband is a Mason, just like Julian, just like the Royal Family and members of the Government and the Civil Service, and not forgetting all sorts of rich people from the City of London. And he is a member of the lodge that is in the basement of the Imperial. And of course they do their silly rituals down there and exchange gossip, and I'm sure raise some money for charity too, because that's what they say they do.

And so there are a lot of very important people down there in that basement . . . and in other basement temples around the city, because they like basements best! It goes without saying it is a very powerful group, these lodges, a very powerful octopus with its arms stretching all over the place . . .

And these people are not easily impressed . . . You understand me, Louis?

LOUIS: I'm sure they're not, no.

JOSEPHINE: Not easily impressed at all. But just before the great financial crash, in the lodge that is in the basement of the Imperial, there was a new member who'd just joined, a little man called Mr Luke.

And he did the most extraordinary thing, he prophesied the crash, and not just that, he was right about every firm that went under and *every* firm that managed to survive. He was advising all the other members of the lodge what to do with their stocks and shares but nobody listened to him.

But Mr Luke was right, he made money when everybody else was hurt by the most grievous losses.

And naturally everybody in the lodge was amazingly impressed, because a lot of them had lost their whole fortune. Of course most of them still had their country estates, but life looked for a time rather uncertain. And here was Mr Luke – the wizard – whom nobody had listened to.

But after a time, because he was such a funny little man, and his manners were very abrupt, they stopped holding him in such awe, and started referring to him as the Fluke. And even though we're in the middle of a great depression, most of the people in the lodge found out they were still quite rich, they could sell a few of their assets, life was good again. And so not only did they not look to Mr Luke for advice, they began to ignore him, wish he wasn't part of the lodge, that he would go elsewhere. They began to refer to him as the *Complete Fluke*.

And so he has remained, the Complete Fluke, who nobody really talks to . . . until a few weeks ago that is. *She stops. We cut back to* LOUIS *in the small hotel room.* Are you still there?

LOUIS: Yes, I am.

JOSEPHINE: Sorry . . .

We see alarm in her eyes for a moment. There is a noise outside in the passage. The sound of keys in a lock. And then the sound of more footsteps.

I just had to stop because I thought my husband was coming back . . . and if my husband finds me telling you this . . . I will be in terrible trouble.

She stares around for a moment.

No, it's somebody else, they've gone past . . . but I've got to keep an ear out. (*a husky laugh*) My husband has very small feet, he creeps up.

She stares around again for a moment.

It's all right, I can go on – do you want me to go on?

LOUIS: If you want to go on Josephine.

JOSEPHINE (*her tone suddenly angry*): What kind of answer is that?! I'm risking things to tell you this –

LOUIS: Of course I want you to go on.

JOSEPHINE: So Mr Fluke is ignored in the basement temple. 'He was always so vulgar,' people say to themselves. 'He comes from trade, how did he ever become part of the lodge?'

And then suddenly one day Mr Luke appears and says, 'I've joined another lodge, I won't be here any more,' and people are very relieved. But then he adds, 'It's in a basement just like this, but it is the most beautiful basement I've ever seen, that is where my new lodge is.'

And of course everybody there is rather curious, and some want to know more. He says, 'You can come and join me if you want, you are welcome to come.'

And this splits the lodge down the middle. Some think, 'What does he know that we don't?' Others think, 'Good riddance, go away horrid little man!'

Her voice soft, intense.

But this special temple really *does* exist Louis, and it is extraordinary. I can tell you where it is, its exact location, though I think I'd better not – but I *can* tell you, during the war, because of the airships and their bombs, there were some wonderful subterranean apartments created in central London where a few very rich families could scuttle down when there was a bombing raid. And out of these luxury apartments

below the street, this temple has now been created.
And that's where the Fluke was going.

'Come and follow me,' says Mr Luke, 'to this new
lodge.' And so some of the people, including my
husband, from the Imperial lodge, do follow him,
a few – just to have a look. And they go down the
steps below the pavement and into the new temple
and it is indeed exquisite. And Mr Luke says, 'If you
join me here now in this lodge, you must promise not
to repeat what you are about to hear to anybody,
ever.' And those that have followed him down there,
look around them, see how special it is and feel they
have to agree. They promise.

(*She whispers.*) I think my husband is the only one
to break this promise by telling me. My husband is
often rather drunk and thinks that I forget everything.
She pauses for a moment. We cut back to LOUIS, *not sure
if she has gone. We cut back to* JOSEPHINE.
I'm still here. And then, after they've all promised
they say, but what *is it* we mustn't repeat? And the
little man says, 'Come next door,' and they go into the
room next door which has the black-and-white
masonic floor, but there is nothing else in it – except
an enormous travelling trunk.

And my husband and the few that followed Mr Luke
stare at the trunk as the door is shut behind them.

And then the man they call the Complete Fluke
says: 'Something extraordinary is going to happen
very soon, worse than you can imagine. Many are
going to die, many many millions will die, old horrors
will be repeated, and completely new horrors beyond
your wildest nightmares will start to happen . . .
Whole cities will be destroyed, families you know will
die, your brothers will die, their houses and businesses
wiped out.

'But since we here at this temple know it is coming, we can find a way of staying alive, of protecting what we've got, and of taking advantage of what will follow. Because even in disaster there is *opportunity*. We can, and will be, the lucky few, if we do the following things –

A light suddenly falls on JOSEPHINE*'s face, as if the door to the room has suddenly been opened. Off-screen, a male voice addresses her.*

MALE VOICE: Sarah, who are you talking to?

JOSEPHINE: Nobody darling, just having a good gossip.

Then her voice, hissed and intense, into the phone, and sounding very frightened.

Oh God, Louis, my husband is back, I don't think he heard anything –

MALE VOICE (*steely*): What's that? Are you still on the telephone?

JOSEPHINE (*into the phone*): Oh God . . . He can't have heard, can he?!

Louis . . . ? (*her eyes are full of fear*) I hope you hear from me again.

A dark shadow falls across her face as if somebody is standing over her. Her face turns towards the shadow.

INT. HOTEL ROOM

We cut to LOUIS *in the hotel room. There is silence at the end of the phone.*

LOUIS: Josephine . . . ?

There is a sound like a small muffled scream down the end of the phone. We stay on LOUIS. *A male voice comes through the other end of the phone.*

MALE VOICE: Hello . . . who is there?

LOUIS *does not reply.*

Hello. (*The voice quietly menacing.*) Are you going to tell me who is there?

I would strongly advise you to tell me who you are.

LOUIS *rings off sharply.*

INT. INTERVIEW ROOM
We cut back to LOUIS *and* STANLEY *together.*

STANLEY: What happened to her?

LOUIS: I don't know.

STANLEY: She didn't call back?

LOUIS (*hesitates for a split second*): No.

STANLEY: She was obviously completely barking.

LOUIS: Yes . . . she must have been.

STANLEY (*suddenly the thought strikes him*): You know the Masons hold special dinners for installing their Worshipful Master in this hotel and they sometimes have music too, would you believe. Maybe one day they'll ask for you!

LOUIS (*smiles*): I doubt it . . . but I'm certainly going to go and play to them if they do. I'm really curious now.

STANLEY: Of course it isn't the Masons here that have this special temple . . . The Masons here –

LOUIS: I'm sure are all perfectly jolly fellows!

STANLEY: Well, I doubt they're that! . . . but they're not the people she was talking about. I wonder who they are? Wouldn't it be amazing to find that special luxury temple? At least discover exactly where it is!

LOUIS: It would be.

STANLEY (*suddenly more serious*): Be careful of these people though, Louis, you don't want to cross them in any way.

LOUIS: I do realise that. (*he smiles*) How could I ever cross them, Stanley?

STANLEY: So you're convinced she was just a crazy person?

LOUIS: Yes . . . Having thought about it a bit, yes. That's what she was.

I think she found it rather exciting . . . to try to scare me. She was one of your aroused aristocrats. *He gets up.*

I've got to leave now, Stanley.

STANLEY (*still thinking about what he said*): Maybe . . . an aroused aristocrat, yes.

Have you told me everything?

LOUIS: Yes. (*He turns in the doorway, smiles.*) Almost everything. There was one last phone call . . .

STANLEY: There was?

LOUIS: A very short one.

INT. HOTEL ROOM
The phone rings. LOUIS *picks it up. The receptionist says, 'There is a call for you, Mr Lester.'*

INT. HOTEL ROOM/JOSEPHINE'S ROOM
Suddenly we see JOSEPHINE *in close-up; we only see her face and her shoulders. Her shoulders are bare, naked, her tone is hoarse, there is just blackness behind her.*

JOSEPHINE (*whispers*): Pray for me . . . Will you pray for me, Louis . . . ?

There is a close-up of LOUIS *in the small hotel room.*
The phone at the other end rings off.

INT. INTERVIEW ROOM
We cut back to LOUIS, *standing in the doorway.*

LOUIS: And that is the last I heard from her.

STANLEY: Where was she? In some asylum somewhere? Is that what she was trying to suggest – they'd locked her up? People don't do that sort of thing to their wives any more, surely?!

LOUIS: Who knows what goes on in those big houses Stanley?!

But it was that last call that convinced me she wasn't genuine . . . I'm pretty sure it was just a game on her part.

STANLEY: A strange game to play, isn't it? –

LOUIS: Yes . . . but what I've worked out is this.

I think she probably loved watching the band, she loved the music . . . all that was true. And she wants to escape the life that she has, but she knows there are several women around that ballroom who feel the same.

She wants to be noticed, so she summons up a sort of nightmare so I will remember her.

STANLEY: And you have . . .

LOUIS: I have, yes. (*smiles*) And I know one thing Stanley, you are never going to print this!

We stay on STANLEY *as he thinks about her.*

STANLEY: You're right . . . She must be merely some mad aristo . . . some upper-class nutcase who wants to sleep with you.

LOUIS (*calm smile*): Precisely. Why else would she have chosen me to tell this to? (*He is in the doorway.*) But just in case she isn't a complete madwoman . . . you won't try to find out more from Pamela? I gave Josephine my word.

STANLEY: No, I promised, remember.

LOUIS *moves to leave and then turns in the door.*

LOUIS: See you in a few days, Stanley, and then you can show me what you've dared to write . . .

LOUIS *leaves. We stay on* STANLEY *for a moment.*

EXT./INT. THE IMPERIAL HOTEL

The camera is exploring the passages, the exterior and the interior of the Imperial. A subjective tracking shot dissolving from one area of the Imperial to another, leading us through the massive hotel. As the camera explores the grand interior of the Imperial, we hear STANLEY*'s voice-over.*

STANLEY (*voice-over*): And then of course events engulfed Louis, very soon after our conversation . . . a matter of days really. And quite a big part of what happened to him was connected to the Masons and their ability to look after their own. Or at least that's my view of how Julian Luscombe was protected. And that would have continued if Julian hadn't killed himself.

And as I write this, I'm not at all sure Louis wasn't right.

I may not have the guts to publish Josephine's story. After all, Louis is safely out of the country now and I am not. I am still here and have every intention of staying.

The camera moving through the hotel.

The Masons have fled the Imperial at the moment, because of its loss of reputation. And that great big crumbling palace of a place, which for a couple of years really burst with life and was so full of possibilities, is just hanging on like a beached creature, hoping the next tide will make it buoyant again.

The camera moves around the ballroom, the sound of distant voices.

And if that happens, will the Masons return?

The camera curling around the basement passage and into the empty Imperial masonic temple.

STANLEY (*voice-over*): One thing I can't stop thinking about is, does Mr Luke really exist? Or was he a figment of this woman's imagination, as Louis believed?

At the moment I've kept the promise not to try to make Pamela tell me more – anything that might lead me to Josephine. Or at least I've half kept the promise, I've asked her in a roundabout way and she said she hadn't a clue what I was talking about . . .

After her brother Julian's death, it is obviously an impossible subject for me to really press her on.

The camera travelling deep into the hotel.

But if Mr Luke does exist, does he really know something we don't? Or is he a complete fraud, the Complete Fluke?

We cut to STANLEY. *He is staring straight at us.*

I think I might just try to find him.

Fade out on STANLEY*'s face staring directly at us.*